∷study**sync**®

Reading & Writing Companion

GRADE 12 UNITS 1–3

What's Next?

Uncovering Truth

Against the Wind

studysync.com

Send all inquiries to:
BookheadEd Learning, LLC
610 Daniel Young Drive
Sonoma, CA 95476

ISBN 978-1-97-016269-1
MHID 1-97-016269-4

3 4 5 6 7 8 9 LWI 24 23 22 21 20

A

Contents

What's Next?

How can we transform the future?

UNIT 1

Uncovering Truth

How do challenges cause us to reveal our true selves?

UNIT 2

Against the Wind

How do leaders fight for their ideas?

UNIT 3

Please note that excerpts and passages in the StudySync® library and this workbook are intended as touchstones to generate interest in an author's work. The excerpts and passages do not substitute for the reading of entire texts, and StudySync® strongly recommends that students seek out and purchase the whole literary or informational work in order to experience it as the author intended. Links to online resellers are available in our digital library. In addition, complete works may be ordered through an authorized reseller by filling out and returning to StudySync® the order form enclosed in this workbook.

Reading & Writing Companion

iii

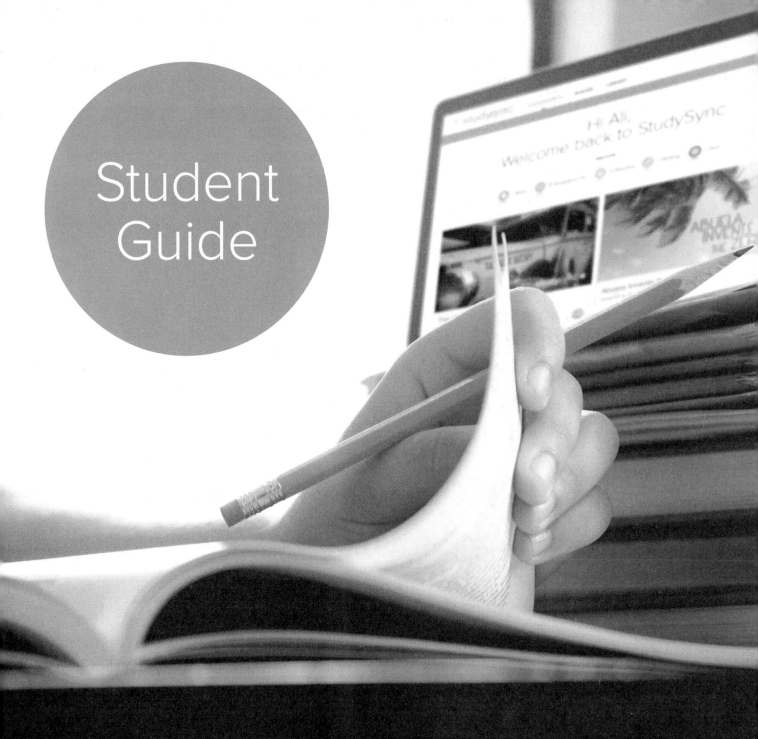

Student Guide

Getting Started

Welcome to the StudySync Reading & Writing Companion! In this book, you will find a collection of readings based on the theme of the unit you are studying. As you work through the readings, you will be asked to answer questions and perform a variety of tasks designed to help you closely analyze and understand each text selection. Read on for an explanation of each

Close Reading and Writing Routine

In each unit, you will read texts that share a common theme, despite their different genres, time periods, and authors. Each reading encourages a closer look through questions and a short writing assignment.

Are the New 'Golden Age' TV Shows the New Novels?

INFORMATIONAL TEXT
Adam Kirsch and Mohsin Hamid
2014

Introduction   study

Adam Kirsch (b. 1976) is a magazine editor, educator, and poet. He is also a literary critic, winning the Roger Shattuck Prize for Criticism in 2010. Mohsin Hamid (b. 1971) is a novelist, known best for *The Reluctant Fundamentalist*, *Exit West*, and his PEN/Hemingway Award finalist *Moth Smoke*. In this op-ed essay from the *New York Times*, both writers share their thoughts on how contemporary TV has changed how we think about the novel. Through a discussion of the style of Charles Dickens' writing, and an examination of novelistic features, both authors present persuasive arguments for their answer to the question "Are the New 'Golden Age' TV Shows the New Novels?"

Are the New 'Golden Age' TV Shows the New Novels?

> To liken TV shows
> to novels suggests an odd
> ambivalence toward both genres.

By Adam Kirsch

One criticism that could be leveled against quality cable TV is that it is not nearly as formally adventurous as Dickens himself.

Television was so bad for so long, it's no surprise that the arrival of good television has caused the culture to lose its head a bit. Since the debut of "The Sopranos" in 1999, we have been living, so we are regularly informed, in a "golden age" of television. And over the last few years, it's become common to hear variations on the idea that quality cable TV shows are the new novels. Thomas Doherty, writing in *The Chronicle of Higher Education*, called the new genre "Arc TV"—because its stories follow long, complex arcs of development—and insisted that "at its best, the world of Arc TV is as exquisitely calibrated as the social matrix of a Henry James novel."

To liken TV shows to novels suggests an odd **ambivalence** toward both genres. Clearly, the comparison is intended to honor TV, by associating it with the prestige and complexity that traditionally belong to literature. But at the same time, it is covertly a form of aggression against literature, suggesting that novels have ceded their role to a younger, more popular, more dynamic art form. Mixed feelings about literature — the desire to annex its virtues while simultaneously belittling them — are typical of our culture today, which doesn't know quite how to deal with an art form, like the novel, that is both democratic and demanding.

It's not surprising that the novelist most often mentioned in this context is Charles Dickens. Dickens, like Shakespeare, was both a writer of genius and a popular entertainer, proving that seriousness of purpose didn't preclude accessibility. His novels appeared in serial installments, like episodes of TV shows, and teemed with minor characters, the literary equivalent of character actors. "The Wire," in particular, has been likened to a Dickens novel, for its

Skill
Textual Evidence

Before 1999, television was generally lower quality than the innovative television shows after 1999. The pre-1999 shows did not follow complex story arcs throughout a season the way that a novel does from start to finish.

Copyright © BookheadEd Learning, LLC

1 Introduction

An Introduction to each text provides historical context for your reading as well as information about the author. You will also learn about the genre of the text and the year in which it was written.

2 Notes

Many times, while working through the activities after each text, you will be asked to **annotate** or **make annotations** about what you are reading. This means that you should highlight or underline words in the text and use the "Notes" column to make comments or jot down any questions you have. You may also want to note any unfamiliar vocabulary words here.

You will also see sample student annotations to go along with the Skill lesson for that text.

  Reading & Writing Companion

③ First Read

During your first reading of each selection, you should just try to get a general idea of the content and message of the reading. Don't worry if there are parts you don't understand or words that are unfamiliar to you. You'll have an opportunity later to dive deeper into the text.

④ Think Questions

These questions will ask you to start thinking critically about the text, asking specific questions about its purpose, and making connections to your prior knowledge and reading experiences. To answer these questions, you should go back to the text and draw upon specific evidence to support your responses. You will also begin to explore some of the more challenging vocabulary words in the selection.

⑤ Skills

Each Skill includes two parts: Checklist and Your Turn. In the Checklist, you will learn the process for analyzing the text. The model student annotations in the text provide examples of how you might make your own notes following the instructions in the Checklist. In the Your Turn, you will use those same instructions to practice the skill.

---

③ First Read

Read "Are the New 'Golden Age' TV Shows the New Novels?" After you read, complete the Think Questions below.

④ ▲ THINK QUESTIONS

1. What does Kirsch say about how TV has changed recently? What is the "new genre" he mentions? Use evidence from the text to support your answer.

2. Why do people often compare "good" TV to the writing of Charles Dickens? What does Kirsch say about Dickens's writing that welcomes this comparison? Use evidence from the text to support your answer.

3. What are the reasons Hamid gives for watching more television than in the past? Use evidence from the text to support your answer.

4. What is the meaning of the word **capacious** as it is used in the text? Write your best definition here, along with a brief explanation of how you inferred its meaning through context.

5. Read the following dictionary entry:

idiom
id•i•om /ˈidēəm/ *noun*

1. a group of words, that when used together, have an unclear meaning when read literally
2. a form of expression natural to a language, person, or group of people
3. the dialect of a people or part of a country
4. a characteristic mode of expression in music, literature or art

Which definition most closely matches the meaning of idiom as it is used in paragraph 4? Write the correct definition of idiom here and explain how you figured out its meaning.

---

⑤ Skill: Informational Text Elements

Use the Checklist to analyze Informational Text Elements in "Are the New 'Golden Age' TV Shows the New Novels?" Refer to the sample student annotations about Informational Text Elements in the text.

••• CHECKLIST FOR INFORMATIONAL TEXT ELEMENTS

In order to identify characteristics and structural elements of informational texts, note the following:

✓ key details in the text that provide information about individuals, events, and ideas

✓ interactions between specific individuals, ideas, or events

✓ important developments over the course of the text

✓ transition words and phrases that signal interactions between individuals, events, and ideas, such as *because*, *as a consequence*, or *as a result*

✓ similarities and differences of types of information in a text

To analyze a complex set of ideas or sequence of events and explain how specific

✓ individuals, ideas, or events interact and develop over the course of the text, consider the following questions:

✓ How does the author present the information as a sequence of events?

✓ How does the order in which ideas or events are presented affect the connections between them?

✓ How do specific individuals, ideas, or events interact and develop over the course of the text?

✓ What other features, if any, help readers to analyze the events, ideas, or individuals in the text?

⟳ YOUR TURN

1. What does the author's use of the transition phrase "for instance" tell the reader?

   ○ A. that the sentence includes an example to support the idea in the sentence before it
   ○ B. that the sentence includes an example to support the idea in the sentence after it
   ○ C. that the author's main point in the paragraph is explained in the sentence.
   ○ D. that the second half of the paragraph discusses a new topic

2. Why does the author compare Gilbert Osmond to Tony Soprano in paragraph 5?

   ○ A. to conclude that Soprano is a more likeable character than Osmond
   ○ B. to show a counterexample to his thesis that he then refutes
   ○ C. to give clear and concrete evidence to support his thesis
   ○ D. to refer to a character in a novel that all Americans have read

---

ARE THE NEW 'GOLDEN AGE' TV SHOWS THE NEW NOVELS?

Close Read

6

Reread "Are the New 'Golden Age' TV Shows the New Novels?" As you reread, complete the Skills Focus questions below. Then use your answers and annotations from the questions to help you complete the Write activity.

◎ SKILLS FOCUS

1. What are the advantages and disadvantages of how TV shows are structured? Use textual evidence to support your answer.

2. Mohsin Hamid believes that TV shows pose a real threat for novelists, and that novelists will need to find a way to adapt in the future. How does Hamid structure his argument?

3. Highlight two examples of supporting evidence in Kirsch's essay. How does the author connect these pieces of evidence to other parts of his argument?

4. Although the authors have different ideas about the role of literature in our lives, they both see a future for both novels and TV shows. What direction would each author give to these artforms? Highlight and annotate examples from the text to support your answer.

✎ WRITE

7

EXPLANATORY ESSAY: Select one of the articles. Analyze how the author uses examples, explanations, and concluding remarks to support his thesis and provide direction to his ideas. Remember to use textual evidence to support your points.

Reading & Writing Companion **13**

Fate or Foolishness
FICTION

Introduction

An accident creates a violent element that threatens the planet. Can a human and a computerized bird restore things to normal?

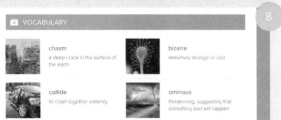

📷 VOCABULARY

chasm
a deep crack in the surface of the earth

bizarre
extremely strange or odd

collide
to crash together violently

ominous
threatening; suggesting that something bad will happen

6

Close Read & Skills Focus

After you have completed the First Read, you will be asked to go back and read the text more closely and critically. Before you begin your Close Read, you should read through the Skills Focus to get an idea of the concepts you will want to focus on during your second reading. You should work through the Skills Focus by making annotations, highlighting important concepts, and writing notes or questions in the "Notes" column. Depending on instructions from your teacher, you may need to respond online or use a separate piece of paper to start expanding on your thoughts and ideas.

7

Write

Your study of each selection will end with a writing assignment. For this assignment, you should use your notes, annotations, personal ideas, and answers to both the Think and Skills Focus questions. Be sure to read the prompt carefully and address each part of it in your writing.

8

English Language Learner

The English Language Learner texts focus on improving language proficiency. You will practice learning strategies and skills in individual and group activities to become better readers, writers, and speakers.

Extended Writing Project and Grammar

This is your opportunity to use genre characteristics and craft to compose meaningful, longer written works exploring the theme of each unit. You will draw information from your readings, research, and own life experiences to complete the assignment.

1 Writing Project

After you have read all of the unit text selections, you will move on to a writing project. Each project will guide you through the process of writing your essay. Student models will provide guidance and help you organize your thoughts. One unit ends with an **Extended Oral Project** which will give you an opportunity to develop your oral language and communication skills.

2 Writing Process Steps

There are four steps in the writing process: Plan, Draft, Revise, and Edit and Publish. During each step, you will form and shape your writing project, and each lesson's peer review will give you the chance to receive feedback from your peers and teacher.

3 Writing Skills

Each Skill lesson focuses on a specific strategy or technique that you will use during your writing project. Each lesson presents a process for applying the skill to your own work and gives you the opportunity to practice it to improve your writing.

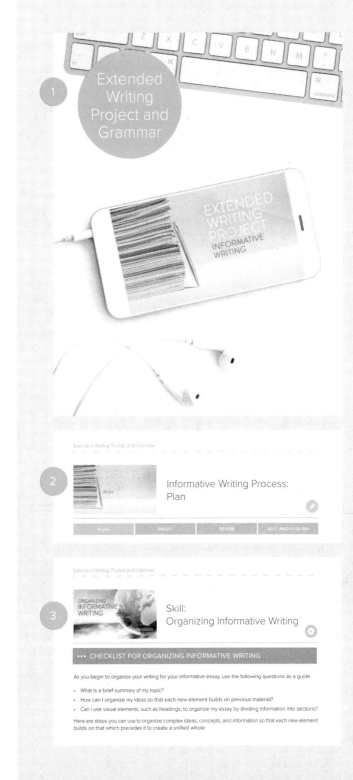

:: study**sync**®

UNIT 1

What's Next?

How can we transform the future?

Genre Focus: INFORMATIONAL

Texts

 Paired Readings

Extended Writing Project and Grammar

Unit 1: What's Next?

How can we transform the future?

CHIMAMANDA NGOZI ADICHIE

Chimamanda Ngozi Adichie (b. 1977) is a writer from Nigeria, who grew up in the house formerly owned by world-famous author Chinua Achebe. She attended college and graduate school in the United States and writes novels, short stories, and essays. In 2013, a speech Adichie gave for TEDxEuston called "We Should All Be Feminists" was sampled in the song "Flawless" by Beyoncé. In 2014, Adichie adapted the speech into a book-length essay of the same name.

FREDERICK DOUGLASS

A vital leader in the abolitionist movement, Frederick Douglass (1818–1895) was the first African American to serve as a United States official and was nominated for vice president of the United States. He was well-regarded in his time as a brilliant and eloquent speaker. Douglass's autobiographical writings, including *Narrative of the Life of Frederick Douglass, An American Slave* (1845), offer a portrait of slavery from the point of view of the enslaved, a much-needed contribution to literature that continues to be widely read.

MOHSIN HAMID

Mohsin Hamid (b. 1971) is a Pakistani American author of four novels. He drafted his first book in a college fiction workshop taught by the writer Toni Morrison, and he believes in the power of literature to visualize different and better ways to live. In an interview published in *The New Yorker,* Hamid stated, "Part of the great political crisis we face in the world today is a failure to imagine plausible desirable futures."

FRANZ KAFKA

Franz Kafka (1883–1924) was born into a middle-class, German-speaking Jewish family in Prague. He was educated as a lawyer and worked for an insurance company, writing on the side, until his death at age forty from tuberculosis. Kafka's stories often feature an isolated protagonist in a nightmarish situation, fusing realism and fantasy. Much of the work Kafka is known for was published posthumously by his friend Max Brod, who had been entrusted to burn the writer's work.

JOHN F. KENNEDY

John F. Kennedy (1917–1963) was the 35th president of the United States, whose brief time in office was colored by Cold War tensions with the Soviet Union and its allies. Shortly after Kennedy's term began in 1961, Russian cosmonaut Yuri Gagarin became the first man in space, and many Americans perceived the United States was losing the so-called space race. Kennedy declared that sending an American to the moon would allow the United States to "catch up and overtake" the Soviet Union in the unclaimed frontier of outer space.

ANNE LAMOTT

As a child growing up in San Francisco, Anne Lamott (b. 1954) was encouraged by her father, also a writer, to take a disciplined approach to the practice—to write every day, and to commit to finishing the pieces she started. By the age of twenty-six, Lamott was a published novelist and has since authored nearly twenty works of fiction and nonfiction. Her best-known book, *Bird by Bird: Some Instructions on Writing and Life* (1994), offers advice on everything from "Getting Started" to "Writer's Block" to "Finding Your Voice."

URSULA MCPIKE

Ursula McPike (b. 1961) grew up in the Detroit area and has always loved to travel. She has lived in Chicago for the last 30+ years, after first visiting the city as a girl and falling in love with the Museum of Science and Industry. She is influenced by reading about cultural differences and topics that draw debate. "Reading a book," according to McPike, "is the closest you can get to making a new friend."

DENA SIMMONS

Dena Simmons (b. 1983) grew up in the Bronx, in a one-bedroom apartment with her two sisters and her mother, who had immigrated to New York from Antigua. When she became the recipient of a scholarship to a majority white boarding school, despite her abundant qualifications, Simmons experienced the feelings of inadequacy and fraud associated with "imposter syndrome." Her career thereafter has been staked in activism and education, as she works to promote culturally responsive practices in the classroom.

ELISSA WASHUTA

Elissa Washuta (b. 1985), a member of the Cowlitz Indian tribe, grew up during a time when Hollywood put forth problematic images of indigenous characters in films like *The Last of the Mohicans* (1992), *Pocahontas* (1995), and *The Indian in the Cupboard* (1995), among others. Washuta is a writer of personal essays and memoir, and her work questions narratives of Native peoples as well as a range of contemporary issues.

MADDIE BADEN, CONNOR BALTHAZOR, GINA MATHEW, TRINA PAUL, KALI POENITSKE, AND PATRICK SULLIVAN

In 2017, high school investigative journalists Maddie Baden, Connor Balthazor, Gina Mathew, Trina Paul, Kali Poenitske, and Patrick Sullivan exposed their newly-hired principal for providing credentials from a false institution. Their story became national news, the principal resigned, and the district hired a replacement. Students at Pittsburg High School are now granted independent control over their editorial content, by the Kansas Student Publications Act, including articles that challenge or criticize the school.

ADAM KIRSCH

Adam Kirsch (b. 1979) is a Los Angeles–born poet, editor, and literary critic who started penning poems at the age of fourteen. He believes literature does not, like science or technology, advance with each new discovery. In an article for *The Atlantic*, Kirsch wrote, "Homer is just as groundbreaking today as he was 2,500 years ago." His work reveals a deep interest in the preservation of traditional literary forms, as shown in his use of meter and rhyme in his three published collections of poetry.

Are the New
'Golden Age' TV
Shows the New
Novels?

INFORMATIONAL TEXT
Adam Kirsch and Mohsin Hamid
2014

Introduction

studysync

A dam Kirsch (b. 1976) is a magazine editor, educator, and poet. He is also a literary critic, winning the Roger Shattuck Prize for Criticism in 2010. Mohsin Hamid (b. 1971) is a novelist, known best for *The Reluctant Fundamentalist*, *Exit West,* and his PEN/Hemingway Award finalist *Moth Smoke*. In this op-ed essay from the *New York Times*, both writers share their thoughts on how contemporary TV has changed how we think about the novel. Through a discussion of the style of Charles Dickens' writing, and an examination of novelistic features, both authors present persuasive arguments for their answer to the question "Are the New 'Golden Age' TV Shows the New Novels?"

To liken TV shows to novels suggests an odd ambivalence toward both genres.

By Adam Kirsch

One criticism that could be leveled against quality cable TV is that it is not nearly as formally adventurous as Dickens himself.

1 Television was so bad for so long, it's no surprise that the arrival of good television has caused the culture to lose its head a bit. Since the debut of "The Sopranos" in 1999, we have been living, so we are regularly informed, in a "golden age" of television. And over the last few years, it's become common to hear variations on the idea that quality cable TV shows are the new novels. Thomas Doherty, writing in *The Chronicle of Higher Education*, called the new genre "Arc TV"—because its stories follow long, complex arcs of development—and insisted that "at its best, the world of Arc TV is as exquisitely calibrated as the social matrix of a Henry James novel."

2 To liken TV shows to novels suggests an odd **ambivalence** toward both genres. Clearly, the comparison is intended to honor TV, by associating it with the prestige and complexity that traditionally belong to literature. But at the same time, it is covertly a form of aggression against literature, suggesting that novels have ceded their role to a younger, more popular, more dynamic art form. Mixed feelings about literature — the desire to annex its virtues while simultaneously belittling them — are typical of our culture today, which doesn't know quite how to deal with an art form, like the novel, that is both democratic and demanding.

3 It's not surprising that the novelist most often mentioned in this context is Charles Dickens. Dickens, like Shakespeare, was both a writer of genius and a popular entertainer, proving that seriousness of purpose didn't preclude accessibility. His novels appeared in serial installments, like episodes of TV shows, and teemed with minor characters, the literary equivalent of character actors. "The Wire," in particular, has been likened to a Dickens novel, for its attention to the details of poverty and class in America. Bill Moyers was echoing what has become conventional wisdom when he said that what Dickens was "to the smoky mean streets of Victorian London, David Simon is to America today."

Skill:
Textual Evidence

Before 1999, television was generally lower quality than the innovative television shows after 1999. The pre-1999 shows did not follow complex story arcs throughout a season the way that a novel does from start to finish.

Reading & Writing Companion

NOTES

Skill:
Textual
Evidence

Dickens's episodic storytelling is similar to cable TV shows' narrative structure. For example, Dickens was able to weave scenes together in a way that is similar to a video montage of shorter scenes put together into a whole.

Skill:
Text-Dependent
Responses

Kirsch supports his argument by listing characteristics unique to literature, such as "voice" and "tone." He thinks TV is still good, but watching TV is not the same experience as reading literature.

4   Ironically, the comparison to Dickens, which is meant to suggest that TV has reached a new level of quality, harks back to the very beginning of modern filmmaking. Already in 1944, Sergei Eisenstein suggested in a landmark essay that the film grammar invented by D. W. Griffith was deeply indebted to Dickens's narrative strategies. Dickens, he wrote, was the real inventor of montage. If today's best TV feels Dickensian, that may be because the conventions of filmed storytelling themselves derive from Dickens — who in turn, Eisenstein points out, was influenced by the stage **melodramas** of his day. Indeed, one criticism that could be leveled against quality cable TV is that it is not nearly as formally adventurous as Dickens himself. Its visual **idiom** tends to be conventional even when its subject matter is ostentatiously provocative.

5   But comparing even the best TV shows with Dickens, or Henry James, also suggests how much the novel can achieve that TV doesn't even attempt. Televised evil, for instance, almost always takes melodramatic form: Our anti-heroes are mobsters, meth dealers or terrorists. But this has nothing to do with the way we encounter evil in real life, which is why a character like Gilbert Osmond, in "The Portrait of a Lady," is more chilling in his bullying egotism than Tony Soprano with all his stranglings and shootings.

6   Spectacle and melodrama remain at the heart of TV, as they do with all arts that must reach a large audience in order to be economically viable. But it is voice, tone, the sense of the author's mind at work, that are the essence of literature, and they exist in language, not in images. This doesn't mean we shouldn't be grateful for our good TV shows; but let's not fool ourselves into thinking that they give us what only literature can.

The writing has improved remarkably, as have the acting, direction and design.

By Mohsin Hamid

Ask novelists whether they spend more time watching TV or reading fiction and prepare yourself to hear them say the unsayable.

7 Movies have always seemed to me a much tighter form of storytelling than novels, requiring greater compression, and in that sense falling somewhere between the short story and the novel in scale. To watch a feature film is to be immersed in its world for an hour and a half, or maybe two, or exceptionally three. A novel that takes only three hours to read would be a short novel indeed, and novels that last five times as long are commonplace.

8 Television is more **capacious**. Episode after episode, and season after season, a serial drama can uncoil for dozens of hours before reaching its end. Along the way, its characters and plot have room to develop, to change course, to congeal. In its near limitlessness, TV rivals the novel.

9 What once sheltered the novel were differences in the quality of writing. Films could be well written, but they were smaller than novels. TV was big, but its writing was clunky. The novel had "Pride and Prejudice"; TV had "Dynasty." But television has made enormous leaps in the last decade or so. The writing has improved remarkably, as have the acting, direction and design.

10 Recently we've been treated to many shows that seem better than any that came before: the brilliant ethnography of "The Wire," the dazzling sci-fi of "Battlestar Galactica," the gorgeous period re-creation of "Mad Men," the gripping fantasy of "Game of Thrones," the lacerating self-exploration of "Girls." Nor is TV's rise confined to shows originating in only one country. Pakistani, Indian, British and dubbed Turkish dramas are all being devoured here in Pakistan. Thanks to downloads, even Denmark's "Borgen" has found its local niche.

11 I now watch a lot of TV. And I'm not alone, even among my colleagues. Ask novelists today whether they spend more time watching TV or reading fiction and prepare yourself, at least occasionally, to hear them say the unsayable.

NOTES

NOTES

12 That this represents a crisis for the novel seems to me undeniable. But a crisis can be an opportunity. It **incites** change. And the novel needs to keep changing if it is to remain novel. It must, pilfering a phrase from TV, boldly go where no one has gone before.

13 In the words of the Canadian writer Sheila Heti: "Now that there are these impeccable serial dramas, writers of fiction should feel let off the hook more — not feel obliged to worry so much about plot or character, since audiences can get their fill of plot and character and story there, so novelists can take off in other directions, like what happened with painting when photography came into being more than a hundred years ago. After that there was an incredible flourishing of the art, in so many fascinating directions. The novel should only do what the serial drama could never do."

14 Television is not the new novel. Television is the old novel.

Skill:
Informational Text
Elements

Hamid tells novelists to embrace the novel's "weirdness" to stay relevant "in the future." Hamid believes the novel is weird because it is intimate yet vast. TV, in contrast, is a "small world."

15 In the future, novelists need not abandon plot and character, but would do well to bear in mind the novel's weirdness. . . . Novels are characterized by their intimacy, which is extreme, by their scale, which is vast, and by their form, which is linguistic and synesthetic. . . .

16 Television gives us something that looks like a small world, made by a group of people who are themselves a small world. The novel gives us sounds pinned down by hieroglyphs, refracted flickerings inside an individual.

17 Sufis tell of two paths to transcendence: One is to look out at the universe and see yourself, the other is to look within yourself and see the universe. Their destinations may converge, but television and the novel travel in opposite directions.

Skill: Text-Dependent Responses

Use the Checklist to analyze Text-Dependent Responses in "Are the New 'Golden Age' TV Shows the New Novels?" Refer to the sample student annotations about Text-Dependent Responses in the text.

••• CHECKLIST FOR TEXT-DEPENDENT RESPONSES

In order to identify strong and thorough textual evidence that supports an analysis, note the following:

✓ strong and thorough details from the text to make an inference or draw a conclusion. Inferences are sound, logical assumptions about information in a text that is not explicitly stated. To practice, you should:

- read closely and consider why an author provides or excludes particular details and information
- apply textual evidence and your own knowledge and experiences to help you figure out what the author does not state directly
- cite several pieces of textual evidence that offer strong support for your analysis
- note where textual evidence is lacking, leaving some matters uncertain

✓ strong and thorough details to support your ideas and opinions about a text

✓ explicit evidence of an author's ideas in an informational text

- explicit evidence is stated directly and must be cited accurately to support a text-dependent response

To cite strong and thorough textual evidence to support an analysis, including determining where the text leaves matters uncertain, consider the following questions:

✓ What strong and thorough textual evidence can I use to support an analysis of a text?

✓ Where does the text leave matters uncertain? How will that affect my analysis?

✓ If I infer things in the text that the author does not state directly, what evidence can I use to support my analysis?

Please note that excerpts and passages in the StudySync® library and this workbook are intended as touchstones to generate interest in an author's work. The excerpts and passages do not substitute for the reading of entire texts, and StudySync® strongly recommends that students seek out and purchase the whole literary or informational work in order to experience it as the author intended. Links to online resellers are available in our digital library. In addition, complete works may be ordered through an authorized reseller by filling out and returning to StudySync® the order form enclosed in this workbook.

Reading & Writing Companion

5

Skill: Text-Dependent Responses

Reread paragraphs 7–11 of "Are the New 'Golden Age' TV Shows the New Novels?" Then, using the Checklist on the previous page, answer the multiple-choice questions below.

⟳ YOUR TURN

1. In paragraph 7, Hamid reveals that "Movies have always seemed to me a much tighter form of storytelling than novels, requiring greater compression, and in that sense falling somewhere between the short story and the novel in scale." Which commentary best responds to this textual evidence?

   - ○ A. This textual evidence shows that storytelling in movies is more like a short story than a novel.
   - ○ B. This textual evidence shows that storytelling in movies is tighter and smaller in scope than novels.
   - ○ C. This textual evidence shows that storytelling in movies is similar to storytelling in television.
   - ○ D. This textual evidence shows that storytelling in movies is greater in scale and larger in scope than novels.

2. Which evidence best supports the idea that television is more like a novel than a movie because there is more time to develop characters?

   - ○ A. "A novel that takes only three hours to read would be a short novel indeed, and novels that last five times as long are commonplace."
   - ○ B. "Episode after episode, and season after season, a serial drama can uncoil for dozens of hours before reaching its end."
   - ○ C. "Films could be well written, but they were smaller than novels."
   - ○ D. "Ask novelists whether they spend more time watching TV or reading fiction and prepare yourself to hear them say the unsayable."

First Read

Read "Are the New 'Golden Age' TV Shows the New Novels?" After you read, complete the Think Questions below.

THINK QUESTIONS

1. What does Kirsch say about how TV has changed recently? What is the "new genre" he mentions? Use evidence from the text to support your answer.

2. Why do people often compare "good" TV to the writing of Charles Dickens? What does Kirsch say about Dickens's writing that welcomes this comparison? Use evidence from the text to support your answer.

3. What are the reasons Hamid gives for watching more television than in the past? Use evidence from the text to support your answer.

4. What is the meaning of the word **capacious** as it is used in the text? Write your best definition here, along with a brief explanation of how you inferred its meaning through context.

5. Read the following dictionary entry:

idiom

id•i•om /ˈidēəm/ *noun*

1. a group of words, that when used together, have an unclear meaning when read literally
2. a form of expression natural to a language, person, or group of people
3. the dialect of a people or part of a country
4. a characteristic mode of expression in music, literature or art

Which definition most closely matches the meaning of idiom as it is used in paragraph 4? Write the correct definition of idiom here and explain how you figured out its meaning.

Skill:
Textual Evidence

Use the Checklist to analyze Textual Evidence in "Are the New 'Golden Age' TV Shows the New Novels?" Refer to the sample student annotations about Textual Evidence in the text.

••• CHECKLIST FOR TEXTUAL EVIDENCE

In order to support an analysis by citing evidence that is explicitly stated in the text, do the following:

- ✓ read the text closely and critically

- ✓ identify what the text says explicitly

- ✓ find the most relevant textual evidence that supports your analysis

- ✓ consider why an author explicitly states specific details and information

- ✓ cite the specific words, phrases, sentences, or paragraphs from the text that support your analysis

- ✓ determine where evidence in the text still leaves certain matters uncertain or unresolved

In order to interpret implicit meanings in a text by making inferences, do the following:

- ✓ combine information directly stated in the text with your own knowledge, experiences, and observations

- ✓ cite the specific words, phrases, sentences, or paragraphs from the text that led to and support this inference.

In order to cite textual evidence to support an analysis of what the text says explicitly as well as inferences drawn from the text, consider the following questions:

- ✓ Have I read the text closely and critically?

- ✓ What inferences am I making about the text?

- ✓ What textual evidence am I using to support these inferences?

- ✓ Am I quoting the evidence from the text correctly?

- ✓ Does my textual evidence logically relate to my analysis or the inference I am making?

- ✓ Does evidence in the text still leave certain matters unanswered or unresolved? In what ways?

Please note that excerpts and passages in the StudySync® library and this workbook are intended as touchstones to generate interest in an author's work. The excerpts and passages do not substitute for the reading of entire texts, and StudySync® strongly recommends that students seek out and purchase the whole literary or informational work in order to experience it as the author intended. Links to online resellers are available in our digital library. In addition, complete works may be ordered through an authorized reseller by filling out and returning to StudySync® the order form enclosed in this workbook.

Reading & Writing
Companion

9

Skill:
Textual Evidence

Reread paragraphs 7–9 of "Are the New 'Golden Age' TV Shows the New Novels?" Then, using the Checklist on the previous page, answer the multiple-choice questions below.

 YOUR TURN

1. According to the text, a novel is similar to a television series because—

   ○ A. the writing is consistently excellent for both.
   ○ B. the storytelling must be concise and compressed in both.
   ○ C. they both appeal to people who dislike watching movies.
   ○ D. they both allow for effective character and plot development.

2. In paragraph 9, which word best supports the author's claim that television used to be inferior to novels?

   ○ A. "sheltered"
   ○ B. "smaller"
   ○ C. "clunky"
   ○ D. "leaps"

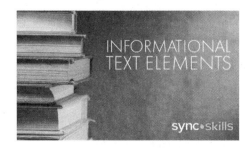

Skill: Informational Text Elements

Use the Checklist to analyze Informational Text Elements in "Are the New 'Golden Age' TV Shows the New Novels?" Refer to the sample student annotations about Informational Text Elements in the text.

••• CHECKLIST FOR INFORMATIONAL TEXT ELEMENTS

In order to identify characteristics and structural elements of informational texts, note the following:

- ✓ key details in the text that provide information about individuals, events, and ideas

- ✓ interactions between specific individuals, ideas, or events

- ✓ important developments over the course of the text

- ✓ transition words and phrases that signal interactions between individuals, events, and ideas, such as *because*, *as a consequence*, or *as a result*

- ✓ similarities and differences of types of information in a text

To analyze a complex set of ideas or sequence of events and explain how specific

- ✓ individuals, ideas, or events interact and develop over the course of the text, consider the following questions:

- ✓ How does the author present the information as a sequence of events?

- ✓ How does the order in which ideas or events are presented affect the connections between them?

- ✓ How do specific individuals, ideas, or events interact and develop over the course of the text?

- ✓ What other features, if any, help readers to analyze the events, ideas, or individuals in the text?

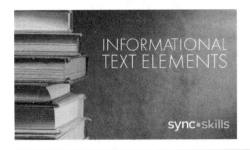

Skill: Informational Text Elements

Reread paragraphs 5 and 6 of "Are the New 'Golden Age' TV Shows the New Novels?" Then, using the Checklist on the previous page, answer the multiple-choice questions below.

⟳ YOUR TURN

1. What does the author's use of the transition phrase "for instance" tell the reader?

   ○ A. that the sentence includes an example to support the idea in the sentence before it
   ○ B. that the sentence includes an example to support the idea in the sentence after it
   ○ C. that the author's main point in the paragraph is explained in the sentence.
   ○ D. that the second half of the paragraph discusses a new topic

2. Why does the author compare Gilbert Osmond to Tony Soprano in paragraph 5?

   ○ A. to conclude that Soprano is a more likeable character than Osmond
   ○ B. to show a counterexample to his thesis that he then refutes
   ○ C. to give clear and concrete evidence to support his thesis
   ○ D. to refer to a character in a novel that all Americans have read

Close Read

Reread "Are the New 'Golden Age' TV Shows the New Novels?" As you reread, complete the Skills Focus questions below. Then use your answers and annotations from the questions to help you complete the Write activity.

◎ SKILLS FOCUS

1. What are the advantages and disadvantages of how TV shows are structured? Use textual evidence to support your answer.

2. Mohsin Hamid believes that TV shows pose a real threat for novelists, and that novelists will need to find a way to adapt in the future. How does Hamid structure his argument?

3. Highlight two examples of supporting evidence in Kirsch's essay. How does the author connect these pieces of evidence to other parts of his argument?

4. Although the authors have different ideas about the role of literature in our lives, they both see a future for both novels and TV shows. What direction would each author give to these artforms? Highlight and annotate examples from the text to support your answer.

✎ WRITE

EXPLANATORY ESSAY: Select one of the articles. Analyze how the author uses examples, explanations, and concluding remarks to support his thesis and provide direction to his ideas. Remember to use textual evidence to support your points.

Please note that excerpts and passages in the StudySync® library and this workbook are intended as touchstones to generate interest in an author's work. The excerpts and passages do not substitute for the reading of entire texts, and StudySync® strongly recommends that students seek out and purchase the whole literary or informational work in order to experience it as the author intended. Links to online resellers are available in our digital library. In addition, complete works may be ordered through an authorized reseller by filling out and returning to StudySync® the order form enclosed in this workbook.

Reading & Writing Companion   **13**

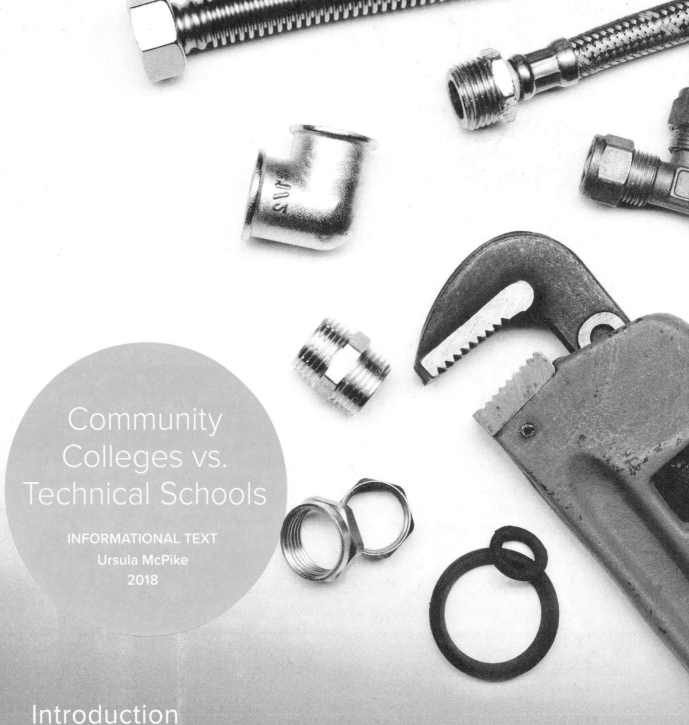

Community Colleges vs. Technical Schools

INFORMATIONAL TEXT
Ursula McPike
2018

Introduction

Before students begin the college application process, it is important that they are aware of the options available to them. This text offers key information and comparisons between what one will find at a community college and what one will find at a technical school. While both provide strong educational foundations, the curricula, cost, duration, and outcomes offered differ between these institutions. "Community Colleges vs. Technical Schools" encourages students to consider these and other factors when deciding where to get an education.

"If you do some research on two-year schools, you might find one that is just right for you."

Community Colleges vs. Technical Schools

1   If you or your bank account has decided that enrolling in a four-year college is not for you, don't despair. You still have options. One choice is a community college, also called a junior college. Another choice is a technical school, also called a **vocational** or trade school. These schools offer programs that take two years or less to complete, and they serve a surprising number of students. According to the National Center for Educational Statistics, 6.1 million undergraduates (36%) were enrolled in two-year colleges in Fall 2016. To compare, 10.8 million (64%) were enrolled in four-year colleges. If you do some research on two-year schools, you might find one that is just right for you.

Community Colleges

2   A community college is a two-year government-supported college that offers an associate's degree and draws its students from a particular community. It usually offers general academic courses in English, writing, and math. It may also provide **technical** training for a specific job, such as emergency medical technician (EMT) or paralegal.

3   Admission at a community college is non-selective, meaning it is much easier to get admitted there than at a four-year college. Additionally, tuition costs at a community college are much lower than those at an in-state four year institution—typically less than half as much. Often people go to community colleges with the intention of transferring to a four-year college once they receive their associate's degree, ultimately achieving a four-year degree for much less than the typical student. Students who don't intend to transfer look forward to starting their careers (and cashing their paychecks) sooner than graduates of four-year colleges.

Things to Consider About Community Colleges

4   Although community colleges offer many benefits, some aspects of these schools need to be considered carefully. With the right financial aid package,

the cost of a four-year college can be brought down to the cost of a community college. With their flexible hours and lack of student housing, community colleges were designed for working students and do not offer the athletic programs and rich social life that a four-year college does.

5   There is also a stigma, or bad perception, attached to community colleges, with many people believing that their students and teachers are less intelligent than those at four-year "regular" colleges. Secondly, although community college students start working sooner, students from traditional colleges eventually catch up with them in earnings. And if students plan to move on to a four-year institution, not all credits may transfer. It usually takes a transfer student an extra (fifth) year to **obtain** a bachelor's degree. Even if credits do transfer, it is is still difficult to get a degree from a four-year school after starting out at a community college. The educational research firm EAB found that out of 100 applicants to a two-year college, only nine completed their associate's degree, and only seven eventually gained a bachelor's degree from a four-year school.

Technical Colleges

6   A technical college is career-focused, giving hands-on training to students in fields such as cosmetology, culinary arts, and skilled trades such as welding. Their programs usually last two years or less. Such schools are usually private and for-profit. Their costs vary widely, but the average cost is about $33,000. Many technical school students learn their jobs through apprenticeships, where they work under an expert in their field. Technical school students find work very quickly, since there is a labor shortage of skilled workers. For the same reason, technical school students also have more job security once they begin working. Moreover, many careers in technical fields are high-paying; for instance, the U.S. Bureau of Labor Statistics reports that the median salary for an air traffic controller is $124,540, and the median salary for a dental hygienist is $74,070.

Things to Consider About Technical Colleges

7   Unlike community colleges, which offer a wide variety of courses and room to change and explore, trade schools won't let you have a do-over. If you began a nursing program and then decided you wanted to be a lab technician, you would have to start all over again. You should also keep in mind that preferred skills and school standings change rapidly. A program considered the best in one year may not be considered the best in the next year. A skill that is in high demand at one time may not be desirable later (think typewriter repair or an outdated programming language).

8 Although technical school graduates, like community college graduates, can start their careers sooner than four-year graduates and with less debt, the four-year graduate eventually catches up to and surpasses them in earnings. Statistics about earnings also hide that most high-paying vocational jobs are held by men, whereas women cluster in low-paying jobs such as nursing aides.

9 Keep in mind that there is a stigma against technical schools, as there is against community colleges. Many people today still hold the same attitudes about graduates from vocational schools that early 20th-century thinker John Dewey expressed:

> "[Vocational training] fits them to become cogs in the industrial machine. Free men need liberal education to make a good use of their freedom."

10 Maybe, maybe not. Distaste for vocational and community colleges can be seen as ironic now, as graduates of two-year colleges do some of the most necessary work in a community—drawing blood, repairing computers, operating water treatment plants, and countless other tasks that keep us all alive and well.

11 Furthermore, a focus on technical education can revive a community. Walla Walla Community College, faced with a decline in local industries such as agriculture, food processing, and lumber, and a rise in the numbers of workers needing to be retrained, **expanded** the number of programs it offered. It created more than 100 programs, with 60% in technical areas. One popular program was in enology and viticulture (winemaking). Over time, the number of wineries in the area grew from 16 to 200 and the hospitality sector ballooned. Hundreds of thousands of wine tourists visited, and hotels and restaurants sprang up to **accommodate** them. The town regained prosperity, due in (large) part to its additional technical education offerings.

Which type of college is better for you?

12 Take this quiz to find out. Check the box under the answer that best fits you. Most "Yes" answers indicate that a community college would be a better choice for you. Most "No" answers indicate that a technical college would be more suitable.

Yes	No	
_____	_____	Are you unsure of the exact job you desire?
_____	_____	Do you require a low tuition?

NOTES

Yes	No	
_____	_____	Do you plan to transfer to a four-year school?
_____	_____	Can you take an extra (fifth) year to get a four-year degree?
_____	_____	Do you have somewhere to live for the time you are in school?
_____	_____	Will your credits transfer to your chosen four-year school?
_____	_____	Do you want to get a job as soon as possible?
_____	_____	Would you like knowing you have contributed to your local economy?
_____	_____	Would you prefer general academic classes over an apprenticeship?

✏ WRITE

PERSONAL RESPONSE: Write a journal entry in which you weigh your options after high school. Consider your hopes for the future as well as the resources and supports that will be available to you. Which experiences would best prepare you for your career, or perhaps help inform your decision? What might your next steps be?

Overcoming Impostor Syndrome

INFORMATIONAL TEXT
Dena Simmons
2018

Introduction

Impostor syndrome is not a mental illness. It is a common set of negative behavioral responses to achievement. When individuals don't give themselves credit for their successes—internalizing their failures instead—they may come to see success as undeserved, or just a stroke of luck. To doubt oneself is human. But to constantly filter one's experiences so that the bad is earned and the good is undeserved is what doctors and psychologists call "impostor syndrome." Impostor syndrome is estimated to affect three out of every four people at some point in their lives. But is there hope for those that suffer from it? Author Dena Simmons reviews the syndrome and shares concrete advice for combating it.

"If you struggle with impostor experiences, you are not alone."

Skill:
Informational Text
Structure

Using headings to structure the text into categories, the author tells readers how to overcome impostor syndrome. This helps readers understand what impostor syndrome is before determining if they are affected by it.

What is impostor syndrome?

1 Do you ever sit in class and say to yourself, "I'm not smart enough to be here"? Do you ever feel like your accomplishments are mere luck, or that you simply do not deserve them? Do you back down from challenges because you fear being evaluated? If you answered "yes" to any of these questions, it is likely that you have impostor syndrome.

2 Now, you might be thinking, "What is impostor syndrome?" Well, impostor syndrome—first described in a 1978 academic paper by Dr. Pauline Clance and her colleague, Dr. Suzanne Imes—is characterized by intense feelings that make you believe that you are inadequate or a fraud, even if your accomplishments prove otherwise. Essentially, people with impostor syndrome do not **internalize** their success. Impostor syndrome goes by numerous names: impostor phenomenon, impostorism, impostor feelings, impostor experiences, impostor fears, and perceived fraudulence. Though there are slight distinctions to these constructs, the common element is having the internal experience of incompetence and fraudulence specifically related to achievement situations like school and the workplace (Sakulkum and Alexander 2011; Harvey 1985).

3 In sum, based on a 2011 article in the *International Journal of Behavioral Science* that reviewed the definitions and characteristics of impostorism (Sakulkum and Alexander 2011), people with impostor syndrome:

- feel like a fraud and believe that others think more favorably of their successes and achievements than they do.

- fear that other people will discover that they are a fraud and believe that they are a failure just as they believe themselves to be.

- have difficulty internalizing their successes, and as a result, attribute their achievements to external factors.

What impostor syndrome is not

4   People generally assume that impostor syndrome is a mental health disorder because of the use of the word *syndrome*. However, it is not a mental illness. In fact, impostor syndrome is not listed in the *Diagnostic and Statistical Manual of Mental Disorders*, which is the main authority on psychiatric **diagnoses** published by the American Psychiatric Association. However, impostor syndrome can interfere with your psychological well-being and lead to depression (Henning, Ey, and Shaw 1998) and low self-esteem (Sonnak and Towell 2001). Some people with impostor syndrome might also engage in maladaptive behaviors—behaviors that get in the way of a person's ability to function well in everyday activities, such as procrastination or over-working.

Who struggles with impostor feelings?

5   When impostor syndrome was first studied in 1978, researchers Drs. Clance and Imes believed that it was a phenomenon that only high-achieving women experienced. However, over the years, numerous studies have found that both men and women (Langford 1990) and people across different cultures (Clance et al. 1995) and occupations (Fried-Buchalter 1992; Topping 1983; Prata and Gietzen 2007) admit to feeling like an impostor at some point in their lives. Essentially, as discussed in a 1981 academic paper by Dr. Harvey, anyone can identify as an impostor as long as they fail to internalize their success. Dr. Harvey (1981) also found that impostor syndrome is not limited to highly successful people.

6   In fact, if you struggle with impostor experiences, you are not alone. According to a 1985 paper by Dr. Gail Matthew and Dr. Clance, about 70% of the sample expressed having impostor feelings at some point in their lives. In addition, notable, successful people have admitted to experiencing impostorism including author Maya Angelou, technology leader Sheryl Sandberg, and actor Tom Hanks. Though diverse groups of people have struggled with impostorism, people from marginalized backgrounds tend to experience it more. This can be a result of **discrimination**, stereotype threat, or microaggressions[1] that potentially lead marginalized groups to internalize feelings of fraudulence and not belonging.

What emotions are common for people who have impostor syndrome?

7   Two emotions that people with impostor syndrome commonly feel are anxiety and fear (Clance 1985). When people feel anxious, they feel uncertain about the future. Anxiety can manifest in tension in the body, an increased heartbeat, an inability to stay still and focus, and hurried speech. People with impostor

Skill: Central or Main Idea

This seems like a central idea because it answers the question in the sub-heading. It also relates to defining impostor syndrome, which the previous paragraphs also do. This shows how various main ideas can build on one another.

---

1. **microaggressions** commonplace verbal or physical slights or insults that communicate a prejudice toward a marginalized group

syndrome experience anxiety because they are not sure what will happen when and if someone finds out that they are a fraud. On the other hand, when people are fearful, they feel there is impending danger. Fear can result in tense bodies, sweaty palms, an increased heartbeat, and wide eyes. People who suffer from impostorism might be fearful about what will happen if they fail or are evaluated poorly. Will they get kicked out of a program or class? Will they be bullied? Will they be embarrassed in front of others? People with impostor syndrome also tend to experience self-doubt, shame, and frustration.

What can we do to overcome our impostor feelings?

1. Talk to others.

Skill:
Informational Text
Structure

Subheadings and clearly labeled steps are effective in helping readers follow the author's instructions, which fulfills the author's purpose for writing: to teach readers how to identify and combat impostor syndrome.

8 When you share your impostor experiences with others, you realize you are not the only one struggling through it. Learning that you are not alone and that other people experience self-doubt as well as impostor feelings can be liberating. In the process of sharing impostor experiences with others, you build community and a safe space. You also begin to believe your successes and achievements are well-deserved.

How to begin:
- With friends that you trust, start a conversation where you share your own experiences of feeling like a fraud and impostor, and invite others to share theirs
- Then, together with your friends, discuss what strategies others have used to tackle their challenges and come up with a way to support each other.

2. Engage in positive self-talk.

Skill:
Central or Main
Idea

The main idea here involves coping with impostor syndrome. The strategy interacts with the idea that anyone can experience impostor syndrome, so speaking about it should be natural and will help you realize you are not alone.

9 People with impostor syndrome generally engage in negative self-talk, the mean and discouraging comments they say to themselves. Some examples of negative self-talk include: "I'm not smart enough to get into my first-choice college!" or "They only accepted me because they felt bad for me." To begin to confront impostor experiences, people need to be kinder to themselves by engaging in positive self-talk, which involves saying encouraging and uplifting statements to yourself. Some examples of positive self-talk include: "You worked hard, and you earned your accomplishments!" and "You are smart enough to be in this class!" By engaging in positive self-talk, you unlock optimism and self-confidence.

How to begin:
- Make a list of the negative comments that you say to yourself often.
- Then, next to each negative comment, write a positive message to yourself instead.
- Afterwards, devise a plan to interrupt your negative self-talk with positive self-talk.

3. Build an emotion management strategy tool box.

10 People who have impostor syndrome tend to feel anxious, frustrated, ashamed, and fearful. These emotions feel unpleasant and can distract people from achieving their goals. That's why it is important to develop strategies to manage emotions, especially the uncomfortable emotions that come with impostorism. To manage emotions effectively, it is important to have a toolbox of strategies from which you can choose.

Emotion management strategies include:
1. Action strategies. These are ways you use your body to regulate emotions, like seeking social support, going for a run, or taking a deep breath.

2. Thought strategies. These are ways you use your mind to regulate emotions, like **visualizing** a successful outcome or reframing everything you do as a learning experience.

How to begin:
- Write a list of thought and action strategies that you already use to manage uncomfortable emotions.

- Put an asterisk next to those strategies that you can employ whenever you are beginning to feel like an impostor in any situation or environment.

4. Leverage your strengths to tackle the areas where you feel like an impostor.

11 Undoubtedly, you are great at something. To begin to confront your impostor feelings, it is helpful to think about your strengths as a way to build the confidence needed to tackle those areas that make you feel like an impostor.

How to begin:
- Make a list of all of your strengths. Then, next to each strength, write down what steps you took to get good at that specific skill or activity.

- Afterwards, write a list of the goals you want to accomplish with an action plan, leveraging some of the steps you took to develop your strengths.

5. Be self-compassionate.

12 Clance (1985) found that people who experience impostor syndrome tend to aim for perfectionism. As such, when things do not go as planned, people who struggle with impostorism feel overwhelmed or disappointed and tend to generalize their inability to meet their perfectionistic goals as evidence that they are a failure. Instead of focusing on being perfect, it is helpful to

remind yourself that everyone is entitled to make mistakes—even you. And, when you do well, do something amazing for yourself.

How to begin:

- When working on an assignment or another task, evaluate your goals by asking yourself the following questions:

  > Can I accomplish this by the deadline if there is a deadline? If you cannot, consider making changes to have a more realistic goal.

  > Will I enjoy myself while doing this task or am I just doing it to stand out among my peers? If you are not enjoying yourself, it is best you consider coming up with a goal that both challenges you accordingly and brings you joy.

  > Do I have the resources to complete the task at hand? If you do not have the resources, either create a plan to attain them or consider another task that you can complete with the resources that you have.

13 These are just some of the ways that you can begin to confront your inner impostor. You might find your own ways to manage your impostor syndrome, but whatever you do, the goal is to develop strategies to promote your personal growth, **enhance** your wellbeing, build positive relationships, and contribute to your desired goals.

References:

Clance, Pauline Rose, and Suzanne Ament Imes. "The Imposter Phenomenon in High Achieving Women: Dynamics and Therapeutic Intervention." *Psychotherapy: Theory, Research & Practice,* vol. 15, no. 3, 1978, pp. 241–247.

Clance, Pauline Rose. *The Imposter Phenomenon: Overcoming the Fear That Haunts Your Success.* Peach Tree Pub Ltd., 1985.

Clance, Pauline Rose, et al. "Imposter Phenomenon in an Interpersonal/Social Context." *Women & Therapy,* vol. 16, no. 4, 1995, pp. 79–96.

Fried-Buchalter, Sharon. "Fear of Success, Fear of Failure, and the Impostor Phenomenon Among Male and Female Marketing Managers."ikm *Sex Roles,* vol. 37, no. 11, 1997, pp. 847–859.

Harvey, J. C. *The Impostor Phenomenon and Achievement: A Failure to Internalize Success.* Dissertation, Temple University, 1981. UMI, 42. ATT 4969B.

Kolligian, John, and Robert J. Sternberg. "Perceived Fraudulence in Young Adults: Is there an "Impostor Syndrome"?" *Journal of Personality Assessment,* vol. 56, no. 2, 1991, pp. 308–326.

Langford, Joe. *The Need to Look Smart: The Impostor Phenomenon and Motivations for Learning.* Dissertation, Georgia State University, 1990. UMI, 51. ATT 3604B.

Leary, Mark R., et al."The Impostor Phenomenon: Self-Perceptions, Reflected Appraisals, and Interpersonal Strategies." *Journal of Personality,* vol. 68, no. 4, 2000, pp. 725–756.

Matthews, Gail, and Pauline Rose Clance. "Treatment of the Impostor Phenomenon in Psychotherapy Clients." *Psychotherapy in Private Practice,* vol. 3, no. 1, 1985, pp. 71–81.

Prata, John, and Jonathan W. Gietzen. "The Imposter Phenomenon in Physician Assistant Graduates." *The Journal of Physician Assistant Education,* vol. 18, no. 4, 2007, pp. 33–36.

Sakulkum, Jaruwan, and James Alexander. "The Impostor Phenomenon." *International Journal of Behavioral Science,* vol. 6, no. 1, 2011, pp. 75–97.

Sonnak, Carina, and Tony Towell. "The Impostor Phenomenon in British University Students: Relationships Between Self-Esteem, Mental Health, Parental Rearing Style and Socioeconomic Status." *Personality and Individual Differences*, vol. 31, no. 6, 2001, pp. 863–874.

Topping, Mary Elaine Harvey. *The Impostor Phenomenon: A Study of its Construct and Incidence in University Faculty Members.* Doctoral Dissertation, University of South Florida, 1983. UMI, 44. ATT 1948B–1949B.

Dena Simmons, Ed.D., is an activist, educator, and student of life from the Bronx, New York. She serves as the Assistant Director of the Yale Center for Emotional Intelligence. She writes and speaks nationally about social justice and culturally responsive and sustaining pedagogy, as well as creating emotionally intelligent and safe classrooms within the context of equity.

Please note that excerpts and passages in the StudySync® library and this workbook are intended as touchstones to generate interest in an author's work. The excerpts and passages do not substitute for the reading of entire texts, and StudySync® strongly recommends that students seek out and purchase the whole literary or informational work in order to experience it as the author intended. Links to online resellers are available in our digital library. In addition, complete works may be ordered through an authorized reseller by filling out and returning to StudySync® the order form enclosed in this workbook.

Reading & Writing Companion

25

OVERCOMING
IMPOSTOR SYNDROME

First Read

Read "Overcoming Impostor Syndrome." After you read, complete the Think Questions below.

THINK QUESTIONS

1. According to the author, what is "maladaptive behavior" and how does it impact an individual? What are some other maladaptive behaviors besides the ones provided in the text? Refer to the text to support your thinking.

2. In what ways might a person with impostor syndrome worry about the future? Support your answer with examples from the text.

3. What kinds of words or actions would be helpful to a friend who is dealing with impostor syndrome? Why and how would these words or actions help? Use the text to support your answer.

4. What is the meaning of the word **diagnoses** as it is used in the text? Write your best definition here, along with a brief explanation of how you arrived at its meaning.

5. Use context clues to figure out the definition of the word **enhance** as it is used in this text. Write your definition here, then check a dictionary to confirm your understanding.

Skill: Informational Text Structure

Use the Checklist to analyze Informational Text Structure in "Overcoming Impostor Syndrome." Refer to the sample student annotations about Informational Text Structure in the text.

••• CHECKLIST FOR INFORMATIONAL TEXT STRUCTURE

In order to determine the structure an author uses in his or her exposition or argument, note the following:

- ✓ where the author introduces and clarifies their argument

- ✓ sentences and paragraphs that reveal the text structure the author uses to frame the argument

- ✓ whether the text structure is effective in presenting all sides of the argument, and makes his or her points clear, convincing and engaging

To analyze and evaluate the effectiveness of the structure an author uses in his or her exposition or argument, including whether the structure makes points clear, convincing, and engaging, consider the following questions:

- ✓ Did I have to read a particular sentence or phrase over again? Where?

- ✓ Did I find myself distracted or uninterested while reading the text? When?

- ✓ Did the structure the author used make their points clear, convincing, and engaging? Why or why not?

- ✓ Was the author's exposition or argument effective? Why or why not?

Please note that excerpts and passages in the StudySync® library and this workbook are intended as touchstones to generate interest in an author's work. The excerpts and passages do not substitute for the reading of entire texts, and StudySync® strongly recommends that students seek out and purchase the whole literary or informational work in order to experience it as the author intended. Links to online resellers are available in our digital library. In addition, complete works may be ordered through an authorized reseller by filling out and returning to StudySync® the order form enclosed in this workbook.

Reading & Writing
Companion

27

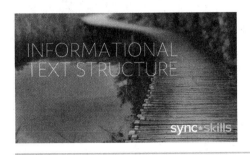

Skill: Informational Text Structure

Reread paragraph 12 of "Overcoming Impostor Syndrome." Then, using the Checklist on the previous page, answer the multiple-choice questions below.

⟳ YOUR TURN

1. Which statement best relates the author's text structure to her purpose in this excerpt?

   ○ A. The author classifies people according to whether or not they have impostor syndrome to present information about unpleasant emotions.

   ○ B. The author structures the text by dividing it into describing the problem then explaining solutions to the problem.

   ○ C. The author structures the text by explaining the advantages and disadvantages of emotion management strategies.

   ○ D. The author structures the text by comparing and contrasting people who are not affected by impostor syndrome with people who are.

2. Does the author effectively use text structure to achieve her purpose in this excerpt?

   ○ A. Yes, because the author explains how people who have impostor syndrome tend to feel anxious and ashamed.

   ○ B. Yes, because the author uses subheadings and gives organized lists of both examples and ways to begin using the strategies.

   ○ C. No, because the author should have written the entire excerpt in bulleted format, instead of alternating lists with prose.

   ○ D. No, because the author does not provide ways of using these emotional management strategies.

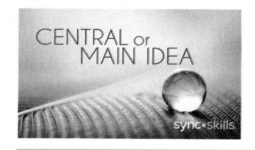

Skill: Central or Main Idea

Use the Checklist to analyze Central or Main Idea in "Overcoming Impostor Syndrome." Refer to the sample student annotations about Central or Main Idea in the text.

••• CHECKLIST FOR CENTRAL OR MAIN IDEA

In order to identify two or more central ideas of a text, note the following:

- ✓ the main idea in each paragraph or group of paragraphs

- ✓ key details in each paragraph or section of text, noticing what they have in common

- ✓ whether the details contain information that could indicate more than one main idea in a text

  - a science text, for example, may provide information about a specific environment and also a message on ecological awareness

  - a biography may contain equally important ideas about a person's achievements, influence, and the time period in which the person lives or lived

- ✓ when each central idea emerges

- ✓ ways that the central ideas interact and build on one another

To determine two or more central ideas of a text and analyze their development over the course of the text, including how they interact and build on one another to provide a complex analysis, consider the following questions:

- ✓ What main idea(s) do the details in each paragraphs explain or describe?

- ✓ What central or main ideas do all the paragraphs support?

- ✓ How do the central ideas interact and build on one another? How does that affect when they emerge?

- ✓ How might you provide an objective summary of the text? What details would you include?

Please note that excerpts and passages in the StudySync® library and this workbook are intended as touchstones to generate interest in an author's work. The excerpts and passages do not substitute for the reading of entire texts, and StudySync® strongly recommends that students seek out and purchase the whole literary or informational work in order to experience it as the author intended. Links to online resellers are available in our digital library. In addition, complete works may be ordered through an authorized reseller by filling out and returning to StudySync® the order form enclosed in this workbook.

Reading & Writing Companion   **29**

Skill: Central or Main Idea

Reread paragraph 4 of "Overcoming Impostor Syndrome." Then, using the Checklist on the previous page, answer the multiple-choice questions below.

⟳ YOUR TURN

1. This question has two parts. First, answer Part A. Then, answer Part B.

   Part A: Which sentence or phrase from the excerpt best expresses the main idea of this section of the article?

   ○ A. "impostor syndrome is a mental health disorder"

   ○ B. "[impostor syndrome] is not a mental illness"

   ○ C. "impostor syndrome can interfere with your psychological well-being"

   ○ D. "Some people with impostor syndrome might also engage in maladaptive behaviors"

   Part B: How does referring to the American Psychiatric Association support the main idea that you identified in Part A?

   ○ A. The writer assumes that most readers will not be familiar with this professional organization.

   ○ B. The writer assumes that most readers will be familiar with this professional organization.

   ○ C. Citing a professional organization weakens the writer's assertion that impostor syndrome is not a mental disorder.

   ○ D. "Citing a professional organization strengthens the writer's assertion that impostor syndrome is not a mental disorder.

Skill: Compare and Contrast

Use the Checklist to analyze Compare and Contrast in "Overcoming Impostor Syndrome." Refer to the sample student annotations about Compare and Contrast in the text.

••• CHECKLIST FOR COMPARE AND CONTRAST

In order to determine how to compare and contrast informational articles, use the following steps:

- ✓ first, choose two or more articles from reputable sources

- ✓ next, identify the main idea in each article

- ✓ after, identify the theme and purpose presented in each article

- ✓ then, identify the rhetorical features in each article, and the use of figures of speech and other compositional techniques that are designed to have a persuasive or impressive effect on readers

- ✓ finally, explain the similarities and differences between two or more of these articles, including their use of rhetoric, the themes each article explores, and their purposes.

To analyze informational articles, consider the following questions:

- ✓ Are the articles from reputable sources or written by reputable individuals?

- ✓ What themes or topics are apparent in each of these articles?

- ✓ What is the purpose of each article?

- ✓ Are there any rhetorical features in these articles? In what ways are these features similar and different?

- ✓ How are the themes, topics, and purpose in these articles similar and different?

Please note that excerpts and passages in the StudySync® library and this workbook are intended as touchstones to generate interest in an author's work. The excerpts and passages do not substitute for the reading of entire texts, and StudySync® strongly recommends that students seek out and purchase the whole literary or informational work in order to experience it as the author intended. Links to online resellers are available in our digital library. In addition, complete works may be ordered through an authorized reseller by filling out and returning to StudySync® the order form enclosed in this workbook.

Reading & Writing Companion

31

Skill: Compare and Contrast

Reread paragraph 13 of "Overcoming Impostor Syndrome" and paragraph 12 of "Community Colleges vs. Technical Schools." Then, using the Checklist on the previous page, answer the multiple-choice questions below.

⟳ YOUR TURN

1. Compare the conclusions from each essay. How are these two conclusions similar?

   ○ A. Both conclusions suggest there is one best way to approach these topics.
   ○ B. Both conclusions suggest that readers need to answer yes/no questions.
   ○ C. Both conclusions focus on getting readers to seek professional help.
   ○ D. Both conclusions focus on getting readers to find their own answers.

2. Contrast the conclusions from each essay. How are these two conclusions different from each other?

   ○ A. "Overcoming Impostor Syndrome" uses the conclusion to summarize ideas, while "Community Colleges vs. Technical Schools" uses it to ask readers reflective questions.
   ○ B. "Overcoming Impostor Syndrome" uses the conclusion to ask readers reflective questions, while "Community Colleges vs. Technical Schools" uses it to summarize ideas.
   ○ C. "Overcoming Impostor Syndrome" uses the conclusion to suggest further reading, while "Community Colleges vs. Technical Schools" uses it to summarize ideas.
   ○ D. "Overcoming Impostor Syndrome" uses the conclusion to ask the reader reflective questions, while "Community Colleges vs. Technical Schools" uses it to suggest further reading.

3. What do your answers to questions 1 and 2 tell you about the authors' approaches to their topics?

   ○ A. "Overcoming Impostor Syndrome" is more about taking action to help yourself, while "Community Colleges vs. Technical Schools" is more about processing information to make a decision.
   ○ B. "Overcoming Impostor Syndrome" is more about processing information to make a decision, while "Community Colleges vs. Technical Schools" is more about taking action to help yourself.
   ○ C. "Overcoming Impostor Syndrome" is more about taking action to help yourself, while "Community Colleges vs. Technical Schools" is more about helping others help themselves.
   ○ D. "Overcoming Impostor Syndrome" is more about doing research to master a subject, while "Community Colleges vs. Technical Schools" is more about processing information to make a decision.

Close Read

Reread "Overcoming Impostor Syndrome." As you reread, complete the Skills Focus questions below. Then use your answers and annotations from the questions to help you complete the Write activity.

◎ SKILLS FOCUS

1. Highlight an example of a specific kind of text structure that appears at least twice in "Overcoming Impostor Syndrome," and explain how using this type of structure helps make the author's points clear, convincing, and engaging.

2. Highlight a detail that supports a central idea in "Overcoming Impostor Syndrome," and explain why it is effective supporting evidence.

3. Highlight a paragraph that helped you identify text structure in "Overcoming Impostor Syndrome." Write a sentence that explains the relationship between the text structure and the main idea of the article.

4. Compare and contrast the use of sub-headings in both "Overcoming Impostor Syndrome" and "Community Colleges vs. Technical Schools". Using textual evidence from "Overcoming Impostor Syndrome" and your memory of "Community Colleges vs. Technical Schools", explain why the authors chose to use subheadings.

5. Both "Overcoming Impostor Syndrome" and "Community Colleges vs. Technical Schools" address decisions and mindsets that are important as high school seniors prepare for their future. How can the main ideas in these articles help you transform your own future?

✏ WRITE

RESEARCH: Select a topic related to your life after high school that you would like to learn more about (for example, how to find a job or how to select a dorm roommate). Then write an informational article about this topic, applying informational text structures to your article and to support your main idea or claim.

The Metamorphosis

FICTION
Franz Kafka
1915

Introduction

zech author Franz Kafka (1883–1924) asked friend and biographer Max Brod to destroy his writings after he died, but Brod thought better of it—otherwise readers would be robbed of the brilliance of Kafka's dark vision. *The Metamorphosis* is typical of Kafka's work, with nightmarish themes of surrealism, confusion, and oppression. In this excerpt, Gregor Samsa awakens to find himself

'O God,' he thought, 'what a demanding job I've chosen!'

1   One morning, as Gregor Samsa was waking up from anxious dreams, he discovered that in bed he had been changed into a monstrous verminous bug. He lay on his armour-hard back and saw, as he lifted his head up a little, his brown, arched abdomen divided up into rigid bow-like sections. From this height the blanket, just about ready to slide off completely, could hardly stay in place. His numerous legs, pitifully thin in comparison to the rest of his circumference, flickered helplessly before his eyes.

Franz Kafka, 1906

2   'What's happened to me,' he thought. It was no dream. His room, a proper room for a human being, only somewhat too small, lay quietly between the four well-known walls. Above the table, on which an unpacked collection of sample cloth goods was spread out (Samsa was a traveling salesman) hung the picture which he had cut out of an illustrated magazine a little while ago and set in a pretty gilt frame. It was a picture of a woman with a fur hat and a fur boa. She sat erect there, lifting up in the direction of the viewer a solid fur muff into which her entire forearm disappeared.

3   Gregor's glance then turned to the window. The dreary weather (the rain drops were falling audibly down on the metal window ledge) made him quite melancholy. 'Why don't I keep sleeping for a little while longer and forget all this foolishness,' he thought. But this was entirely impractical, for he was used to sleeping on his right side, and in his present state he couldn't get himself into this position. No matter how hard he threw himself onto his right side, he always rolled again onto his back. He must have tried it a hundred times, closing his eyes, so that he would not have to see the wriggling legs, and gave up only when he began to feel a light, dull pain in his side which he had never felt before.

NOTES

**Skill:
Story Structure**

Kafka begins the story after the metamorphosis has taken place. So I can assume that the story will be about living life as an insect rather than becoming one. This kind of beginning makes the story surprising and humorous.

**Skill:
Connotation and Denotation**

The words proper and well-known often have positive or neutral connotations, but I think Kafka might be implying a more negative connotation. I think the message might be that Gregor has had a rather mundane and monotonous life.

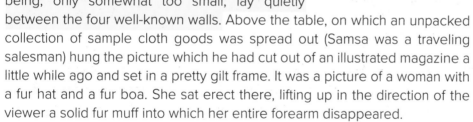
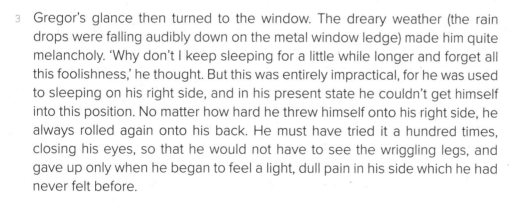

Copyright © BookheadEd Learning, LLC

4 'O God,' he thought, 'what a demanding job I've chosen! Day in, day out on the road. The stresses of trade are much greater than the work going on at head office, and, in addition to that, I have to deal with the problems of traveling, the worries about train connections, irregular bad food, temporary and constantly changing human relationships which never come from the heart. To hell with it all!' He felt a slight itching on the top of his abdomen. He slowly pushed himself on his back closer to the bed post so that he could lift his head more easily, found the itchy part, which was entirely covered with small white spots (he did not know what to make of them), and wanted to feel the place with a leg. But he retracted it immediately, for the contact felt like a cold shower all over him.

5 He slid back again into his earlier position. 'This getting up early,' he thought, 'makes a man quite idiotic. A man must have his sleep. Other traveling salesmen live like harem women. For **instance**, when I come back to the inn during the course of the morning to write up the necessary orders, these gentlemen are just sitting down to breakfast. If I were to try that with my boss, I'd be thrown out on the spot. Still, who knows whether that mightn't be really good for me. If I didn't hold back for my parents' sake, I would've quit ages ago. I would've gone to the boss and told him just what I think from the bottom of my heart. He would've fallen right off his desk! How weird it is to sit up at the desk and talk down to the employee from way up there. The boss has trouble hearing, so the employee has to step up quite close to him. Anyway, I haven't completely given up that hope yet. Once I've got together the money to pay off the parents' debt to him—that should take another five or six years—I'll do it for su[re. Then I'll make the big break. In any case, right now I have to get up. My train leaves at five o'clock.'

6 And he looked over at the alarm clock ticking away by the chest of drawers. 'Good God,' he thought. It was half past six, and the hands were going quietly on. It was past the half hour, already nearly quarter to. Could the alarm have failed to ring? One saw from the bed that it was properly set for four o'clock. Certainly it had rung. Yes, but was it possible to sleep through this noise that made the furniture shake? Now, it's true he'd not slept quietly, but evidently he'd slept all the more deeply. Still, what should he do now? The next train left at seven o'clock. To catch that one, he would have to go in a mad rush. The sample collection wasn't packed up yet, and he really didn't feel particularly fresh and active. And even if he caught the train, there was no avoiding a blow up with the boss, because the firm's errand boy would've waited for the five o'clock train and reported the news of his absence long ago. He was the boss's minion, without backbone or intelligence. Well then, what if he reported in sick? But that would be extremely embarrassing and **suspicious**, because during his five years' service Gregor hadn't been sick even once. The boss

NOTES

would certainly come with the doctor from the health insurance company and would reproach his parents for their lazy son and cut short all objections with the insurance doctor's comments; for him everyone was completely healthy but really lazy about work. And besides, would the doctor in this case be totally wrong? Apart from a really excessive drowsiness after the long sleep, Gregor in fact felt quite well and even had a really strong appetite.

7   As he was thinking all this over in the greatest haste, without being able to make the decision to get out of bed (the alarm clock was indicating exactly quarter to seven) there was a cautious knock on the door by the head of the bed.

8   'Gregor,' a voice called (it was his mother!) 'it's quarter to seven. Don't you want to be on your way?' The soft voice! Gregor was startled when he heard his voice answering. It was clearly and unmistakably his earlier voice, but in it was intermingled, as if from below, an irrepressibly painful squeaking which left the words positively distinct only in the first moment and distorted them in the reverberation, so that one didn't know if one had heard correctly. Gregor wanted to answer in detail and explain everything, but in these circumstances he **confined** himself to saying, 'Yes, yes, thank you mother. I'm getting up right away.' Because of the wooden door the change in Gregor's voice was not really noticeable outside, so his mother calmed down with this explanation and shuffled off. However, as a result of the short conversation the other family members became aware of the fact that Gregor was unexpectedly still at home, and already his father was knocking on one side door, weakly but with his fist. 'Gregor, Gregor,' he called out, 'what's going on?' And after a short while he urged him on again in a deeper voice. 'Gregor! Gregor!' At the other side door, however, his sister knocked lightly. 'Gregor? Are you all right? Do you need anything?' Gregor directed answers in both directions, 'I'll be ready right away.' He made an effort with the most careful articulation and by inserting long pauses between the individual words to remove everything remarkable from his voice. His father turned back to his breakfast. However, the sister whispered, 'Gregor, open the door, I beg you.' Gregor had no intention of opening the door, but congratulated himself on his precaution, acquired from traveling, of locking all doors during the night, even at home.

9   First he wanted to stand up quietly and undisturbed, get dressed, above all have breakfast, and only then consider further action, for (he noticed this clearly) by thinking things over in bed he would not reach a reasonable conclusion. He remembered that he had already often felt a light pain or other in bed, perhaps the result of an awkward lying position, which later turned out to be purely imaginary when he stood up, and he was eager to see how his present fantasies would gradually dissipate. That the change in his voice was nothing other than the onset of a real chill, an occupational illness of commercial travelers, of that he had not the slightest doubt.

Skill:
Textual Evidence

The exclamation mark might indicate that Gregor is surprised by his mother's voice. But why? Maybe he hears differently now that he is a bug. Or perhaps it gives him comfort in his current condition. I'll need to read more.

10   It was very easy to throw aside the blanket. He needed only to push himself up a little, and it fell by itself. But to continue was difficult, particularly because he was so unusually wide. He needed arms and hands to push himself upright. Instead of these, however, he had only many small limbs which were **incessantly** moving with very different motions and which, in addition, he was unable to control. If he wanted to bend one of them, then it was the first to extend itself, and if he finally succeeded doing with this limb what he wanted, in the meantime all the others, as if left free, moved around in an excessively painful agitation. 'But I must not stay in bed uselessly,' said Gregor to himself.

11   At first he wanted to get of the bed with the lower part of his body, but this lower part (which he incidentally had not yet looked at and which he also couldn't picture clearly) proved itself too difficult to move. The attempt went so slowly. When, having become almost frantic, he finally hurled himself forward with all his force and without thinking, he chose his direction incorrectly, and he hit the lower bedpost hard. The violent pain he felt revealed to him that the lower part of his body was at the moment probably the most sensitive.

12   Thus, he tried to get his upper body out of the bed first and turned his head carefully toward the edge of the bed. He managed to do this easily, and in spite of its width and weight his body mass at last slowly followed the turning of his head. But as he finally raised his head outside the bed in the open air, he became anxious about moving forward any further in this manner, for if he allowed himself eventually to fall by this process, it would take a miracle to prevent his head from getting injured. And at all costs he must not lose consciousness right now. He preferred to remain in bed.

13   However, after a similar effort, while he lay there again sighing as before and once again saw his small limbs fighting one another, if anything worse than before, and didn't see any chance of imposing quiet and order on this **arbitrary** movement, he told himself again that he couldn't possibly remain in bed and that it might be the most reasonable thing to sacrifice everything if there was even the slightest hope of getting himself out of bed in the process. At the same moment, however, he didn't forget to remind himself from time to time of the fact that calm (indeed the calmest) reflection might be better than the most confused decisions. At such moments, he directed his gaze as precisely as he could toward the window, but unfortunately there was little confident cheer to be had from a glance at the morning mist, which concealed even the other side of the narrow street. 'It's already seven o'clock' he told himself at the latest striking of the alarm clock, 'already seven o'clock and still such a fog.' And for a little while longer he lay quietly with weak breathing, as if perhaps waiting for normal and natural conditions to re-emerge out of the complete stillness.

First Read

Read *The Metamorphosis*. After you read, complete the Think Questions below.

☁ THINK QUESTIONS

1. Is Gregor's transformation real or imagined? How does Kafka's writing style affect the believability of the story? Explain your reasoning in a few sentences, including specific examples from the text.

2. What is Gregor Samsa's attitude toward his chosen work as a traveling salesman? Use evidence from the text to explain his feelings about his job and his place in society.

3. Is Gregor's "metamorphosis" an inexplicable occurrence? Or does Kafka give any clues or insights to suggest why this may have happened or what might have caused it? Cite specific examples from the excerpt in your response.

4. Use context clues to determine the meaning of **confined** as it is used in paragraph 8 of *The Metamorphosis*. Write your definition of *confined* here and explain which context clues helped you determine its meaning.

5. The Latin verb cessare means "to cease or stop." Knowing this, along with any other common affixes and/or roots, what do you think the adverb **incessantly** means? Write your best definition here, along with any other related words with a similar origin.

Please note that excerpts and passages in the StudySync® library and this workbook are intended as touchstones to generate interest in an author's work. The excerpts and passages do not substitute for the reading of entire texts, and StudySync® strongly recommends that students seek out and purchase the whole literary or informational work in order to experience it as the author intended. Links to online resellers are available in our digital library. In addition, complete works may be ordered through an authorized reseller by filling out and returning to StudySync® the order form enclosed in this workbook.

Reading & Writing Companion   **39**

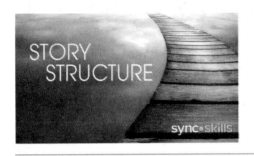

Skill:
Story Structure

Use the Checklist to analyze Story Structure in *The Metamorphosis*. Refer to the sample student annotations about Story Structure in the text.

••• CHECKLIST FOR STORY STRUCTURE

In order to identify the choices an author makes when structuring specific parts of a text, note the following:

- ✓ the choices an author makes to organize specific parts of a text such as where to begin and end a story, or whether the ending should be tragic, comic, or inconclusive

- ✓ the author's use of literary devices, such as:

  - foreshadowing: a way of hinting at what will come later
  - flashback: a part of a story that shows something that happened in the past
  - pacing: how quickly or slowly the events of a story unfold

- ✓ how the overall structure of the text contributes to its meaning as well as its aesthetic impact

  - the effect structure has on the impact it makes on the reader, such as the creation of suspense through the use of pacing
  - the use of flashback to reveal hidden dimensions of a character that affect the theme

To analyze how an author's choices concerning how to structure specific parts of a text contribute to its overall structure and meaning as well as its aesthetic impact, consider the following questions:

- ✓ How does the author structure the text overall? How does the author structure specific parts of the text?

- ✓ Does the author incorporate literary elements such as flashback or foreshadowing?

- ✓ How do these elements affect the overall text structure and the aesthetic impact of the text?

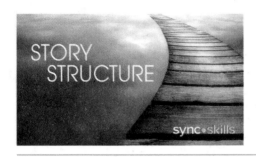

Skill: Story Structure

Reread paragraph 5 of *The Metamorphosis*. Then, using the Checklist on the previous page, answer the multiple-choice questions below.

⟳ YOUR TURN

1. Which of the following sentences is most likely to be an example of foreshadowing?

   ○ A. "This getting up early," he thought, "makes a man quite idiotic."
   ○ B. Other traveling salesmen live like harem women.
   ○ C. For **instance**, when I come back to the inn during the course of the morning to write up the necessary orders, these gentlemen are just sitting down to breakfast.
   ○ D. If I were to try that with my boss, I'd be thrown out on the spot.

2. What is the most likely reason that Kafka has his main character mention his parents' debt before the parents appear in the story?

   ○ A. So the reader will understand why Gregor was turned into a bug-like creature.
   ○ B. So the reader will learn about the relationship between Gregor and his parents.
   ○ C. So the reader will understand how poor Gregor's family is and feel bad for them.
   ○ D. So the reader will learn about the social structures that were prevalent at the time in which this story is set.

3. This passage consists largely of a long, unhurried series of thoughts from Gregor Samsa. What is the most likely reason Kafka uses such slow pacing at the opening of this story?

   ○ A. It helps the reader understand precisely how Gregor feels about the other traveling salesmen he regularly encounters.
   ○ B. It helps reveal many aspects of Gregor's life, and it helps reveal the absurdity of his fear of losing his job when he should be more concerned about being a bug.
   ○ C. It helps the reader understand that this story might become monotonous, with long, drawn-out passages consisting largely of Gregor's thoughts.
   ○ D. It helps reveal the author's feelings about common vices, such as laziness and uncleanliness.

Skill:
Textual Evidence

Use the Checklist to analyze Textual Evidence in *The Metamorphosis*. Refer to the sample student annotations about Textual Evidence in the text.

••• CHECKLIST FOR STORY STRUCTURE

In order to support an analysis by citing evidence that is explicitly stated in the text, do the following:

- ✓ read the text closely and critically

- ✓ identify what the text says explicitly

- ✓ find the most relevant textual evidence that supports your analysis

- ✓ consider why an author explicitly states specific details and information

- ✓ cite the specific words, phrases, sentences, or paragraphs from the text that support your analysis

- ✓ determine where evidence in the text still leaves certain matters uncertain or unresolved

In order to interpret implicit meanings in a text by making inferences, do the following:

- ✓ combine information directly stated in the text with your own knowledge, experiences, and observations

- ✓ cite the specific words, phrases, sentences, or paragraphs from the text that led to and support this inference.

In order to cite textual evidence to support an analysis of what the text says explicitly as well as inferences drawn from the text, consider the following questions:

- ✓ Have I read the text closely and critically?

- ✓ What inferences am I making about the text?

- ✓ What textual evidence am I using to support these inferences?

- ✓ Am I quoting the evidence from the text correctly?

- ✓ Does my textual evidence logically relate to my analysis or the inference I am making?

- ✓ Does evidence in the text still leave certain matters unanswered or unresolved? In what ways?

Copyright © BookheadEd Learning, LLC

Skill:
Textual Evidence

Reread paragraph 9 of *The Metamorphosis*. Then, using the Checklist on the previous page, answer the multiple-choice questions below.

⟳ YOUR TURN

1. Which of the following sentences would provide the best textual evidence for the inference that Gregor Samsa still doesn't want to believe he has turned into a bug?

   - ○ A. "First he wanted to stand up quietly and undisturbed, get dressed, above all have breakfast, and only then consider further action . . ."
   - ○ B. ". . . for (he noticed this clearly) by thinking things over in bed he would not reach a reasonable conclusion."
   - ○ C. "He remembered that he had already often felt a light pain or other in bed . . ."
   - ○ D. "That the change in his voice was nothing other than the onset of a real chill, an occupational illness of commercial travelers, of that he had not the slightest doubt."

Read the inferences in the chart below. Then, complete the chart by matching the textual evidence that best supports each inference.

⟳ YOUR TURN

Textual Evidence Options	
A	He remembered that he had already often felt a light pain or other in bed, perhaps the result of an awkward lying position . . .
B	. . . above all have breakfast, and only then consider further action . . .
C	. . . he was eager to see how his present fantasies would gradually dissipate.
D	First he wanted to stand up quietly and undisturbed . . .

Inference	Textual Evidence
Gregor doesn't reason well on an empty stomach.	
Gregor has previously had trouble sleeping.	
Gregor wants to keep his condition secret.	
Gregor does not believe he is actually a bug.	

Skill: Connotation and Denotation

Use the Checklist to analyze Connotation and Denotation in *The Metamorphosis*. Refer to the sample student annotations about Connotation and Denotation in the text.

••• CHECKLIST FOR CONNOTATION AND DENOTATION

In order to identify the denotative meanings of words, use the following steps:

- ✓ first, note unfamiliar words and phrases, key words used to describe important characters, events, and ideas, or words that inspire an emotional reaction

- ✓ next, determine and note the denotative meaning of words by consulting a reference material such as a dictionary, glossary, or thesaurus

- ✓ finally, analyze nuances in the meaning of words with similar denotations

To better understand the meaning of words and phrases as they are used in a text, including connotative meanings, use the following questions as a guide

- ✓ What is the genre or subject of the text? Based on context, what do you think the meaning of the word is intended to be?

- ✓ Is your inference the same or different from the dictionary definition?

- ✓ Does the word create a positive, negative, or neutral emotion?

- ✓ What synonyms or alternative phrasing help you describe the connotative meaning of the word?

To determine the meaning of words and phrases as they are used in a text, including connotative meanings, use the following questions as a guide:

- ✓ What is the denotative meaning of the word? Is that denotative meaning correct in context?

- ✓ What possible positive, neutral, or negative connotations might the word have, depending on context?

- ✓ What textual evidence signals a particular connotation for the word?

Skill: Connotation and Denotation

Reread paragraph 13 of *The Metamorphosis*. Then, using the Checklist on the previous page, answer the multiple-choice questions below.

🔁 YOUR TURN

1. Which of the following words is most likely to have a negative connotation in the context of this passage?

   ○ A. confidence
   ○ B. cheer
   ○ C. concealed
   ○ D. street

2. Which word in the passage can be interpreted figuratively, and with a negative connotation, to describe unclear thinking?

   ○ A. gaze
   ○ B. window
   ○ C. street
   ○ D. fog

3. Which of the following denotative meanings of *fog* best fits how the word is used in this paragraph?

   ○ A. a thick cloud close to the earth's surface
   ○ B. to cover with steam
   ○ C. to treat something with a spray
   ○ D. something that confuses a thought process

Close Read

Reread *The Metamorphosis*. As you reread, complete the Skills Focus questions below. Then use your answers and annotations from the questions to help you complete the Write activity.

◎ SKILLS FOCUS

1. This excerpt, which is the very beginning of Kafka's *The Metamorphosis*, focuses on the main character's first morning as a "monstrous verminous bug." Why do you think Kafka chooses to spend so much time on this particular moment of the character's day? What effect does this have on the reader? Highlight and annotate details in the text that show how Kafka uses this moment in the character's day to develop the plot.

2. Throughout the passage, Gregor Samsa expresses his feelings about his job. Highlight three pieces of textual evidence that implicitly or explicitly inform you about Samsa's feelings toward his work, his colleagues, and his boss. Annotate your highlights to explain what this textual evidence helps you understand about Samsa and his job.

3. Find and highlight three words in this excerpt that tell you (through connotation or denotation) how Samsa feels about his family members. Use the annotation feature to explain what these words tell you about this feelings toward his family members.

4. Gregor Samsa wakes up to an incredible transformation. Highlight and annotate textual evidence to support your response to the following questions: What aspects of Samsa's life was he unable to change before this moment? In what ways was Samsa unable to transform his own future? How will his transformation into a "monstrous verminous bug" change his future?

✏ WRITE

LITERARY ANALYSIS: An allegory is a literary device used to convey a symbolic message that comments on some aspect of human life and society. In an allegory, characters represent ideas. Kafka uses the literary device of allegory to structure this story. What do you think the character of Gregor Samsa represents? What message might the author be conveying about human life and society? Focus on specific words that connote or denote an opinion about human life and society. Use textual evidence to support your ideas.

Blast: In Your Hands

What are the challenges of planning for life after high school?

ⓘ BACKGROUND

Listen to the What's Next podcast associated with this Blast in your digital account.

Are you a high school student? If so, you've probably fantasized about what it will be like to walk across the stage in a tasseled cap and long gown, proudly accepting a diploma after 13 years of hard work. But how much have you thought about what will happen after you step off the stage?

Finishing high school is a momentous achievement that many anticipate eagerly, but it can be tougher to picture what life will look like after graduation.

Every year, more than 3 million American students graduate high school, according to the National Center for Education Statistics. Nationwide, seniors are faced with questions they have never confronted face-to-face before: What will I do once I finish high school? How will I chase my passions, and what am I passionate about? What does my future hold? It can feel scary and intimidating when all these questions lie ahead. Luckily, there are countless resources to help you along the way. Some of the most valuable resources are people who have gone through the process themselves.

StudySync's "What's Next?" Blast and podcast series follows ten high school students — nine seniors, one junior — from September to May. Throughout the year, StudySync documents these students as they encountered the challenges of planning for life after high school. From an aspiring esthetician eager to start her career in California to a risk-taking Texan with his sights set on a private university, these seven students have a wide variety of backgrounds, interests, motivations, and goals. Their advice can help you start answering some of the toughest questions you face as you decide your next steps. Listening to their stories can help you start planning your own.

Below, read a brief description and listen to a one-minute audio clip introducing each student.

Diana-Nicole Ramirez is a senior at the Academy of Finance and Enterprise in Queens, New York. She loves reading, writing, and classic rock. After graduating, she plans to attend college in New York City to study journalism and communications.

DJ Frost is a senior at Blue Springs South High School in Blue Springs, Missouri. After graduation, he plans to attend the Air Force Academy in Colorado to play football and major in business.

Felicia Horn is a senior at Paul VI High School in Haddonfield, New Jersey. Inspired by hospital visits with her mom, who has multiple sclerosis, Horn aspires to be a nurse, and eventually a nurse anesthetist.

Katherine Carlo is a senior at Nease High School in St. Augustine, Florida. She's applying to schools in Florida and the surrounding states, as well as Ivy League schools, and hopes to get a scholarship to pay for college.

Kiana Griffin is a senior at Pleasant Grove High School in Elk Grove, California. After graduation, she hopes to play basketball at a D1 university.

Lyssa Nix is a senior at Classical Academy High School in Escondido, California. After graduation, she will attend cosmetology school to become an esthetician and begin a career close to home.

Makalya Adams is a senior at William B. Murrah High School in Jackson, Mississippi. She aspires to become a nurse, and is torn between attending a local community college, which she prefers, or a local private college, which her mom thinks is best.

Patrick Cadogan is a junior at Westford Academy in Westford, Massachusetts. With the goal of attending a four-year college in-state, he will spend this year taking the SAT, building a strong application and narrowing down where he would like to apply.

Shamora Rogers is a senior at Warren High School in San Antonio, Texas. She is applying to four-year public universities in state and is excited to study theater, film, and television in college.

NOTES

Zac Walsdorf is a senior at John Marshall High School in San Antonio, Texas. A student with many interests and a love for trying new things, he plans to apply to various elite private universities out of state.

After listening to each of the students at the start of their school year, whom do you relate to most? Did any of their comments resonate with you? What are the biggest obstacles that lie ahead in your journey toward adult life? What are the challenges of planning for life after high school?

NUMBER CRUNCH

45

QUIKPOLL

Do you feel prepared for adult life?

☐ Absolutely. I've been waiting for high school graduation for years, and I couldn't be more ready. I can't wait for the next steps.

☐ Mostly. I know I have the skills I need for adult life, but I'm also a little nervous.

☐ Not really. I'm excited for the future, but I know I still have a lot of preparing to do.

☐ Not at all. I'm terrified for adult life. Do I have to graduate?

✳ CREATE YOUR BLAST

What are the challenges of planning for life after high school?

_____

_____

_____

_____

Blast: The Future Awaits

What do you want to do after you graduate high school?

Listen to the What's Next podcast associated with this Blast in your digital account.

When you imagine your life five years from now, what do you picture?

Do you envision yourself as a newly minted college graduate launching a career in your dream industry, or a passionate volunteer traveling the world and serving those less fortunate? Maybe you see yourself rising in rank in the military, building a business, saving money for the future, or starting a family. Perhaps you're totally uncertain about what your life will look like — after all, how can you know what you'll be doing years down the road when you're still trying to navigate the immediate day-to-day challenges of high school?

Selecting a course of action after graduation — whether it's college, employment, volunteering, a gap year, or something else — is one of the most consequential decisions most seniors in high school have ever made, so it's normal to be overwhelmed and unsure, according to Kristen Flemer, a counselor at Skyline High School in Sammamish, Washington.

Flemer says one way to start narrowing down future plans is to reflect on what you enjoy doing now. "Start with questions," she said. "What do you love? What do you do on the weekends? If you could do one thing for the rest of your life, what would you do? What do you not like doing? Would you rather be outdoors or indoors? Would you rather be on a computer or talking with someone? Would you rather be up and moving or sitting at a desk?" Once

Please note that excerpts and passages in the StudySync® library and this workbook are intended as touchstones to generate interest in an author's work. The excerpts and passages do not substitute for the reading of entire texts, and StudySync® strongly recommends that students seek out and purchase the whole literary or informational work in order to experience it as the author intended. Links to online resellers are available in our digital library. In addition, complete works may be ordered through an authorized reseller by filling out and returning to StudySync® the order form enclosed in this workbook.

Reading & Writing Companion

51

NOTES

you've identified and solidified goals for a future lifestyle, Flemer says, you can figure out a career that suits those goals, and work backwards to devise an action plan for how to arrive at that lifestyle.

It might seem like all your peers are pursuing the same path after high school, but that doesn't necessarily have to mean this path is right for you — and Kelly Kaye, the operations manager of a financial planning firm in Los Angeles, knows this firsthand. When she was a senior in high school in Buffalo, New York, most of her friends were pursuing college degrees at expensive and elite private universities. However, her family didn't have the financial means to afford that kind of education, so Kaye created a new plan: She moved to California after graduating high school, worked at a bank to save money and establish residency in the state, and then enrolled a year later in community college in Santa Monica. From there, she transferred to a state university and earned a Bachelor's degree. Even though Kaye opted for a different path than her friends, she gained independence, made money over the course of a gap year, and ended up in a career she enjoys. "Listen to what other people have to say, but don't make your decision based on somebody else's opinion," Kaye says. "Do what feels right to you, even if that's going against the grain."

So, do you see yourself going to college, pursuing a career, joining the military, working to save for college, or something else? Have you already crafted a plan for life after graduation, or are you still weighing options? What do you want to do after you graduate high school?

NUMBER CRUNCH

69.7

◕ QUIKPOLL

Which of the following best fits your plan for life after graduation?

☐ Four-year college

☐ Two-year college or trade school

☐ Gap year, traveling, or joining the military

☐ Working

☐ Something else

✹ CREATE YOUR BLAST

What do you want to do after you graduate high school?

_____

_____

_____

_____

Blast: Your Perfect Path

What are the benefits of college alternatives?

ⓘ BACKGROUND

Listen to the What's Next podcast associated with this Blast in your digital account.

In 1980 in Anchorage, Alaska, a young man named Mark Begich graduated from high school. While some of his peers chased dreams of higher education, Begich pursued a different path.

Already a thriving entrepreneur, Begich chose not to go to college. Instead, he began managing his family's real estate properties. He also grew his own businesses, including a jewelry business and an 18-and-under club in Anchorage that he had run since the age of 14. As he became more successful in business over the years, he grew more involved in local politics as well. Eventually, he became the city's mayor. In 2008, Begich took his political aspirations even further, campaigning for the United States Senate. When he won, Begich became the only sitting U.S. senator without a college degree.

During your senior year of high school, it might seem like you have to go to college in order to be successful in a career one day. However, the reality is that plenty of Americans, including former U.S. Senator Mark Begich, have flourished professionally without graduating from college. College is a popular path because it allows students to deepen their education, make connections, and obtain a certificate that some jobs require. Still, other options like career and technical education or employment can be just as beneficial — and at a much lower cost.

NOTES

For students who don't have the financial means or academic record needed to attend college, or for students whose career goals don't require a higher degree, it can be wise to consider options besides college after high school. For example, career and technical education — sometimes called trade school or vocational school — can teach specific technical skills needed for a particular job. Career and technical education can usually be completed in a shorter period of time than traditional college and at a lower cost. These programs can certify people to pursue industrial careers, like becoming an electrician or a welder. They can also train people in the arts or in hands-on careers, like culinary arts or cosmetology.

If you're not sure whether you want to go to college yet, or want a break before jumping back into school, a gap year is another option. Tens of thousands of American students take advantage of a gap year every year. The American Gap Association defines a gap year as "a structured period of time when students take a break from formal education to increase self-awareness, learn from different cultures, and experiment with possible careers. Typically, these are achieved by a combination of traveling, volunteering, interning, or working." While gap years are particularly common in Europe and Australia, they have gained popularity in the U.S. in recent years. Ethan Knight, founder of the American Gap Association, says "everybody stands to benefit from a gap year." However, he advises students to think carefully and seek out resources to decide whether or not it's the right decision for them.

With the emphasis placed on college in America's high schools today, it can seem like everyone is applying to college. Begich encourages students to consider college as an option, but he also points out that success in life can be reached without a degree. "If you have the ability, with or without a college degree, you can achieve great things," he said. "If you decide not to go to college, don't let people make it sound like it's a bad thing. You have choices in life, you made a choice, and now you're going to take it to a new level."

So, what do you think? Have you ever thought that college might not be the right fit for you? Why might students consider a path besides college after high school? What are the benefits of college alternatives?

NUMBER CRUNCH
30,000 TO 40,000

Please note that excerpts and passages in the StudySync® library and this workbook are intended as touchstones to generate interest in an author's work. The excerpts and passages do not substitute for the reading of entire texts, and StudySync® strongly recommends that students seek out and purchase the whole literary or informational work in order to experience it as the author intended. Links to online resellers are available in our digital library. In addition, complete works may be ordered through an authorized reseller by filling out and returning to StudySync® the order form enclosed in this workbook.

Reading & Writing Companion 55

NOTES

QUIKPOLL

Have you considered pursuing career and technical education in place of a two-year or four-year degree?

☐ Yes. I have thought about career and technical education as an alternative that might suit my current situation and career goals.

☐ No, but I might look into it. I am curious to see whether career and technical education could be a good fit for me.

☐ No. Based on what I want to do in the future, career and technical education is not the right path for me.

CREATE YOUR BLAST

What are the benefits of college alternatives?

_____

_____

_____

_____

Bird by Bird:
Some Instructions on Writing and Life

INFORMATIONAL TEXT
Anne Lamott
1995

Introduction

Anne Lamott (b. 1954) is a *New York Times* bestselling author who has written several books and novels. In addition to her fictional work, Lamott is known for her books aimed at imparting writing advice to aspiring writers. In this excerpt from *Bird by Bird: Some Instructions on Writing and Life*, Lamott describes what happens in her mind when she sits down to write, and how she deals with the sometimes overwhelming nature of her thoughts.

"Bird by bird, buddy. Just take it bird by bird."

NOTES

1   Often when you sit down to write, what you have in mind is an autobiographical novel about your childhood, or a play about the immigrant experience, or a history of—oh, say—say women. But this is like trying to **scale** a glacier. It's hard to get your footing, and your fingertips get all red and frozen and torn up. Then your mental illnesses arrive at the desk like your sickest, most secretive relatives. And they pull up chairs in a semicircle around the computer, and they try to be quiet but you know they are there with their weird coppery breath, leering at you behind your back.

2   What I do at this point, as the panic mounts and the jungle drums begin beating and I realize that the well has run dry and that my future is behind me and I'm going to have to get a job only I'm completely unemployable, is to stop. First I try to breathe, because I'm either sitting there panting like a lapdog or I'm unintentionally making slow asthmatic death rattles. So I just sit there for a minute, breathing slowly, quietly. I let my mind wander. After a moment I may notice that I'm trying to decide whether or not I am too old for orthodontia and whether right now would be a good time to make a few calls, and then I start to think about learning to use makeup and how maybe I could find some boyfriend who is not a total and complete fixer-upper and then my life would be totally great and I'd be happy all the time, and then I think about all the people I should have called back before I sat down to work, and how I should probably at least check in with my agent and tell him this great idea I have and see if he thinks it's a good idea, and see if he thinks I need orthodontia— if that is what he is actually thinking whenever we have lunch together. Then I think about someone I'm really annoyed with, or some financial problem that is driving me crazy, and decide that I must resolve this before I get down to today's work. So I become a dog with a chew toy, worrying it for a while, wrestling it to the ground, flinging it over my shoulder, chasing it, licking it, chewing it, flinging it back over my shoulder. I stop just short of actually barking. But all of this only takes somewhere between one and two minutes, so I haven't actually wasted that much time. Still, it leaves me winded. I go back to trying to breathe, slowly and calmly, and I finally notice the one-inch picture frame that I put on my desk to remind me of short assignments.

3   It reminds me that all I have to do is to write down as much as I can see through a one-inch picture frame. This is all I have to bite off for the time being. All I am going to do right now, for example, is write that one paragraph that sets the story in my hometown, in the late fifties, when the trains were still running. I am going to paint a picture of it, in words, on my word processor[1]. Or all I am going to do is to describe the main character the very first time we meet her, when she first walks out the front door and onto the porch. I am not even going to describe the expression on her face when she first notices the blind dog sitting behind the wheel of her car—just what I can see through the one-inch picture frame, just one paragraph describing this woman, in the town where I grew up, the first time we **encounter** her.

4   E. L. Doctorow once said that "writing a novel is like driving a car at night. You can see only as far as your headlights, but you can make the whole trip that way." You don't have to see where you're going, you don't have to see your destination or everything you will pass along the way. You just have to see two or three feet ahead of you. This is right up there with the best advice about writing, or life, I have ever heard.

5   So after I've completely exhausted myself thinking about the people I most resent in the world, and my more arresting financial problems, and, of course, the orthodontia, I remember to pick up the one-inch picture frame and to figure out a one-inch piece of my story to tell, one small scene, one memory, one exchange. I also remember a story that I know I've told elsewhere but that over and over helps me to get a grip: thirty years ago my older brother, who was ten years old at the time, was trying to get a report on birds written that he'd had three months to write, which was due the next day. We were out at our family cabin in Bolinas, and he was at the kitchen table close to tears, surrounded by binder paper and pencils and unopened books on birds, **immobilized** by the hugeness of the task ahead. Then my father sat down beside him, put his arm around my brother's shoulder, and said, "Bird by bird, buddy. Just take it bird by bird."

6   I tell this story again because it usually makes a dent in the tremendous sense of being **overwhelmed** that my students experience. Sometimes it actually gives them hope, and hope, as Chesterton said, "is the power of being cheerful in circumstances that we know to be **desperate**." Writing can be a pretty desperate endeavor, because it is about some of our deepest needs: our need to be visible, to be heard, our need to make sense of our lives, to wake up and grow and belong. It is no wonder if we sometimes tend to take ourselves perhaps a bit too seriously.

---

1. **word processor** a standalone device or machine used for writing and printing written documents before the invention of the personal computer

Excerpted from *Bird by Bird: Some Instructions on Writing and Life* by Anne Lamott, published by Anchor Books.

 WRITE

EXPLANATORY ESSAY: The author uses several examples of figurative language to describe her ongoing experience with anxiety. Identify three instances of figurative language, explain their meaning, and evaluate how effective these examples are in supporting the writer's thesis.

We Choose to Go to the Moon

ARGUMENTATIVE TEXT

John F. Kennedy

1962

Introduction

After the Soviet Union's successful launch of *Sputnik* in October of 1957, the United States entered the Space Race, quickly forming the National Aeronautics and Space Administration (NASA) and working to launch its own satellites. Within five years, both the U.S. and U.S.S.R. had launched manned spacecraft. The Soviets initially soared ahead, putting the first man in space and successfully penetrating the Moon's atmosphere. Landing a man on the Moon was the most coveted prize of all, however, and President John F. Kennedy (1917–1963) was determined for America to accomplish it first. At Houston's Rice University, in September of 1962, he spoke of this quest before an audience of 35,000 people. His impassioned speech ignited the country, inspiring Americans everywhere to embrace the challenge of putting a man on the Moon. His impassioned speech ignited the country, inspiring Americans everywhere to embrace the challenge of putting a man on the Moon by highlighting America's spirit of determination and innovation.

"The greater our knowledge increases, the greater our ignorance unfolds."

Skill:
Author's Purpose
and Point of View

The president appeals to his audience with a repetitive assertion of the values of the place he is speaking in. This both sets the purpose for his speech, and emotionally flatters his audience.

1   We meet at a college noted for knowledge, in a city noted for progress, in a state noted for strength, and we stand in need of all three, for we meet in an hour of change and challenge, in a decade of hope and fear, in an age of both knowledge and ignorance. The greater our knowledge increases, the greater our ignorance unfolds.

2   Despite the striking fact that most of the scientists that the world has ever known are alive and working today, despite the fact that this Nation's own scientific manpower is doubling every 12 years in a rate of growth more than three times that of our population as a whole, despite that, the vast stretches of the unknown and the unanswered and the unfinished still far outstrip our collective comprehension. . . .

3   Surely the opening **vistas** of space promise high costs and hardships, as well as high reward. So it is not surprising that some would have us stay where we are a little longer to rest, to wait. But this city of Houston, this state of Texas, this country of the United States, was not built by those who waited and rested and wished to look behind them. This country was conquered by those who moved forward—and so will space.

4   . . . [M]an, in his quest for knowledge and progress, is determined and cannot be deterred. The exploration of space will go ahead, whether we join in it or not, and it is one of the great adventures of all time, and no nation which expects to be the leader of other nations can expect to stay behind in this race for space.

5   Those who came before us made certain that this country rode the first waves of the industrial revolution, the first waves of modern invention, and the first wave of nuclear power, and this generation does not intend to **founder** in the backwash of the coming age of space. We mean to be a part of it—we mean to lead it. For the eyes of the world now look into space, to the Moon and to the planets beyond, and we have vowed that we shall not see it governed by a **hostile** flag of conquest, but by a banner of freedom and peace. We have vowed that we shall not see space filled with weapons of mass destruction, but with instruments of knowledge and understanding.

6   Yet the vows of this Nation can only be fulfilled if we in this Nation are first, and, therefore, we intend to be first. In short, our leadership in science and industry, our hopes for peace and security, our obligations to ourselves as well as others, all require us to make this effort, to solve these mysteries, to solve them for the good of all men, and to become the world's leading space-faring nation.

7   We set sail on this new sea because there is new knowledge to be gained, and new rights to be won, and they must be won and used for the progress of all people. For space science, like nuclear science and all technology, has no conscience of its own. Whether it will become a force for good or ill depends on man, and only if the United States occupies a position of pre-eminence can we help decide whether this new ocean will be a sea of peace or a new terrifying theater of war. . .

**Skill:
Arguments and
Claims**

The president builds on his previous argument by elaborating on why these ambitious goals and accepted realities are impactful and effective. The further this argument goes logically, the more effective it is.

8   There is no strife, no prejudice, no national conflict in outer space as yet. Its hazards are hostile to us all. Its conquest deserves the best of all mankind, and its opportunity for peaceful cooperation many never come again. But why, some say, the Moon? Why choose this as our goal? And they may well ask why climb the highest mountain? Why, 35 years ago, fly the Atlantic? Why does Rice play Texas?

9   We choose to go to the Moon. We choose to go to the Moon in this decade and do the other things, not because they are easy, but because they are hard, because that goal will serve to organize and measure the best of our energies and skills, because that challenge is one that we are willing to accept, one we are unwilling to postpone, and one which we intend to win, and the others, too.

10   It is for these reasons that I regard the decision last year to shift our efforts in space from low to high gear as among the most important decisions that will be made during my incumbency in the office of the Presidency. . .

11   Within these last 19 months at least 45 satellites have circled the earth. Some 40 of them were "made in the United States of America" and they were far more sophisticated and supplied far more knowledge to the people of the world than those of the Soviet Union . . .

12   We have had our failures, but so have others, even if they do not admit them. And they may be less public.

13   To be sure, we are behind, and will be behind for some time in manned flight. But we do not intend to stay behind, and in this decade, we shall make up and move ahead.

**Skill:
Rhetoric**

In this passage I see ethos: he was President! He also uses pathos when he appeals to patriotism by talking about how good American satellites are. He uses logos when he says that being behind doesn't mean we can't catch up.

NOTES

14 The growth of our science and education will be enriched by new knowledge of our universe and environment, by new techniques of learning and mapping and observation, by new tools and computers for industry, medicine, the home as well as the school. Technical institutions, such as Rice, will reap the harvest of these gains.

15 And finally, the space effort itself, while still in its infancy, has already created a great number of new companies, and tens of thousands of new jobs. . .

16 To be sure, all this costs us all a good deal of money. This year's space budget is three times what it was in January 1961, and it is greater than the space budget of the previous eight years combined. . .

17 But if I were to say, my fellow citizens, that we shall send to the Moon, 240,000 miles away from the control station in Houston, a giant rocket more than 300 feet tall, the length of this football field, made of new metal alloys, some of which have not yet been invented, capable of standing heat and stresses several times more than have ever been experienced, fitted together with a precision better than the finest watch, carrying all the equipment needed for propulsion, guidance, control, communications, food and survival, on an untried mission, to an unknown **celestial** body, and then return it safely to earth, re-entering the atmosphere at speeds of over 25,000 miles per hour, causing heat about half that of the temperature of the sun—almost as hot as it is here today—and do all this, and do it right, and do it first before this decade is out—then we must be bold. . .

Edwin "Buzz" Aldrin becomes the second man to walk on the moon, July 21, 1969

18 Many years ago the great British explorer George Mallory, who was to die on Mount Everest, was asked why did he want to climb it. He said, "Because it is there."

19 Well, space is there, and we're going to climb it, and the Moon and the planets are there, and new hopes for knowledge and peace are there. And, therefore, as we set sail we ask God's blessing on the most hazardous and dangerous and greatest adventure on which man has ever **embarked**.

Skill:
Author's Purpose
and Point of View

I imagine that, for the audience, who are living in a time before humans had explored space, this would have felt impossible but also very exciting.

First Read

Read "We Choose to Go to the Moon." After you read, complete the Think Questions below.

☁ THINK QUESTIONS

1. According to President Kennedy, what are some of the drawbacks to space travel? Support your answer with evidence from paragraphs 3, 8, and 16.

2. Why does President Kennedy believe it is vital for the United States to be the leader in space travel? Support your answer with evidence from paragraphs 5 and 6.

3. President Kennedy refers to the Soviet Union by name only once in this excerpt. Yet he refers to them indirectly in paragraphs 5 and 13. Based on these indirect references, what can you infer about how Kennedy feels about the Soviet Union?

4. Use context to determine the meaning of the word **founder** as it is used in "We Choose to Go to the Moon." Write your definition of *founder* here and explain which context clues helped you determine its meaning.

5. Use context to determine the meaning of the word **embarked** as it is used in "We Choose to Go to the Moon." Then verify your definition by consulting a print or digital dictionary.

Skill:
Author's Purpose and Point of View

Use the Checklist to analyze Author's Purpose and Point of View in "We Choose to Go to the Moon." Refer to the sample student annotations about Author's Purpose and Point of View in the text.

••• CHECKLIST FOR AUTHOR'S PURPOSE AND POINT OF VIEW

In order to identify author or speaker's purpose and point of view, note the following:

- ✓ whether the writer is attempting to establish trust by citing his or her experience or education

- ✓ whether the evidence the author or speaker provides is convincing and the argument or position is logical

- ✓ what words and phrases the author or speaker uses to appeal to emotions

- ✓ the author or speaker's use of rhetoric, or the art of speaking and writing persuasively, such as the use of repetition to drive home a point, as well as allusion and alliteration

- ✓ the author or speaker's use of rhetoric to contribute to the power, persuasiveness, or beauty of the text

To determine the author or speaker's purpose and point of view, consider the following questions:

- ✓ How does the author or speaker try to convince me that he or she has something valid and important for me to read?

- ✓ What words or phrases express emotion or invite an emotional response? How or why are they effective or ineffective?

- ✓ What words and phrases contribute to the power, persuasiveness, or beauty of the text? Is the author or speaker's use of rhetoric successful? Why or why not?

Skill:
Author's Purpose and
Point of View

Reread paragraphs 3 and 4 of "We Choose to Go to the Moon." Then, using the Checklist on the previous page, answer the multiple-choice questions below.

⟳ YOUR TURN

1. Which of the following sentences from the speech is the best statement of president Kennedy's purpose?

   ○ A. "This country was conquered by those who moved forward—and so will space."

   ○ B. ". . . [M]an, in his quest for knowledge and progress, is determined and cannot be deterred."

   ○ C. "So it is not surprising that some would have us stay where we are a little longer to rest, to wait."

   ○ D. "But this city of Houston, this state of Texas, this country of the United States, was not built by those who waited and rested and wished to look behind them."

2. Which of the following sentences is the best example of the president appealing to his audience's emotions?

   ○ A. "This country was conquered by those who moved forward—and so will space."

   ○ B. "But this city of Houston, this state of Texas, this country of the United States, was not built by those who waited and rested and wished to look behind them."

   ○ C. "The exploration of space will go ahead, whether we join in it or not, and it is one of the great adventures of all time, and no nation which expects to be the leader of other nations can expect to stay behind in this race for space."

   ○ D. "Surely the opening **vistas** of space promise high costs and hardships, as well as high reward."

3. Why is the emotional appeal in Question 2 likely to be effective?

   ○ A. In this appeal, the president appeals to the audience's hopes and fears.

   ○ B. In this appeal, the president makes historical references.

   ○ C. In this appeal, the president speaks indirectly to the Soviet Union.

   ○ D. In this appeal, the president speaks directly to the pride of Houston, Texas, and the entire country.

Reading & Writing
Companion

Skill:
Rhetoric

Use the Checklist to analyze Rhetoric in "We Choose to Go to the Moon." Refer to the sample student annotations about Rhetoric in the text.

••• CHECKLIST FOR RHETORIC

In order to identify the rhetorical appeals in a text, note the following:

- ✓ the purpose of the text

- ✓ the way in which a writer phrases, or constructs, what he or she wants to say

- ✓ details and statements that identify the author or speaker's point of view or purpose

To identify how the author or speaker uses rhetorical appeals, look for:

- ✓ the three elements of persuasion as defined by Aristotle: ethos, pathos, and logos. Ethos relies on the authority or credibility of the person making the argument to try to convince an audience. Pathos is an appeal to emotion. Logos is an appeal to reason or logic.

- ✓ words that appeal to the senses or emotions and can create a vivid picture in the minds of readers and listeners, and persuade them to accept a specific point of view

- ✓ a specific style, such as the use of assonance or the repetition of certain words can be used to create catchphrases, something that can be widely or repeatedly used and is easily remembered

- ✓ when the author or speaker's use of rhetorical appeal is particularly effective

In order to identify the rhetorical appeals in a text, note the following:

- ✓ Which rhetorical appeals can you identify in the text?

- ✓ How does this writer or speaker use rhetorical devices or appeals to persuade an audience?

- ✓ Do the rhetorical devices or appeals work to make the argument or position sound? Why or why not?

- ✓ How does the use of rhetorical devices or appeals affect the way the text is read and understood?

- ✓ In what way are the rhetorical devices particularly effective?

Skill:
Rhetoric

Reread paragraphs 17–19 of "We Choose to Go to the Moon." Then, using the Checklist on the previous page, answer the multiple-choice questions below.

⟳ YOUR TURN

1. The use of word repetition in paragraph 17 is most obvious in the phrase—

   ○ A. "Well, space is there, and we're going to climb it, and the Moon and the planets are there."
   ○ B. "with a precision better than the finest watch."
   ○ C. "propulsion, guidance, control, communications, food and survival."
   ○ D. "and do all this, and do it right, and do it first."

2. Paragraph 19 is mostly an example of what form of rhetorical appeal:

   ○ A. ethos
   ○ B. logos
   ○ C. pathos
   ○ D. word repetition

3. The final sentence of paragraph 19 is persuasive largely because—

   ○ A. it includes logical fallacies, such as the claim that boats can sail into space.
   ○ B. Kennedy was one of the world's leading experts on space science.
   ○ C. it appeals to emotion by describing the wonders of a trip to the Moon.
   ○ D. it appeals to reason by giving facts and figures about the trip to the Moon.

Please note that excerpts and passages in the StudySync® library and this workbook are intended as touchstones to generate interest in an author's work. The excerpts and passages do not substitute for the reading of entire texts, and StudySync® strongly recommends that students seek out and purchase the whole literary or informational work in order to experience it as the author intended. Links to online resellers are available in our digital library. In addition, complete works may be ordered through an authorized reseller by filling out and returning to StudySync® the order form enclosed in this workbook.

Reading & Writing
Companion

69

Skill:
Arguments and Claims

Use the Checklist to analyze Arguments and Claims in "We Choose to Go to the Moon." Refer to the sample student annotations about Arguments and Claims in the text.

••• CHECKLIST FOR ARGUMENTS AND CLAIMS

In order to delineate the premises, purposes, and arguments in works of public advocacy, note the following:

✓ in works of public advocacy, an individual or group tries to influence or support a cause or policy

✓ the premise, or the basis of the proposal the individual or group makes, must be based on logical reasoning

✓ isolate the premise in a work of public advocacy

✓ identify the purpose of the text and the position the writer takes

✓ determine whether the premise is based on logical reasoning

To evaluate the premises, purposes, and arguments in works of public advocacy, consider the following questions:

✓ What position does the writer take?

✓ How does the writer use logical reasoning to support his or her position?

✓ In a work of public advocacy, how does the individual or group try to influence or support a cause or policy?

Skill:
Arguments and Claims

Reread paragraphs 11–14 of "We Choose to Go to the Moon." Then, using the Checklist on the previous page, answer the multiple-choice questions below.

↻ YOUR TURN

1. What is the most likely reason the president shares that "Within these last 19 months at least 45 satellites have circled the earth. Some 40 of them were 'made in the United States of America'"?

   ○ A. He shares this timeline and numbers to create anxiety.

   ○ B. He shares this timeline and numbers to give the audience a logical premise and reason to hope.

   ○ C. He shares this timeline and numbers to create additional jobs for Americans.

   ○ D. He shares this timeline and numbers to give Americans another reason to compete with the Soviet Union.

2. Why does the president share the failures and challenges that we will face?

   ○ A. The president shares the failures and challenges because the perils of space exploration were largely unknown.

   ○ B. The president shares the failures and challenges because he wants those involved in the space program to admit their mistakes.

   ○ C. The president shares the failures and challenges because a real description will prevent future failures.

   ○ D. The president shares the failures and challenges because a real description of the situation acknowledges the challenges ahead, but also provides an argument for action.

3. Which of the following sentences best supports the president's argument that the benefits of the space program will be felt by his audience?

   ○ A. "Technical institutions, such as Rice, will reap the harvest of these gains."

   ○ B. "Some 40 of them were "made in the United States of America" and they were far more sophisticated and supplied far more knowledge to the people of the world than those of the Soviet Union. . . "

   ○ C. "To be sure, we are behind, and will be behind for some time in manned flight. But we do not intend to stay behind, and in this decade, we shall make up and move ahead."

   ○ D. "We have had our failures, but so have others, even if they do not admit them. And they may be less public."

Close Read

Reread "We Choose to Go to the Moon." As you reread, complete the Skills Focus questions below. Then use your answers and annotations from the questions to help you complete the Write activity.

◎ SKILLS FOCUS

1. Reread paragraph 5. What does the president reveal is part of his purpose in this paragraph? What emotion would this appeal to in his audience? Do you think it's effective?

2. Highlight and annotate two examples in which the president uses pathos to appeal to the audience's emotions. Explain whether you find these appeals persuasive and why.

3. Reread the second half of the speech. Find a sentence that appeals to the audience's sense of reason or logic. Explain why Kennedy might have chosen to use this rhetorical device, and whether or not it is effective.

4. In several key moments of this speech, the president chooses to use timelines, numbers, and statistics. Highlight two examples of this, and in your annotation explain why these numbers are useful to the president's argument. How would these numbers influence his audience?

5. In this speech, president Kennedy argues for a goal that will require tons of energy, effort, and resources. What is the future that the president is envisioning? Why is it a motivating future, if it can be attained? Why does Kennedy need to convince his audience of the possibility of this future? Remember to use textual evidence in your response

✏ WRITE

RHETORICAL ANALYSIS: Examine the reasons President Kennedy lists for wanting to **cultivate** the space program and send Americans to the Moon by the end of the 1960s. Based on his speech, what do you think motivates him? Do you find his arguments and use of rhetoric persuasive? Use evidence from the text to support your answer.

Please note that excerpts and passages in the StudySync® library and this workbook are intended as touchstones to generate interest in an author's work. The excerpts and passages do not substitute for the reading of entire texts, and StudySync® strongly recommends that students seek out and purchase the whole literary or informational work in order to experience it as the author intended. Links to online resellers are available in our digital library. In addition, complete works may be ordered through an authorized reseller by filling out and returning to StudySync® the order form enclosed in this workbook.

Reading & Writing Companion

73

Blast: The Write Stuff

How do you tell the story of who you are and who you want to become?

 BACKGROUND

Listen to the What's Next podcast associated with this Blast in your digital account.

When you finally click "Submit" and send your personal statement into the abyss of an online application portal, where does it go?

Anxious college applicants might imagine their essays go to a panel of harsh, judgmental, easily bored professors. However, this isn't accurate, according to Will Dix, a longtime college admissions counselor. "For a lot of admission people, it's kind of the dessert of a college application," says Dix. "We want to like your essay. We're not there to make corrections with red pens and so on. We do notice whether you're writing well or not, but we want to hear your voice, and that's always the primary thing."

So, how do you make sure your voice shines through in a short essay? First, pick a topic that actually matters to you. The four years you spent playing baseball might sound impressive, but unless you truly care about the game, the essay will fall flat. Rachel Toor, a creative writing professor at Eastern Washington University, says unconventional topics often make for great essays. "Write about whatever keeps you up at night," Toor writes. "That might be cars, or coffee. It might be your favorite book or the Pythagorean theorem."

Second, use anecdotes to tell a compelling story. Instead of writing a broad overview of your life, pick a moment to zoom in on. Be sure to pick a moment that symbolizes what you want to convey. "Most students think of their college essay as a major motion picture. They feel they need to cover the highlights (or, too often, the tragedies) of years of experience," Parke Muth, senior assistant dean and director of international admissions at the University of Virginia, tells U.S. News and World Report "The problem is that to write about a life in 500 words will result in a cinematic long shot . . . I tell students it is not a movie they are making but a Nike ad." Muth explains that the best essays make it easy to "hear, see, touch, taste, and sometimes even smell" the student's world.

Finally, write your essay well. Use vibrant words, clear sentence structure and correct spelling, grammar and punctuation. Many experts recommend having one or two teachers or trusted family members read over your essay. They can help you revise and edit.

In the end, Toor says, "most essays are typical. Many are boring. Some are just plain bad. But occasionally one will make an admissions officer tear down the hallway to find a colleague to whom she can say, 'You have to read what this Math Olympiad girl said about Hamlet.' Your goal is to write an essay that makes someone fall in love with you."

So, what do you think? How do you show who you are and what makes you special in just a few hundred words? How will you make your essay shine? How do you tell the story of who you are and who you want to become?

NUMBER CRUNCH
650

QUIKPOLL

What are you most likely to write your college essay about?

- ☐ Academics or activities at school
- ☐ My family or childhood
- ☐ My friends or social life outside of school
- ☐ An experience that changed the way I see the world
- ☐ Something else

✳ CREATE YOUR BLAST

How do you tell the story of who you are and who you want to become?

I would tell my story by saying that I love to work, it's my life and I love my job because I'm a baker and my other passion is animals and after I take a gap year after high school I'm going to college to become a vet tech or veterinarian.

Blast: Narrowing the Field

What qualities do you look for in a college?

 BACKGROUND

Listen to the What's Next podcast associated with this Blast in your digital account.

What is the longest amount of time you have spent preparing for something? Maybe you spent a month learning a language for a trip out of the country. Maybe you spent weeks planning for a family trip. Both situations involve a fair amount of patience and effort. The desired payoff is having an experience that is worth every penny. You will need those same skills if you plan on applying to colleges.

The college application process requires patience and effort on a much broader scale. Finding the right fit in a college requires thinking about many different factors. It also requires thinking about many different schools. There are about 3,000 four-year colleges and universities in the United States, not including the estimated 1,600 two-year institutions, according to the National Center for Education Statistics. You may want to approach your search with specific requirements. Are there certain regions of the country you would prefer to live in? Do you like the idea of a small liberal arts school or a large public university? These questions can narrow your search significantly. Online tools, such as the U.S. Department of Education's College Scorecard, account for a wide range of preferences in college searches.

There is not one single college characteristic that is universally important to every college applicant. Martha O'Connell is the executive director of college advisory organization Colleges That Change Lives. She says that you need to ask yourself four main questions about your reasons for going to college

Please note that excerpts and passages in the StudySync® library and this workbook are intended as touchstones to generate interest in an author's work. The excerpts and passages do not substitute for the reading of entire texts, and StudySync® strongly recommends that students seek out and purchase the whole literary or informational work in order to experience it as the author intended. Links to online resellers are available in our digital library. In addition, complete works may be ordered through an authorized reseller by filling out and returning to StudySync® the order form enclosed in this workbook.

Reading & Writing Companion

77

before you start your search. "Why, really, are you going? What are your abilities and strengths? What are your weaknesses," O'Connell asked in NPR. "What do you want out of life — something tangible or intangible?"

Your ideal college lifestyle is an important step in college decisions. How much will it cost to head far from home? What does the campus offer? Take a look at internship opportunities, entertainment options and the availability of public transportation. It's also valuable to check and see if there are established clubs or organizations that you'd want to participate in at different universities.

Accounting for a college lifestyle that works for you is vital, but so is picking a school with the right program and potential major. These choices will impact your life long after graduation. However, many high schoolers aren't ready to commit to a career track right away. Roughly 30 percent of college students change their major at least once before graduation, according to a 2017 study by the Department of Education. If you feel unsure about your dream job, then do not stress about how one business school stacks up against another. But if you do have a good idea of what you want to do, you can balance the benefits that come with attending a university that has a strong reputation in a certain department versus the university's other qualities.

For some students, the average annual cost of college is the most weighty and important factor. O'Connell recommends not ruling any university based on the sticker price of tuition. "Online resources, as well as financial aid workshops sponsored by high schools in local communities, are widely available to get you started," O'Connell says. "Investigate early and ask for help." Look for scholarships and grants that prospective schools offer, in-state versus out-of-state tuition, and the cost of living in different areas of the country.

Finally, as hard as it might be, try not to latch too strongly onto a dream school. *The Atlantic* analyzed a 2015 study published in the journal Contemporary Economic Policy about whether the prestige of a degree really helps students make more money. Its conclusion was that "for certain majors, going to a top-tier institution is invaluable. But for many career paths, it just doesn't matter where a person got his or her education."

What do you think? How do you research colleges? Which colleges are you interested in? What qualities do you look for in college?

NUMBER CRUNCH
40%

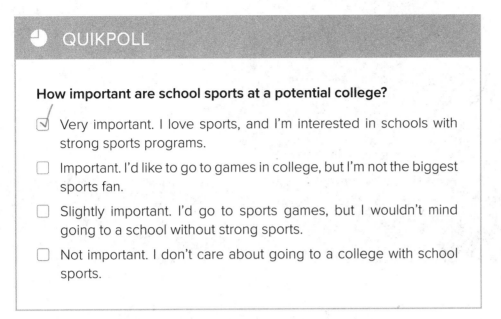

QUIKPOLL

How important are school sports at a potential college?

☑ Very important. I love sports, and I'm interested in schools with strong sports programs.

☐ Important. I'd like to go to games in college, but I'm not the biggest sports fan.

☐ Slightly important. I'd go to sports games, but I wouldn't mind going to a school without strong sports.

☐ Not important. I don't care about going to a college with school sports.

✳ CREATE YOUR BLAST

What qualities do you look for in a college?

A good atmosphere to be in, a place where I actually
want to get out of bed and go to class. Where there is
good people and professors to be around.

Please note that excerpts and passages in the StudySync® library and this workbook are intended as touchstones to generate interest in an author's work. The excerpts and passages do not substitute for the reading of entire texts, and StudySync® strongly recommends that students seek out and purchase the whole literary or informational work in order to experience it as the author intended. Links to online resellers are available in our digital library. In addition, complete works may be ordered through an authorized reseller by filling out and returning to StudySync® the order form enclosed in this workbook.

Reading & Writing
Companion

79

Blast: Filling in the Blanks

How can you best represent yourself in an application?

NOTES

ⓘ BACKGROUND

Listen to the What's Next podcast associated with this Blast in your digital account.

One of the most exciting and nerve-wracking parts of graduating high school is figuring out what, exactly, comes next. By the time graduation comes, you have likely had many different experiences. You might have tried out for a sports team, a role in a play, or a leadership position in a club.

All of your experiences in school — and outside of school — are all important preparations for college and job applications. Each type of application has unique challenges. However, there are common tips that can help you stand out, no matter which path you choose to take.

You should feel fully comfortable with your background and your body of work before the application process starts, according to Diane Anci, the dean of admissions at Kenyon College. This can boost your confidence. "Knowing who you are provides a protective armor in a process that can be overwhelming," Anci says. "Not only are you inundated with communication from the colleges, everyone you know has an opinion of what is a good college and what is not, and they feel very free to express it."

It might be tempting to throw a laundry list of extracurriculars onto your application, but it can be more beneficial to hone in on the things you are most passionate about, or those skills that are most applicable to the specific college or job. Stuart Schmill is the dean of admissions at the Massachusetts

Institute of Technology. He says that selective colleges, especially, "want students who prioritize quality over quantity."

You can also make an impression and best represent yourself by personalizing your application for each college and job you are interested in. Jessica Yeager is a graduate of the Massachusetts Institute of Technology and Harvard University. She says that general responses in an essay or cover letter are not exciting to admissions officers. For colleges, she recommends "doing deep research, visiting campuses if you can, and trying to connect with professors or coaches," she said. "Weave all this information into your supplemental essays."

Supplemental essays or responses can highlight aspects of your personality or experience that do not shine through in the rest of your application. Stephen Farmer is the executive vice chancellor and provost at the University of North Carolina. He provided essay-writing advice to The New York Times. "My advice to students is to first show your essay to a friend and ask, 'Can you hear my voice in this? Could you pick my essay from a stack of 200?' The essay doesn't have to be about something life-changing or confessional," Farmer said. "Smaller topics, written well, almost always work best."

Finally, make sure that you take your time with your application. Yale University's admissions office also recommends getting constructive feedback from those you trust. "Share your essays with at least one or two people who know you well — such as a parent, teacher, counselor, or friend — and ask for feedback," the official admissions website says. A simple error can invalidate an otherwise superb application.

It is also important to remember to not get upset over rejected applications. You are not a failure if you do not get accepted to a certain school or job. Swarthmore College, for instance, rejected former President Barack Obama — and he transferred from a liberal arts college to an Ivy League university for his junior year. On average, a corporate opening leads to roughly 250 applications, according to job search website Glassdoor. Only four to six people are called in for interviews for that one position. The application process can be competitive and stressful. However, it will be worth it when you find the right fit. But don't take rejection too much to heart.

What do you think? Who do you trust to proofread your applications? Which of your life experiences are most important to highlight on your applications? How can you best represent yourself in an application?

NUMBER CRUNCH
2.9

Please note that excerpts and passages in the StudySync® library and this workbook are intended as touchstones to generate interest in an author's work. The excerpts and passages do not substitute for the reading of entire texts, and StudySync® strongly recommends that students seek out and purchase the whole literary or informational work in order to experience it as the author intended. Links to online resellers are available in our digital library. In addition, complete works may be ordered through an authorized reseller by filling out and returning to StudySync® the order form enclosed in this workbook.

Reading & Writing Companion

81

QUIKPOLL

Do you think the most interesting thing about you would best show your potential in the field of STEM, the Humanities, Business, or Education?

- ☐ I think the most interesting thing about me would show my potential in the field of STEM.
- ☐ I think the most interesting thing about me would show my potential in the field of the Humanities.
- ☐ I think the most interesting thing about me would show my potential in the field of Business.
- ☐ I think the most interesting thing about me would show my potential in the field of Education.

CREATE YOUR BLAST

How can you best represent yourself in an application?

_____

_____

_____

_____

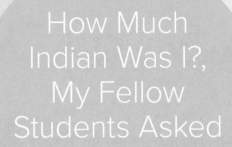

How Much Indian Was I?, My Fellow Students Asked

INFORMATIONAL TEXT
Elissa Washuta
2013

Introduction

Elissa Washuta is a lecturer at the University of Washington and teaches creative writing at the Institute of American Indian Arts. Her writings, primarily autobiographical essays and memoirs, include the Washington State Book Award finalist *My Body Is a Book of Rules*. In her short essay "How Much Indian Was I?, My Fellow Students Asked," Washuta, a nearly perfect student, receives a prestigious scholarship. The resulting journey to reconcile her success with her status as a Cowlitz tribe member is an exploration of race, culture, and identity in

"I'll never know why Maryland gave me a full scholarship. But is it so bad to think they wanted me?"

1   I came into my own as a Native American woman in high school. My skin being on the fair side of plain Yoplait, I **designated** my dark-brown hair as the body part that would legitimize me, letting its split ends shoot for my waist. The U.S. Census Bureau reported that in 2000, three Native Americans lived in Liberty Township, N.J.: my mom, my brother, and me, all enrolled members of the Cowlitz tribe.

2   In early 2003, I was a high-school senior. My only grade below an A was in gym class; on my report card, next to the B, the gym teacher wrote, "Works to ability." After nearly 13 years of academic perfectionism, I finally got a glimpse of the payoff when the University of Maryland at College Park sent me a letter inviting me to interview for a scholarship.

3   Inside the honors building I immediately noticed all the dark skin in the waiting room. I sat on the couch between my parents, wondering whether I should have worn some dream-catcher[1] earrings. My letter had said that this was an interview for a merit scholarship, with no mention of diversity. I worried that the interviewers were going to quiz me about my favorite Indian ceremonies. If they wanted me to speak in my native tongue, I would have to make something up on the spot. There was a lot of money on the line.

4   That day I wondered, what was so special about me that the adults would want to hand me what amounted to a sack filled with money? Not my poems, or my miniature clay sculptures of the members of Nirvana, or my gleaming transcripts. There were probably plenty of kids in the room who knew how to use their graphing calculators for purposes other than playing Tetris.

5   The interviewers greeted me with smiles. They asked about our drive from New Jersey and what I'd been reading. I talked about a book about Pine Ridge Reservation and my desire to work in Indian country. I told the nodding adults all about poverty, tradition, alcohol, and loss.

6   An ancient people in southwest Washington, the Cowlitz tribe maintains vibrant cultural practices and social and conservation programs despite its

---

1. **dream-catcher** a handmade item of spiritual significance in some Native American cultures, typically featuring a web or net woven into a willow hoop and adorned with feathers or beads

lack of a reservation land base. My Cowlitz mom, who had lived in the Columbia River Gorge her whole life, met my East Coast dad in college in Seattle, and afterward they moved to New Jersey.

7   I didn't know how to talk about the histories embedded in my bones: the damming of our language that coincided with the damming of the Columbia River, my wordless conversations with the towering **petroglyph** woman by the water, my belly's swell that my mother told me was an Indian thing while I battled it with Weight Watchers point counts. I thought that if I spoke the truth, they would think all the Indianness had evaporated from my family line, leaving me pale and dry. So I said, "I want to do something for my people," and two weeks later, I received a thin letter thick with the promise of more money than I could imagine: four years of tuition, room, board, and books.

8   Not long after I hung my bell-bottom jeans and shower tote in my cinderblock closet, I told the kids on my floor of the honors dorm that in order to keep my scholarship, I'd have to obsess over every grade point. That money never went to white kids, they said, so I must be an undercover genius. I'm not all white, I said. What was my SAT score, they wanted to know. My GPA? Extracurriculars? How much Indian was I? The first thing I learned in college was that white boys don't care if you're legitimately Indian if they think you robbed them of $100,000 in scholarship money that they'd earned holding a tuba for countless hours on a high-school football field.

9   I threw myself into super-Indianness, taking both of the Native-studies courses offered by the university's **anthropology** department. I participated in a summer internship program for Native students and scored a part-time job in tribal relations with the U.S. Department of Agriculture. I graduated with a 4.0 GPA. If the university had wanted to reel in an Indian who could bring the numbers, I figured they had gotten what they paid for, as long as I became the Indian I had promised they were getting.

10   I didn't take any time off before shipping myself to Seattle for graduate school in creative writing at the University of Washington. The master's program offered me no teaching assistantship, and I told the program director I couldn't sign on unless the price tag was slashed. She came through with a university program committed to serving underrepresented graduate students. After I sent over a photocopy of my tribal card to add to the application, the grant program awarded me a generous partial scholarship. Creative-writing programs are notorious for the feelings of resentment that brew when students feel like a bunch of blood-hungry dogs made to scrap over funds granted on the basis of artistic **prowess**, but my colleagues were supportive of my scholarship.

11   In my application essay, I said that part of Washington's allure was its proximity to my tribe. I meant it. In the five years I have been at Washington, I have been attending Cowlitz general-council meetings and learning to participate. During

Please note that excerpts and passages in the StudySync® library and this workbook are intended as touchstones to generate interest in an author's work. The excerpts and passages do not substitute for the reading of entire texts, and StudySync® strongly recommends that students seek out and purchase the whole literary or informational work in order to experience it as the author intended. Links to online resellers are available in our digital library. In addition, complete works may be ordered through an authorized reseller by filling out and returning to StudySync® the order form enclosed in this workbook.

Reading & Writing Companion

85

my second year, I was a graduate assistant for the department of American Indian studies, and I now serve as the undergraduate adviser. I also teach classes that focus on Native literature and film representations of Natives.

12 I'd love to see more Native students at Washington and elsewhere. Native people deserve to be educated in spite of the extraordinary challenges many face because of uniquely broken educational systems wrapped up in the mangled trust relationship that sets Indian identity apart from other racial or ethnic distinctions. Native people hold an elemental piece of this nation's life story, and universities will suffer without an indigenous presence.

13 Those interviewers back at Maryland would be happy with my academic career, I think. My work these days comes with a clear mission: to help the students I teach learn who we are and who we are not, and to help them—especially those who were least prepared because of their backgrounds—navigate the academic maze. I wish my students could stop worrying about money—who's getting it, why, and how they're going to get some of their own—so they can focus on learning to write killer essays and getting smarter than they ever thought possible.

14 I'll never know why Maryland gave me a full scholarship. But is it so bad to think they wanted me? As my gym teacher noticed, I "work to ability." I pull out all the stops in every class. Perhaps the interviewers sensed my yearning to go for broke and to stuff every synapse with academic pleasures.

15 From my family and Native communities, I have learned about the gifting tradition. In our culture, accepting a gift with grace and giving meaningful gifts are skills more important, and more difficult to **cultivate**, than learning to graph calculus problems. So I have stopped apologizing for the gifts I receive. I accept them. And now I have my own gifting to do.

✏ WRITE

PERSONAL RESPONSE: Today, many people are turning to online services such as Ancestry.com to discover their backgrounds. Do you think that knowing your ethnic makeup and cultural heritage is important in order to forge your identity? Why or why not? Write an essay of 300 or more words arguing your position. Use details from this selection and from your own life to develop your ideas.

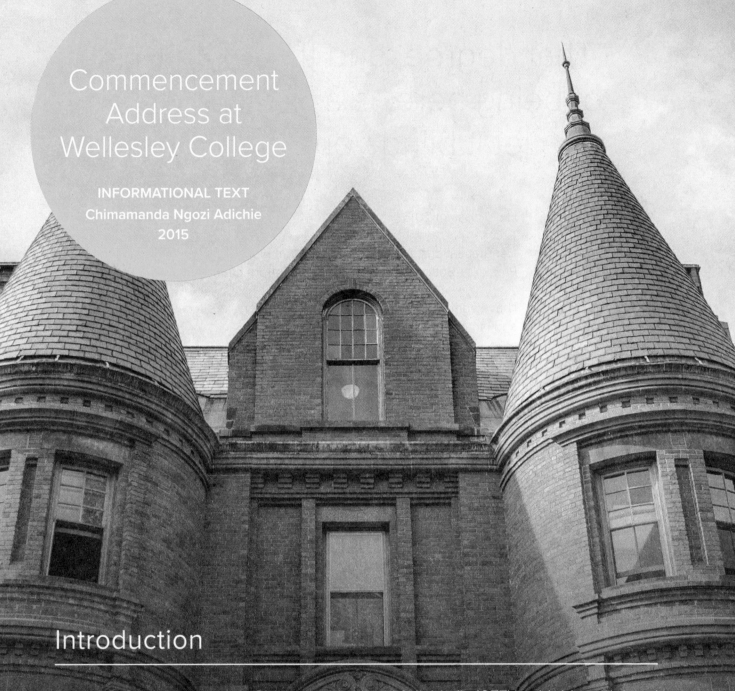

Commencement Address at Wellesley College

INFORMATIONAL TEXT
Chimamanda Ngozi Adichie
2015

Introduction

Nigerian-born author Chimamanda Ngozi Adichie (b. 1977) is a highly acclaimed novelist, short-story writer, and critic whose advocacy on behalf of gender equality was first introduced to mass audiences in the 2013 Beyoncé song "Flawless," which samples an Adichie speech entitled "We Should All Be Feminists." In this commencement address to the 2015 graduating class of Wellesley College—a women's college in Massachusetts—she outlines the unprecedented challenges and opportunities young women encounter in society today.

"That degree, and the experience of being here, is a privilege. Don't let it blind you too often."

Copyright © BookheadEd Learning, LLC

1   Hello class of 2015.

2   Congratulations! And thank you for that wonderful welcome. And thank you President Bottomly for that wonderful introduction.

3   I have admired Wellesley—its mission, its story, its successes—for a long time and I thank you very much for inviting me.

4   You are ridiculously lucky to be graduating from this bastion of excellence and on these beautiful acres.

5   I'm truly, truly happy to be here today, so happy, in fact, that when I found out your class color was yellow, I decided I would wear yellow eyeshadow. But on second thoughts, I realized that as much as I admire Wellesley, even yellow eyeshadow was a bit too much of a gesture. So I dug out this yellow—yellowish—headwrap instead.

6   Speaking of eyeshadow, I wasn't very interested in makeup until I was in my twenties, which is when I began to wear makeup. Because of a man. A loud, unpleasant man. He was one of the guests at a friend's dinner party. I was also a guest. I was about 23, but people often told me I looked 12. The conversation at dinner was about traditional Igbo culture, about the custom that allows only men to break the kola nut, and the kola nut[1] is a deeply symbolic part of Igbo cosmology[2].

7   I argued that it would be better if that honor were based on achievement rather than **gender**, and he looked at me and said, dismissively, "You don't know what you are talking about, you're a small girl."

8   I wanted him to disagree with the substance of my argument, but by looking at me, young and female, it was easy for him to dismiss what I said. So I decided to try to look older.

---

1. **kola nut** fruit of the kola tree, used in beverages, gum, medicine, and religious practices of West Africa
2. **cosmology** study of the universe, its foundations and physics

9 So I thought lipstick might help. And eyeliner.

10 And I am grateful to that man because I have since come to love makeup, and its wonderful possibilities for temporary transformation.

11 So, I have not told you this anecdote as a way to illustrate my discovery of gender injustice. If anything, it's really just an ode to makeup.

12 It's really just to say that this, your graduation, is a good time to buy some lipsticks—if makeup is your sort of thing—because a good shade of lipstick can always put you in a slightly better mood on dark days.

13 It's not about my discovering gender injustice because of course I had discovered years before then. From childhood. From watching the world.

14 I already knew that the world does not extend to women the many small courtesies that it extends to men.

15 I also knew that victimhood is not a virtue. That being **discriminated** against does not make you somehow morally better.

16 And I knew that men were not inherently bad or evil. They were merely privileged[3]. And I knew that privilege blinds because it is the nature of privilege to blind.

17 I knew from this personal experience, from the class privilege I had of growing up in an educated family, that it sometimes blinded me, that I was not always as alert to the nuances of people who were different from me.

18 And you, because you now have your beautiful Wellesley degree, have become privileged, no matter what your background. That degree, and the experience of being here, is a privilege. Don't let it blind you too often. Sometimes you will need to push it aside in order to see clearly.

• • •

19 I bring greetings to you from my mother. She's a big admirer of Wellesley, and she wishes she could be here. She called me yesterday to ask how the speech-writing was going and to tell me to remember to use a lot of lotion on my legs today so they would not look ashy.

20 My mother is 73 and she retired as the first female registrar of the University of Nigeria—which was quite a big deal at the time.

---

3. **privileged** in possession of rights or advantages not accessible to everyone

Copyright © BookheadEd Learning, LLC

21 My mother likes to tell a story of the first university meeting she chaired. It was in a large conference room, and at the head of the table was a sign that said CHAIRMAN. My mother was about to get seated there when a clerk came over and made to remove the sign. All the past meetings had of course been chaired by men, and somebody had forgotten to replace the CHAIRMAN with a new sign that said CHAIRPERSON. The clerk apologized and told her he would find the new sign, since she was not a chairman.

22 My mother said no. Actually, she said, she WAS a chairman. She wanted the sign left exactly where it was. The meeting was about to begin. She didn't want anybody to think that what she was doing in that meeting at that time on that day was in any way different from what a CHAIRMAN would have done.

23 I always liked this story, and admired what I thought of as my mother's fiercely feminist choice. I once told the story to a friend, a card-carrying feminist, and I expected her to say bravo to my mother, but she was troubled by it.

24 "Why would your mother want to be called a chairman, as though she needed the MAN part to validate her?" my friend asked.

25 In some ways, I saw my friend's point.

26 Because if there were a Standard Handbook published annually by the Secret Society of Certified Feminists, then that handbook would certainly say that a woman should not be called, nor want to be called, a CHAIRMAN.

27 But gender is always about context and **circumstance**.

28 If there is a lesson in this anecdote, apart from just telling you a story about my mother to make her happy that I spoke about her at Wellesley, then it is this: Your standardized **ideologies** will not always fit your life. Because life is messy.

• • •

29 When I was growing up in Nigeria I was expected, as every student who did well was expected, to become a doctor. Deep down I knew that what I really wanted to do was to write stories. But I did what I was supposed to do and I went into medical school.

30 I told myself that I would tough it out and become a psychiatrist and that way I could use my patients' stories for my fiction.

31 But after one year of medical school I fled. I realized I would be a very unhappy doctor and I really did not want to be responsible for the inadvertent death of

my patients. Leaving medical school was a very unusual decision, especially in Nigeria where it is very difficult to get into medical school.

32 Later, people told me that it had been very courageous of me, but I did not feel courageous at all.

33 What I felt then was not courage but a desire to make an effort. To try. I could either stay and study something that was not right for me. Or I could try and do something different. I decided to try. I took the American exams and got a scholarship to come to the US where I could study something else that was NOT related to medicine. Now it might not have worked out. I might not have been given an American scholarship.

34 My writing might not have ended up being successful. But the point is that I tried.

35 We can not always bend the world into the shapes we want but we can try, we can make a concerted and real and true effort. And you are privileged that, because of your education here, you have already been given many of the tools that you will need to try. Always just try. Because you never know.

36 And so as you graduate, as you deal with your excitement and your doubts today, I urge you to try and create the world you want to live in.

37 Minister to the world in a way that can change it. Minister radically in a real, active, practical, get your hands dirty way.

38 Wellesley will open doors for you. Walk through those doors and make your strides long and firm and sure.

39 Write television shows in which female strength is not depicted as remarkable but merely normal.

40 Teach your students to see that vulnerability is a HUMAN rather than a FEMALE trait.

41 Commission magazine articles that teach men HOW TO KEEP A WOMAN HAPPY. Because there are already too many articles that tell women how to keep a man happy. And in media interviews make sure fathers are asked how they balance family and work. In this age of 'parenting as guilt,' please spread the guilt equally. Make fathers feel as bad as mothers. Make fathers share in the glory of guilt.

42 Campaign and agitate for paid paternity leave everywhere in America.

Please note that excerpts and passages in the StudySync® library and this workbook are intended as touchstones to generate interest in an author's work. The excerpts and passages do not substitute for the reading of entire texts, and StudySync® strongly recommends that students seek out and purchase the whole literary or informational work in order to experience it as the author intended. Links to online resellers are available in our digital library. In addition, complete works may be ordered through an authorized reseller by filling out and returning to StudySync® the order form enclosed in this workbook.

Reading & Writing
Companion

91

43 Hire more women where there are few. But remember that a woman you hire doesn't have to be exceptionally good. Like a majority of the men who get hired, she just needs to be good enough.

. . .

44 Recently a feminist organization kindly nominated me for an important prize in a country that will remain unnamed. I was very pleased. I've been fortunate to have received a few prizes so far and I quite like them especially when they come with shiny presents. To get this prize, I was required to talk about how important a particular European feminist woman writer had been to me. Now the truth was that I had never managed to finish this feminist writer's book. It did not speak to me. It would have been a lie to claim that she had any major influence on my thinking. The truth is that I learned so much more about feminism from watching the women traders in the market in Nsukka where I grew up than from reading any **seminal** feminist text. I could have said that this woman was important to me, and I could have talked the talk, and I could have been given the prize and a shiny present.

45 But I didn't.

46 Because I had begun to ask myself what it really means to wear this FEMINIST label so publicly.

47 Just as I asked myself after excerpts of my feminism speech were used in a song by a talented musician whom I think some of you might know. I thought it was a very good thing that the word 'feminist' would be introduced to a new generation.

48 But I was startled by how many people, many of whom were academics, saw something troubling, even menacing, in this.

49 It was as though feminism was supposed to be an elite little cult, with esoteric rites of membership.

50 But it shouldn't. Feminism should be an inclusive party. Feminism should be a party full of different feminisms.

51 And so, class of 2015, please go out there and make Feminism a big raucous inclusive party.

. . .

52 The past three weeks have been the most emotionally difficult of my life. My father is 83 years old, a retired professor of statistics, a lovely kind man. I am an absolute Daddy's girl. Three weeks ago, he was kidnapped near his home

in Nigeria. And for a number of days, my family and I went through the kind of emotional pain that I have never known in my life. We were talking to threatening strangers on the phone, begging and negotiating for my father's safety and we were not always sure if my father was alive. He was released after we paid a ransom. He is well, in fairly good shape and in his usual lovely way, is very keen to reassure us all that he is fine.

53   I am still not sleeping well, I still wake up many times at night, in panic, worried that something else has gone wrong, I still cannot look at my father without fighting tears, without feeling this profound relief and gratitude that he is safe, but also rage that he had to undergo such an indignity to his body and to his spirit.

54   And the experience has made me rethink many things, what truly matters, and what doesn't. What I value, and what I don't.

55   And as you graduate today, I urge you to think about that a little more. Think about what really matters to you. Think about what you WANT to really matter to you.

56   I read about your rather lovely tradition of referring to older students as "big sisters" and younger ones as "little sisters." And I read about the rather strange thing about being thrown into the pond—and I didn't really get that—but I would very much like to be your honorary big sister today.

57   Which means that I would like to give you bits of advice as your big sister:

58   All over the world, girls are raised to be make themselves likeable, to twist themselves into shapes that suit other people.

59   Please do not twist yourself into shapes to please. Don't do it. If someone likes that version of you, that version of you that is false and holds back, then they actually just like that twisted shape, and not you. And the world is such a gloriously multifaceted, diverse place that there are people in the world who will like you, the real you, as you are.

60   I am lucky that my writing has given me a platform that I choose to use to talk about things that I care about, and I have said a few things that have not been so popular with a number of people. I have been told to shut up about certain things – such as my position on the equal rights of gay people on the continent of Africa, such as my deeply held belief that men and women are completely equal. I don't speak to provoke. I speak because I think our time on earth is short and each moment that we are not our truest selves, each moment we pretend to be what we are not, each moment we say what we do not mean because we imagine that is what somebody wants us to say, then we are wasting our time on earth.

NOTES

61 I don't mean to sound precious but please don't waste your time on earth, but there is one exception. The only acceptable way of wasting your time on earth is online shopping.

62 Okay, one last thing about my mother. My mother and I do not agree on many things regarding gender. There are certain things my mother believes a person should do, for the simple reason that said person 'is a woman.' Such as nod occasionally and smile even when smiling is the last thing one wants to do. Such as strategically give in to certain arguments, especially when arguing with a non-female. Such as get married and have children. I can think of fairly good reasons for doing any of these. But 'because you are a woman' is not one of them. And so, Class of 2015, never ever accept 'Because You Are A Woman' as a reason for doing or not doing anything.

63 And, finally I would like to end with a final note on the most important thing in the world: love.

64 Now girls are often raised to see love only as giving. Women are praised for their love when that love is an act of giving. But to love is to give AND to take.

65 Please love by giving and by taking. Give and be given. If you are only giving and not taking, you'll know. You'll know from that small and true voice inside you that we females are so often socialized to silence.

66 Don't silence that voice. Dare to take.

67 Congratulations.

WRITE

PERSONAL RESPONSE: In her speech, Chimamanda Ngozi Adichie uses personal memories and stories to explain how small gestures of resistance (wearing makeup, or wanting to be called a "chairman" instead of "chairperson," for example) have helped her and her mother be true to themselves, notwithstanding other people's attempts to transform them into something they are not. Think about your own identity. Has anyone ever pushed you to be something other than your true self? Write a brief speech that describes this situation and the outcome. Were you able to remain true to yourself, or did you have to compromise? Why is it important to be true to yourself? Why is it important for others to acknowledge your true self? (If you have never experienced such a situation, please imagine one and write your speech based on that.)

I've always tried hard to remain true to myself but there has been a few situations where it was hard to do so. Most of the time it's hard for me to remain true to myself but it is very important to do so.

Please note that excerpts and passages in the StudySync® library and this workbook are intended as touchstones to generate interest in an author's work. The excerpts and passages do not substitute for the reading of entire texts, and StudySync® strongly recommends that students seek out and purchase the whole literary or informational work in order to experience it as the author intended. Links to online resellers are available in our digital library. In addition, complete works may be ordered through an authorized reseller by filling out and returning to StudySync® the order form enclosed in this workbook.

Reading & Writing Companion   95

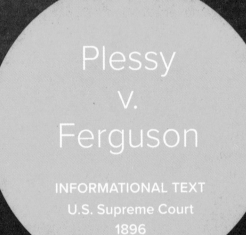

Plessy v. Ferguson

INFORMATIONAL TEXT
U.S. Supreme Court
1896

Introduction

Plessy v. Ferguson was an 1896 U.S. Supreme Court case that allowed segregation of public facilities under the doctrine of "separate but equal." The underlying case was orchestrated by a committee of concerned citizens who opposed a Louisiana law that required separate railroad cars for blacks and whites. Plaintiff Homer Plessy, a man with one-eighth African blood, challenged that law when he attempted to ride as a passenger on a whites-only car on the East Louisiana Railroad and refused requests to leave. He was found guilty by Judge John Howard Ferguson, who ruled that Louisiana had the right to regulate railroad companies that operated within the state. The Supreme Court's ruling that "separate but equal" was not in violation of the constitution was eventually invalidated by

"The judgment of the court below is therefore affirmed."

From the majority opinion of the Court, delivered by Justice Henry Billings Brown:

Copyright © BookheadEd Learning, LLC

1   The constitutionality[1] of this act is attacked upon the ground that it conflicts both with the thirteenth amendment of the constitution, abolishing slavery, and the fourteenth amendment[2], which prohibits certain restrictive legislation on the part of the states.

A man drinks from a streetcar station water fountain labeled "COLORED" in 1939, over forty years after the Plessy v. Ferguson decision.

2   1. That it does not conflict with the thirteenth amendment, which abolished slavery and involuntary servitude, except as a punishment for crime, is too clear for argument. Slavery implies involuntary servitude,—a state of bondage; the ownership of mankind as a chattel, or, at least, the control of the labor and services of one man for the benefit of another, and the absence of a legal right to the disposal of his own person, property, and services. This amendment was said in the Slaughter-House Cases to have been intended primarily to abolish slavery, as it had been previously known in this country and that it equally forbade Mexican peonage or the Chinese coolie trade, when they amounted to slavery or involuntary servitude, and that the use of the word "servitude" was intended to prohibit the use of all forms of involuntary slavery, of whatever class or name. It was **intimated,** however, in that case, that this amendment was regarded by the statesmen of that day as insufficient to protect the colored race from certain laws which had been enacted in the Southern states, imposing upon the colored race **onerous** disabilities and burdens, and curtailing their rights in the pursuit of life, liberty, and property to such an

NOTES

Skill:
Reasons and
Evidence

Justice Brown argues that the act (by plaintiff Homer Plessy) is unconstitutional. He supports his opinion by referring to two constitutional amendments. His position seems clear and based on constitutional reasoning.

1. **constitutionality** the extent to which something adheres to the rules and principles laid forth in a Constitution
2. **amendment** an addition or addendum to the U.S. Constitution (there have been 27 to date)

NOTES

extent that their freedom was of little value; and that the fourteenth amendment was devised to meet this **exigency.**

. . .

3   2. By the fourteenth amendment, all persons born or naturalized in the United States, and subject to the jurisdiction[3] thereof, are made citizens of the United States and of the state wherein they reside; and the states are forbidden from making or enforcing any law which shall **abridge** the privileges or immunities of citizens of the United States, or shall deprive any person of life, liberty, or property without due process of law, or deny to any person within their jurisdiction the equal protection of the laws.

. . .

4   The object of the amendment was undoubtedly to enforce the absolute equality of the two races before the law, but, in the nature of things, it could not have been intended to abolish distinctions based upon color, or to enforce social, as distinguished from political, equality, or a commingling of the two races upon terms unsatisfactory to either. Laws permitting, and even requiring, their separation, in places where they are liable to be brought into contact, do not necessarily imply the inferiority of either race to the other, and have been generally, if not universally, recognized as within the competency of the state legislatures in the exercise of their police power. The most common instance of this is connected with the establishment of separate schools for white and colored children, which have been held to be a valid exercise of the legislative power even by courts of states where the political rights of the colored race have been longest and most earnestly enforced.

. . .

Skill:
Rhetoric

Brown's argument continues in a logical progression. He says that equality cannot be achieved by legally-enforced commingling. Can equality be achieved by legally-enforced separation? There is a breakdown in logic and rhetoric.

5   We consider the underlying **fallacy** of the plaintiff's argument to consist in the assumption that the enforced separation of the two races stamps the colored race with a badge of inferiority. If this be so, it is not by reason of anything found in the act, but solely because the colored race chooses to put that construction upon it. The argument necessarily assumes that if, as has been more than once the case, and is not unlikely to be so again, the colored race should become the dominant power in the state legislature, and should enact a law in precisely similar terms, it would thereby **relegate** the white race to an inferior position. We imagine that the white race, at least, would not acquiesce in this assumption. The argument also assumes that social prejudices may be overcome by legislation, and that equal rights cannot be secured to the negro except by an enforced commingling of the two races. We cannot

3. **jurisdiction** an area in which a government has power or a set of laws is used

accept this proposition. If the two races are to meet upon terms of social equality, it must be the result of natural affinities, a mutual appreciation of each other's merits, and a voluntary consent of individuals. As was said by the court of appeals of New York in People v. Gallagher: 'This end can neither be accomplished nor promoted by laws which conflict with the general sentiment of the community upon whom they are designed to operate. When the government, therefore, has secured to each of its citizens equal rights before the law, and equal opportunities for improvement and progress, it has accomplished the end for which it was organized, and performed all of the functions respecting social advantages with which it is endowed.' Legislation is powerless to **eradicate** racial instincts, or to abolish distinctions based upon physical differences, and the attempt to do so can only result in accentuating the difficulties of the present situation. If the civil and political rights of both races be equal, one cannot be inferior to the other civilly or politically. If one race be inferior to the other socially, the constitution of the United States cannot put them upon the same plane.

6   It is true that the question of the proportion of colored blood necessary to constitute a colored person, as distinguished from a white person, is one upon which there is a difference of opinion in the different states; some holding that any visible admixture of black blood stamps the person as belonging to the colored race; others, that it depends upon the preponderance of blood; and still others, that the predominance of white blood must only be in the proportion of three-fourths. But these are questions to be determined under the laws of each state, and are not properly put in issue in this case. Under the allegations of his petition, it may undoubtedly become a question of importance whether, under the laws of Louisiana, the petitioner belongs to the white or colored race.

7   The judgment of the court below is therefore affirmed.

From Justice John Marshall Harlan's dissenting opinion:

8   The thirteenth amendment does not permit the withholding or the deprivation of any right necessarily inhering in freedom. It not only struck down the institution of slavery as previously existing in the United States, but it prevents the imposition of any burdens or disabilities that constitute badges of slavery or servitude. It decreed universal civil freedom in this country. This court has so adjudged. But, that amendment having been found inadequate to the protection of the rights of those who had been in slavery, it was followed by the fourteenth amendment, which added greatly to the dignity and glory of American citizenship, and to the security of personal liberty, by declaring that 'all persons born or naturalized in the United States, and subject to the jurisdiction thereof, are citizens of the United States and of the state wherein they reside,' and that 'no state shall make or enforce any law which shall

Skill:
Technical
Language

The use of the word right is crucial to Harlan's argument. This is a Supreme Court opinion so it has major consequences for civil rights in America. He uses the Thirteenth Amendment to argue for all rights associated with freedom.

Copyright © BookheadEd Learning, LLC

abridge the privileges or immunities of citizens of the United States; nor shall any state deprive any person of life, liberty or property without due process of law, nor deny to any person within its jurisdiction the equal protection of the laws.' These two amendments, if enforced according to their true intent and meaning, will protect all the civil rights that pertain to freedom and citizenship. Finally, and to the end that no citizen should be denied, on account of his race, the privilege of participating in the political control of his country, it was declared by the fifteenth amendment that 'the right of citizens of the United States to vote shall not be denied or abridged by the United States or by any state on account of race, color or previous condition of servitude.'

9 These notable additions to the fundamental law were welcomed by the friends of liberty throughout the world. They removed the race line from our governmental systems. They had, as this court has said, a common purpose, namely, to secure 'to a race recently emancipated, a race that through many generations have been held in slavery, all the civil rights that the superior race enjoy.' They declared, in legal effect, this court has further said, 'that the law in the states shall be the same for the black as for the white; that all persons, whether colored or white, shall stand equal before the laws of the states; and in regard to the colored race, for whose protection the amendment was primarily designed, that no discrimination shall be made against them by law because of their color.' We also said: 'The words of the amendment, it is true, are prohibitory, but they contain a necessary implication of a positive immunity or right, most valuable to the colored race,—the right to exemption from unfriendly legislation against them distinctively as colored; exemption from legal discriminations, implying inferiority in civil society, lessening the security of their enjoyment of the rights which others enjoy; and discriminations which are steps towards reducing them to the condition of a subject race.' It was, consequently, adjudged that a state law that excluded citizens of the colored race from juries, because of their race, however well qualified in other respects to discharge the duties of jurymen, was repugnant to the fourteenth amendment. At the present term, referring to the previous adjudications, this court declared that 'underlying all of those decisions is the principle that the constitution of the United States, in its present form, forbids, so far as civil and political rights are concerned, discrimination by the general government or the states against any citizen because of his race. All citizens are equal before the law.'

10 The decisions referred to show the scope of the recent amendments of the constitution. They also show that it is not within the power of a state to prohibit colored citizens, because of their race, from participating as jurors in the administration of justice.

NOTES

11 It was said in argument that the statute of Louisiana does not discriminate against either race, but prescribes a rule applicable alike to white and colored citizens. But this argument does not meet the difficulty. Every one knows that the statute in question had its origin in the purpose, not so much to exclude white persons from railroad cars occupied by blacks, as to exclude colored people from coaches occupied by or assigned to white persons. Railroad corporations of Louisiana did not make discrimination among whites in the matter of commodation for travelers. The thing to accomplish was, under the guise of giving equal accommodation for whites and blacks, to compel the latter to keep to themselves while traveling in railroad passenger coaches. No one would be so wanting in candor as to assert the contrary. The fundamental objection, therefore, to the statute, is that it interferes with the personal freedom of citizens. 'Personal liberty,' it has been well said, 'consists in the power of locomotion, of changing situation, or removing one's person to whatsoever places one's own inclination may direct, without imprisonment or restraint, unless by due course of law.' If a white man and a black man choose to occupy the same public conveyance on a public highway, it is their right to do so; and no government, proceeding alone on grounds of race, can prevent it without infringing the personal liberty of each.

12 The sure guaranty of the peace and security of each race is the clear, distinct, unconditional recognition by our governments, national and state, of every right that inheres in civil freedom, and of the equality before the law of all citizens of the United States, without regard to race. State enactments regulating the enjoyment of civil rights upon the basis of race, and cunningly devised to defeat legitimate results of the war, under the pretense of recognizing equality of rights, can have no other result than to render permanent peace impossible, and to keep alive a conflict of races, the continuance of which must do harm to all concerned.

Skill:
Technical
Language

Harlan uses *right* again, this time with a specific example. He associates the term with personal liberty and with freedom. He states that legislating the separation of races infringes on the liberty and freedom of all races.

Please note that excerpts and passages in the StudySync® library and this workbook are intended as touchstones to generate interest in an author's work. The excerpts and passages do not substitute for the reading of entire texts, and StudySync® strongly recommends that students seek out and purchase the whole literary or informational work in order to experience it as the author intended. Links to online resellers are available in our digital library. In addition, complete works may be ordered through an authorized reseller by filling out and returning to StudySync® the order form enclosed in this workbook.

Reading & Writing
Companion

101

First Read

Read *Plessy v. Ferguson.* After you read, complete the Think Questions below.

THINK QUESTIONS

1. Refer to one or more details from the text to explain what Justice Brown believes to be the limitations of the Supreme Court's power. What words and phrases hint at why he feels the Court has this limit?

2. According to Justice Brown, who is at fault if one group of people feels inferior to another? How do you think he would suggest Plessy deal with the segregation laws? Support your answer with textual evidence.

3. According to Justice Harlan, what did the railroad claim was its motivation for the decision to separate passengers? How does Harlan feel about that claim, and what does he think the real motivation was? Use details from the text to describe Justice Harlan's response to the railroad's actions and the arguments made in court.

4. Use sentence clues, such as contextual definitions or restatements, to determine the meaning of the word **relegate**. Verify that your determined meaning makes sense by checking it in the context of the sentence or paragraph. Write your definition here and explain how you determined and verified it.

5. Use contextual clues to determine the meaning of the word **eradicate**. Write your definition here and tell how you found it. Then, consult a reference work, such as a dictionary, to check your definition and trace the etymology of "eradicate." Explain how knowing the word's Latin roots helps you to understand its full meaning.

Skill:
Reasons and Evidence

Use the Checklist to analyze Reasons and Evidence in *Plessy v. Ferguson*. Refer to the sample student annotations about Reasons and Evidence in the text.

••• CHECKLIST FOR REASONS AND EVIDENCE

In order to delineate and evaluate the reasoning in seminal (influential) U.S. texts, note the following:

✓ the writer's position and determine how he or she uses legal reasoning to interpret the law

- legal reasoning includes the thinking processes and strategies used by lawyers and judges when arguing and deciding legal cases, and is based on constitutional principles, or laws written down in the U.S. Constitution

✓ a Supreme Court judge that disagrees with the legal reasoning behind the majority opinion in a legal case writes a dissent, expressing opposition

- a dissent must follow constitutional principles, or the laws set down in the Constitution

✓ determine whether the premise is based on legal reasoning and constitutional principles

To evaluate the reasoning in seminal (influential) U.S. texts, including the application of constitutional principles and use of legal reasoning, consider the following questions:

✓ What position does the writer take?

✓ How does the writer use constitutional principles and legal reasoning to support his or her position?

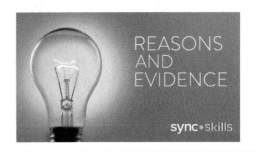

Skill:
Reasons and Evidence

Reread paragraph 5 of *Plessy v. Ferguson*. Then, using the Checklist on the previous page, answer the multiple-choice questions below.

⟳ YOUR TURN

1. This question has two parts. First, answer Part A. Then, answer Part B.

    Part A: Why does Justice Brown quote the previous Supreme Court decision *People v. Gallagher* during this part of his argument?

    ○ A. He uses a previous Supreme Court decision to support his argument that courts can only enforce political and not social equality.

    ○ B. He uses a previous Supreme Court decision to support his argument that the racial discrimination in public places should be outlawed.

    ○ C. He uses a previous Supreme Court decision to refute the Louisiana state law.

    ○ D. He uses a previous Supreme Court decision to support his argument that the U.S. Constitution should make distinctions based on race.

    Part B: Which of the following statements best represents Justice Brown's reasoning in relation to the answer in Part A?

    ○ A. "If the two races are to meet upon terms of social equality, it must be the result of natural affinities, a mutual appreciation of each other's merits, and a voluntary consent of individuals."

    ○ B. "If one race be inferior to the other socially, the constitution of the United States cannot put them upon the same plane."

    ○ C. "If the civil and political rights of both races be equal, one cannot be inferior to the other civilly or politically."

    ○ D. "Legislation is powerless to eradicate racial instincts, or to abolish distinctions based upon physical differences, and the attempt to do so can only result in accentuating the difficulties of the present situation."

Skill: Rhetoric

Use the Checklist to analyze Rhetoric in *Plessy v. Ferguson*. Refer to the sample student annotations about Rhetoric in the text.

••• CHECKLIST FOR RHETORIC

In order to identify an author's point of view or purpose in a text, note the following:

- ✓ the purpose of the text

- ✓ the way in which a writer phrases, or constructs, what he or she wants to say

- ✓ details and statements that identify the author's point of view or purposes

To identify how the author uses rhetorical appeals, look for:

- ✓ the three elements of persuasion as defined by Aristotle: ethos, pathos, and logos. Ethos relies on the authority or credibility of the person making the argument to try to convince an audience. Pathos is an appeal to emotion. Logos is an appeal to reason or logic

- ✓ a specific style, such as the use of assonance or the repetition of certain words can be used to create catchphrases, something that can be widely or repeatedly used and is easily remembered

- ✓ when the author's use of rhetorical appeal is particularly effective

To determine the rhetorical appeal(s) in a text in which the rhetoric is particularly effective, consider the following questions:

- ✓ Which rhetorical appeals can you identify in the text?

- ✓ How does this writer or speaker use rhetorical devices or appeals to persuade an audience?

- ✓ In what way are the rhetorical devices particularly effective?

Skill: Rhetoric

Reread paragraph 9 of *Plessy v. Ferguson*. Then, using the Checklist on the previous page, answer the multiple-choice questions below.

⟳ YOUR TURN

1. Which of the following states the main rhetorical strategy of the passage?

   ○ A. An appeal to emotions causing a sense of disgust
   ○ B. An appeal to shared beliefs based on the concept of freedom
   ○ C. An appeal to morals causing a sense of guilt
   ○ D. An appeal to the intellect based on data and statistics

2. Which sentence or phrase from the passage best supports your answer to Question 1?

   ○ A. These notable additions to the fundamental law were welcomed by the friends of liberty throughout the world.
   ○ B. They declared, in legal effect, this court has further said, "that the law in the states shall be the same for the black as for the white."
   ○ C. "That all persons, whether colored or white, shall stand equal before the laws of the states."
   ○ D. All of the above

Skill:
Technical Language

Use the Checklist to analyze Technical Language in *Plessy v. Ferguson*. Refer to the sample student annotations about Technical Language in the text.

••• CHECKLIST FOR TECHNICAL LANGUAGE

In order to determine the meaning of words and phrases as they are used in a text, including key terms and technical meanings, note the following:

- ✓ the subject of the book or article

- ✓ any unfamiliar words that you think might be technical terms

- ✓ words that have multiple meanings that change when used with a specific subject

- ✓ the possible contextual meaning of a word, or the definition from a dictionary

- ✓ key terms that are used repeatedly throughout the text

To determine the meaning of words and phrases as they are used in a text, including key terms and technical meanings, consider the following questions:

- ✓ What is the subject of the informational text?

- ✓ How does the use of technical language help establish the author as an authority on the subject?

- ✓ Are there any key terms or technical words that have an impact on the meaning and tone of the book or article?

- ✓ Does the author use the same term several times, refining its meaning and adding layers to it over the course of the text?

Skill: Technical Language

Reread paragraph 2 of *Plessy v. Ferguson*. Then, using the Checklist on the previous page, answer the multiple-choice questions below.

⟳ YOUR TURN

1. What is the most likely reason why Justice Brown defines the term *slavery* in his argument?

   ○ A. Justice Brown defines the term *slavery* because he believes the opposing argument wants to make slavery legal again in America.

   ○ B. Justice Brown defines the term *slavery* because making a technical term of slavery allows Justice Brown to argue that the Thirteenth amendment is not being violated.

   ○ C. Justice Brown defines the term *slavery* because he wants the court to understand how the separation of the races is similar to slavery.

   ○ D. Justice Brown defines the term *slavery* because making a technical term of slavery allows him to argue that the Thirteenth amendment is being violated.

2. What does Justice Brown state is the function of the technical term *involuntary servitude* in the Thirteenth Amendment?

   ○ A. *Involuntary servitude* provides a more specific definition of the concept of slavery so that the Thirteenth Amendment only protects some individuals.

   ○ B. *Involuntary servitude* refutes the claim that slavery was involuntary servitude, so the Thirteenth Amendment should be abolished.

   ○ C. *Involuntary servitude* generalizes the concept of slavery to protect the freedom of any person, whether they are legally designated as "slaves" or not.

   ○ D. *Involuntary servitude* has multiple contextual meanings, so it is important to understand what it means in the context of the Thirteenth Amendment.

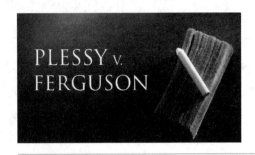

Close Read

Reread *Plessy v. Ferguson*. As you reread, complete the Skills Focus questions below. Then use your answers and annotations from the questions to help you complete the Write activity.

SKILLS FOCUS

1. Explain why Justice Harlan, in the first two paragraphs of the dissenting opinion, also mentions the Fifteenth Amendment. How does this relate to the case of *Plessy v. Ferguson*? Use the annotation tool to highlight details from the text that helped you form your explanation.

2. How do Justices Brown and Harlan use the Thirteenth Amendment to provide reasons and evidence for their arguments? Do they agree or disagree with each other on how the Thirteenth Amendment relates to the case at hand? Highlight textual evidence that expresses their interpretations and their similarities or differences.

3. Reread the last paragraph of the reading selection. Summarize Justice Harlan's argument here and explain what kind of rhetorical strategy he uses to discredit the Louisiana railroad's statute and the claims of Justice Brown's majority opinion. Highlight textual evidence that supports your explanation.

4. Throughout their arguments, Justice Brown and Justice Harlan both refer extensively to several amendments. What is the effect of using the technical term "amendment" on their speech and reasoning? Do both justices use the term in the same way? Highlight textual evidence to support your answer.

5. Reread the last two paragraphs of Justice Harlan's argument. In what way might Harlan's position reflect changing attitudes toward American citizenship and American values? How does Harlan's understanding of race and equal rights suggest the potential for a different kind of future in America? Highlight textual evidence to support your answer.

WRITE

COMPARE AND CONTRAST: Compare and contrast the arguments in Justice Brown's majority opinion with Justice Harlan's dissenting opinion in *Plessy v. Ferguson*. Which rhetorical strategies does each use most effectively to advance their arguments? Which arguments or instances of legal reasoning don't seem to have withstood the test of time? Explain your response using textual evidence from each argument.

Booster Staff Investigates

INFORMATIONAL TEXT
Maddie Baden, Connor Balthazor,
Gina Mathew, Trina Paul,
Kali Poenitske, & Patrick Sullivan
2017

Introduction

Juniors and seniors from Pittsburg High School in Pittsburg, Kansas made headlines, and history, in March of 2017. Six members of the high school newspaper—Maddie Baden, Connor Balthazor, Gina Mathew, Trina Paul, Kali Poenitske and Patrick Sullivan—uncovered the fraudulent past of their newly inducted principal with a lot of determination and a little help from Google. These members of *The Booster Redux* staff contributed to this article, which not only shed light on the discrepancies of the new administrator's educational credentials but also took down a "university" that wasn't what it seemed. The students' hard-hitting journalism caught the attention of news outlets around the world, proving that determined young people can make a difference.

"*The Booster* staff found inconsistencies in Robertson's credentials."

1 Following the hiring of incoming Pittsburg High School (PHS) principal Dr. Amy Robertson on March 6, discrepancies arose between Robertson's personal accounts of her education and information provided by education institutions she said she attended. The discrepancies cast doubt on the **accreditation** of a university she said she attended and the degrees she listed. Robertson said she currently works as the CEO of an education consulting firm known as Atticus I S Consultants in Dubai, and has resided there for over 20 years. According to a Pittsburg Community Schools press release on Thursday, Robertson "gained leadership and management experience at the international equivalence of a building administrator and superintendent. As CEO, she advised global companies on education projects, including writing and implementing curriculum and school policies, developing and executing professional development, and advising on school construction and renovation projects."

2 Robertson said she will arrive in the US in April and is eager for the new experience. "I'm excited about the opportunity," Robertson said. "I could easily stay [in Dubai] for another 10 years working in schools as a principal here, but I want to come home. I want to be in the US, and I want to be a part of a community. Pittsburg is the right community to put down roots in." *The Booster Redux* staff typically introduces each new administrator at PHS with a news story. During the interview process with Robertson, *The Booster* staff found **inconsistencies** in Robertson's credentials. The staff presented these concerns to Pittsburg Community School superintendent Destry Brown, who encouraged *The Booster* reporters to reach out to Robertson. On March 16, *The Booster* staff held a conference call with the incoming principal. *Booster* adviser Emily Smith and Brown were also present. During the call, Robertson presented incomplete answers, conflicting dates and inconsistencies in her responses.

3 After the conference call interview, the staff conducted further research online and by phone interview to confirm her credentials. These are the findings.

Educational Background

4   Robertson said in the conference call interview she earned a Master's degree in Comparative Literature and a Ph.D. in English from Corllins University. Corllins, however, has been under fire in the national media for its lack of **legitimacy**. Furthermore, the Better Business Bureau's website said, "This business is not BBB accredited." The posting online in 2010 also stated, "The true physical address of Corllins University is unknown." Robertson said during the conference call interview that the majority of her education through this university was done online, but that she also occasionally traveled to the onsite campus in Stockton, Calif. "In 1994, I was living in Spain," Robertson said during the conference call interview. "I kept my apartment in New York at the time. I would fly back and forth [from Spain] to New York and California all the time."

5   When asked by Brown if she took classes in Stockton, Calif. during two different summers, Robertson replied that she had. However, a check of the records at the City of Stockton's Community Development Department **indicated** that no business license or building permit existed for Corllins University, as stated by City of Stockton permit technician Carmen Davila.

6   "If they're going to do business, then they need to have a business license," Davila said via phone interview. "I don't have any business license under that name. I don't think we have a [Corllins University] here in the area."

7   Stockton is located in San Joaquin County. The San Joaquin Community Development Department records also indicated that no such university ever existed in Stockton.

8   "In our business records, we have no such record of Corllins University existing," Megan Aguirre, an associate planner of the department in San Joaquin County, said via phone interview with *The Booster*. Corllins is not accredited by the U.S. Department of Education. Accreditation is a status given to colleges and universities deemed **valid** educational institutions. The department's online database of both accredited online and traditional colleges and universities returned no past or current record of Corllins. When asked if a degree from Corllins University would be accepted, Pittsburg State University Registrar Debbie Greve could not find any record of the existence of Corllins. "[Corllins] is not in the book at all, so I would doubt the accreditation of that school," Greve said. "[If they had ever been accredited], they would be listed in this book. Because if they had ever been accredited, it lists them as accredited and it shows the period of time in which they were accredited. It sounds like they're trying to pass themselves off as accredited but, in fact, they maybe fell short of that."

9   Further research seems to show Corllins University is considered a diploma mill, or a "business that sells fake college degrees," according to Oregon

NOTES

Live, the website of *The Oregonian*. The university is listed as one of the "top 10 sources of invalid degree reports or **inquiries**" received by the Oregon Office of Degree Authorization. According to its website, Corllins University has two accreditation agencies, the Global Accreditation Bureau and the Accreditation Panel for Online Colleges and Universities. However, those accreditation agencies were also listed as fraudulent by retired FBI agent Allen Ezell in his article, "Recent Developments With Degree Mills" published in the educational journal, *College and University*. Many diploma and accreditation mills, including "Corllins University," were also listed. The spelling of Corllins listed in the article does not exactly match the spelling of the university provided by Robertson. Also, search results on the Council for Higher Education Accreditation's (CHEA) database found "Pittsburg State University" and "University of Kansas." A search for "Corllins University" returned no results. CHEA is used by colleges and universities to verify accreditation. "When I went [to Corllins], it was an accredited university," Robertson said. "Otherwise, you can't get any degree authenticated." During the conference call interview, Brown said, "I think [Corllins University] lost its accreditation at some point." In an email to *The Booster*, Robertson also said she had a teacher certification from the University of Cambridge UK. The University of Cambridge confirmed that they offer that degree. Also during the conference call interview, Robertson said she received a bachelor's of fine arts (BFA) in theater arts from the University of Tulsa (UT) in 1991. *The Booster* continued to fact check Robertson's education and contacted UT. According to the registrar's office, a BFA has never been offered at the institution. The university was specific in the degrees offered; only a bachelor of arts in theater was available at that time, not a BFA.

10   After the conference call interview, Brown stated that assistant superintendent Ronda Fincher would serve as the principal of record for the 2017-2018 school year because Robertson currently does not hold a Kansas administrator's license. According to Robertson's contract approved by the USD 250 school board, an "administrator must be licensed in Kansas by August 1, 2018." Whether she can attain a teaching or administrator's license by August 2018 to become an administrator is still in question. According to Brown, she must complete a number of college credit hours to obtain her licensure.

Local Reaction

11   Over the past two weeks, the *The Morning Sun* has also covered questions about Robertson's hiring.

12   On March 20, *The Morning Sun* published a story about Robertson's questioned qualifications inspired by an anonymous letter sent by "Pittsburg Citizen X." PHS band director Cooper Neil responded in *The Morning Sun* Tuesday with a letter to the editor addressing a lack of evidence in the original article. Chance

Hoener, the original author, published a response on Wednesday apologizing for failing "to bring closure to . . . rumors via the facts." On Thursday, Pittsburg Community Schools Public Relations director Zach Fletcher issued a press release detailing Robertson's prior professional experience.

13 "When talking with previous supervisors and Dr. Robertson, the Board felt she was a great fit for PHS and the future of our students," Brown, the superintendent, said in the press release. "The high school staff and students who sat in on interviews also felt she was the right pick. We are excited to have her join our team of administrators."

14 In an interview with *The Booster*, French teacher Chris Colyer expressed reservations regarding Robertson. "It concerns me a lot as to how she's going to take all the classes she needs because she's going to have a lot of duties as principal, and that's a full time, and overtime, job," Colyer said. "The fact that she has never taught in a US school does concern me because our schools are different from what she [found] in Dubai." Marjorie Giffin teaches history and social studies at PHS and served on the interview committee for the new principal. "I thought she interviewed very well," Giffin said in an interview with *The Booster*, in reference to Robertson's interview with the committee. "I thought she had all the answers."

15 Brown held a faculty meeting March 17 to address administrative changes, which ended up raising questions for Giffin. "[The meeting] made me more uneasy after than it had before," Giffin continued. "The more [Brown] talked about making us feel at ease about the process made me more worried because I didn't know she wasn't really accredited." "I want some real leadership and I am hoping she can provide it," Giffin said. "I want her to be successful because I want [the school] to get back on track." According to the contract, Robertson begins work at the district July 1.

 WRITE

RHETORICAL ANALYSIS: Select two or three pieces of evidence presented in the article that you found particularly convincing, and explain why you think the evidence is strong. Use details from the text and your knowledge about reasons and evidence to support your response.

Blast: Saving Smart

How will you finance your future?

 BACKGROUND

Listen to the What's Next podcast associated with this Blast in your digital account.

You may have worked a summer job or earn an allowance for doing chores around the house. You could have chosen to spend a portion of that money to go see a movie or buy a video game, or perhaps you saved up for something more expensive. After high school, you'll still be making similar choices, but with additional expenses to account for, like rent, transportation, insurance and groceries.

The impact and total cost of those expenses depends first and foremost on whether you want to go to college. It also depends on which schools you're deciding between. Community college is typically the most affordable option. The sticker price of an in-state public school is lower than an out-of-state public school or a private school, according to CNBC news. Applying for merit-based or financial scholarship and grants can help to ease the high costs of higher education. You do not need to repay scholarships and grants.

For many college students and their families, however, even a scholarship isn't enough to cover the cost. This is where student loans typically enter the picture. Student loans can help to pay for college. These loans can also be difficult to manage. "Over 44 million Americans collectively hold nearly $1.5 trillion in student debt," a February 2018 CNBC article reports. "That means that roughly one in four American adults are paying off student loans."

Some student loans are more manageable than others. Subsidized options, for instance, don't gather interest while you're in college, and have generally lower interest rates after college. This is because the federal government helps to keep costs down, according to Forbes magazine. Unsubsidized loans, on the other hand, do gather interest while you're still in school. This means you will eventually need to pay more than your original loan amount.

Another step after graduating high school may be applying for a credit card. "Credit cards provide an easy opportunity to build credit, which is important when it's time to buy a car or a house," writer Lindsay Konsko says.

However, there are drawbacks to credit cards. Like student loans, you have to carefully read the fine print of the terms. Otherwise, you run the risk of getting stuck with high interest rates. Mark Munzenberger is a financial education specialist. "Obtaining a credit card . . . can be a great way for a young person to establish a good credit history, provided that all payments are made on time and that balances are kept low," Munzenberger told the Detroit Free Press. "Only charge what you can afford to pay off in one month, no matter what," Konsko says. "This is easier to do if you're carefully tracking your spending and keeping it in line with your income."

Assessing the risks associated with student loans and credit cards is part of a longer-term outlook about your financial future. However, the short-term matters, too. Gaby Dunn is the host of the personal finance podcast "Bad with Money." She recommends learning how to budget while in high school. "Now is the least expenses you'll ever have," Dunn says. "You're only making money at this point. That will end very soon."

What do you think? If you plan on going to college, how do you plan to finance it? How long do you think young people should wait to get a credit card? How much do you know about budgeting? How will you finance your future?

NUMBER CRUNCH

37,172

QUIKPOLL

Which of the following is the most important financial decision for a high school graduate to make?

☐ Deciding whether to go to college or get a full-time job

☐ Deciding whether to acquire a credit card

☐ Coming up with a weekly budget and sticking to it

☐ Plotting out how much student loan debt you're willing to take on

CREATE YOUR BLAST

How will you finance your future?

_____

_____

_____

_____

Blast: Choices, Choices

How will you decide what your future holds?

 NOTES

ⓘ BACKGROUND

Listen to the What's Next podcast associated with this Blast in your digital account.

When you imagine choosing a single path for your life after college, how do you react?

If you get nervous at the idea of making a decision about your future life path, you are not alone. Your life after high school could involve college, a career, travel or any number of options. Deciding on one can seem intimidating. However, author Mike Whitaker believes it is important to learn how to make strategic decisions. "Decisions are forks in the road," Whitaker told Fast Company. "Life doesn't happen to us; we are an active participant. We get out of life what we choose."

People who struggle with decisions may experience a fear of loss, according to psychologist Daniel Kahneman. He says that this is due to loss aversion. This is a difference in value between wins and losses. His research suggests that loss aversion is influential in decision making. "In my classes, I say: 'I'm going to toss a coin, and if it's tails, you lose $10," Kahneman says in a 2013 interview. "How much would you have to gain on winning in order for this gamble to be acceptable to you?'" He says that, on average, people will only accept the gamble if they can win $20 or more. This means that people are willing to lose more money to avoid losing. "People really discriminate sharply between gaining and losing and they don't like losing," Kahneman says.

So, how can you get over that fear of making the wrong life decision? Writers Kate Douglas and Dan Jones argue that most decisions have a much smaller impact than you believe. "Remember also that whatever the future holds, it will probably hurt or please you less than you imagine," Douglas and Jones write in magazine New Scientist.

Writer Elaina Giolando believes that you should think about your motivations. She recommends asking yourself two questions. "Am I doing this because I really want to, or because it would look good," she asked in Fortune. "Am I doing this because I'm just too scared to say no?" Giolando says that these questions can help you to figure out what makes you lean towards one choice.

Philosopher Ruth Chang says that people commonly fear the unknown in decisions. She thinks this fear relies on a misunderstanding of hard choices. "Hard choices are hard not because of us or our ignorance; they're hard because there is no best option," Chang says in a 2014 TEDSalon speech.

There are no best decisions in a lot of scenarios. One example is choosing a college. This choice requires you to consider a lot of different factors. The importance of these factors is different for everyone. You may have to weigh factors like the school's location, tuition and social life. Mike Myatt is a leadership advisor with N2Growth. Myatt says that you should consider four sources of information when making a choice. He ranks these sources from least to most important: gut instincts, data, information and knowledge. Myatt believes that gut instincts can be unreliable. However, he says that instincts can provide a gut check against biased sources. Knowledge, on the other hand, "is information that has been refined by analysis such that it has been assimilated, tested and/or validated," Myatt said.

In the end, Chang says that hard decisions help you shape your identity. She says that hard choices are opportunities. Choices are not always correct or incorrect. When we have a hard choice to make, "we have the power to create reasons for ourselves to become the distinctive people that we are," Chang says.

So, what do you think? How do you typically make decisions? How can you improve your decision-making process? How will you decide what your future holds?

NUMBER CRUNCH

2014

◔ QUIKPOLL

Is it typically easy for you to make a decision?

☐ Yes. It's easy to make decisions because I can always weigh my options and pick one.

☐ Sometimes. I don't always make decisions easily, but I don't agonize over most decisions.

☐ No. It's really hard for me to make decisions, because it always seems like I have too many options.

✳ CREATE YOUR BLAST

How will you decide what your future holds?

_____

_____

_____

_____

Blast: Going Forth

What should all high schoolers know?

 BACKGROUND

Listen to the What's Next podcast associated with this Blast in your digital account.

Senior year of high school is a time of mixed emotions — joy and exhaustion, pride and regret, excitement and anxiety. As you navigate big decisions at the end of high school, chances are you'll reflect on where you've been, where you are, and where you're going.

This was a common experience for the students featured in StudySync's "What's Next?" Blast and podcast series. Students looked back at their senior year and realized how their perspectives had changed and how they'd grown as people.

For some students — like Kiana Griffin — plans for life after high school changed drastically over the course of nine months. At the beginning of the school year, Griffin expected to go to a four-year D1 university to play basketball on a full scholarship. However, a knee injury forced her to consider different options, and she ultimately went with a community college.

For other students — like DJ Frost — their mindset remained consistent all year. Frost had his post-grad plan locked in before his senior year began. So, he spent the year focusing on solidifying friendships, finishing academically strong and preparing for the year ahead.

Listen to the final podcast in the "What's Next?" series. Then, read about each student's final plans below:

Diana-Nicole Ramirez will attend Adelphi University on Long Island, New York to study journalism and communications. In the spring, a rejection letter from New York University devastated Diana-Nicole. However, when she visited Adelphi, she fell in love. She says her senior year made her a more positive person.

DJ Frost will attend the Air Force Academy in Colorado to play football and major in business. Since his decision was made before his senior year began, DJ focused on finishing strong and looking ahead. DJ said his goal is to "become the best me that I can be while helping as many people as I can."

Felicia Horn will attend Fairfield University in Connecticut to study nursing. Eventually, she wants to become a nurse anesthetist. Felicia got deferred from Fairfield University initially, but she wrote the school expressing her interest and conducted an interview with the admissions team. She got accepted. In April, she struggled to decide between Fairfield University and Sacred Heart University. In the end, she chose Fairfield because it had more name recognition and her gut said it was the better choice.

Katherine Carlo will attend the University of Florida on a full scholarship. She doesn't know what she wants to study yet, but she's starting with classes in business. Katherine applied to prestigious universities and scholarships throughout the East Coast. When she got rejected from some of the bigger scholarships she applied to, and learned she would have merit-based financial aid at UF, she knew the school was the right move for her.

Kiana Griffin will attend Sacramento City College to play basketball, in hopes of one day transferring to a four-year university to play D1. After her injury and surgery, Kiana decided that community college was the best decision directly out of high school. Once she heals and can play to her full potential again, she hopes to build back her basketball career and transfer to a larger school.

Lyssa Nix will attend Bellus Academy, a cosmetology school in San Diego, and join their esthetician program. Lyssa knew from the beginning of the year that she wanted to pursue being an esthetician. However, she wasn't sure where she wanted to go or how to apply. After touring schools and talking to mentors, she's preparing to start a program she's excited about.

Makalya Adams will attend Hinds Community College in Jackson, Mississippi, where she hopes to get prerequisite credits before transferring to nursing school. Makalya had a good feeling about Hinds Community College from the beginning, but her mom pushed back. Her mom wanted her to go to a private university. However, Makalya knew she should make the decision that felt right to her, and she's proud that she made that decision on her own.

Patrick Cadogan will begin his senior in high school at Westford Academy in Westford, Massachusetts. Patrick began the year wanting to go to college close to home, but after touring a few schools further away, he's opened his mind to more options. After taking the SAT this year, he's ready to get started on college applications over the summer.

Shamora Rogers will attend Stephen F. Austin University in Nacogdoches, Texas to study theater, film and television. Shamora prioritized a strong theater program and affordability when she applied to college. Those priorities helped her choose Stephen F. Austin University in the end. Financial aid will help her pay for school, and she's still waiting to hear back from various outside scholarships as well.

Zac Walsdorf will attend Notre Dame University in South Bend, Indiana and study psychology. After getting rejected from several of his top choices, Zac narrowed down his college choices to his state school and Notre Dame University. When he visited Notre Dame and met some of the other students, he knew he could make it his home for four years.

As you've seen and heard, the students we interviewed are moving into their adult lives with all kinds of different mindsets, goals and road maps. But they're all graduating with insights and advice for other students going through the same things.

What do you think? What did you learn from the students featured in the "What's Next?" podcast series? What do you think every student should keep in mind during their senior year? How will you make your last year of high school count? What should all high schoolers know?

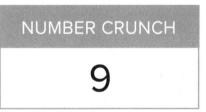

NUMBER CRUNCH

9

◔ QUIKPOLL

What do you think is the most important part of the high school experience?

☐ Academics and learning new things

☐ Joining clubs or sports teams

☐ Making lifelong friends

☐ Self-reflection and figuring out who you really are

☐ Something else

✳ CREATE YOUR BLAST

What should all high schoolers know?

_____

_____

_____

_____

Extended
Writing
Project and
Grammar

EXTENDED
WRITING
PROJECT
INFORMATIVE
WRITING

Informative Writing Process: Plan

PLAN	DRAFT	REVISE	EDIT AND PUBLISH

Humans are complex beings, shaped by the many facets of life. Born with incredibly similar genetic material, we develop into strikingly different personalities with singular, often divergent goals. These goals, shaped by our past, guide us into the future and into the ways we will transform this world.

WRITING PROMPT

How will our understanding of who we are shape the goals we develop for ourselves?

Reflect on your background, identity, interests, and talents. Think through experiences you have had and obstacles you have faced. Which of these aspects of life have had the greatest impact on who you are now? Select two to four of these aspects. Describe what you learned from them, how you developed as a result of them, and how they affect the goals you are setting for your future self. Your personal essay should include the following:

- a strong thesis statement
- an introduction
- a clear organizational structure
- supporting details
- a conclusion

Introduction to Informative Writing

Informative writing includes a main idea or thesis statement that focuses on a particular aspect of a topic. Informative texts use evidence—such as definitions, quotations, examples, and facts—that clarifies and supports the thesis statement. In personal essays, authors use many of the attributes used in informative writing, but they also use anecdotes and commentary on actual events to support their thesis statement. However, the purpose of informative writing is to inform readers about real people, places, things, and events, so authors of personal essays still need to organize their ideas, concepts, and information in a logical way.

Writers carefully choose an organizational structure, such as definition, classification, compare/contrast, or cause and effect, that best suits their material. Often, informative writing includes visual elements such as headings, graphics, and/or tables to communicate complex ideas or information. The characteristics of informative writing include:

- an introduction with a clear thesis statement
- a clear and logical organizational structure that includes supporting details
- transitions that link sections of text and support the organization of complex ideas
- precise language and a formal or informal style appropriate to the topic
- a conclusion that unifies ideas

Writers also carefully craft their work so that each new element builds on that which precedes it to create a unified whole. In a personal essay, authors often have a more subjective point of view and informal style that readers can easily identify. Effective personal essays combine these informative genre characteristics and craft to engage the reader.

As you continue with this Extended Writing Project, you'll receive more instruction and practice in crafting each of the characteristics of informative writing to create your own personal essay.

Please note that excerpts and passages in the StudySync® library and this workbook are intended as touchstones to generate interest in an author's work. The excerpts and passages do not substitute for the reading of entire texts, and StudySync® strongly recommends that students seek out and purchase the whole literary or informational work in order to experience it as the author intended. Links to online resellers are available in our digital library. In addition, complete works may be ordered through an authorized reseller by filling out and returning to StudySync® the order form enclosed in this workbook.

Reading & Writing Companion

127

Before you get started on your own personal essay, read this personal essay that one student, Monica, wrote in response to the writing prompt. As you read the Model, highlight and annotate the features of informative writing that Monica included in her personal essay.

NOTES

☰ STUDENT MODEL

My So-Called Introverted Life

1 When you look in the mirror, what do you see? I see dark brown hair, hazel eyes, and a somewhat crooked smile. Beneath the surface, though, I see a loyal heart, fierce determination, and an introverted personality. Those are the things that make me Monica, but I haven't always appreciated the qualities that make me *me*. Since I grew up in a loud, gregarious family, I always thought something was wrong with me because I didn't want to spend all of my time around other people, especially new people. My family seemed to agree and would shake their heads when I tried to get away from the noise on holidays. During my junior year of high school, however, I learned that being different doesn't mean I'm flawed. Sometimes the qualities that others consider to be your greatest weaknesses turn out to be your greatest strengths.

Background and Identity

2 School work has always come easy to me. Making new friends has not. My teachers praised my talent for language but always noted that I am uncomfortable working in groups, especially if my best friend wasn't also involved. Kayla and I have been inseparable since elementary school. We were assigned to share a cubby in first grade, and we've been partners ever since. My family warned me against forming such a close attachment with just one friend. What would happen if the relationship fell apart? I stubbornly refused to seek other companions. My friendship with Kayla always felt like a safety net. With Kayla, I could always be myself. She understood if I needed space and encouraged me to take care of myself. It felt disloyal to look for other friends when Kayla gave me all the support I needed. As we grew older, though, we started growing apart. Although Kayla and I have always been extremely close—our classmates even jokingly referred to us as "Kaylica"—we are also very different. Kayla is friendly and outgoing, while I am more reserved. She loves science

and working in the community garden on weekends, but I'd much rather curl up with a good book or write a short story. Last year, Kayla's aptitude in science led her to apply to a STEM program at a local private high school. She was accepted, and while I was thrilled for her, I was overwhelmed by the idea of having to begin a new school year without my best friend by my side.

Interests and Talents

3   The first days of junior year were hard. Although I enjoy being by myself, the school day can feel incredibly long if you have no one else to talk to. Each night, Kayla would call to tell me about the new friends she was making and the new adventures she was having. My heart sank as I realized she was thriving without me. My family's criticism of my introversion and stubborn insistence to remain loyal to a single friend came flooding back. I'd never felt so alone. That's when I made a decision. Like Kayla, I needed to find a new group who shared my interests and who would accept me for who I am.

4   The school's newspaper seemed like a natural fit, so I signed up. I'd thought about joining the paper before but was intimidated by the newsrooms I'd seen on television and in movies. If I can't handle Sunday night dinner with my extended family, how was I supposed to work amid the hustle and bustle of such a high-stakes environment? After I dragged myself to my first newspaper meeting, though, I quickly realized how silly I had been. The newspaper office was actually small and unintimidating. Four students sat at computers, silently working on their own individual assignments. When I walked in, they looked up and offered small smiles before returning their eyes to their screens. These students were all part of the same team, working toward a shared goal, but they were doing so at their own pace and in their own spaces. It was perfect for me.

Self-Acceptance

5   In the following weeks, I began to look forward to newspaper meetings as much as I looked forward to my nightly calls with Kayla. My assignments were tough, especially when I had to interview strangers for a story. Yet my determination to succeed kept me focused, and knowing that I planned to spend time alone to write about each new experience kept me motivated. I also developed strong feelings of loyalty toward the newspaper staff. They might not

be my best friends, but they were my new team. With each passing day, it became clearer that I didn't have to change who I am in order to be happy. My loyalty, determination, and introverted personality might not be the best qualities in every situation, but it turned out that they are the perfect recipe for a reporter. Before I walked into the newspaper office, I had no idea what I wanted to do after graduation, but now I know. I want to study journalism and become a correspondent for a newspaper.

6 Facing the world without Kayla always by my side was scarier than a proud introvert like me would like to admit, but I am grateful that I went through the difficult experience. It showed me that my loyal heart, fierce determination, and introverted personality could be assets for my future. Instead of causing me to be alone and unengaged, my personality can actually help me connect with others because the way I see the world helps me write stories about the world. Now that I know this, when I cross the stage at graduation, I believe that I'll have the confidence to pursue a bright future on my own.

✏ WRITE

Writers often take notes about their ideas before they sit down to write. Think about what you've learned so far about organizing informative writing to help you begin prewriting.

- **Purpose:** How do you see yourself? What experiences had the greatest impact on who you are now?

- **Audience:** Who is your audience, and how might your audience connect to your essay? How will you engage your audience?

- **Introduction:** How will you clearly introduce the topic and the main idea of your essay? What language can you use that is both personal and intriguing?

- **Thesis Statement:** How did your experiences affect you? What two to four aspects of life have had the greatest impact on you?

- **Organizational Text Structure:** What strategies will you use to organize your response to the prompt? Will you explain your experiences chronologically or by ideas?

- **Evidence, Examples, and Anecdotes:** What evidence or examples relate to your thesis? What anecdotes exemplify your ideas?

- **Conclusion:** How does the information in the body of your essay relate to your thesis? How can you connect the ideas in your personal essay to your audience or to a larger idea about society?

Response Instructions

Use the questions in the bulleted list to write a one-paragraph summary. Your summary should describe what you will explain in your personal essay.

Don't worry about including all of the details now; focus only on the most essential and important elements. You will refer to this short summary as you continue through the steps of the writing process.

Skill:
Organizing Informative Writing

••• CHECKLIST FOR ORGANIZING INFORMATIVE WRITING

As you begin to organize your writing for your informative essay, use the following questions as a guide:

- What is a brief summary of my topic?

- How can I organize my ideas so that each new element builds on previous material?

- Can I use visual elements, such as headings, to organize my essay by dividing information into sections?

Here are steps you can use to organize complex ideas, concepts, and information so that each new element builds on that which precedes it to create a unified whole:

- definitions

  > first, define a subject or concept

  > second, define the qualities of the subject or concept

  > third, provide examples, focusing on showing different aspects of the subject or concept

- categories

  > first, identify the main idea or topic

  > second, divide the main idea or topic into categories, focusing on how you want to explain your ideas

  > third, use the categories to provide descriptive details and deepen your reader's understanding

- comparisons

  > first, identify two texts about similar topics to compare

  > second, identify the similarities and differences between the texts

  > third, determine how those comparisons reveal larger ideas about the topic of the texts

- cause and effect

  > first, determine what happened in a text, including the order of events

  > second, identify the reasons that something happened

  > third, connect what happened and the reasons for it to the main idea or claim

⟳ YOUR TURN

Read the statements in the first column in the chart below. Then, in the second column, write the corresponding letter for the organizational structure that would be most appropriate for the purpose and topic of each statement.

Organizational Structure Options	
A	Compare and contrast
B	Advantages and disadvantages
C	Definition or classification
D	Categories and subcategories
E	Cause and effect

Statement	Organizational Structure
Kayla's aptitude in science led her to apply to a STEM program.	
Sometimes the qualities that others consider to be your greatest weaknesses turn out to be your greatest strengths.	
Although Kayla and I have always been extremely close—our classmates even jokingly referred to us as "Kaylica"—we are also very different.	
During my junior year of high school, however, I learned that being different doesn't mean I'm flawed.	
Beneath the surface, though, I see a loyal heart, fierce determination, and an introverted personality. Those are the things that make me Monica, but I haven't always appreciated the qualities that make me *me*.	

↻ YOUR TURN

Complete the chart below by writing key ideas to include in each paragraph of your essay.

Paragraph	Key Idea
Introduction	
Body Paragraph 1	
Body Paragraph 2	
Body Paragraph 3	
Conclusion	

Skill:
Thesis Statement

••• CHECKLIST FOR THESIS STATEMENT

Before you begin writing your thesis statement, ask yourself the following questions:

- What is the prompt asking me to write about?
- What claim do I want to make about the topic of this essay?
- Is my claim precise and informative? How is it specific to my topic? How does it inform the reader about my topic?
- Does my thesis statement introduce the body of my essay?
- Where should I place my thesis statement?

Here are some steps for introducing and developing a topic as well as a precise and informative claim:

- think about your central claim of your essay
  - > identify a clear claim you want to introduce, thinking about:
    - ○ how closely your claim is related to your topic and how specific it is to your supporting details
    - ○ how your claim includes necessary information to guide the reader through the topic
- your thesis statement should:
  - > let the reader anticipate the content of your essay
  - > help you begin your essay in an organized manner
  - > present your opinion clearly
  - > respond completely to the writing prompt
- consider the best placement for your thesis statement
  - > if your response is short, you may want to get right to the point and present your thesis statement in the first sentence of the essay
  - > if your response is longer (as in a formal essay), you can build up to your thesis statement and place it at the end of your introductory paragraph

↻ YOUR TURN

Read the statements below. Then, complete the chart by sorting the statements into two categories: thesis statements and details. Write the corresponding letter for each statement in the appropriate column.

	Statement Options
A	I prefer to keep to myself, but at the same time my friends know that I am loyal.
B	I am someone who prefers to read a book than socialize with a large group of people.
C	Although some people consider my shy personality a weakness, I consider it a strength.
D	It turned out that those qualities are the perfect recipe for a reporter.
E	Sometimes our personalities just need the right context in which to flourish.
F	All of my characteristics, both the positive and the negative, are what make me a strong person.

Thesis Statement	Details

✎ WRITE

Use the checklist to draft a thesis statement for your personal essay.

Skill:
Supporting Details

CHECKLIST FOR SUPPORTING DETAILS

As you look for supporting details to develop your topic, claim, or thesis statement, ask yourself the following questions:

- What is my main idea about this topic?
- What does a reader need to know about the topic in order to understand the main idea?
- What details will support my thesis?
- What other kinds of information could I provide?
- Does this information help to develop and refine my main idea?
- Does this information relate closely to my thesis or claim?
- Are the supporting details I have included sufficient to support my thesis or claim?

Here are some suggestions for how you can develop your topic:

- review your thesis or claim
- consider what your audience may already know about the topic
- note what the audience will need to know to understand the topic
- develop your topic thoroughly and accurately, taking into consideration all of its aspects
- use different types of supporting details, such as:
  - > the most significant and relevant facts that are specific to your topic, make an impact in your discussion, and fully support your thesis or claim
  - > concrete details that will add descriptive material to your topic
  - > quotations to directly connect your thesis statement or claim to the text
  - > examples and other information to deepen the audience's knowledge

Please note that excerpts and passages in the StudySync® library and this workbook are intended as touchstones to generate interest in an author's work. The excerpts and passages do not substitute for the reading of entire texts, and StudySync® strongly recommends that students seek out and purchase the whole literary or informational work in order to experience it as the author intended. Links to online resellers are available in our digital library. In addition, complete works may be ordered through an authorized reseller by filling out and returning to StudySync® the order form enclosed in this workbook.

Reading & Writing
Companion

137

⟳ YOUR TURN

Choose the best answer to each question.

The following sentence is from a draft of a student's personal essay on the impact of having parents who speak a different language. Select the supporting detail below that best supports the topic.

> Growing up with parents who speak a language besides English has helped me appreciate the many diverse cultures in our school and community.

○ A. Many students at school only know English, and this makes it hard for us to all get to know each other because many people in our community speak another language at home.

○ B. My parents want me to take Spanish classes at school so I can talk with our neighbors down the street and make friends with their children, who are my age.

○ C. At home, my parents speak Polish, and seeing how they have become close friends with the many diverse people in our neighborhood has encouraged me to be open-minded.

○ D. Do you ever feel like you are the only person who has non-English-speaking parents?

⟳ YOUR TURN

Complete the chart below by listing ideas and relevant supporting details that will help your audience understand these ideas in your essay. The first row presents an example.

Ideas	What the Audience Needs to Know	Supporting Details
Speaking two languages also means you connect with two cultures.	My audience needs to understand how speaking two languages helps you connect with cultures better.	Saying *thanks* in English means that you are "giving thanks" and acknowledgement to someone. In Portuguese, *obrigado* is the way we say "thank you," but it translates as "I am obligated to you." This is just one example of how knowing just one word in each language can help you understand each culture.

Informative Writing Process: Draft

PLAN	DRAFT	REVISE	EDIT AND PUBLISH

You have already made progress toward writing your personal essay. Now it is time to draft your personal essay.

✏ WRITE

Use your plan and other responses in your Binder to draft your essay. You may also have new ideas as you begin drafting. Feel free to explore those new ideas as you have them. You can also ask yourself these questions to ensure that your writing is focused, organized, and detailed:

Draft Checklist:

☐ **Purpose and Focus:** Have I made my thesis clear to readers?

☐ **Organization:** Does the organizational structure in my essay make sense? Will readers be interested in the way I present information and my commentary? Does my writing flow together naturally, or is it choppy?

☐ **Ideas and Details:** Will my readers be able to easily follow and understand my ideas? Have I included only relevant examples?

Before you submit your draft, read it over carefully. You want to be sure that you've responded to all aspects of the prompt.

Please note that excerpts and passages in the StudySync® library and this workbook are intended as touchstones to generate interest in an author's work. The excerpts and passages do not substitute for the reading of entire texts, and StudySync® strongly recommends that students seek out and purchase the whole literary or informational work in order to experience it as the author intended. Links to online resellers are available in our digital library. In addition, complete works may be ordered through an authorized reseller by filling out and returning to StudySync® the order form enclosed in this workbook.

Reading & Writing Companion **139**

Here is Monica's personal essay draft. As you read, notice how Monica develops her draft to be focused, organized, and detailed. As she continues to revise and edit her personal essay, she will improve the style of her writing, as well as correct any grammatical mistakes.

STUDENT MODEL: FIRST DRAFT

Weaknesses are Strengths

~~I grew up in a loud family, and I always thought something was wrong with me because I liked being by myself. My family seemed to agree and would shake their heads when I tried to get away from the noise on holidays. During my junior year of high school, however, I learned that being different doesnt mean Im flawed. Parts of my personality used to seem like weaknesses, but later I learned that they were actually my strengths.~~

Skill:
Introductions

Monica strengthens her introduction by adding a hook. She provides an intriguing question and uses it to describe her appearance and her personality. These changes make her introduction more interesting and better introduce the ideas she will develop in her essay.

When you look in the mirror, what do you see? I see dark brown hair, hazel eyes, and a somewhat crooked smile. Beneath the surface, though, I see a loyal heart, fierce determination, and an introverted personality. Those are the things that make me Monica, but I haven't always appreciated the qualities that make me *me*. Since I grew up in a loud, gregarious family, I always thought something was wrong with me because I didn't want to spend all of my time around other people, especially new people. My family seemed to agree and would shake their heads when I tried to get away from the noise on holidays. During my junior year of high school, however, I learned that being different doesn't mean I'm flawed. Sometimes the qualities that others consider to be your greatest weaknesses turn out to be your greatest strengths.

Background and Identity

~~School work has always come easy to me. Making new friends has not. My teachers praised my talent for language but always noted that I am uncomfortable working in groups. Kayla and I have been inseparateable since elementary school. We were assigned to share a cubby in first grade, and weve been partners ever since. My family warned me against forming such a close attachment with just one friend. What would happen if the relationship fell apart? I would not seek other companions. My friend-ship with Kayla always seemed~~

~~very important to me and I did not feel as comfortable with anyone else. With Kayla, I could always be myself. She understood if I needed space and let me take care of myself. It didn't feel right to look for other friends when Kayla gave me all the support I needed. As we grew older, though, started growing apart. Kayla and I have always been extremily close. Our classmates even jokingly referred to us as "Kaylica." We are also very different. Kayla is friendly and outgoing while I am more reserved. Last year, Kaylas aptitude in science led her to aply to a STEM program at a local privat high school. She was accepted. I was thrilled for her. I was scared of the idea of having to begin a new school year without my best friend by my side.~~

School work has always come easy to me. Making new friends has not. My teachers praised my talent for language but always noted that I am uncomfortable working in groups, especially if my best friend wasn't also involved. Kayla and I have been inseparable since elementary school. We were assigned to share a cubby in first grade, and we've been partners ever since. My family warned me against forming such a close attachment with just one friend. What would happen if the relationship fell apart? I stubbornly refused to seek other companions. My friendship with Kayla always felt like a safety net. With Kayla, I could always be myself. She understood if I needed space and encouraged me to take care of myself. It felt disloyal to look for other friends when Kayla gave me all the support I needed. As we grew older, though, we started growing apart. Although Kayla and I have always been extremely close—our classmates even jokingly referred to us as "Kaylica"—we are also very different. Kayla is friendly and outgoing, while I am more reserved. She loves science and working in the community garden on weekends, but I'd much rather curl up with a good book or write a short story. Last year, Kayla's aptitude in science led her to apply to a STEM program at a local private high school. She was accepted, and while I was thrilled for her, I was overwhelmed by the idea of having to begin a new school year without my best friend by my side.

Interests and Talents

The first days of junior year were hard. Although I enjoy being by myself, the school day can feel incredibley long if you have no one else to talk to. Each night, Kayla would call to tell me about the new

Skill:
Precise Language

Monica replaces the sentence "My friendship with Kayla always seemed very important to me . . . ." with a simile. She can now better convey the significance of their relationship and the impact that Kayla's absence will have on her.

Skill:
Transitions

Monica inserts the transition although *to express the change or contradiction in her relationship with Kayla more clearly. She also adds the transition* while *at the end of the paragraph to better express her conflicting emotions.*

friends she was making and the new adventures she was having. My heart sank as I realized she was thriving without me. My familys criticism of my shyness and insistentce to remain close to a single freind came flooding back. Never felt so alone. That's when I made a decision. Like Kayla, I needed to find a new group who shared my interests and who would accept me for who I am.

After I dragged myself to my first newspaper meeting, though, I quickly realized how silly I had been. Id thought about joining the paper before but was intimidated by the newsrooms Id seen on television and in movies. If I cant handle Sunday night dinner with my extended family, how was I supposed to work amid the hustle and bustle of such a high-stakes environment? The school's newspaper seemed like a natural fit, though, so I signed up. The newspaper office was actually small. It was also unintimidating. Four students sat at computers. They silently working on their own invidual assignments. When I walked in, they looked up. They offered small smiles. Then returned their eyes to their screens. These students were all part of the same team and they worked toward a shared goal and they were doing so at their own pace and in their own spaces. It was perfict for me.

Self-Acceptance

In the following weeks, I began to look forward to newspaper meetings. I also looked forward to my nightly calls with Kayla. My assignments were tough. I had to inter view strangers. My desire to succeed kept me focused. I spent time alone to write about each new exspereince. They might not be my best friends, but they were my new team. I also developed strong feelings of commitment toward the newspaper staff. With each passing day, it became clearer that I didnt have to change who I am in order to be happy. My desire to be alone and my shy personality might not be the best qualitys in every situation. It turned out that they are the perfect recipe for a reporter. Before I walked into the newspaper office, I had no idea what I wanted to do after graduation. Now I know. I want to study journalism and become a correspondent for a newspaper.

~~My desire to be a good friend and shy personality can be assets for my future. Sometimes the qualities that others consider to be your greatest weaknesses turn out to be your greatest strengths. Now~~

~~that I know this, when I cross the stage at graduation, I believe that I'll have the confidence to pursue a bright future on my own.~~

Facing the world without Kayla always by my side was scarier than a proud introvert like me would like to admit, but I am grateful that I went through the difficult experience. It showed me that my loyal heart, fierce determination, and introverted personality could be assets for my future. Instead of causing me to be alone and unengaged, my personality can actually help me connect with others because the way I see the world helps me write stories about the world. Now that I know this, when I cross the stage at graduation, I believe that I'll have the confidence to pursue a bright future on my own.

Skill:
Conclusions

Monica strengthens her final paragraph by creating a smoother transition between her body paragraphs and conclusion. She also rephrases her thesis, adding specific details to reinforce the significance of her topic and leave her audience with a memorable idea.

Skill:
Introductions

••• CHECKLIST FOR INTRODUCTIONS

Before you write your introduction, ask yourself the following questions:

- What is my claim? In addition:

  > How can I make it more precise and informative?

  > Have I included why my claim is significant to discuss? How does it help the reader understand the topic better?

- How can I introduce my topic? Have I organized complex ideas, concepts, and information so that each new element builds on the previous element and creates a unified whole?

- How will I "hook" my reader's interest? I might:

  > start with an attention-grabbing statement

  > begin with an intriguing question

  > use descriptive words to set a scene

Below are two strategies to help you introduce your precise claim and topic clearly in an introduction:

- Peer Discussion

  > Talk about your topic with a partner, explaining what you already know and your ideas about your topic.

  > Write notes about the ideas you have discussed and any new questions you may have.

  > Review your notes, and think about what your claim or controlling idea will be.

  > Briefly state your precise and informative claim, establishing why it is important.

  > Write a possible "hook."

- Freewriting

  > Freewrite for 10 minutes about your topic. Don't worry about grammar, punctuation, or having fully formed ideas. The point of freewriting is to discover ideas.

  > Review your notes, and think about what your claim or controlling idea will be.

  > Briefly state your precise and informative claim, establishing why it is important.

  > Write a possible "hook."

YOUR TURN

Choose the best answer to each question about the following introduction from a previous draft of Monica's personal essay.

> Growing up, I was always quiet. I preferred reading books and writing furiously in my notebook over joining neighborhood baseball games and talking loudly at family parties. People would always comment on how quiet I was and I started to think that something was wrong with me. In high school, though, I found an activity that allowed me to use my quieter skills. Soon I learned that there were other people who thought like me.

1. Which sentence could Monica add to the beginning of the paragraph to help her engage her audience's attention?
   - ○ A. My weakness has always been my quiet personality.
   - ○ B. My personality is way different from the rest of my family's.
   - ○ C. Do you think journalists are loud people or quiet people like me?
   - ○ D. Do you ever feel like you are the only person who thinks the way you do?

2. Identify the best sentence that Monica could add to the beginning of the introduction to make it clear to the audience why the claim is significant to discuss.

   - ○ A. I have always struggled to explain and defend my shy personality.
   - ○ B. I am blessed that I am able to work alone.
   - ○ C. Most teenagers have friends who move away.
   - ○ D. Do you ever wonder why you are so different from your brothers and sisters?

WRITE

Use the questions in the checklist to revise the introduction of your personal essay.

Please note that excerpts and passages in the StudySync® library and this workbook are intended as touchstones to generate interest in an author's work. The excerpts and passages do not substitute for the reading of entire texts, and StudySync® strongly recommends that students seek out and purchase the whole literary or informational work in order to experience it as the author intended. Links to online resellers are available in our digital library. In addition, complete works may be ordered through an authorized reseller by filling out and returning to StudySync® the order form enclosed in this workbook.

Reading & Writing
Companion

145

Skill: Transitions

••• CHECKLIST FOR TRANSITIONS

Before you revise your current draft to include transitions, think about:

- the key ideas you discuss
- the major sections of your essay
- the organizational structure of your essay
- the relationships between complex ideas and concepts

Next, reread your current draft and note places in your essay where:

- the organizational structure is not yet apparent
    > For example, if you are comparing and contrasting two ideas or life experiences, your explanations about how they are similar and different should be clearly stated
- the relationship between ideas from one paragraph to the next is unclear
    > For example, when you describe a process in sequential order, you should clarify the order of steps using transitional words like *first, then, next,* and *finally*
- your ideas are not creating cohesion, or a unified whole
- your transition and/or syntax is inappropriate

Revise your draft to use appropriate and varied transitions and syntax to link the major sections of your essay, create cohesion, and clarify the relationships between complex ideas and concepts, using the following questions as a guide:

- What kind of transitions should I use to make the organizational structure clear to readers?
- Are my transitions linking the major sections of my essay?
- What transitions create cohesion between complex ideas and concepts?
- Are my transitions and syntax varied and appropriate?
- Have my transitions clarified the relationships between complex ideas and concepts?

↻ YOUR TURN

Choose the best answer to each question.

1. Below is a section from a previous draft of Monica's essay. The connection between the ideas is unclear. What transition should Monica add to the beginning of the third sentence to make her writing more coherent and appropriate for the purpose, topic, and context of her essay, as well as her audience?

> (1) I knew I had to attend the newspaper meeting, but was scared and really didn't want to go. (2) It wasn't what I thought it would be. (3) When I met the other students, I realized how silly I had been.

- ○ A. Eventually
- ○ B. As a matter of fact
- ○ C. On balance
- ○ D. Another key point

2. Below is a section from a previous draft of Monica's essay. The connection between the ideas in the second and third sentences is unclear. What transitions should Monica add to the beginning of the second and third sentences to make her writing more coherent?

> (1) It's impossible to predict what will happen in the future. (2) Walking into the newspaper office, I had no idea what I wanted to do after graduation. (3) I want to study journalism and become a correspondent for a newspaper.

- ○ A. Eventually, Prior to
- ○ B. As a matter of fact, Including
- ○ C. Before, Now
- ○ D. Another key point, In the meantime

✎ WRITE

Use the questions in the checklist to revise your use of transitions in a section of your personal essay.

Skill:
Precise Language

••• CHECKLIST FOR PRECISE LANGUAGE

As you consider precise language, domain-specific vocabulary, and techniques related to a complicated subject or topic, use the following questions as a guide:

- What information am I trying to explain to my audience?

- What domain-specific vocabulary is relevant to my topic?

- Have I determined the complexity of the subject matter and whether any words and domain-specific vocabulary need additional explanation?

- How can I use techniques such as metaphors, similes, or analogies to help explain difficult concepts?

- Where can I use more precise vocabulary in my explanation?

Here are some suggestions for using precise language, domain-specific vocabulary, and techniques such as metaphors, similes, and analogies to help make complex topics clear:

- determine your topic or area of study

- determine the complexity of the subject matter and whether any words and domain-specific vocabulary need additional explanation in order to make concepts clear

- replace vague, general, or overused words and phrases with more precise, descriptive, and domain-specific language

- try to use metaphors, similes, or analogies to make information easier to understand

  > an example of an analogy for a scientific concept is *a cell membrane is similar to the bricks that make up the outside of a building*

  > a metaphor such as *there is an endless battle between thermodynamics and gravity* can help readers begin to understand the meaning of *thermodynamics*

↻ YOUR TURN

Choose the best answer to each question.

1. After reviewing the checklist, a student realizes he needs to revise the statement below by using more precise, domain-specific language. Select the best answer that uses domain-specific language to express the ideas in the underlined portion of the sentence.

> <u>I will be the first person to go to college in my family</u>, so my goal is to become a doctor and give back as much as possible to my parents and my community.

- ○ A. I will attend college before any of my siblings have,
- ○ B. Previously, no one in my family has attended school past high school,
- ○ C. I will be a first-generation college graduate,
- ○ D. A diploma post-high school is a dream no one in my family has realized,

2. After reviewing the checklist, a student decides to use a metaphor or simile to explain his idea in the passage below. Select the best revision of the underlined portion of the passage.

> It is thanks to the efforts of my entire neighborhood that I am the person I am today. <u>For some reason, I feel responsible to my community</u> when I complete my college degree.

- ○ A. Like a bird finally leaving the nest for the first time after being taught how to fly by family and friends, I feel responsible to my community
- ○ B. Like the recipient of a gift who wants to write a thank-you note, I feel responsible to my community
- ○ C. I'm a shooting star in the night sky and a rainbow on a cloudy day, so I feel responsible to my community
- ○ D. I feel responsible to my community, which is like an old book that you keep returning to for more lessons,

Please note that excerpts and passages in the StudySync® library and this workbook are intended as touchstones to generate interest in an author's work. The excerpts and passages do not substitute for the reading of entire texts, and StudySync® strongly recommends that students seek out and purchase the whole literary or informational work in order to experience it as the author intended. Links to online resellers are available in our digital library. In addition, complete works may be ordered through an authorized reseller by filling out and returning to StudySync® the order form enclosed in this workbook.

Reading & Writing
Companion

149

YOUR TURN

Complete the chart below by revising a sentence or paragraph from your essay draft.

Instruction	Original Sentence/Paragraph	Revised Sentence/Paragraph
Write a precise description of the topic of your essay.		
Revise a sentence or paragraph to include a metaphor, simile, or analogy to help explain your topic.		
Revise a sentence or paragraph to include more precise vocabulary related to your topic.		

Skill:
Conclusions

••• CHECKLIST FOR CONCLUSIONS

Before you write your conclusion, ask yourself the following questions:

- How can I rephrase the thesis or main idea?
- How can I write my conclusion so that it supports and follows from the information I presented?
- How can I communicate the importance of my topic? What information do I need?

Below are two strategies to help you provide a concluding statement or section that follows from and supports the information or explanation presented:

- Peer Discussion

  > After you have written your introduction and body paragraphs, talk with a partner about what you want readers to remember, writing notes about your discussion.

  > Think about how you can articulate, or express, the significance of your topic in the conclusion.

  > Rephrase your main idea to show the depth of your thinking and support for the information you presented.

  > Write your conclusion.

- Freewriting

  > Freewrite for 10 minutes about what you might include in your conclusion. Don't worry about grammar, punctuation, or having fully formed ideas. The point of freewriting is to discover ideas.

  > Think about how you can articulate, or express, the significance of your topic in the conclusion.

  > Rephrase your main idea to show the depth of your thinking and support for the information you presented.

  > Write your conclusion.

YOUR TURN

Choose the best answer to each question.

1. The following conclusion is from a previous draft of Monica's essay. Monica would like to add a sentence that addresses how being an introvert is beneficial, not only to her, but to people around her. Which sentence could she add after the last sentence to help achieve this goal?

> Albert Einstein was an introvert and look where that got him—the world's more revered physicist! However, there are obstacles too. People don't often discuss the challenges associated with being an introvert. Perhaps we don't talk about it because we are afraid or we think we won't be taken seriously. I am not sure. The gifts that come from such a personality extend beyond me and can positively impact society as a whole.

   ○ A. All challenges also present opportunities for reflection and growth.

   ○ B. Being an introvert has its constraints and takes immense amounts of determination to overcome.

   ○ C. Like Albert Einstein, I have my talents that could benefit the world if they are given the right space to grow and flourish.

   ○ D. I have learned that my introversion and determination allow me to investigate challenging news stories while being sensitive to the people with whom I speak.

2. The following conclusion is from a previous draft of Monica's essay. Monica would like to add a sentence that addresses the part of the writing prompt about goals for the future. Which sentence could she add after the last sentence to help achieve this aim?

> After my time at the newspaper, I started to trust parts of myself that I used to view as weaknesses. Now my heart, determination, and introverted personality help me tell important, true stories. I can finally see that these qualities are some of my greatest strengths.

   ○ A. I wish I could tell my past self that everything would turn out all right.

   ○ B. Even though we have different interests, I know that Kayla and I will still be friends in the future.

   ○ C. As I leave high school, I know that I have the skills to pursue journalism and tell even more stories, because now I embrace every part of what makes me *me*.

   ○ D. Although my introverted personality can be a weakness, I know that it is my greatest strength as a friend and as a school newspaper reporter.

 WRITE

Use the questions in the checklist to revise the conclusion of your personal essay.

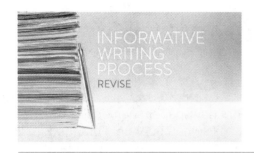

Informative Writing Process: Revise

| PLAN | DRAFT | REVISE | EDIT AND PUBLISH |

You have written a draft of your personal essay. You have also received input from your peers about how to improve it. Now you are going to revise your draft.

◀ REVISION GUIDE

Examine your draft to find areas for revision. Use the guide below to help you review:

Review	Revise	Example
Clarity		
Highlight each example or event. Annotate any places where the connection between the example or event and your main idea is unclear.	Include transition words and explanatory phrases to show how examples and events connect to the main ideas in your essay.	My teachers praised my talent for language but always noted that I am uncomfortable working in groups, especially if my best friend wasn't also involved. Kayla and I have been inseparateable since elementary school.
Development		
Identify ideas or events that might need further explanation for your audience to understand.	Make sure you convey your personal experiences using details that help the reader understand what you were thinking and feeling at the time.	Kayla is friendly and outgoing while I am more reserved. She loves science and working in the community garden on weekends, but I'd much rather curl up with a good book or write a short story.

Please note that excerpts and passages in the StudySync® library and this workbook are intended as touchstones to generate interest in an author's work. The excerpts and passages do not substitute for the reading of entire texts, and StudySync® strongly recommends that students seek out and purchase the whole literary or informational work in order to experience it as the author intended. Links to online resellers are available in our digital library. In addition, complete works may be ordered through an authorized reseller by filling out and returning to StudySync® the order form enclosed in this workbook.

Reading & Writing Companion   153

Review	Revise	Example

Organization

Review	Revise	Example
Review your body paragraphs. Are they coherent? Identify and annotate any sentences within and across paragraphs that don't flow in a clear and logical way.	Rewrite the sentences so they appear in a clear and logical order.	The school's newspaper seemed like a natural fit, so I signed up. ~~After I dragged myself to my first newspaper meeting, though, I quickly realized how silly I had been.~~ Id thought about joining the paper before but was intimidated by the newsrooms Id seen on television and in movies. If I cant handle Sunday night dinner with my extended family, how was I supposed to work amid the hustle and bustle of such a high-stakes environment? After I dragged myself to my first newspaper meeting, though, I quickly realized how silly I had been. ~~The school's newspaper seemed like a natural fit, though, so I signed up.~~

Style: Word Choice

Review	Revise	Example
Identify repetitive words or imprecise words that do not clearly convey your ideas and experiences to the reader.	Replace weak and repetitive words and phrases with more descriptive ones that better convey your ideas.	I ~~would not~~ stubbornly refused to seek other companions. My friend-ship with Kayla ~~always seemed very important to me and I did not feel as comfortable with anyone else~~ always felt like a safety net. With Kayla, I could always be myself. She understood if I needed space and encouraged ~~let~~ me to take care of myself. It ~~didn't feel right~~ felt disloyal to look for other friends when Kayla gave me all the support I needed.

Review	Revise	Example
Style: Sentence Fluency		
Read aloud your writing and listen to the way the text sounds. Does it sound choppy? Or does it flow smoothly? Is the emphasis on important details and events?	Rewrite a key passage, making your sentences longer or shorter to achieve a better flow of writing.	In the following weeks, I began to look forward to newspaper meetings: as much as I ~~also~~ looked forward to my nightly calls with Kayla. My assignments were tough:, especially when I had to inter view strangers for a story. Yet my ~~My desire~~ determination to succeed kept me focused:, and knowing that I planned to spend ~~I spent~~ time alone to write about each new exspereince kept me motivated.

✏ WRITE

Use the revision guide, as well as your peer reviews, to help you evaluate your personal essay to determine areas that should be revised.

Skill:
Style

••• CHECKLIST FOR STYLE

First, reread the draft of your personal essay and identify the following:

- slang, colloquialisms, contractions, abbreviations, or a conversational tone
- places where you could use precise language in order to help inform your readers
- the use of the first-person (*I*) or second person (*you*) or third person (*he, she, they*)
- places where you could vary sentence structure and length, emphasizing compound, complex, and compound-complex sentences
    > for guidance on effective ways of varying syntax, use a reference such as Tufte's *Artful Sentences*
- incorrect uses of the conventions of standard English for grammar, spelling, capitalization, and punctuation

Establish and maintain a formal style in your essay, using the following questions as a guide:

- Have I used academic language when informing my audience and a personal, conversational tone only when appropriate?
- Did I consistently use the same perspective (for example, using third-person pronouns) throughout my essay?
- Have I used varied sentence lengths and different sentence structures? Did I consider using reference sources, such as Tufte's *Artful Sentences,* to learn about effective ways of varying syntax?
    > Where should I make some sentences longer by using conjunctions to connect independent clauses, dependent clauses, and phrases?
    > Where should I make some sentences shorter by separating independent clauses?
- Did I follow the conventions of standard English?

↻ YOUR TURN

Choose the best answer to each question.

1. Below is a sentence from another draft of Monica's essay. How can she rewrite the sentence to eliminate slang and non-academic language?

> School work was a breeze, something that I rocked even when I was young, but high fiving kids in class wasn't my thing.

- ○ A. School work came easy to me, something that I never bombed even when I was young, but celebrating other students or conversing with them wasn't something I felt comfortable doing.
- ○ B. School work was a breeze, something that I excelled at even when I was young, but high fiving kids in class wasn't my thing.
- ○ C. School work came easy to me, something that I excelled at even when I was young, but celebrating other students or conversing with them wasn't something I felt comfortable doing.
- ○ D. School work was easy for me, something that I excelled at even when I was young, but getting to chit-chat with kids in class was more difficult.

2. Below is a section of a paragraph from another draft of Monica's essay. Which of the following sentences uses an inconsistent perspective?

> (1) A female student sat at a computer, silently working on her own individual assignment. (2) She was concentrating. (3) When you walk in, she looks up and offers you a small smile before returning her eyes to her screen. (4) She and I were part of the same team. (5) The newspaper office became a place I love.

- ○ A. Sentence 1
- ○ B. Sentence 2
- ○ C. Sentence 3
- ○ D. Sentence 5

✏ WRITE

Use the checklist to revise a paragraph of your personal essay to establish and maintain a style and tone.

Grammar:
Sentence Variety

One way to create a more interesting style when writing or editing a draft is to vary the syntax, or structure, of sentences.

English sentences have four basic structures: simple sentences, compound sentences, complex sentences, and compound-complex sentences. When writers use only one type of sentence, readers may disengage from the text. This is especially evident when authors rely heavily on simple sentences. However, with a knowledge of sentence structures, writers can employ a variety of sentences. In the example below, the writer has revised for greater sentence variety and improved the flow of the text.

Edited for Sentence Variety	Not Yet Edited for Sentence Variety
Ronald Reagan was born in Illinois. He graduated from Eureka College in 1932 and worked as an actor for nearly three decades before entering politics in the 1960s. Because he was considered an effective speaker, he was asked to give a speech at the 1964 Republican National Convention. This speech made him more popular and contributed to his being elected Governor of California in 1966.	Ronald Reagan was born in Illinois. He graduated from Eureka College in 1932. He worked as an actor for nearly three decades. He entered politics in the 1960s. He was considered an effective speaker. In 1964, he was asked to give a speech at the Republican National Convention. This speech made him more popular. He was elected Governor of California in 1966.

Notice that the writer applies the strategies of coordination and subordination to combine sentences. The edited second sentence combines information from three sentences but is still easy to read and understand because it includes the word *before* to show that the relationship between the three events in Reagan's life is chronological.

Another particularly helpful strategy for constructing effective sentences is using parallelism.

Strategy	Text
Use parallel construction to emphasize ideas that are related and equal in importance through the use of similarly constructed clauses, phrases, or single words.	**Black** and **ageless**, he sat rocking **day in** and **day out** in a mindless stupor, lulled by the monotonous squeak-squawk of the chair. Marigolds

⟳ YOUR TURN

1. How were these sentences edited for structure?

> Sample Sentences: The plane landed. The passengers departed the plane. The passengers entered the terminal.
>
> Edited Text: After the plane landed, the passengers departed the plane, and they entered the terminal.

- ○ A. The sample sentences were combined to create a compound sentence.
- ○ B. The sample sentences were combined to create a compound-complex sentence.
- ○ C. The sample sentences were combined to create a complex sentence.
- ○ D. The sample sentences were combined to create one longer simple sentence.

2. How were these sentences edited for sentence variety?

> Sample Sentences: The graduating class gave a talent show. Some of the students performed. Other students worked behind the scenes.
>
> Edited Text: The graduating class gave a talent show. Some of the students performed, and others worked behind the scenes.

- ○ A. Two of the sample sentences were combined to create a complex sentence.
- ○ B. Two of the sample sentences were combined to create a compound-complex sentence.
- ○ C. Two of the sample sentences were combined to create a simple sentence.
- ○ D. Two of the sample sentences were combined to create a compound sentence.

3. How were these sentences edited for sentence variety?

> Sample Sentences: I want to work on the project with Michael. He can work quickly. His work is accurate. He is also effective at making decisions.
>
> Edited Text: I want to work on the project with Michael. He can work quickly, accurately, and decisively.

- ○ A. Three sentences were combined to create a compound sentence.
- ○ B. Three sentences were combined into a pair of parallel clauses.
- ○ C. Three sentences were combined to create a series of parallel phrases.
- ○ D. Three sentences were combined to create a series of parallel adverbs.

Grammar:
Basic Spelling Rules I

Rule	Text	Explanation
When adding a suffix that begins with a vowel to a word that ends with a silent *e*, usually drop the *e*. When adding a suffix that begins with a consonant to a word that ends with a silent *e*, keep the *e*.	Therefore begrudging neither augury Nor other **divination** that is thine, O save thyself, thy country, and thy king, Save all from this **defilement** of blood shed. Oedipus Rex	*Divination* drops the final silent *e* of *divine*, because the suffix starts with a vowel. *Defilement* keeps the silent *e*, because the suffix starts with a consonant.
Always keep the original spelling of the word when you add a prefix, even if the prefix causes a double letter.	It is the Nation's resilience, not its rigidity, that Texas sees reflected in the flag—and it is that resilience that we **reassert** today. Texas v. Johnson	The prefix *re-* does not change the spelling of the base word *assert*.
When adding a suffix that begins with *a* or *o* to a word that ends with *ce* or *ge*, usually keep the *e*.	The different accidents of life are not so **changeable** as the feelings of human nature. Frankenstein	The final silent *e* remains after the suffix is added to *change*.
When a word ends in a consonant + *y*, change the *y* to *i* before adding a suffix. Usually, when *i* and *e* appear together in one syllable, the *i* comes before the *e*. However, there are many exceptions to this rule.	The earliest epics date back to a time when most people were illiterate. Recited by poets, probably with musical **accompaniment**, these epics were the **movies** of their day. The Epic and the Epic Hero	The final *y* in *accompany* is changed to *i* when the suffix is added. In *movies*, the *i* comes before the *e*.

↻ YOUR TURN

1. How should this sentence be changed?

> The typical superhero is the personifycation of masculinity, noted for strength, prowess, endurance, and every other virtue except humility.

- ○ A. The typical superhero is the personification of masculinity, noted for strength, prowess, endurance, and every other virtue except humility.
- ○ B. The typical superhero is the personifycation of masculenity, noted for strength, prowess, endurance, and every other virtue except humility.
- ○ C. The typical superhero is the personifycation of masculinity, noted for strength, prowess, endurence, and every other virtue except humility.
- ○ D. No change needs to be made to this sentence.

2. How should this sentence be changed?

> Shakespeare and his peers inhabited an unstable world in which humans were prey to unknown microrganisms that could swiftly terminate their lives.

- ○ A. Shakespeare and his peers inabited an unstable world in which humans were prey to unknown microrganisms that could swiftly terminate their lives.
- ○ B. Shakespeare and his peers inhabited an unstable world in which humans were prey to unnown microrganisms that could swiftly terminate their lives.
- ○ C. Shakespeare and his peers inhabited an unstable world in which humans were prey to unknown microorganisms that could swiftly terminate their lives.
- ○ D. No change needs to be made to this sentence.

3. How should this sentence be changed?

> Browning writes of loving to the depth and breadth and height of the soul, quietly, yet with a passion that replaces past greifs.

- ○ A. Browning writes of loving to the depth and breadth and hieght of the soul, quietly, yet with a passion that replaces past greifs.
- ○ B. Browning writes of loving to the depth and breadth and height of the soul, queitly, yet with a passion that replaces past greifs.
- ○ C. Browning writes of loving to the depth and breadth and height of the soul, quietly, yet with a passion that replaces past griefs.
- ○ D. No change needs to be made to this sentence.

Please note that excerpts and passages in the StudySync® library and this workbook are intended as touchstones to generate interest in an author's work. The excerpts and passages do not substitute for the reading of entire texts, and StudySync® strongly recommends that students seek out and purchase the whole literary or informational work in order to experience it as the author intended. Links to online resellers are available in our digital library. In addition, complete works may be ordered through an authorized reseller by filling out and returning to StudySync® the order form enclosed in this workbook.

Reading & Writing Companion   161

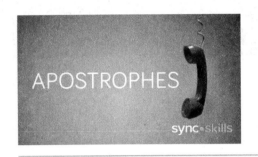

Grammar: Apostrophes

Rule	Text
Use an apostrophe and an *s* to form the possessive of a singular noun.	Is this the custom in King Arthur**'s** house? The Canterbury Tales
Use an apostrophe and an *s* to form the possessive of a plural noun that does not end in *s*. Do not use an apostrophe in a possessive pronoun.	She had been long enough in bondage to other people**'s** pleasure to be considerate of those who depended on **hers**, and in her bitter moods it sometimes struck her that she and her maid were in the same position, except that the latter received her wages more regularly. The House of Mirth
Use an apostrophe alone to form the possessive of a plural noun that ends in *s*.	And so his sons would do after him, and his son**s'** sons, to the final generation. Grendel
Use an apostrophe and an *s* to form the possessive of a singular indefinite pronoun.	"Depending upon one another**'s** hearts, he had still hoped that virtue were not all a dream." Young Goodman Brown
If two or more partners possess something jointly, use the possessive form for the last partner named.	Simon and Garfunkel**'s** list of hit songs is extensive.
If two or more partners possess something individually, put each one's name in the possessive form.	When it comes to tennis, Venus**'s** and Serena**'s** records speak for themselves.
Use an apostrophe to replace letters that have been omitted in a contraction.	The Irish had a hero something like Arthur, Finn MacCool, and stories of Finn spread to Scotland, but that**'s** as far as they went. Conversation with Geoffrey Ashe re: King Arthur

↻ YOUR TURN

1. How should this sentence be changed?

> New Mexico is a state whose history, cultural traditions, and natural beauty deserve to be better known.

- ○ A. New Mexico is a state who's history, cultural traditions, and natural beauty deserve to be better known.
- ○ B. New Mexicos' is a state whose history, cultural traditions, and natural beauty deserve to be better known.
- ○ C. New Mexico's is a state whose history, cultural traditions, and natural beauty deserve to be better known.
- ○ D. No change needs to be made to this sentence.

2. How should this sentence be changed?

> The reputation of Taos as an artists mecca and Georgia O'Keeffes home helps attract visitors.

- ○ A. The reputation of Taos as an artists mecca and Georgia O'Keeffe's home helps attract visitors.
- ○ B. The reputation of Taos as an artist's mecca and Georgia O'Keeffes home helps attract visitors.
- ○ C. The reputation of Taos as an artists' mecca and Georgia O'Keeffe's home helps attract visitors.
- ○ D. No change needs to be made to this sentence.

3. How should this sentence be changed?

> De Niza's and Estevan's one journey did not, however, yield any discoveries of gold or silver.

- ○ A. De Niza and Estevan's one journey did not, however, yield any discoveries of gold or silver.
- ○ B. De Niza and Estevan one journey did not, however, yield any discoveries of gold or silver.
- ○ C. De Niza's and Estevan's one journey did not, however, yield any discoverie's of gold or silver.
- ○ D. No change needs to be made to this sentence.

Informative Writing Process: Edit and Publish

PLAN	DRAFT	REVISE	EDIT AND PUBLISH

You have revised your personal essay based on your peer feedback and your own examination.

Now, it is time to edit your personal essay. When you revised, you focused on the content of your personal essay. You probably examined how to improve your introduction and conclusion as well as how to make your writing cohesive. When you edit, you focus on the mechanics of your essay, paying close attention to things like grammar and punctuation.

Use the checklist below to guide you as you edit:

☐ Have I used a variety of sentences?

☐ Have I followed basic spelling rules?

☐ Have I used apostrophes correctly throughout the essay?

☐ Do I have any sentence fragments or run-on sentences?

Notice some edits Monica has made:

- Used an apostrophe to make a contraction

- Corrected a spelling error

- Used a variety of sentences

With each passing day, it became clearer that I didn't ~~didnt~~ have to change who I am in order to be happy. My loyalty, determination, and introverted personality might not be the best qualities ~~qualitys~~ in every situation~~,~~ but it ~~It~~ turned out that they are the perfect recipe for a reporter. Before I walked into the newspaper office, I had no idea what I wanted to do after graduation~~,~~ but now ~~Now~~ I know. I want to study journalism and become a correspondent for a newspaper.

✏ WRITE

Use the questions on the previous page, as well as your peer reviews, to help you evaluate your personal essay to determine areas that need editing. Then, edit your personal essay to correct those errors.

Once you have made all your corrections, you are ready to publish your work. You can distribute your writing to family and friends, hang it on a bulletin board, or post it on your blog. If you publish online, share the link with your family, friends, and classmates.

Fate or Foolishness

FICTION

Introduction

An accident creates a violent element that threatens the planet. Can a human

VOCABULARY

chasm
a deep crack in the surface of the earth

bizarre
extremely strange or odd

collide
to crash together violently

ominous
threatening; suggesting that something bad will happen

calamity
a disaster; an event that causes great harm

READ

NOTES

1 In those days, every human unit was warned to stay away from the EDGE, the Eastern Dangerous Galaxy Enclosure. The EDGE had existed since the twenty-first century. At that time, a ghastly event happened. An explosion happened aboveground. A vast **chasm** appeared, and tunnels cracked open. The planet shook, releasing blasts of bright, flaming energy that **collided** violently in the atmosphere. Half the planet was destroyed. Since then, no one has entered the area of the catastrophe that we call the singularity. It has an intense gravitational pull, so nothing can escape from it. The EDGE was the barrier set up to isolate the **calamity**.

2 Once upon a midnight dreary, I foolishly believed that I could repair the planet and destroy the EDGE. In those days, human units had created machines that were advanced for their time. The machines were programmed well. They did many things for human units. No longer did the units have to know mathematics. The machines calculated for them. No longer did they need dictionaries. The machines "knew" the definition and spelling of every word.

NOTES

But, according to the designers and manufacturers, the machines could not think for themselves.

3   I took a different approach with my experiments. I focused on true "artificial intelligence." I built Lenore, a birdlike thinking machine. At first visitors to my laboratory laughed in mockery. "A raven is such a **bizarre** pet for a scientist!" They did not recognize that Lenore was not a real raven. They could not guess that she would change their existence. I taught Lenore to make decisions. She became my dear friend.

4   This explains why I was standing on a desolate plain near the EDGE. It was a dark and stormy night. Sizzling bits of energy seemed to float above the singularity. No plant, nor tree, nor blade of grass grew on the bleak plain. The earth was scorched and stripped bare. The singularity sucked the energy from all living creatures. Merciless blasts of wind rocked my body, but Lenore rested safely under my jacket. **Ominous** cracking and creaking sounds filled me with terror. Yet, I had come to fulfill my destiny. Perhaps I was correct in my actions. I will never know.

5   The beating of my fearful heart drowned out the relentless sounds of the singularity. I moved as close as I dared to the flashing, rippling nightmare that had ruined my beloved planet. Slowly, with shaking fingers, I opened my jacket. Lenore looked at me, wide-eyed, unafraid. Tonight I would lose my friend forever. Yet, I knew if she were successful, my planet would be healed.

6   I eased Lenore out and placed her on my shoulder. I whispered one final goodbye. Then I shouted, "Lenore, do what you must!" She rose into the turbulent air, strong against the violent wind. Her instructions were simple. She was to fly into the singularity and do what was needed to destroy it. She could think and reason. She would know what to do once inside. She circled twice and flew straight into the center. Suddenly, flames exploded, feeding on the oxygen in the air. I struggled to breathe. Horrid shrieks roared and howled. Time and space flew apart, breaking into a million pieces before slamming back together with an ear-splitting scream.

7   The singularity disappeared. The desolate plain was gone, too. I was standing next to an apple tree, and somewhere a raven was making a cawing sound. Stunned, I began walking, not knowing or caring where I was. I picked an apple from the tree and took a bite. Taking a deep breath I looked around. I was in a beautiful garden. It seemed like now there would be a new beginning.

First Read

Read "Fate or Foolishness." After you read, complete the Think Questions below.

☁ THINK QUESTIONS

1. What is the EDGE? Why does it exist?

   The EDGE is _____.

   It exists because _____.

2. Who is Lenore?

   Lenore is _____.

3. What happens at the end of the story?

   At the end of the story, _____

   _____.

4. Use context to confirm the meaning of the word *calamity* as it is used in "Fate or Foolishness." Write your definition of *calamity* here.

   Calamity means_____.

   A context clue is _____.

5. What is another way to say that something is *ominous*?

   Something is _____

   _____.

Please note that excerpts and passages in the StudySync® library and this workbook are intended as touchstones to generate interest in an author's work. The excerpts and passages do not substitute for the reading of entire texts, and StudySync® strongly recommends that students seek out and purchase the whole literary or informational work in order to experience it as the author intended. Links to online resellers are available in our digital library. In addition, complete works may be ordered through an authorized reseller by filling out and returning to StudySync® the order form enclosed in this workbook.

Reading & Writing
Companion

169

Skill:
Analyzing Expressions

★ DEFINE

When you read, you may find English expressions that you do not know. An **expression** is a group of words that communicates an idea. Three types of expressions are idioms, sayings, and figurative language. They can be difficult to understand because the meanings of the words are different from their **literal**, or usual, meanings.

An **idiom** is an expression that is commonly known among a group of people. For example, "It's raining cats and dogs" means it is raining heavily. **Sayings** are short expressions that contain advice or wisdom. For instance, "Don't count your chickens before they hatch" means do not plan on something good happening before it happens. **Figurative** language is when you describe something by comparing it with something else, either directly (using the words *like* or *as*) or indirectly. For example, "I'm as hungry as a horse" means I'm very hungry. None of the expressions are about actual animals.

••• CHECKLIST FOR ANALYZING EXPRESSIONS

To determine the meaning of an expression, remember the following:

✓ If you find a confusing group of words, it may be an expression. The meaning of words in expressions may not be their literal meaning.

  • Ask yourself: Is this confusing because the words are new? Or because the words do not make sense together?

✓ Determining the overall meaning may require that you use one or more of the following:

  • context clues

  • a dictionary or other resource

  • teacher or peer support

✓ Highlight important information before and after the expression to look for clues.

⟳ YOUR TURN

Read the following excerpt from "Fate or Foolishness". Then, complete the multiple-choice questions below.

---

from "Fate or Foolishness"

The beating of my fearful heart drowned out the relentless sounds of the singularity. I moved as close as I dared to the flashing, rippling nightmare that had ruined my beloved planet. Slowly, with shaking fingers, I opened my jacket. Lenore looked at me, wide-eyed, unafraid. Tonight I would lose my friend forever. Yet, I knew if she were successful, my planet would be healed.

---

1. An example of personification is—

   ○ A. "fearful heart"
   ○ B. "beloved planet"
   ○ C. "shaking fingers"
   ○ D. "planet would be healed"

2. According to context clues in the passage, the meaning of this personification is—

   ○ A. loud
   ○ B. afraid
   ○ C. dangerous
   ○ D. unexpected

3. The figurative meaning of the word *nightmare* in this passage is—

   ○ A. a bad dream
   ○ B. an evil spirit
   ○ C. a difficult task
   ○ D. something scary

4. A context clue that best supports this meaning is—

   ○ A. "moved as close as I dared"
   ○ B. "I opened my jacket."
   ○ C. "Lenore looked at me, wide-eyed, unafraid."
   ○ D. "lose my friend forever"

Please note that excerpts and passages in the StudySync® library and this workbook are intended as touchstones to generate interest in an author's work. The excerpts and passages do not substitute for the reading of entire texts, and StudySync® strongly recommends that students seek out and purchase the whole literary or informational work in order to experience it as the author intended. Links to online resellers are available in our digital library. In addition, complete works may be ordered through an authorized reseller by filling out and returning to StudySync® the order form enclosed in this workbook.

Reading & Writing
Companion

171

Skill:
Conveying Ideas

★ DEFINE

Conveying ideas means communicating a **message** to another person. When speaking, you might not know what word to use to convey your ideas. When you do not know the exact English word, you can try different strategies. For example, you can ask for help from classmates or your teacher. You may use gestures and physical movements to act out the word. You can also try using **synonyms** or **defining** and describing the meaning you are trying to express.

••• CHECKLIST FOR CONVEYING IDEAS

To convey ideas for words you do not know when speaking, use the following learning strategies:

✓ Request help.

✓ Use gestures or physical movements.

✓ Use a synonym for the word.

✓ Describe what the word means using other words.

✓ Give an example of the word you want to use.

↻ YOUR TURN

Match each example with its correct strategy for conveying the meaning of the word *destroy*.

	Example Options
A	The person rips up a piece of paper.
B	The person says it is like when you break the screen on your phone.
C	The person uses the similar word *ruin*.
D	The person explains that the word means causing a lot of damage to something.

Strategy	Example
Use gestures or physical movements.	
Use a synonym for the word.	
Describe what the word means using other words.	
Give examples of the word you want to use.	

Please note that excerpts and passages in the StudySync® library and this workbook are intended as touchstones to generate interest in an author's work. The excerpts and passages do not substitute for the reading of entire texts, and StudySync® strongly recommends that students seek out and purchase the whole literary or informational work in order to experience it as the author intended. Links to online resellers are available in our digital library. In addition, complete works may be ordered through an authorized reseller by filling out and returning to StudySync® the order form enclosed in this workbook.

Reading & Writing Companion   **173**

Close Read

✏ **WRITE**

PERSONAL RESPONSE: In "Fate or Foolishness," using Lenore to save the planet seemed like a good idea, but it could have ended in failure. Tell about a time you acted on a good idea that ended well, although it could have just as easily ended in disaster. Recount the events from your experience and connect them to details in the story. Pay attention to and edit for spelling patterns.

Use the checklist below to guide you as you write.

☐ What is a risky decision that you made?

☐ Why was your idea or action risky?

☐ How did you feel when it ended well?

☐ How can you connect this to details in 'Fate or Foolishness'?

Use the sentence frames to organize and write your personal response.

A risky decision that I made was _____.

It was risky because _____.

I felt very _____.

It could have ended badly if _____.

Instead it ended well when _____.

Afterward, I felt _____.

A First in Space

INFORMATIONAL TEXT

Introduction

Children often dream about what they want to be when they grow up. Sally Ride turned her dream into a reality, and in the process helped establish a role for women in the field of science. Learn more about Sally

VOCABULARY

limitation

disadvantage that limits the effectiveness of something or someone

cope

to deal effectively with problems or responsibilities

potential

possible; capable of becoming real

direct

guide, oversee, or manage something, such as a project

candidate

someone competing for a position or prize

NOTES

≡ READ

1   The word "trailblazer" once referred to someone who explored an area and created a trail to guide those who followed. Today the word refers to a person who is the first to do something. It also describes someone who has ignored **limitations** and opened a new path. Sally Ride was a trailblazer, an amazing one.

2   When Sally Ride was little, she didn't ask for typical toys. Instead, she wanted a chemistry set. She also wanted a telescope to study the sky. She might have even wondered what it would be like to travel in space and look down on Earth. Sally was fascinated by science, and her parents supported and encouraged her. She enjoyed sports and competed in junior tennis tournaments. All of these things worked together as Sally pursued different careers.

3   In 1977, Sally was working on her Ph.D. in physics at Stanford University when she noticed an advertisement in the paper. NASA was looking for **potential** astronauts. Until then, only men had been accepted into the program, and they all had to have been military pilots. Then the rules changed. Scientists and engineers were encouraged to apply and so were women. Sally sent in

her application, along with 8,000 others. Only thirty-five individuals, including six women, were chosen as **candidates** for the program.

4   Being an astronaut means being physically able to **cope** with unusual situations, so the training is challenging. Sally learned parachute jumping and water survival. She learned how to deal with the weightlessness that occurs in a zero-gravity situation. She trained in navigation and radio communications. She became part of a team that built a robotic arm designed to launch and retrieve satellites. The arm was to be used on the shuttle, a vehicle that circled and then returned to Earth.

5   In 1979, Sally was approved for assignment to a flight crew. She would be a mission specialist on board the orbiter *Challenger*. Her responsibilities would involve performing experiments using the robotic arm she designed. While she waited for her scheduled launch, she worked as a communications officer for two other space flights. She sent messages and instructions from mission control to the flight crews.

6   Finally, in 1983, Sally soared into space. Her job was to control the robotic arm and perform the same experiments she had practiced on Earth. Using the arm, she sent several satellites into space. She also retrieved other units from space. Sally was the first American woman astronaut. At 32, she was also the youngest individual to travel into space. She became a role model in a job previously performed only by men, and she was on a grand adventure that shaped her life.

7   Sally's second flight took place in 1984. She then began training for yet another voyage. Sadly, in 1986, the *Challenger* exploded as it took off. Sally was not on the flight, but all upcoming assignments were canceled, including Sally's.

8   In 1987, Sally began teaching and devoted herself to helping students who wanted to study science. She started writing science books for children. She began and **directed** education projects including the EarthKAM, which allowed middle school students to take pictures of Earth from a camera on the International Space Station. In 2001, she co-founded *Sally Ride Science* to encourage girls in science, technology, engineering, and math. The company organizes science festivals, creates publications, and develops science programs for students.

9   Sally was made a member of the National Women's Hall of Fame. She was given the Jefferson Award for Public Service. She received two medals for her space flights. In 2003, she became a member of the Astronaut Hall of Fame where pioneering space travelers are remembered and honored for what they accomplished.

Please note that excerpts and passages in the StudySync® library and this workbook are intended as touchstones to generate interest in an author's work. The excerpts and passages do not substitute for the reading of entire texts, and StudySync® strongly recommends that students seek out and purchase the whole literary or informational work in order to experience it as the author intended. Links to online resellers are available in our digital library. In addition, complete works may be ordered through an authorized reseller by filling out and returning to StudySync® the order form enclosed in this workbook.

Reading & Writing Companion   177

First Read

Read "A First in Space." After you read, complete the Think Questions below.

☁ **THINK QUESTIONS**

1. Who was Sally Ride? Why was she a role model?

   Sally Ride was _____.

   She was a role model because _____.

2. Write two or three sentences to describe the training Sally Ride did.

   Sally trained by learning _____

   _____.

3. What did Sally Ride do after her time as an astronaut?

   After her time as an astronaut, Sally Ride _____

   _____.

4. Use context to confirm the meaning of the word *potential* as it is used in "A First in Space." Write your definition of *potential* here.

   Potential means_____.

   A context clue is _____.

5. What is another way to say that someone *coped* with a difficult situation?

   Someone _____.

Copyright © Bookheaded Learning, LLC

Skill:
Language Structures

★ DEFINE

In every language, there are rules that tell how to **structure** sentences. These rules define the correct order of words. In the English language, for example, a **basic** structure for sentences is subject, verb, and object. Some sentences have more **complicated** structures.

You will encounter both basic and complicated **language structures** in the classroom materials you read. Being familiar with language structures will help you better understand the text.

••• CHECKLIST FOR LANGUAGE STRUCTURES

To improve your comprehension of language structures, do the following:

✓ Monitor your understanding.

- Ask yourself: Why do I not understand this sentence? Is it because I do not understand some of the words? Or is it because I do not understand the way the words are ordered in the sentence?

✓ Break down the sentence into its parts.

- In English, many sentences share this basic pattern: subject + verb + object.

  > The **subject** names who or what is doing the action.

  > The **verb** names the action or state of being.

  > The **object** answers questions such as Who?, What?, Where?, and When?

- Ask yourself: What is the action? Who or what is doing the action? What details do the other words provide?

✓ Confirm your understanding with a peer or teacher.

⟳ YOUR TURN

Read each sentence below. Then, complete the chart by identifying the verb and object of each sentence.

Word and Phrase Options					
pursued	wanted	two medals	different careers	received	chemistry set

Sentence	Verb	Object
Instead, **she** wanted a chemistry set.		
All of these things worked together as **Sally** pursued different careers.		
She received two medals for her space flights.		

Skill:
Retelling and Summarizing

★ DEFINE

You can retell and summarize a text after reading to show your understanding. **Retelling** is telling a story again in your own words. **Summarizing** is giving a short explanation of the most important ideas in a text.

Keep your retelling or summary **concise**. Only include important information and key words from the text. By summarizing and retelling a text, you can improve your comprehension of the text's ideas.

••• CHECKLIST FOR RETELLING AND SUMMARIZING

In order to retell or summarize a text, note the following:

✓ Identify the main events of the text.

- Ask yourself: What happens in this text? What are the main events that happen at the beginning, the middle, and the end of the text?

✓ Identify the main ideas in a text.

- Ask yourself: What are the most important ideas in the text?

✓ Determine the answers to the six WH questions.

- Ask yourself: After reading this text, can I answer Who?, What?, Where?, When?, Why?, and How? questions?

YOUR TURN

Read the following excerpt from "A First in Space". Then, place the events in the correct order to retell what happened first, next, and last.

---

from **"A First in Space"**

In 1977, Sally was working on her Ph.D. in physics at Stanford University when she noticed an advertisement in the paper. NASA was looking for potential astronauts. Until then, only men had been accepted into the program, and they all had to have been military pilots. Then the rules changed. Scientists and engineers were encouraged to apply and so were women. Sally sent in her application, along with 8,000 others. Only thirty-five individuals, including six women, were chosen as candidates for the program.

Event Options	
A	NASA encouraged women to apply to become astronauts.
B	Sally Ride was chosen as a candidate for the astronaut program.
C	Sally Ride worked on her Ph.D.

First	Next	Last

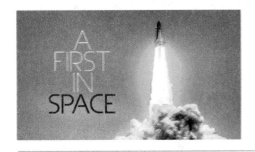

Close Read

✏️ **WRITE**

ARGUMENTATIVE: The author of "A First in Space" calls Sally Ride a trailblazer. Do you agree? Support your opinion with events and evidence from the text. Pay attention to and edit for subject-verb agreement.

Use the checklist below to guide you as you write.

☐ What is a *trailblazer*?

☐ Do you agree that Sally Ride was a trailblazer?

☐ What events and evidence from the text support your opinion?

Use the sentence frames to organize and write your argument.

A *trailblazer* is a person who _____

an area and makes a path for others to follow. I _____

that Sally Ride was a trailblazer. She was the first American _____

astronaut. She was also the _____

person to travel into space for the United States. These facts show that she was a trailblazer because she

was the _____ to do something important.

UNIT 2

Uncovering Truth

How do challenges cause us to reveal our true selves?

Genre Focus: FICTION

Texts

 Paired Readings

Extended Writing Project and Grammar

English Language Learner Resources

How do challenges cause us to reveal our true selves?

SIMON ARMITAGE

Simon Armitage (b. 1963) has written poems, novels, plays, and even a script for a puppet opera. He published his critically-acclaimed translation of the 14th-century Arthurian chivalric poem, *Sir Gawain and the Green Knight,* in 2008, which has sold over 100,000 copies worldwide. Originally written in alliterative verse, its author remains unknown. Armitage, who was elected to serve as Professor of Poetry at Oxford, has also taught at the University of Leeds and the University of Iowa's Writer's Workshop.

BILL BRYSON

Born in Iowa, Bill Bryson (b. 1951) has lived in Britain since the 1970s, when he decided to move there following a four-month backpacking trip of Europe. A trained journalist, he has written a number of popular nonfiction books on subjects ranging from travel to science to language. His 2007 biography of William Shakespeare investigates some of the controversies surrounding the playwright and poet, such as the well-rehearsed authorship debate.

GEOFFREY CHAUCER

Known as the first English author, Geoffrey Chaucer (c. 1343–1400) elected to write in English, the language of the lower-class Saxons, when Latin was commonly spoken and the aristocracy spoke mainly in French. The son of a middle-class wine merchant and a squire in the court of Elizabeth, Countess of Ulster, Chaucer was attentive to subtle class distinctions, which was often the basis of his stories. His best-known work, *The Canterbury Tales* (1387), has an innovative form, distinguished by the wide-ranging social ranks of its characters.

T. S. ELIOT

One of the most highly regarded poets of his time, T. S. Eliot (1888–1965) was also a playwright and an influential literary critic. In his 1919 essay on Shakespeare's *Hamlet*, he put forward his concept of the "objective correlative"—a set of objects, a situation, or a chain of events that evokes a certain emotion in an audience. When asked in a *Paris Review* interview about the difference between plays and poems, Eliot replied, "There is all the difference in the world between writing a play for an audience and writing a poem, in which you're writing primarily for yourself."

SHAQUEM GRIFFIN

NFL football player Shaquem Griffin (b. 1995) overcame major obstacles on his journey to becoming a professional football player. Born with a congenital illness that prevented his left hand from fully developing, he often faced discrimination from other players and coaches. He penned an open letter to the general managers of the NFL in 2018 about his experiences fighting adversity. Several weeks later, he was selected in the 2018 NFL Draft by the Seattle Seahawks.

SEAMUS HEANEY

Poet, scholar, and translator, Seamus Heaney (1939–2013) grew up a Catholic in Protestant Northern Ireland. Though he would later live in Dublin for many years, the often-violent political conflict that surrounded him in his youth was at the core of much of his writing. Heaney published over twenty volumes of poetry and criticism and several anthologies, but is perhaps best known for his translation of the epic Anglo-Saxon poem *Beowulf*. Heaney's translation of this foundational Old English text is groundbreaking for its use of modern language.

GARETH HINDS

Illustrator Gareth Hinds (b. 1971) has adapted numerous literary classics into critically-acclaimed graphic novels. His rendition of Beowulf, written by an unknown Anglo-Saxon poet around the 10th or 11th century, dramatically depicts a series of epic battles featuring the hero Beowulf. *A Publishers Weekly* reviewer describes Hinds's perspectives and palettes as lending the book "an almost overwhelming sense of menace."

NAOMI SHIHAB NYE

After the World Trade Center attacks in 2001, writer Naomi Shihab Nye (b. 1952) became an active advocate for Arab Americans, voicing her opposition to both terrorism and prejudice. Her 2005 book, *You & Yours*, was divided into sections addressing her personal experience as a mother and traveler and conditions in the Middle East. Born in St. Louis and raised in both San Antonio, Texas, and Jerusalem, Nye focuses on cultural difference, local life, and the everyday in her work, which spans poetry, fiction, essays, and translations.

WILLIAM SHAKESPEARE

William Shakespeare (1564–1616) is widely regarded as the greatest playwright of all time. His work, which coincided in large part with the reign of England's Queen Elizabeth I, came to define that period in literary history. In addition to comedies and tragedies, he also wrote plays based on major events in English history. *Richard III*, the last in a sequence of four plays set in the late 14th and early 15th centuries, opens with a soliloquy in which Richard discloses his plans to seize the throne through murder, lies, and betrayal.

RABINDRANATH TAGORE

A native of Calcutta, India, Rabindranath Tagore (1861–1941) was the first non-European to win the Nobel Prize in Literature, in 1913. His numerous novels, stories, plays, songs, and poems were influenced by both Western modernism and Indian storytelling traditions, and he is known for introducing colloquial language into Bengali literature. His frequent encounters with the village folk in present-day Bangladesh, where he lived for ten years, formed the basis for much of his later writing.

JESMYN WARD

A native of the Mississippi Gulf Coast, Jesmyn Ward (b. 1977) experienced Hurricane Katrina first hand. This devastating event features prominently in her work, especially her 2011 novel, *Salvage the Bones*, as a focal point for broader inquiries into race and class struggles. Her complex characters and poetic language reflect the depth of experience that constitutes life along the Gulf Coast.

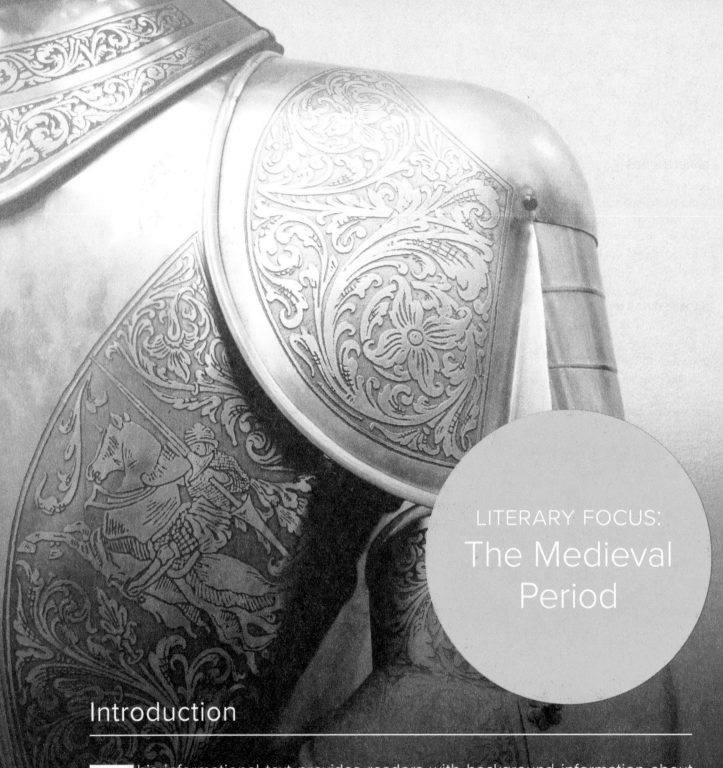

The Medieval Period

Introduction

This informational text provides readers with background information about the history and culture of medieval literature, focusing on the intricacies of the societies that gave rise to heroes like Beowulf, Sir Gawain, and King Arthur. Readers will explore some of the earliest written works of the English language, including epic poetry and medieval romances. For those interested in the earliest foundations of modern epic heroes like Black Panther or Tris Prior, this introduction to medieval literature explains the context in which many of our classic

"The epic hero almost always defeats his enemies."

1   What are some of your favorite movies? Do any of these movies tell the story of an amazing hero with superhuman abilities? There have been many recent blockbusters about extraordinary heroes like Black Panther, Tris Prior, and Harry Potter—to name a few. These modern-day heroes are part of a long lineage of heroes and legends celebrated in literature throughout history and across cultures. Traveling back all the way to the English Middle Ages we find Beowulf, an Anglo-Saxon warrior, and King Arthur, a legendary medieval king—heroic figures who still capture our imagination and remain **relevant** in today's entertainment industry.

Anglo-Saxon Warriors

2   The English Middle Ages ranged from the end of the fifth century to 1485. The Romans had conquered Britain, but they left when the Roman Empire began to fall. Meanwhile, invaders from a mix of tribes from Germany, Denmark, and the Netherlands came to Britain in ships across the North Sea. The three biggest tribes were the Angles, the Saxons, and the Jutes, and today they are collectively referred to as the **Anglo-Saxons.**

3   The Anglo-Saxons brought their language, culture, and literary traditions to Britain. Anglo-Saxon storytellers created heroic songs describing warriors' great deeds and celebrating qualities such as strength, courage, and loyalty. Minstrels performed these songs during banquets in the mead-halls of Anglo-Saxon rulers. In a mostly illiterate society, such songs served as entertainment. They also provided models for warriors to emulate and a goal to pursue— namely, to win fame and be remembered after death for one's deeds. During this period, an unknown poet composed *Beowulf,* the oldest known **epic** poem in England.

Christianity and Pilgrimages

4   In 596 CE Pope Gregory I sent missionaries to convert the Anglo-Saxons to Christianity. By 650 CE, most of England was Christian, though many people retained some pagan beliefs and traditions. One way people expressed their religious devotion during the Middle Ages was to undertake a pilgrimage, or journey to a sacred site. One of the most important destinations for English

pilgrims was Canterbury Cathedral. In fact, the pilgrims described in Chaucer's *The Canterbury Tales* are journeying to this holy site.

Knights and Chivalry

5   The Anglo-Saxon era ended in 1066 when William the Conqueror landed with his army in England and attacked and defeated the Anglo-Saxons to become the first Norman king of England. The Normans introduced the system of **feudalism**, under which land was divided among the nobility. Knights pledged their wealth and services to barons, who in turn provided use of the land. Constant warfare in the Middle Ages involved troops of heavily armed knights fighting each other. Given their role in society, knights enjoyed great social prestige in the feudal aristocracy system. It was during this time period that English writers produced romances about the legendary King Arthur and his Knights of the Round Table, with *Sir Gawain and the Green Knight* as one of the most highly regarded verse romances in English.

William I, King of England, also known
as William the Conqueror

Major Concepts

6   • **Anglo-Saxon virtues**—Anglo-Saxon culture was a warrior society. They were under constant attack, such as during the Viking raids of the eighth and ninth centuries. Courage, loyalty, and physical strength were important virtues and through them it was believed that a warrior could achieve fame and immortality.

    • **The Power of Faith**—The Christian church shaped the culture of medieval England, influencing all aspects of life: politics, warfare, education, business, art, literature, folkways, and recreation.

NOTES

- **Code of Chivalry—**During the time period of feudalism, knights enjoyed a high social status and were expected to exhibit exemplary behavior. The code of **chivalry,** an ideal of civilized behavior among the nobility, encouraged knights to be honorable, generous, brave, skillful in battle, and respectful to women.

Style and Form

Epic Poetry

7 • *Beowulf* is considered an epic poem—a long narrative poem that recounts the **exploits** of a larger-than-life hero. It is characterized by poetic lines with regular meter and formal, lofty language.

- The earliest epics date back to a time when most people were illiterate. These epics were recited by poets and likely included musical accompaniment.

- Epic plots typically involve supernatural events, long periods of time, distant journeys, and life-and-death struggles between good and evil.

- The epic hero is a man—women take a subordinate role in traditional epics—of high social status whose fate affects the destiny of his people. He embodies the ideals and values of his people. Through physical strength, skill as a warrior, nobility of character, and quick wits, the epic hero almost always defeats his enemies.

A Collection of Tales

8 • In a collection of tales, several stories are framed by a larger story. A collection is not specific to writing in the medieval period. It is a traditional storytelling form that has been used by cultures worldwide.

- Geoffrey Chaucer's *The Canterbury Tales* is a well-known collection, which is highly representative of medieval culture and values. In *The Canterbury Tales*, the larger story frame is that of a group of pilgrims. Each tale is an individual story told by one of the pilgrims.

- Chaucer's tales are written mostly in verse, although some are in prose.

- Chaucer's characters represent a diversity of views as well as different social classes.

Medieval Romance

9 • *Sir Gawain and the Green Knight* is a medieval romance. **Medieval romances** often told romantic tales about legendary heroes, such as King Arthur and his knights. They were written in both verse and prose. The

Please note that excerpts and passages in the StudySync® library and this workbook are intended as touchstones to generate interest in an author's work. The excerpts and passages do not substitute for the reading of entire texts, and StudySync® strongly recommends that students seek out and purchase the whole literary or informational work in order to experience it as the author intended. Links to online resellers are available in our digital library. In addition, complete works may be ordered through an authorized reseller by filling out and returning to StudySync® the order form enclosed in this workbook.

Reading & Writing Companion   **193**

emphasis on chivalry and courtly love distinguishes medieval romance from other types of epics.

- Romance was the most popular literary genre in medieval England among the upper classes.

- The knight usually goes on a quest and in the course of his adventures, undergoes a process of self-discovery and self-improvement.

- The romance hero follows a strict code of conduct, demonstrating absolute loyalty to his king and an unwavering adherence to his oaths as well as exhibiting courtly manners toward women and protecting and aiding the defenseless.

The Knight's Progress of Arthurian Legend

10 Epic poems, medieval romances, and pilgrims' tales were the movies of their day. Audiences were enthralled by stories of epic warriors, legendary knights, courtly love, supernatural monsters, perilous journeys, and fierce battles. Epic poems, romances, and folk tales have continued to captivate readers throughout literary history. Where do you notice the influence of medieval literature on today's films and literature?

LITERARY FOCUS:
THE MEDIEVAL
PERIOD

Literary Focus

Read "Literary Focus: The Medieval Period." After you read, complete the Think Questions below.

☁ THINK QUESTIONS

1. What specific themes, characters, and plot points might audiences of medieval literature find in a typical epic poem or medieval romance? Cite evidence from the text as support.

2. What were the expectations of knights in medieval times? Why do you think they were expected to behave this way? Explain, citing textual evidence to support your response.

3. How did the fact that Anglo-Saxon society was largely illiterate affect entertainment during this time period? Explain.

4. Use context clues to determine the meaning of the word **chivalry** as it is used in this text. Write your definition here, along with the words and phrases that were most helpful in coming to your conclusion. Finally, consult a dictionary to confirm your understanding.

5. The word **exploit** has multiple meanings. Use a print or digital resource to clarify and validate which meaning is used in this text. Cite any context clues that were helpful in determining the word's meaning.

Please note that excerpts and passages in the StudySync® library and this workbook are intended as touchstones to generate interest in an author's work. The excerpts and passages do not substitute for the reading of entire texts, and StudySync® strongly recommends that students seek out and purchase the whole literary or informational work in order to experience it as the author intended. Links to online resellers are available in our digital library. In addition, complete works may be ordered through an authorized reseller by filling out and returning to StudySync® the order form enclosed in this workbook.

Reading & Writing Companion   195

Beowulf
(A Graphic Novel)

FICTION
Gareth Hinds
2007

Introduction

Gareth Hinds (b. 1971) has adapted numerous literary classics into graphic novel form, including *Beowulf*, an epic poem written in Old English and widely considered to be the most important and enduring work of Old English literature. Though its origin date is contested amongst scholars, a first manuscript is widely believed to have been created sometime between 970 and 1025 A.D. The poem was written by an Anglo-Saxon of unknown identity, but the story itself is set firmly in the Scandinavia of yore. The tale follows the heroic journey of Beowulf, who comes to the aid of a king to defeat the murderous monster, Grendel. In this excerpt, Beowulf confronts the gigantic creature.

"Therefore I shall carry neither sword nor shield nor coat of mail to this battle."

Panel 1

NOTES

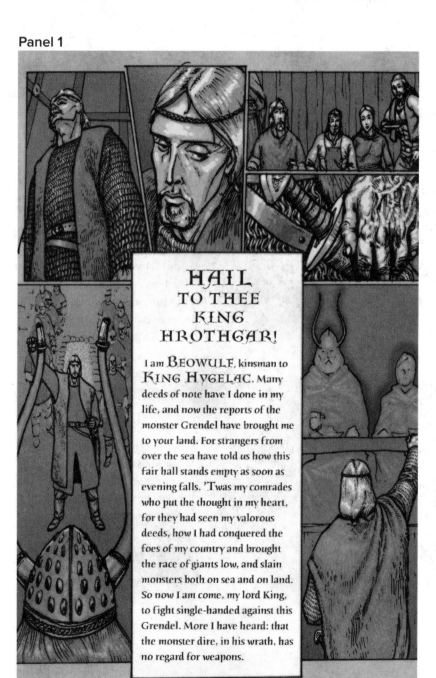

HAIL TO THEE KING HROTHGAR!

I am BEOWULF, kinsman to KING HYGELAC. Many deeds of note have I done in my life, and now the reports of the monster Grendel have brought me to your land. For strangers from over the sea have told us how this fair hall stands empty as soon as evening falls. 'Twas my comrades who put the thought in my heart, for they had seen my valorous deeds, how I had conquered the foes of my country and brought the race of giants low, and slain monsters both on sea and on land. So now I am come, my lord King, to fight single-handed against this Grendel. More I have heard: that the monster dire, in his wrath, has no regard for weapons.

Panel 2

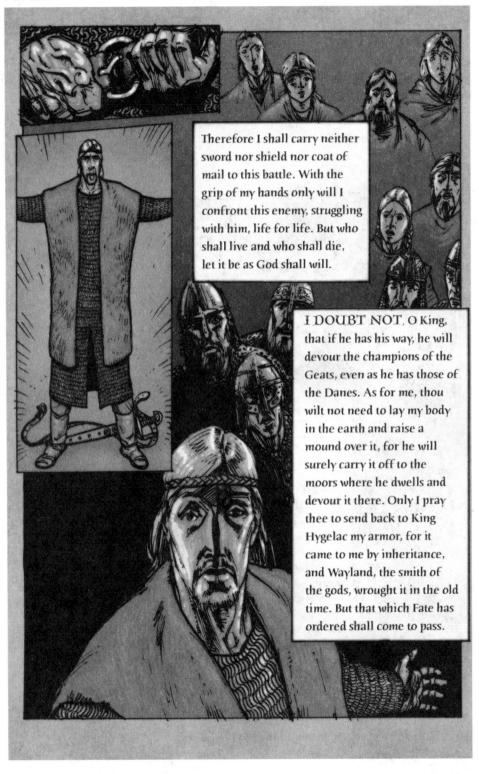

Panel 3

Panel 4

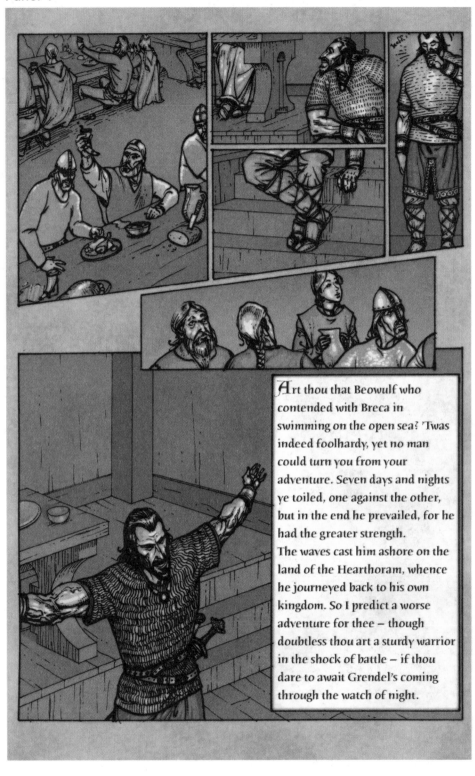

Panel 5

Surely the ale-can has wrought with thee, friend Unferth, that thou hast said such things about Breca. But I say to thee that in buffeting the waves of the sea, I have more strength than any man under heaven.

Now hear the truth. This Breca and I, in our boyhood, were wont to talk of this – how we would test ourselves against the sea – and we made agreement to contend one against the other. So we swam, each holding in one hand a sword to defend himself against the monsters of the sea. Not one whit farther than I could he swim, nor could I outpace him.

So for the space of five days and nights we swam together, but on the sixth day the floods parted us, for the wind blew mightily from the north and the waves were rough. So was I left alone, and the rage of the sea-monsters was roused against me; but my coat of mail stood me in good stead against their attacks. In grimmest grip did one great beast seize me and drag me to the bottom of the sea. Yet strength was given me to pierce the monster with my sword, and I slew him.

1. **Breca** a close, childhood friend of Beowulf

Reading & Writing
Companion

Panel 6

Panel 7

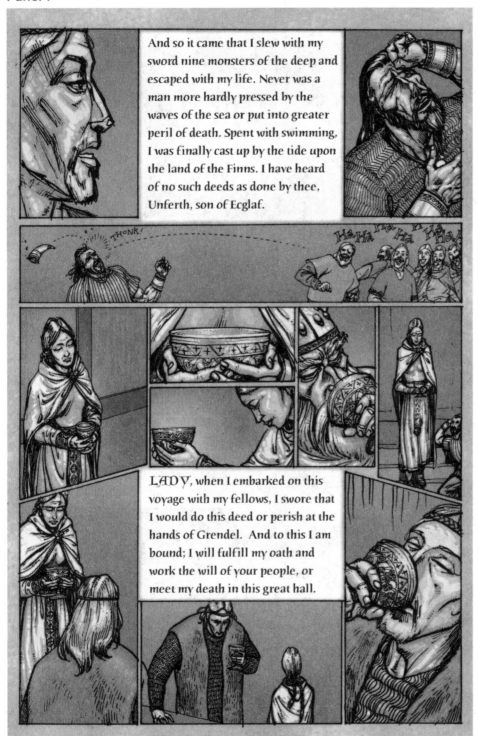

Please note that excerpts and passages in the StudySync® library and this workbook are intended as touchstones to generate interest in an author's work. The excerpts and passages do not substitute for the reading of entire texts, and StudySync® strongly recommends that students seek out and purchase the whole literary or informational work in order to experience it as the author intended. Links to online resellers are available in our digital library. In addition, complete works may be ordered through an authorized reseller by filling out and returning to StudySync® the order form enclosed in this workbook.

Reading & Writing
Companion

203

Panel 8

Panel 9

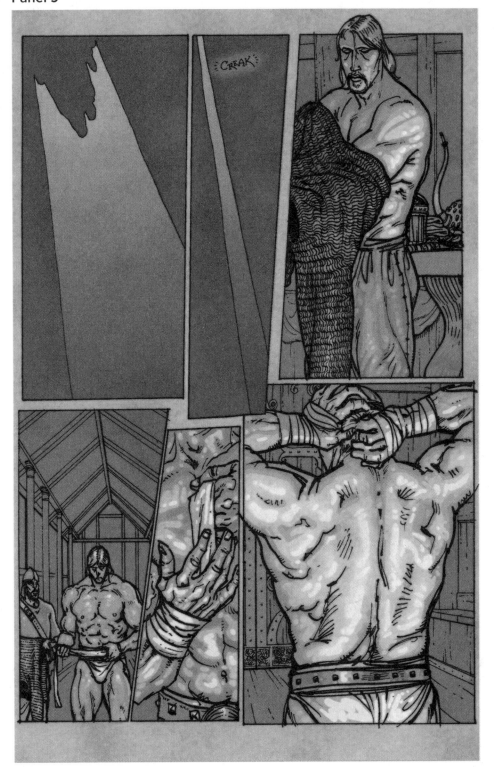

Please note that excerpts and passages in the StudySync® library and this workbook are intended as touchstones to generate interest in an author's work. The excerpts and passages do not substitute for the reading of entire texts, and StudySync® strongly recommends that students seek out and purchase the whole literary or informational work in order to experience it as the author intended. Links to online resellers are available in our digital library. In addition, complete works may be ordered through an authorized reseller by filling out and returning to StudySync® the order form enclosed in this workbook.

Reading & Writing Companion

205

Panel 10

Panel 11

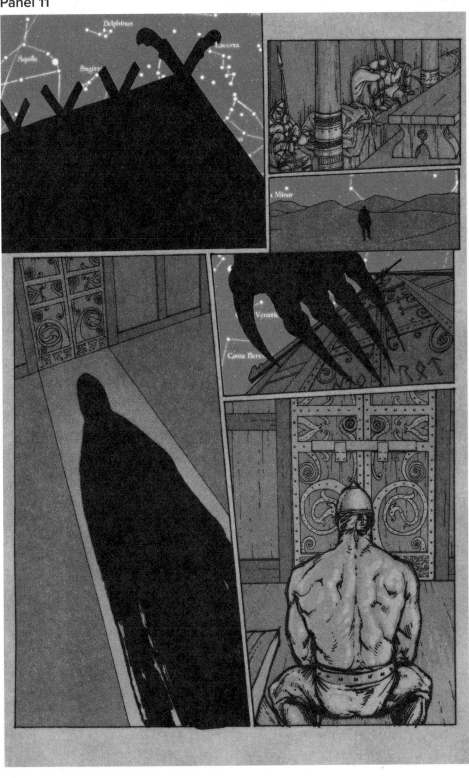

Please note that excerpts and passages in the StudySync® library and this workbook are intended as touchstones to generate interest in an author's work. The excerpts and passages do not substitute for the reading of entire texts, and StudySync® strongly recommends that students seek out and purchase the whole literary or informational work in order to experience it as the author intended. Links to online resellers are available in our digital library. In addition, complete works may be ordered through an authorized reseller by filling out and returning to StudySync® the order form enclosed in this workbook.

Reading & Writing Companion   207

NOTES

Panel 12

Panel 13

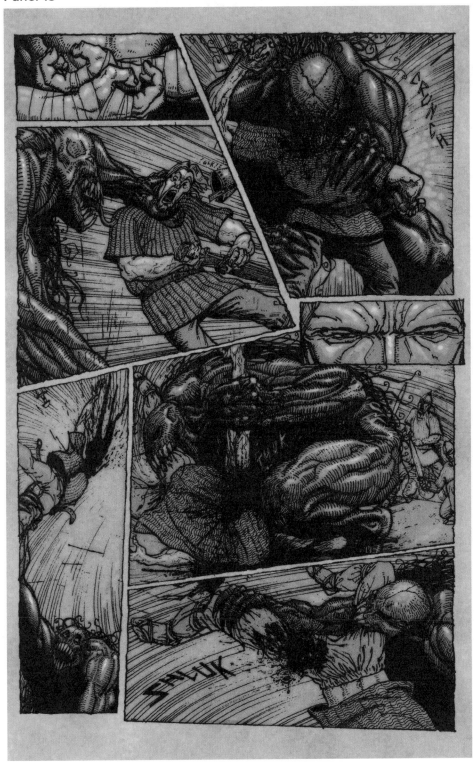

Panel 14

Panel 15

Please note that excerpts and passages in the StudySync® library and this workbook are intended as touchstones to generate interest in an author's work. The excerpts and passages do not substitute for the reading of entire texts, and StudySync® strongly recommends that students seek out and purchase the whole literary or informational work in order to experience it as the author intended. Links to online resellers are available in our digital library. In addition, complete works may be ordered through an authorized reseller by filling out and returning to StudySync® the order form enclosed in this workbook.

Reading & Writing Companion

211

Panel 16

Panel 17

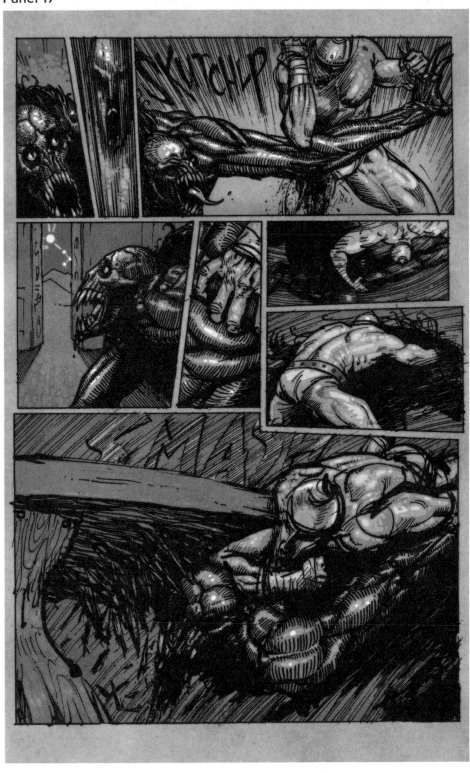

Panel 18

Panel 19

Panel 20

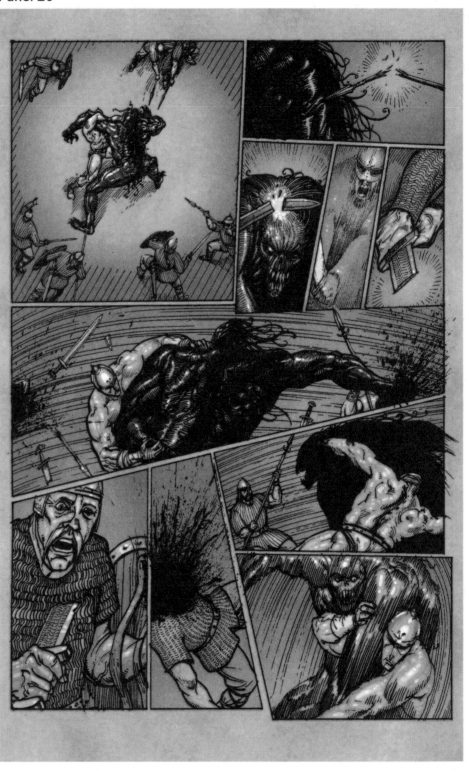

Panel 21

Panel 22

Panel 23

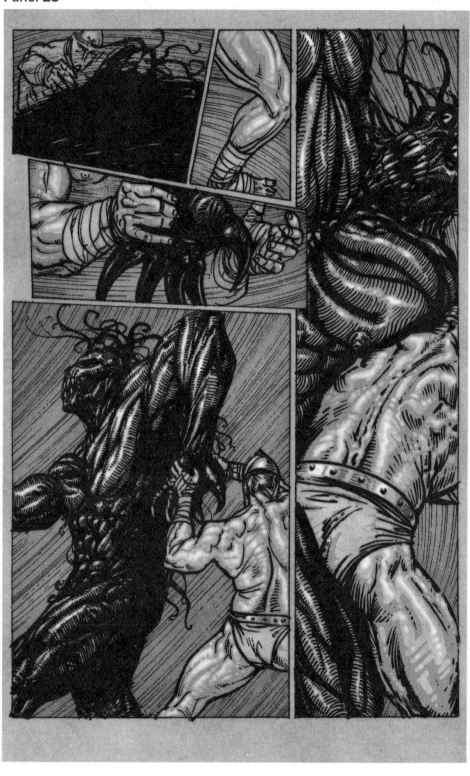

Please note that excerpts and passages in the StudySync® library and this workbook are intended as touchstones to generate interest in an author's work. The excerpts and passages do not substitute for the reading of entire texts, and StudySync® strongly recommends that students seek out and purchase the whole literary or informational work in order to experience it as the author intended. Links to online resellers are available in our digital library. In addition, complete works may be ordered through an authorized reseller by filling out and returning to StudySync® the order form enclosed in this workbook.

Reading & Writing Companion

219

Panel 24

Panel 25

Panel 26

Panel 27

NOTES

Panel 28

Panel 29

Panel 30

BEOWULF. Copyright © 1999, 2000, 2007 by Gareth Hinds. Reproduced by permission of the publisher, Candlewick Press, Somerville, MA.

WRITE

LITERARY ANALYSIS: How does the portrayal of Beowulf in this excerpt reveal the qualities of an Anglo-Saxon hero? Write a response in which you answer this question. Be sure to use textual evidence to defend your analysis of *Beowulf*.

Beowulf
(Lines 144–300)

POETRY
Anglo-Saxon Tradition
(translated by Seamus Heaney)
8th to 11th Centuries

Introduction

A foundational work of Old English literature dating from sometime between the 8th and 11th centuries, *Beowulf* narrates the deeds of a young nobleman from Geatland who comes to rid his Danish neighbors of a marauding monster, Grendel. In this modern translation of the epic poem, readers are introduced to Grendel's twelve-year reign of terror—and to the hero intent on stopping it—courtesy of poet and translator Seamus Heaney (1939–2013), the winner of the 1995 Nobel Prize in Literature. American poet Robert Lowell dubbed Heaney "the most important Irish poet since Yeats."

"No counsellor could ever expect fair reparation from those rabid hands."

144 So Grendel ruled in defiance of right,
145 one against all, until the greatest house
146 in the world stood empty, a deserted wallstead.
147 For twelve winters, seasons of woe,
148 the lord of the Shieldings¹ suffered under
149 his load of sorrow; and so, before long,
150 the news was known over the whole world.
151 Sad lays were sung about the beset king,
152 the vicious raids and ravages of Grendel,
153 his long and unrelenting feud,
154 nothing but war; how he would never
155 parley or make peace with any Dane
156 nor stop his death-dealing nor pay the death-price.
157 No counsellor could ever expect
158 fair **reparation** from those rabid hands.
159 All were endangered; young and old
160 were hunted down by that dark death-shadow
161 who lurked and swooped in the long nights
162 on the misty moors; nobody knows
163 where these reavers from hell roam on their errands.

164 So Grendel waged his lonely war,
165 inflicting constant cruelties on the people,
166 atrocious hurt. He took over Heorot²,
167 haunted the glittering hall after dark,
168 but the throne itself, the treasure-seat,
169 he was kept from approaching; he was the Lord's outcast.

170 These were hard times, heart-breaking
171 for the prince of the Shieldings; powerful counsellors,
172 the highest in the land, would lend advice,

Skill:
Word Patterns and Relationships

The word lays looks like a plural noun, since it comes after the adjective sad and before the verb were. Also, I suspect that lays are like songs, since the poem says they are "sung." I can try swapping lays for songs . . .

---

1. **Shieldings** descendants of a legendary royal family of Danes
2. **Heorot** represents the seat of Hrothgar's power, a mead-hall that is also a residence for the king's warriors

NOTES

173 plotting how best the bold defenders
174 might resist and beat off sudden attacks.
175 Sometimes at pagan shrines they vowed
176 offerings to idols, swore oaths
177 that the killer of souls might come to their aid
178 and save the people. That was their way,
179 their heathenish hope; deep in their hearts
180 they remembered hell. The Almighty Judge
181 of good deeds and bad, the Lord God,
182 Head of the Heavens and High King of the World,
183 was unknown to them. Oh, cursed is he
184 who in time of trouble has to thrust his soul
185 in the fire's embrace, **forfeiting** help;
186 he has nowhere to turn. But blessed is he
187 who after death can approach the Lord
188 and find friendship in the Father's embrace.

189 So that troubled time continued, woe
190 that never stopped, steady **affliction**
191 for Halfdane's son[3], too hard an ordeal.
192 There was panic after dark, people endured
193 raids in the night, riven by the terror.

194 When he heard about Grendel, Hygelac's thane[4]
195 was on home ground, over in Geatland.
196 There was no one else like him alive.
197 In his day, he was the mightiest man on earth,
198 high-born and powerful. He ordered a boat
199 that would ply the waves. He announced his plan:
200 to sail the swan's road and search out that king,
201 the famous prince who needed defenders.
202 Nobody tried to keep him from going,
203 no elder denied him, dear as he was to them.
204 Instead, they inspected omens and spurred
205 his ambition to go, whilst he moved about
206 like the leader he was, enlisting men,
207 the best he could find; with fourteen others
208 the warrior boarded the boat as captain,
209 a canny pilot along coast and currents.

210 Time went by, the boat was on water,
211 in close under the cliffs.

Skill:
Media

Heaney's translation sounds very different from the Old English and the Gummere translation: they sound more like a song. There is a little less alliteration in Heaney's translation. But this translation sounds more contemporary.

---

3. **Halfdane's son** King Hrothgar
4. **Hygelac's thane** a noble who provided military assistance to the King of the Geats, Hygelac

212   Men climbed eagerly up the gangplank,
213   sand churned in surf, warriors loaded
214   a cargo of weapons, shining war-gear
215   in the vessel's hold, then heaved out,
216   away with a will in their wood-wreathed ship.
217   Over the waves, with the wind behind her
218   and foam at her neck, she flew like a bird
219   until her curved prow had covered the distance
220   and on the following day, at the due hour,
221   those seafarers sighted land,
222   sunlit cliffs, sheer crags
223   and looming headlands, the landfall they sought.
224   It was the end of their voyage and the Geats vaulted
225   over the side, out on to the sand,
226   and moored their ship. There was a clash of mail
227   and a thresh of gear. They thanked God
228   for that easy crossing on a calm sea.

229   When the watchman on the wall, the Shieldings' lookout
230   whose job it was to guard the sea-cliffs,
231   saw shields glittering on the gangplank
232   and battle-equipment being unloaded
233   he had to find out who and what
234   the arrivals were. So he rode to the shore,
235   this horseman of Hrothgar's, and challenged them
236   in formal terms, **flourishing** his spear:

237   "What kind of men are you who arrive
238   rigged out for combat in coats of mail,
239   sailing here over the sea-lanes
240   in your steep-hulled boat? I have been stationed
241   as lookout on this coast for a long time.
242   My job is to watch the waves for raiders,
243   any danger to the Danish shore.
244   Never before has a force under arms
245   **disembarked** so openly—not bothering to ask
246   if the sentries allowed them safe passage
247   or the clan had consented. Nor have I seen
248   a mightier man-at-arms on this earth
249   than the one standing here: unless I am mistaken,
250   he is truly noble. This is no mere
251   hanger-on in a hero's armour.
252   So now, before you fare inland
253   as **interlopers**, I have to be informed
254   about who you are and where you hail from.

255 Outsiders from across the water,

256 I say it again: the sooner you tell

257 where you come from and why, the better."

258 The leader of the troop unlocked his word-hoard;

259 the distinguished one delivered this answer:

260 "We belong by birth to the Geat people

261 and owe allegiance to Lord Hygelac[5].

262 In his day, my father was a famous man,

263 a noble warrior-lord named Ecgtheow.

264 He outlasted many a long winter

265 and went on his way. All over the world

266 men wise in counsel continue to remember him.

267 We come in good faith to find your lord

268 and nation's shield, the son of Halfdane.

269 Give us the right advice and direction.

270 We have arrived here on a great errand

271 to the lord of the Danes, and I believe therefore

272 there should be nothing hidden or withheld between us.

273 So tell us if what we have heard is true

274 about this threat, whatever it is,

275 this danger abroad in the dark nights,

276 this corpse-maker mongering death

277 in the Shieldings' country. I come to proffer

278 my wholehearted help and counsel.

279 I can show the wise Hrothgar a way

280 to defeat his enemy and find respite—

281 if any respite is to reach him, ever.

282 I can calm the turmoil and terror in his mind.

283 Otherwise, he must endure woes

284 and live with grief for as long as his hall

285 stands at the horizon, on its high ground."

286 Undaunted, sitting astride his horse,

287 the coast-guard answered, "Anyone with gumption

288 and a sharp mind will take the measure

289 of two things: what's said and what's done.

290 I believe what you have told me: that you are a troop

291 loyal to our king. So come ahead

292 with your arms and your gear, and I will guide you.

293 What's more, I'll order my own comrades

294 on their word of honour to watch your boat

295 down there on the strand—keep her safe

---

5. **Lord Hygelac** King of the Geats and Beowulf's uncle

296 in her fresh tar, until the time comes
297 for her curved prow to preen on the waves
298 and bear this hero back to Geatland.
299 May one so valiant and venturesome
300 come unharmed through the clash of battle."

Excerpted from *Beowulf: A New Verse Translation* by Seamus Heaney, published by W.W. Norton & Company.

Please note that excerpts and passages in the StudySync® library and this workbook are intended as touchstones to generate interest in an author's work. The excerpts and passages do not substitute for the reading of entire texts, and StudySync® strongly recommends that students seek out and purchase the whole literary or informational work in order to experience it as the author intended. Links to online resellers are available in our digital library. In addition, complete works may be ordered through an authorized reseller by filling out and returning to StudySync® the order form enclosed in this workbook.

Reading & Writing
Companion

233

First Read

Read *Beowulf*. After you read, complete the Think Questions below.

☁ THINK QUESTIONS

1. What violence did Grendel inflict on the Danes? Use specific details from the text to support your answer.

2. How do the Shieldings attempt to protect themselves? How effective are these means of protection? Be sure to cite textual evidence.

3. What is the coast-guard's initial opinion of the Geatland sailors? How does he react to their sudden arrival? Use evidence from the text to justify your answer.

4. Use context to determine the meaning of **affliction** as it is used in the text. Write your definition of *affliction* here and explain which context clues helped you determine its meaning.

5. Use context to determine the meaning of the noun **interloper** as it is used in the text. Write your definition of *interloper* here and explain which context clues helped you determine its meaning.

Skill:
Media

Use the Checklist to analyze Media in *Beowulf*. Refer to the sample student annotations about Media in the text.

••• CHECKLIST FOR MEDIA

In order to identify multiple interpretations of a story, drama, or poem, do the following:

- ✓ evaluate how each version interprets the source text

- ✓ consider how, within the same medium, a story can have multiple interpretations if told by writers from different time periods and cultures

- ✓ consider how stories told in the same medium will likely reflect the specific objectives as well as the respective ideas, concerns, and values of each writer

- ✓ note how the same information can be presented in more than one medium

- ✓ use the diverse media to cross-check information

- ✓ consider the skillfulness and artistry of various translations of the same text

To analyze multiple interpretations of a story, drama, or poem, evaluating how each version interprets the source text, consider the following questions:

- ✓ What medium is being used, and how does it affect the interpretation of the source text?

- ✓ What are the similarities and differences between the various versions?

- ✓ If each version is from a different time period/culture, what does each version reveal about the author's objectives, time period and culture in which it was written?

- ✓ How can you integrate multiple sources presented in diverse formats and media in order to inform your own interpretation of the story?

Skill:
Media

To analyze different versions of Beowulf, read an excerpt from the Old English following along with the video, then compare the Gummere equivalent. Next, reread a section from the Heaney translation. Then, using the checklist on the previous page, answer the multiple-choice questions that follow.

 YOUR TURN

From *Beowulf* (Old English version)

Syððan ærest wearð
feasceaft funden, he þæs frofre gebad,
weox under wolcnum, weorðmyndum þah,
oðþæt him æghwylc þara ymbsittendra
ofer hronrade hyran scolde,
gomban gyldan. þæt wæs god cyning.

From *Beowulf,* translated by Francis B. Gummere

Since erst he lay
friendless, a foundling, fate repaid him:
for he waxed under welkin, in wealth he throve,
till before him the folk, both far and near,
who house by the whale-path, heard his
mandate, gave him gifts: a good king he!

From *Beowulf,* (translated by Seamus Heaney)
Note: *These lines are from another section of the poem.*

So Grendel ruled in defiance of right,
one against all, until the greatest house
in the world stood empty, a deserted wallstead.
For twelve winters, seasons of woe,
the lord of the Shieldings suffered under
his load of sorrow; and so, before long,
the news was known over the whole world.
Sad lays were sung about the beset king,
the vicious raids and ravages of Grendel,
his long and unrelenting feud,
nothing but war; how he would never
parley or make peace with any Dane
nor stop his death-dealing nor pay the
death-price.
No counsellor could ever expect
fair reparation from those rabid hands.
All were endangered; young and old
were hunted down by that dark death-shadow
who lurked and swooped in the long nights
on the misty moors; nobody knows
where these reavers from hell roam on their
errands.

1. When watching and listening to the Old English being recited in the video, and reading the same lines in the Gummere translation, how is the translation similar to the original poem?

   ○ A. Gummere attempted to keep the vowel patterns of the original poem the same.
   ○ B. Gummere attempted to use mostly archaic words.
   ○ C. Gummere attempted to keep the alliterative patterns of the original poem the same.
   ○ D. Gummere attempted to make the poem rhyme.

2. When comparing the Old English version to the Heaney translation, how is it different?

   ○ A. Heaney uses conjoined words to keep his text more compact.
   ○ B. Heaney uses fewer archaic words, making his translation more contemporary.
   ○ C. Heaney's version is shorter and more concise.
   ○ D. All of the above

Please note that excerpts and passages in the StudySync® library and this workbook are intended as touchstones to generate interest in an author's work. The excerpts and passages do not substitute for the reading of entire texts, and StudySync® strongly recommends that students seek out and purchase the whole literary or informational work in order to experience it as the author intended. Links to online resellers are available in our digital library. In addition, complete works may be ordered through an authorized reseller by filling out and returning to StudySync® the order form enclosed in this workbook.

Reading & Writing
Companion

237

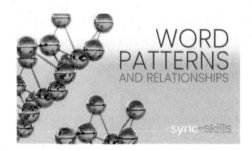

Skill:
Word Patterns and Relationships

Use the Checklist to analyze Word Patterns and Relationships in *Beowulf*. Refer to the sample student annotations about Word Patterns and Relationships in the text.

••• CHECKLIST FOR WORD PATTERNS AND RELATIONSHIPS

In order to identify patterns of word changes to indicate different meanings or parts of speech, do the following:

- ✓ determine the word's part of speech

- ✓ when reading, use context clues to make a preliminary determination of the meaning of the word

- ✓ when writing a response to a text, check that you understand the meaning and part of speech and that it makes sense in your sentence

- ✓ consult a dictionary to verify your preliminary determination of the meanings and parts of speech

- ✓ be sure to read all of the definitions, and then decide which definition, form, and part of speech makes sense within the context of the text

To identify and correctly use patterns of word changes that indicate different meanings or parts of speech, consider the following questions:

- ✓ What is the intended meaning of the word?

- ✓ How do I know that this word form is the correct part of speech? Do I understand the word patterns for this particular word?

- ✓ When I consult a dictionary, can I confirm that the meaning I have determined for this word is correct? Do I know how to use it correctly?

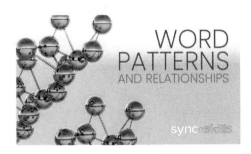

Skill:
Word Patterns and Relationships

Reread the fourth stanza from *Beowulf*. Then, using the Checklist on the previous page, answer the multiple-choice questions below.

⟳ YOUR TURN

1. What part of speech is the word *ordeal*?

   ○ A. noun

   ○ B. verb

   ○ C. adjective

   ○ D. adverb

2. Paying close attention to parts of speech and context, determine which of the following words most closely means *distressed*.

   ○ A. woe

   ○ B. endured

   ○ C. riven

   ○ D. ordeal

Please note that excerpts and passages in the StudySync® library and this workbook are intended as touchstones to generate interest in an author's work. The excerpts and passages do not substitute for the reading of entire texts, and StudySync® strongly recommends that students seek out and purchase the whole literary or informational work in order to experience it as the author intended. Links to online resellers are available in our digital library. In addition, complete works may be ordered through an authorized reseller by filling out and returning to StudySync® the order form enclosed in this workbook.

Reading & Writing Companion   **239**

Close Read

Reread *Beowulf*. As you reread, complete the Skills Focus questions below. Then use your answers and annotations from the questions to help you complete the Write activity.

⊙ SKILLS FOCUS

1. *Beowulf* is an Old English poem that contains many words related to the English words we use today. Translators like Seamus Heaney often choose to keep some of these words, even if they are archaic or not familiar to us. Find two examples of these words in the Heaney translation and use your knowledge of Word Patterns and Relationships to determine their part of speech, and use contextual clues to help you guess a meaning.

2. In Seamus Heaney's translation, Beowulf spends time building up a force of fourteen heavily armed men before traveling to the hall to challenge Grendel. Identify a difference in the way Beowulf's quest is portrayed in the graphic novel, and explain how that difference changes your perception of the character.

3. Find details that show how the historical and social setting of *Beowulf* affects the way Beowulf and other characters interact. Explain which historical and social details you think are particularly effective in developing this part of the plot and why.

4. In the opening lines of this Heaney excerpt, we find out that "These were hard times, heart-breaking for the prince of the Shieldings." It is upon hearing this news that Beowulf decides to travel to the Shieldings and help them. How do these times of challenge reveal the true values of an Anglo-Saxon hero? Highlight and annotate two pieces of textual evidence to support your answer.

✎ WRITE

DISCUSSION: The two excerpts (the Heaney translation and the Hinds graphic novel) of *Beowulf* demonstrate a universal pattern in literature. People are living in fear as an evil force threatens to upset society. Then a brave, strong, and good hero appears to defeat the evil force. What would a hero's arrival look like in a modern-day setting? What would the application of Anglo-Saxon values look like in today's society and culture? Discuss this question with a group of your peers. To prepare for your discussion, use the graphic organizer to write down your ideas about the prompt. Support your ideas with evidence from the text. After your discussion, you will write a reflection in the space below.

Sir Gawain and the Green Knight

POETRY
Anonymous
14th Century
(translated by Simon Armitage)

Introduction

Sir Gawain and the Green Knight is a 14th-century Arthurian romance that has been retold by myriad storytellers since. Originally written in alliterative verse by an unknown author, this translation, in free verse, was published in 2008 by English poet Simon Armitage (b. 1963), an award-winning writer and lecturer from Yorkshire who is most famous for his darkly comedic poetry, drama, and prose. With themes of courage and competition, *Sir Gawain and the Green Knight* weaves together two traditional motifs: the beheading game, and the exchange of winnings. In this particular excerpt, a mysterious visitor arrives during a

"Amazement seized their minds, no soul had ever seen a knight of such a kind—"

NOTES

1   Flavorsome **delicacies** of flesh were fetched in
2   and the freshest of foods, so many in fact
3   there was scarcely space to present the stews
4   or to set the soups in the silver bowls on
5   the cloth.
6   Each guest received his share
7   of bread or meat or broth;
8   a dozen plates per pair—
9   plus beer or wine, or both!

10   Now, on the subject of supper I'll say no more
11   as it's obvious to everyone that no one went without.
12   Because another sound, a new sound, suddenly drew near,
13   which might signal the king to sample his supper,
14   for barely had the horns finished blowing their breath
15   and with starters just spooned to the seated guests,
16   a fearful form appeared, framed in the door:
17   a mountain of a man, immeasurably high,
18   a hulk of a human from head to hips,
19   so long and thick in his loins and his limbs
20   I should genuinely judge him to be a half giant,
21   or a most massive man, the mightiest of mortals.
22   But handsome, too, like any horseman worth his horse,
23   for despite the bulk and brawn of his body
24   his stomach and waist were slender and sleek.
25   In fact in all features he was finely formed
26   it seemed.
27   Amazement seized their minds,
28   no soul had ever seen
29   a knight of such a kind—
30   entirely emerald green.

31   And his gear and garments were green as well:
32   a tight fitting tunic, tailored to his torso,
33   and a cloak to cover him, the cloth fully lined

34 with smoothly shorn fur clearly showing, and faced
35 with all-white ermine, as was the hood,
36 worn shawled on his shoulders, shucked from his head.
37 On his lower limbs his leggings were also green,
38 wrapped closely round his calves, and his sparkling spurs
39 were green-gold, strapped with stripy silk,
40 and were set on his stockings, for this stranger was shoeless.
41 In all vestments he revealed himself veritably verdant!
42 From his belt hooks and buckle to the baubles and gems
43 arrayed so richly around his costume
44 and adorning the saddle, stitched onto silk.
45 All the details of his dress are difficult to describe,
46 embroidered as it was with butterflies and birds,
47 green beads emblazoned on a background of gold.
48 All the horse's tack—harness strap, hind strap,
49 the eye of the bit, each alloy and enamel
50 and the stirrups he stood in were similarly tinted,
51 and the same with the cantle and the skirts of the saddle,
52 all glimmering and glinting with the greenest jewels.
53 And the horse: every hair was green, from hoof
54 to mane.
55 A steed of pure green stock.
56 Each snort and shudder strained
57 the hand-stitched bridle, but
58 his rider had him reined.

59 The fellow in green was in fine fettle.
60 The hair of his head was as green as his horse,
61 fine flowing locks which fanned across his back,
62 plus a bushy green beard growing down to his breast,
63 and his face hair along with the hair of his head
64 was lopped in a line at elbow length
65 so half his arms were gowned in green growth,
66 crimped at the collar, like a king's cape.
67 The mane of his mount was groomed to match,
68 combed and knotted into curlicues
69 then tinseled with gold, tied and twisted
70 green over gold, green over gold. . . .
71 The fetlocks were finished in the same fashion
72 with bright green ribbon braided with beads,
73 as was the tail—to its tippety-tip!
74 And a long, tied thong lacing it tight
75 was strung with gold bells which resounded and shone.
76 No waking man had witnessed such a warrior
77 or weird warhorse—otherworldly, yet flesh

Copyright © BookheadEd Learning, LLC

NOTES

78   and bone.
79   A look of lightning flashed
80   from somewhere in his soul.
81   The force of that man's fist
82   would be a thunderbolt.

83   Yet he wore no helmet and no hauberk either,
84   no armored apparel or plate was apparent,
85   and he swung no sword nor sported any shield,
86   but held in one hand a sprig of holly—
87   of all the evergreens the greenest ever—
88   and in the other hand held the mother of all axes,
89   a cruel piece of kit I kid you not:
90   the head was an ell in length at least
91   and forged in green steel with a gilt finish;
92   the skull-busting blade was so stropped and buffed
93   it could shear a man's scalp and shave him to boot.
94   The handle which fitted that fiend's great fist
95   was inlaid with iron, end to end,
96   with green pigment picking out impressive designs.
97   From stock to neck, where it stopped with a knot,
98   a lace was looped the length of the haft,
99   trimmed with tassels and tails of string
100 fastened firmly in place by forest-green buttons.
101 And he kicks on, canters through that crowded hall
102 towards the top table, not the least bit timid,
103 cocksure of himself, sitting high in the saddle.
104 "And who," he bellows, without breaking breath,
105 "is governor of this gaggle? I'll be glad to know.
106 It's with him and him alone that I'll have
107 my say."
108 The green man steered his gaze
109 deep into every eye,
110 explored each person's face
111 to probe for a reply.

112 The guests looked on. They gaped and they gawked
113 and were mute with amazement: what did it mean
114 that human and horse could develop this hue,
115 should grow to be grass-green or greener still,
116 like green enamel emboldened by bright gold?
117 Some stood and stared then stepped a little closer,
118 drawn near to the knight to know his next move;
119 they'd seen some sights, but this was something special,
120 a miracle or magic, or so they imagined.

121 Yet several of the lords were like statues in their seats,
122 left speechless and rigid, not risking a response.
123 The hall fell hushed, as if all who were present
124 had slipped into sleep or some trancelike state.
125 No doubt
126 not all were stunned and stilled
127 by dread, but duty bound
128 to hold their tongues
129 until their **sovereign** could respond.

130 Then the king acknowledged this curious occurrence,
131 cordially addressed him, keeping his cool.
132 "A warm welcome, sir, this winter's night.
133 My name is Arthur, I am head of this house.
134 Won't you slide from that saddle and stay awhile,
135 and the business which brings you we shall learn of later."
136 "No," said the knight, "it's not in my nature
137 to idle or allack about this evening.
138 But because your acclaim is so loudly chorused,
139 and your castle and brotherhood are called the best,
140 the strongest men to ever mount the saddle,
141 the worthiest knights ever known to the world,
142 both in competition and true combat,
143 and since courtesy, so it's said, is championed here,
144 I'm intrigued, and attracted to your door at this time.
145 Be assured by this hollin stem here in my hand
146 that I mean no menace. So expect no **malice**,
147 for if I'd slogged here tonight to slay and slaughter
148 my helmet and hauberk wouldn't be at home
149 and my sword and spear would be here at my side,
150 and more weapons of war, as I'm sure you're aware;
151 I'm clothed for peace, not kitted out for conflict.
152 But if you're half as honorable as I've heard folk say
153 you'll gracefully grant me this game which I ask for
154 by right."
155 Then Arthur answered, "Knight
156 most **courteous**, you claim
157 a fair, unarmored fight.
158 We'll see you have the same."

159 "I'm spoiling for no scrap, I swear. Besides,
160 the bodies on these benches are just bum-fluffed bairns.
161 If I'd ridden to your castle rigged out for a ruck¹

---

1. **rigged out for a ruck** prepared for a fight

162   these lightweight adolescents wouldn't last a minute.

163   But it's Yuletide—a time of youthfulness, yes?

164   So at Christmas in this court I lay down a challenge:

165   if a person here present, within these premises,

166   is big or bold or red blooded enough

167   to strike me one stroke and be struck in return,

168   I shall give him as a gift this gigantic cleaver

169   and the axe shall be his to handle how he likes.

170   I'll kneel, bare my neck and take the first knock.

171   So who has the gall? The gumption? The guts?

172   Who'll spring from his seat and snatch this weapon?

173   I offer the axe—who'll have it as his own?

174   I'll afford one free hit from which I won't flinch,

175   and promise that twelve months will pass in peace,

176   then claim

177   the duty I deserve

178   in one year and one day.

179   Does no one have the nerve

180   to wager in this way?"

181   Flustered at first, now totally foxed

182   were the household and the lords, both the highborn and the low.

183   Still stirruped, the knight swiveled round in his saddle

184   looking left and right, his red eyes rolling

185   beneath the bristles of his bushy green brows,

186   his beard swishing from side to side.

187   When the court kept its counsel he cleared his throat

188   and stiffened his spine. Then he spoke his mind:

189   "So here is the House of Arthur," he scoffed,

190   "whose virtues reverberate across vast realms.

191   Where's the **fortitude** and fearlessness you're so famous for?

192   And the breathtaking bravery and the big-mouth bragging?

193   The towering reputation of the Round Table,

194   skittled and scuppered by a stranger—what a scandal!

195   You flap and you flinch and I've not raised a finger!"

196   Then he laughed so loud that their leader saw red.

197   Blood flowed to his fine-featured face and he raged

198   inside.

199   His men were also hurt—

200   those words had pricked their pride.

201   But born so brave at heart

202   the king stepped up one stride.

203   "Your request," he countered, "is quite insane,

204   and folly finds the man who flirts with the fool.

205 No warrior worth his salt would be worried by your words,

206 so in heaven's good name hand over the axe

207 and I'll happily fulfill the favor you ask."

208 He strides to him swiftly and seizes his arm;

209 the man-mountain dismounts in one mighty leap.

210 Then Arthur grips the axe, grabs it by its haft

211 and takes it above him, intending to attack.

212 Yet the stranger before him stands up straight,

213 highest in the house by at least a head.

214 Quite simply he stands there stroking his beard,

215 fiddling with his coat, his face without fear,

216 about to be bludgeoned, but no more bothered

217 than a guest at the table being given a goblet

218 of wine.

219 By Guinevere, Gawain

220 now to his king inclines

221 and says, "I stake my claim.

222 This moment must be mine."

223 "Should you call me, courteous lord," said Gawain to his king,

224 "to rise from my seat and stand at your side,

225 politely take leave of my place at the table

226 and quit without causing offence to my queen,

227 then I shall come to your counsel before this great court.

228 For I find it unfitting, as my fellow knights would,

229 when a deed of such daring is dangled before us

230 that you take on this trial—tempted as you are—

231 when brave, bold men are seated on these benches,

232 men never matched in the mettle of their minds,

233 never beaten or bettered in the field of battle.

234 I am weakest of your warriors and feeblest of wit;

235 loss of my life would be grieved the least.

236 Were I not your nephew my life would mean nothing;

237 To be born of our blood is my body's only claim.

238 Such a foolish affair is unfitting for a king,

239 so, being first to come forward, it should fall to me.

240 And if my proposal is improper, let no other person

241 stand blame."

242 The knighthood then unites

243 and each knight says the same:

244 their king can stand aside

245 and give Gawain the game.

246 So the sovereign instructed his knight to stand.

247 Getting to his feet he moved graciously forward

248 and knelt before Arthur, taking hold of the axe.

249 Letting go of it, Arthur then held up his hand

250 to give young Gawain the blessing of God

251 and hope he finds firmness in heart and fist.

252 "Take care, young cousin, to catch him cleanly,

253 use full-blooded force then you needn't fear

254 the blow which he threatens to trade in return."

255 Gawain, with the weapon, walked towards the warrior,

256 and they stood face-to-face, not one man afraid.

257 Then the green knight spoke, growled at Gawain:

258 "Before we compete, repeat what we've promised.

259 And start by saying your name to me, sir,

260 and tell me the truth so I can take it on trust."

261 "In good faith, it's Gawain," said the God-fearing knight,

262 "I heave this axe, and whatever happens after,

263 in twelvemonth's time I'll be struck in return

264 with any weapon you wish, and by you and you

265 alone."

266 The other answers, says

267 "Well, by my living bones,

268 I welcome you Gawain

269 to bring the blade-head home."

270 "Gawain," said the green knight, "by God, I'm glad

271 the favor I've called for will fall from your fist.

272 You've perfectly repeated the promise we've made

273 and the terms of the contest are crystal clear.

274 Except for one thing: you must solemnly swear

275 that you'll seek me yourself; that you'll search me out

276 to the ends of the earth to earn the same blow

277 as you'll dole out today in this decorous hall."

278 "But where will you be? Where's your abode?

279 You're a man of mystery, as God is my maker.

280 Which court do you come from and what are you called?

281 There is knowledge I need, including your name,

282 then by wit I'll work out the way to your door

283 and keep to our contract, so cross my heart."

284 "But enough at New Year. It needs nothing more,"

285 said the war man in green to worthy Gawain.

286 "I could tell you the truth once you've taken the blow;

287 if you smite me smartly I could spell out the facts

288 of my house and home and my name, if it helps,

289 Then you'll pay me a visit and vouch for our pact.

290 Or if I keep quiet you might cope much better,

291 loafing and lounging here, looking no further. But

292 you stall!
293 Now grasp that gruesome axe
294 And show your striking style."
295 He answered, "since you ask,"
296 And touched the tempered steel.

297 In the standing position he prepared to be struck,
298 bent forward, revealing a flash of green flesh
299 as he heaped his hair to the crown of his head,
300 the nape of his neck now naked and ready.
301 Gawain grips the axe and heaves it heavenwards
302 plants his left foot firmly on the floor in front,
303 then swings it swiftly towards the bare skin.
304 The cleanness of the strike cleaved the spinal cord
305 and parted the fat and the flesh so far
306 that the bright steel blade took a bite from the floor.
307 The handsome head tumbles onto the earth
308 and the king's men kick it as it clatters past.
309 Blood gutters brightly against his green gown,
310 yet the man doesn't shudder or stagger or sink
311 but trudges towards them on those tree-trunk legs
312 and rummages around, reaches at their feet
313 and cops hold of his head and hoists it high,
314 and strides to his steed, snatches the bridle,
315 steps into the stirrups and swings onto the saddle
316 still gripping his head by a handful of hair.
317 Then he settles himself in his seat with the ease
318 of a man unmarked, never mind being minus
319 his head!
320 And when he wheeled about
321 his bloody neck still bled.
322 His point was proved. The court
323 was deadened now with dread.

324 For that scalp and skull now swung from his fist;
325 towards the top table he turned the face
326 and it opened its eyelids, started straight ahead
327 and spoke this speech, which you'll hear for yourselves:
328 "Sir Gawain, be wise enough to keep your word
329 and faithfully follow me until I'm found
330 as you vowed in this hall within hearing of these horsemen.
331 You're charged with getting to the Green Chapel,
332 To reap what you've sown. You'll rightfully receive
333 the justice you are due just as January dawns.
334 Men know my name as the Green Chapel knight

NOTES

335 and even a fool couldn't fail to find me.
336 So come, or be called a coward forever."
337 With a tug of the reigns he twisted around
338 and, head still in hand, galloped out of the hall,
339 so the hooves brought the fire from the flame in the flint.
340 Which Kingdom he came from they hadn't a clue,
341 no more than they knew where he made for next.
342 And then?
343 Well, with the green man gone
344 they laughed and grinned again.
345 And yet such goings-on
346 were magic to those men.

347 And although King Arthur was awestruck at heart
348 No signed of it showed. Instead he spoke
349 to his queen of queens with courteous words:
350 "Dear lady, don't be daunted by this deed today,
351 it's in keeping that such strangeness should occur at Christmas
352 between sessions of banter and seasonal song,
353 amid the lively pastimes of ladies and lords.
354 And at the least I'm allowed to eat at last,
355 having witnessed such wonder, wouldn't you say?
356 Then he glanced at Gawain and was **graceful** with his words:
357 "Now hang up your axe—one hack is enough."
358 So it dangled from the drape behind the dais[2]
359 so that men who saw it would be mesmerised and amazed,
360 And give it voice, on its evidence, to the stunning event.
361 Then the two of them turned and walked to the table,
362 the monarch and his man, and were met with food—
363 double dishes apiece, rare delicacies,
364 all manners of meals—and the music of minstrels.
365 And they danced and sang till the sun went down
366 that day.
367 But mind your mood, Gawain,
368 keep blacker thoughts at bay,
369 or lose this lethal game
370 you've promised you will play.

From SIR GAWAIN AND THE GREEN KNIGHT: A NEW VERSE TRANSLATION, translated by Simon Armitage. Copyright © 2007 by Simon Armitage. Used by permission of W. W. Norton & Company, Inc.

2. **dais** a raised platform upon which sits a throne

WRITE

LITERARY ANALYSIS: How does the portrayal of Gawain in this excerpt reveal the values and code of conduct of medieval knights? Use textual evidence and original commentary to support your response.

Please note that excerpts and passages in the StudySync® library and this workbook are intended as touchstones to generate interest in an author's work. The excerpts and passages do not substitute for the reading of entire texts, and StudySync® strongly recommends that students seek out and purchase the whole literary or informational work in order to experience it as the author intended. Links to online resellers are available in our digital library. In addition, complete works may be ordered through an authorized reseller by filling out and returning to StudySync® the order form enclosed in this workbook.

Reading & Writing
Companion
251

Truth Serum

POETRY
Naomi Shihab Nye
2005

Introduction

Naomi Shihab Nye (b. 1952) is an American poet living in San Antonio, Texas. Raised in both Jerusalem and San Antonio, Nye often focuses on ancestry and cultural differences in her writing, celebrating the everyday occurrences of life. She is considered one of the great poets of the American Southwest and has published many critically acclaimed volumes of poetry. "Truth Serum" was included

"That frog song wanting nothing but echo? / We used that."

NOTES

1 We made it from the ground-up corn in the old back **pasture**.
2 Pinched a scent of night jasmine **billowing** off the fence,
3 popped it right in.
4 That frog song wanting nothing but echo?
5 We used that.
6 Stirred it widely. Noticed the clouds while stirring.
7 Called upon our **ancient** great aunts and their long slow eyes
8 of summer. Dropped in their names.
9 Added a mint leaf now and then
10 to hearten the broth. Added a note of cheer and worry.
11 Orange butterfly between the claps of thunder?
12 Perfect. And once we had it,
13 had smelled and tasted the **fragrant** syrup,
14 placing the pan on a back burner for keeping,
15 the sorrow lifted in small ways.
16 We boiled down the lies in another pan till they disappeared.
17 We washed that pan.

Naomi Shihab Nye, "Truth Serum" from You & Yours. Copyright © 2005 by Naomi Shihab Nye. Reprinted with the permission of The Permissions Company, Inc. on behalf of BOA Editions, Ltd., www.boaeditions.org.

✎ WRITE

POETRY: Think about places, people, and experiences that bring truth and happiness into your life. Then write a poem about "Truth Serum" as you see it applied to your life. You may use Naomi Shihab Nye's poem, including her use of sensory details, as a model for your own writing.

Please note that excerpts and passages in the StudySync® library and this workbook are intended as touchstones to generate interest in an author's work. The excerpts and passages do not substitute for the reading of entire texts, and StudySync® strongly recommends that students seek out and purchase the whole literary or informational work in order to experience it as the author intended. Links to online resellers are available in our digital library. In addition, complete works may be ordered through an authorized reseller by filling out and returning to StudySync® the order form enclosed in this workbook.

Reading & Writing Companion   253

Richard III

DRAMA
William Shakespeare
1592

Introduction

I n this famous soliloquy from the opening of Shakespeare's *Richard III*, Richard
muses on his circumstances and his plans to seize the throne from his brother

"Now is the winter of our discontent / Made glorious summer by this son of York."

From Act I, Scene i:

Characters:
RICHARD, DUKE OF GLOUCESTER: brother to the King Edward IV, afterwards King Richard III

Location: *London. A street.*

1   [*Enter* RICHARD DUKE of GLOUCESTER, *solus.*]

2   GLOUCESTER: Now is the winter of our discontent
3   Made glorious summer by this son of York[1];
4   And all the clouds that low'r'd upon our house
5   In the deep bosom of the ocean buried.
6   Now are our brows bound with victorious wreaths,
7   Our bruised arms hung up for monuments,
8   Our stern alarums[2] chang'd to merry meetings,
9   Our dreadful marches to delightful measures.
10   Grim-visag'd War hath smooth'd his wrinkled front;
11   And now, in stead of mounting barded steeds
12   To fright the souls of fearful adversaries,
13   He capers nimbly in a lady's chamber
14   To the **lascivious** pleasing of a lute.
15   But I, that am not shap'd for sportive tricks,
16   Nor made to court an amorous looking-glass;
17   I, that am rudely stamp'd, and **want** love's majesty
18   To strut before a **wanton** ambling nymph;
19   I, that am curtail'd of this fair proportion,
20   Cheated of feature by **dissembling** nature,
21   Deform'd, unfinish'd, sent before my time
22   Into this breathing world, scarce half made up,

Engraving of King Richard III, 1611

1. **son of York** Richard's brother, King Edward IV, of the York family
2. **stern alarums** alarms, or calls to battle

NOTES

23 And that so lamely and unfashionable

24 That dogs bark at me as I halt by them—

25 Why, I, in this weak piping time of peace,

26 Have no delight to pass away the time,

27 Unless to see my shadow in the sun

28 And **descant** on mine own deformity.

29 And therefore, since I cannot prove a lover

30 To entertain these fair well-spoken days,

31 I am determined to prove a villain

32 And hate the idle pleasures of these days.

33 Plots have I laid, inductions dangerous,

34 By drunken prophecies, libels, and dreams,

35 To set my brother Clarence and the King

36 In deadly hate the one against the other;

37 And if King Edward be as true and just

38 As I am subtle, false, and treacherous,

39 This day should Clarence closely be mew'd up

40 About a prophecy, which says that G

41 Of Edward's heirs the murtherer shall be.

42 Dive, thoughts, down to my soul, here Clarence comes!

✎ WRITE

CORRESPONDENCE: In the persona of Richard III, write a confessional letter explaining why you choose to be a villain. Use your own words to paraphrase the reasons stated in the soliloquy, but maintain the meaning and logical order of the original text.

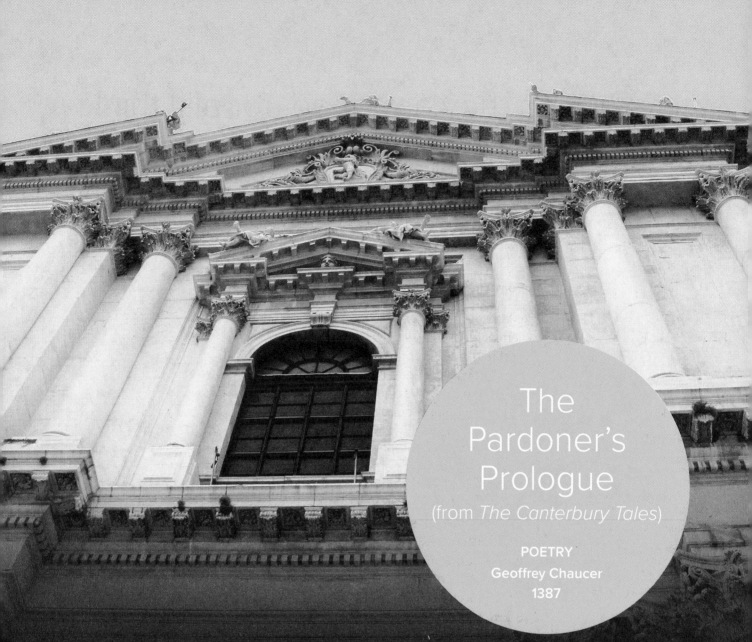

The Pardoner's Prologue

(from *The Canterbury Tales*)

POETRY
Geoffrey Chaucer
1387

Introduction

On a pilgrimage from London to Canterbury Cathedral to visit the shrine of St. Thomas Becket, twenty-nine people from various walks of life engage in a storytelling contest. Despite the fact that they are gathered for a spiritual purpose, many of them seem distracted by more earthly concerns. Their two dozen stories comprise *The Canterbury Tales* by Geoffrey Chaucer (c. 1343–1400), one of the foundational works of English literature. Offering social commentary that is not without humor, irony, and wit, the collection features classic musings like "The Pardoner's Prologue," in which the Pardoner—a sort of preacher who sells promises of salvation for a price—introduces himself to the group by launching into

"When they are dead, for all I think thereon / Their souls may well black-berrying have gone!"

**Skill:
Point of View**

The Pardoner is revealing something to the reader. This stanza suggests he is a performer and has his lines memorized. His audience probably thinks his sermon is honest and isn't aware it's a performance.

**Skill:
Point of View**

This reminds me of the beginning. The relics don't actually have power, but the audience doesn't share that knowledge. He is taking advantage of them and exaggerating the powers of the objects.

1   **from The Prologue of the Pardoner's Tale:**

2   "Masters," quoth he, "in churches, when I preach,
3   I am at pains that all shall hear my speech,
4   And ring it out as roundly as a bell,
5   For I know all by heart the thing I tell.
6   My **theme** is always one, and ever was:
7   '*Radix malorum est cupiditas.*[1]'

8   "First I announce the place whence I have come,
9   And then I show my pardons, all and some.
10 Our liege-lord's seal on my patent perfect,
11 I show that first, my safety to protect,
12 And then no man's so old, no priest nor clerk,
13 As to disturb me in Christ's holy work;
14 And after that my tales I marshal all.
15 Indulgences of pope and cardinal,
16 Of **patriarch** and bishop, these I do
17 Show, and in Latin speak some words, a few,
18 To spice therewith a bit my sermoning
19 And stir men to devotion, marvelling.
20 Then show I forth my hollow crystal-stones,
21 Which are crammed full of rags, aye, and of bones;
22 Relics are these, as they think, every one.
23 Then I've in latten box a shoulder bone
24 Which came out of a holy Hebrew's sheep.
25 'Good men,' say I, 'my words in memory keep;
26 If this bone shall be washed in any well,
27 Then if a cow, calf, sheep, or ox should swell
28 That's eaten snake, or been by serpent stung,
29 Take water of that well and wash its tongue,
30 And 'twill be well anon; and furthermore,
31 Of pox and scab and every other sore

---

1. **Radix malorum est cupiditas** translated from Biblical Latin: "the root of evil is greed"

32   Shall every sheep be healed that of this well
33   Drinks but one draught; take heed of what I tell.
34   And if the man that owns the beasts, I trow,
35   Shall every week, and that before cock-crow,
36   And before breakfast, drink thereof a draught,
37   As that Jew taught of yore in his priestcraft,
38   His beasts and all his store shall multiply.
39   And, good sirs, it's a cure for jealousy;
40   For though a man be fallen in jealous rage,
41   Let one make of this water his pottage
42   And nevermore shall he his wife mistrust,
43   Though he may know the truth of all her lust,
44   Even though she'd taken two priests, aye, or three.

45   " 'Here is a mitten, too, that you may see.
46   Who puts his hand therein, I say again,
47   He shall have increased harvest of his grain,
48   After he's sown, be it of wheat or oats,
49   Just so he offers pence or offers groats.

50   " 'Good men and women, one thing I warn you,
51   If any man be here in church right now
52   That's done a sin so horrible that he
53   Dare not, for shame of that sin **shriven** be,
54   Or any woman, be she young or old,
55   That's made her husband into a cuckold[2],
56   Such folk shall have no power and no grace
57   To offer to my relics in this place.
58   But whoso finds himself without such blame,
59   He will come up and offer, in God's name,
60   And I'll absolve him by authority
61   That has, by bull, been granted unto me.'

62   "By this fraud have I won me, year by year,
63   A hundred marks, since I've been pardoner.
64   I stand up like a scholar in a pulpit,
65   And when the ignorant people all do sit,
66   I preach, as you have heard me say before,
67   And tell a hundred false japes, less or more.
68   I am at pains, then, to stretch forth my neck,
69   And east and west upon the folk I beck,
70   As does a dove that's sitting on a barn.
71   With hands and swift tongue, then, do I so yarn

---

2. **cuckold** has been sexually unfaithful to

Skill:
Connotation
and Denotation

I think the word "fraud" can have negative connotations. The Pardoner seems to admit he has a habit of lying to "ignorant people."

The dictionary definition of "fraud" is "wrongful or criminal deception" which confirms the negative connotation as it is used.

Please note that excerpts and passages in the StudySync® library and this workbook are intended as touchstones to generate interest in an author's work. The excerpts and passages do not substitute for the reading of entire texts, and StudySync® strongly recommends that students seek out and purchase the whole literary or informational work in order to experience it as the author intended. Links to online resellers are available in our digital library. In addition, complete works may be ordered through an authorized reseller by filling out and returning to StudySync® the order form enclosed in this workbook.

Reading & Writing
Companion

259

72   That it's a joy to see my busyness.

73   Of **avarice** and of all such wickedness

74   Is all my preaching, thus to make them free

75   With offered pence, the which pence come to me.

76   For my intent is only pence to win,

77   And not at all for punishment of sin.

78   When they are dead, for all I think thereon

79   Their souls may well black-berrying have gone!

80   For, certainly, there's many a sermon grows

81   Ofttimes from evil purpose, as one knows;

82   Some for folks' pleasure and for flattery,

83   To be advanced by all hypocrisy,

84   And some for vainglory, and some for hate.

85   For, when I dare not otherwise debate,

86   Then do I sharpen well my tongue and sting

87   The man in sermons, and upon him fling

88   My lying **defamations**, if but he

89   Has wronged my brethren or—much worse—wronged me.

90   For though I mention not his proper name,

91   Men know whom I refer to, all the same,

92   By signs I make and other circumstances.

93   Thus I pay those who do us displeasances.

94   Thus spit I out my venom under hue

95   Of holiness, to seem both good and true.

96   "But briefly my intention I'll express;

97   I preach no sermon, save for covetousness.

98   For that my theme is yet, and ever was,

99   *'Radix malorum est cupiditas.'*

100   Thus can I preach against that self-same vice

101   Which I indulge, and that is avarice.

102   But though myself be guilty of that sin,

103   Yet can I cause these other folk to win

104   From avarice and really to repent.

105   But that is not my principal intent.

106   I preach no sermon, save for covetousness;

107   This should suffice of that, though, as I guess.

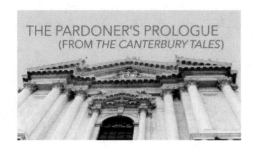

THE PARDONER'S PROLOGUE
(FROM *THE CANTERBURY TALES*)

First Read

Read "The Pardoner's Prologue." After you read, complete the Think Questions below.

☁ THINK QUESTIONS

1. In stanza two, the Pardoner says, "Our liege-lord's seal on my patent perfect, / I show that first, my safety to protect, / And then no man's so old, no priest nor clerk, / As to disturb me in Christ's holy work." What can you infer about the Pardoner's attitude about the bulls, or official public decrees, that he carries? What purpose do they serve for him? Cite evidence from the text to support your explanation.

2. What are the two relics, or religious objects imbued with miraculous powers, that the Pardoner discusses? What are the specific alleged powers of these seemingly banal objects, according to the Pardoner? Cite evidence from the text to support your answer.

3. Citing the Pardoner's own words, what do you think he is most concerned about? How deeply is he invested in the salvation of his congregants?

4. The Latin word *pater* means "father." With this information in mind and using context clues from the text, write your best definition of the word **patriarch** here.

5. What is the meaning of the word **avarice** as it is used in the text? Write your best definition here, along with a brief explanation of how you arrived at its meaning.

Skill:
Point of View

Use the Checklist to analyze Point of View in "The Pardoner's Prologue." Refer to the sample student annotations about Point of View in the text.

••• CHECKLIST FOR POINT OF VIEW

To grasp a character's point of view in which what is directly stated is different from what is really meant, note the following:

✓ Literary techniques intended to provide humor or criticism. Examples of these include:

- Sarcasm or the use of language that says one thing, but means the opposite.

- Irony or a contrast between what one expects to happen and what happens.

- Understatement or an instance where a character deliberately makes a situation seem less important or serious than it is.

- Satire or the use of humor, irony, exaggeration, or ridicule to expose and criticize people's foolishness or vices.

✓ Possible critiques an author might be making about contemporary society through theme or characters' actions and words.

✓ An unreliable narrator or character whose point of view cannot be trusted.

To analyze a case in which grasping a point of view requires distinguishing what is directly stated in a text from what is really meant, consider the following questions:

✓ When do you notice that the reader's point of view differs from that of the character or speaker in this text?

✓ How does a character's or narrator's point of view contribute to a non-literal understanding of the text?

✓ How does the use of sarcasm, understatement, or satire add meaning to the story?

✓ How does the author use these techniques to expose or criticize some aspect of society?

Copyright © Bookheaded Learning, LLC

Skill:
Point of View

Reread lines 14–43 from "The Pardoner's Prologue." Then, using the Checklist on the previous page, answer the multiple-choice questions below.

↻ YOUR TURN

1. The Pardoner uses figurative language when he states "To spice therewith a bit my sermoning / And stir men to devotion, marvelling. . ." Why does the Pardoner use this metaphor?

   ○ A. He uses the metaphor to explain how he makes his sermons more appetizing so he can better trick the churchgoers.

   ○ B. He uses the metaphor to explain the process of using potions and relics in the forgiveness of sin.

   ○ C. The metaphor serves to educate the churchgoers.

   ○ D. He uses the metaphor to persuade the churchgoers.

2. Which of the following phrases make it clear that the Pardoner knows he is a liar?

   ○ A. "And, good sirs, it's a cure for jealousy;"

   ○ B. "Shall every sheep be healed that of this well / Drinks but one draught"

   ○ C. "Then show I forth my hollow crystal-stones,"

   ○ D. "Relics are these, as they think, every one"

3. This question has two parts. First, answer Part A. Then, answer Part B.

   Part A: Which statement best reflects the relationship the Pardoner has with the churchgoers?

   ○ A. He respects them and seeks their advice on religious matters.

   ○ B. He tries to manipulate them and hide his true intentions.

   ○ C. He tries to help them but is concerned they won't accept it.

   ○ D. He believes they are intelligent but immoral.

Part B: Which of the following quotes from the text BEST supports the answer in Part A?

○ A. "Then show I forth my hollow crystal-stones, / Which are crammed full of rags, aye, and of bones; / Relics are these, as they think, every one."

○ B. "Then I've in latten box a shoulder bone / Which came out of a holy Hebrew's sheep."

○ C. "If this bone shall be washed in any well, / Then if a cow, calf, sheep, or ox should swell That's eaten snake, or been by serpent stung, / Take water of that well and wash its tongue."

○ D. "As that Jew taught of yore in his priestcraft, / His beasts and all his store shall multiply."

Skill:
Connotation and Denotation

Use the Checklist to analyze Connotation and Denotation in "The Pardoner's Prologue." Refer to the sample student annotations about Connotation and Denotation in the text.

••• CHECKLIST FOR CONNOTATION AND DENOTATION

In order to identify the denotative meanings of words, use the following steps:

- ✓ first, note unfamiliar words and phrases, key words used to describe important characters, events, and ideas, or words that inspire an emotional reaction

- ✓ next, determine and note the denotative meaning of words by consulting a reference material such as a dictionary, glossary, or thesaurus

- ✓ finally, analyze nuances in the meaning of words with similar denotations

To better understand the meaning of words and phrases as they are used in a text, including connotative meanings, use the following questions as a guide:

- ✓ What is the genre or subject of the text? Based on context, what do you think the meaning of the word is intended to be?

- ✓ Is your inference the same or different from the dictionary definition?

- ✓ Does the word create a positive, negative, or neutral emotion?

- ✓ What synonyms or alternative phrasing help you describe the connotative meaning of the word?

To determine the meaning of words and phrases as they are used in a text, including connotative meanings, use the following questions as a guide:

- ✓ What is the denotative meaning of the word? Is that denotative meaning correct in context?

- ✓ What possible positive, neutral, or negative connotations might the word have, depending on context?

- ✓ What textual details signal a particular connotation for the word?

Skill:
Connotation and Denotation

Reread lines 68–79 from "The Pardoner's Prologue." Then, using the Checklist on the previous page, answer the multiple-choice questions below.

⟳ YOUR TURN

1. In line 70, the metaphor, "As does a dove that's sitting on a barn," connotes:

   ○ A. the churchgoers are naive and easily duped by the pardoner's false sermons,
   ○ B. the churchgoers are commoners who require the guidance of the more-educated pardoner.
   ○ C. the pardoner is a nuisance who annoys churchgoers by continually asking for donations.
   ○ D. the pardoner is a greedy figure who is swindling churchgoers by trying to seem innocent.

2. What does "When they are dead, for all I think thereon," suggest about the Pardoner?

   ○ A. It suggests the Pardoner's job is finished once someone dies.
   ○ B. It suggests the Pardoner is ignorant when it comes to matters related to death and dying.
   ○ C. It suggests the Pardoner does not care about the souls of his followers.
   ○ D. It suggests the Pardoner participates in burial rites.

3. This question has two parts. First, answer Part A. Then, answer Part B.

   Part A: Which sentence best describes the Pardoner's attitude toward the churchgoers?
   ○ A. He is very concerned about helping the churchgoers go to heaven.
   ○ B. He does not really care whether the churchgoers go to heaven.
   ○ C. He is very concerned about helping the churchgoers become good citizens.
   ○ D. He does not really care whether the churchgoers become good citizens.

   Part B: Which of the following quotes from the text best supports the answer in Part A?
   ○ A. "And east and west upon the folk I beck"
   ○ B. "With hands and swift tongue, then, do I so yarn / That it's a joy to see my busyness."
   ○ C. "When they are dead, for all I think thereon / Their souls may well black-berrying have gone!"
   ○ D. "For my intent is only pence to win, / And not at all for punishment of sin."

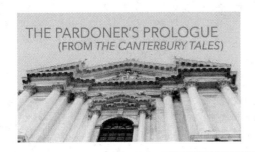

THE PARDONER'S PROLOGUE
(FROM *THE CANTERBURY TALES*)

Close Read

Reread "The Pardoner's Prologue." As you reread, complete the Skills Focus questions below. Then use your answers and annotations from the questions to help you complete the Write activity.

◎ SKILLS FOCUS

1. Sometimes, a character is not completely clear on what they themselves think, and they are wrestling with more than one opinion or point of view. Identify a moment in the text where the Pardoner seems to believe one thing, and then identify a moment in the text where he seems to believe another. Explain why you chose these two passages.

2. Situational irony occurs when the outcome of a situation is the opposite of what was expected. Identify the outcome of the Pardoner's sermons, and explain why it is ironic.

3. The Pardoner makes his living by selling his relics and services to people who believe in him. How does the Pardoner describe his work? What does this reveal about him and what he thinks of his job in the church? Highlight specific words in the text and explain how these words reveal his opinion of the church and his work.

4. The Pardoner tells this story while on a pilgrimage. How does his context — a long journey to a religious destination — cause him to reflect on his true self?

✏ WRITE

MONOLOGUE: In "The Pardoner's Prologue," Chaucer satirizes medieval society by highlighting the greediness of a church official who shamelessly tries to swindle people, convincing them to give him money in exchange for pardons. Think of today's society and imagine a person who represents some sort of corruption or foolishness. Then, write a short satirical monologue to expose that person's true motives.

The English Renaissance

Introduction

This introduction to English Renaissance literature provides readers with the historical and cultural context of the period. The Renaissance movement, inspired by the reign of Queen Elizabeth I and humanist ideals, gave rise to one of the most prolific writers in the English language: William Shakespeare. It was a time in which human experience had more value than ever before. Independent thought, along with scientific and artistic endeavors, were more and more common, contributing to an inspiring culture in which Shakespeare could craft his legendary dramas. Meaning "rebirth" in French, the Renaissance gave birth to some of the most memorable and influential works in the English canon.

"To the humanists, human endeavor had dignity and worth in its own right."

Copyright © BookheadEd Learning, LLC

NOTES

1   In May of 2018, Nielsen reported that 29.2 million Americans watched the wedding of Prince Henry and Meghan Markle. Seven years earlier, 22.8 million Americans tuned in to watch Harry's older brother, William, marry Kate Middleton. Why are so many Americans still interested in the royal family nearly 250 years after the United States broke free from British control? The British royals remain international tastemakers. People from all around the world try to emulate their style and preferences. That remains as true today as it was during the seventeenth century, when the tastes of royals like Queen Elizabeth I helped artistic movements gain fans both at home and abroad.

Tudor England

2   The **Tudors** reigned between the fifteenth and seventeenth centuries in England. The first **monarch** of the Tudor dynasty, Henry VII, came into power in 1485. Henry earned the English crown after defeating Richard III, ending the 30-year civil war known as the War of the Roses. His son, Henry VIII, ruled following Henry VII's death in 1509. Three of Henry VIII's children sat on the English throne between 1547 and 1603. Edward VI immediately succeeded his father. After Edward died of tuberculosis, Mary I ruled for a mere five years before her own death. Mary's rule was brief but intense. She received the nickname "Bloody Mary" due to her persecution of Protestants in an attempt to restore Catholicism as the state religion. Elizabeth I reversed this position when she took control of the country in 1558. Despite the religious and political conflicts that divided the Tudors, by the time Elizabeth took the crown a burst of creative energy brought a golden age of culture to England.

Queen Elizabeth

3   Many people celebrated Elizabeth I's ascension to the throne, which restored peace after Mary I's short, turbulent reign. During her reign, Elizabeth was praised for her wit, eloquence, and intellect. Unlike other girls and young women of the time, Elizabeth received a strong formal education. As a result, she was well-versed in many subjects, including mathematics, history, geography, and astronomy, and literate in Greek, Latin, and several other modern languages.

NOTES

4   Elizabeth's reign was long and eventful. During her 45 years on the throne, she overcame numerous challenges that came from religious conflicts, political intrigue, and threats of war. Many believed that a queen could not rule successfully without a king by her side, but Elizabeth never married. Instead, she proved herself to be more than capable of facing international crises and defending her country. Under Elizabeth's guidance, England became a great sea power capable of defeating its enemies, including the powerful Spanish **Armada** sent by Philip II in an attempt to seize control of England. Additionally, Elizabeth supported a flourishing period of cultural achievement that came to be known as the English **Renaissance**.

Painting of the Spanish Armada in the collection of the National Maritime Museum, Greenwich, England

The Renaissance

5   Spanning the fourteenth and seventeenth centuries, the Renaissance was a vast artistic and cultural movement that started in Italy and spread across Europe. French for "rebirth," the Renaissance marks a period of time between the Middle Ages and the modern world in which there was renewed interest in the sciences and art. During this time, a movement called **humanism** began to take shape. In general, humanists relished new ideas and shared a lively interest in the affairs of the world. This was a shift from medieval art that focused on the afterlife and other religious themes.

6   Humanists also emphasized the ability of the individual to think independently, without guidance from higher authorities. Inspired by political, scientific, and philosophical questions, humanists sought to better understand their own world. During this time period, people painted, sculpted, and composed music as never before as they found their own voices and began to express their own ideas. The value that humanism placed on human experience has permanently altered the way people view and judge the world. For instance,

humanism's emphasis on intellectual questioning and direct observation is a forerunner to modern scientific methods.

Shakespeare's Humanism

7   Perhaps no Renaissance writer is more well-known than William Shakespeare. More than 400 years after his death, the poet and playwright is still said to be the world's favorite author. Shakespeare is beloved for both the characters he created and the language he used in his writing. His ability to absorb and transform different kinds of material, ranging from the political issues of his own time to events from Roman and English history, reflects humanist ideals. Shakespeare's tragedies and histories focus on complex individuals who seek to fulfill their full potential while also grappling with painful, difficult dilemmas. At the same time, his comedies are robust with jokes and songs that provide audiences with an escape from their own problems. From Puck to Hamlet and Falstaff to Lady Macbeth, Shakespeare's canon portrays a complete range of human experiences. Young and old, women and men, good and evil, beggars and kings—characters from all walks of life live in Shakespeare's plays.

Ophelia offering fennel and columbines, engraving from
The Illustrated London News, 1892.

Major Concepts

8   • **Humanism**—To the humanists, human endeavor had dignity and worth in its own right. Influenced by this idea, English writers began to shift their focus from religious concerns and concentrate on secular subjects, such as love, politics, science, and philosophy. Later, in the 18th century, a movement called the Enlightenment builds on the ideas of individual dignity, rational thought, and secular law.

   • **A Bard for the Ages**—William Shakespeare was a singular genius who wrote poems and plays that represent the full flowering of the English Renaissance. His characters, seeking to fulfill their potential, are constantly

Reading & Writing
Companion

probing and striving, demonstrating their wit at court, displaying their courage on the battlefield, falling in love and writing poetry, or devising plots to bring about their deepest desires, whether loving or vengeful.

Style and Form

Shakespearean Drama

9 •   Shakespeare invented little content out of thin air. Instead, he dramatized stories from sources such as Petrarch and Holinshed, often combining elements from multiple accounts of the same story.

•   Shakespeare's plays follow a strict format. Each has five acts, and each of those acts contain scenes. Characters express themselves through dialogue as well as soliloquies and monologues. A soliloquy is a speech delivered directly to the audience in which a character reveals his or her innermost thoughts. A monologue is a long speech delivered to another character.

•   Subplots, or minor plotlines that support the main plot, are common in Shakespearean drama. Conflicts often arise between characters due to misunderstandings or misinformation that stems from an event that takes place in a subplot.

•   Shakespeare's language varies from play to play and sometimes within a play. He is known for writing in iambic pentameter. In this meter, each line has five units, known as feet, and each foot contains an unstressed syllable followed by a stressed syllable. He often uses iambic pentameter to write in blank verse, or writing with a regular meter but without a regular rhyme scheme. He may also include some rhyming couplets for emphasis. However, the language in Shakespeare's plays is not limited to any particular style or meter. He also uses prose, which is ordinary speech without meter or rhyme, when more formal language may seem out of place.

•   Sophisticated, intricate language is a trademark of Shakespearean drama. Many plays include elaborate extended metaphors as well as bawdy puns, word play, and double entendres. Humor is always present, even in his tragedies.

10   In addition to featuring characters from all walks of life, Shakespeare's plays drew crowds made up of members from every level of society. Although most of Shakespeare's works were written after her death, there is proof that Queen Elizabeth I watched several of his plays at court. Elizabeth's successor, James I, even became a patron of Shakespeare's theater company, which was renamed The King's Men. With a focus on individual thought and experiences, it is easy to see why Shakespearean drama and other humanist works were so popular during the Renaissance and continue to be valued. How do the ideas introduced and developed through Renaissance literature continue to inspire audiences today?

Literary Focus

Read "Literary Focus: The English Renaissance." After you read, complete the Think Questions below.

☁ THINK QUESTIONS

1. Why was Elizabeth I an important monarch who is still remembered today? Provide two or three reasons, citing evidence from the text to support your response.

2. What were humanists interested in and inspired by? Explain, citing evidence from the text to support your response.

3. Based on the information in the reading, explain what a soliloquy is. Why do you think Shakespeare was able to make this form of dramatic speech so popular during the Renaissance specifically? Use evidence from the text to help support your explanations.

4. Use context clues to determine the meaning of the word **monarch**. Write your definition here, along with the specific words or phrases that helped you come to your conclusion. Then, check a dictionary to confirm your understanding.

5. What is the meaning of the word **armada** as it used in this text? Write your best definition here, in addition to an explanation of how you arrived at the word's meaning.

Please note that excerpts and passages in the StudySync® library and this workbook are intended as touchstones to generate interest in an author's work. The excerpts and passages do not substitute for the reading of entire texts, and StudySync® strongly recommends that students seek out and purchase the whole literary or informational work in order to experience it as the author intended. Links to online resellers are available in our digital library. In addition, complete works may be ordered through an authorized reseller by filling out and returning to StudySync® the order form enclosed in this workbook.

Reading & Writing Companion   **273**

Shakespeare:
The World as Stage

ARGUMENTATIVE TEXT
Bill Bryson
2007

Introduction

Known for his distinctly humorous writing style, Bill Bryson (b. 1951) is a highly regarded American author of various nonfiction books on travel, science, language, and other topics. Bryson's biography of William Shakespeare, *Shakespeare: The World as Stage*, focuses on what little is known conclusively about the famous playwright and poet. The excerpt here discusses the Shakespeare authorship debate.

"The presumption is that William Shakespeare of Stratford was, at best, an amiable stooge . . ."

From Chapter 9: Claimants

1   There is an extraordinary—seemingly an **insatiable**—urge on the part of quite a number of people to believe that the plays of William Shakespeare were written by someone other than William Shakespeare. The number of published books suggesting—or more often insisting—as much is estimated now to be well over five thousand.

2   Shakespeare's plays, it is held, so brim with expertise—on law, medicine, statesmanship, court life, military affairs, the bounding main, antiquity, life abroad—that they cannot possibly be the work of a single lightly educated **provincial**. The presumption is that William Shakespeare of Stratford was, at best, an amiable **stooge**, an actor who lent his name as cover for someone of greater talent, someone who could not, for one reason or another, be publicly identified as a playwright.

3   The controversy has been given respectful airing in the highest quarters. PBS, the American television network, in 1996 produced an hour-long documentary **unequivocally** suggesting that Shakespeare probably wasn't Shakespeare. *Harper's Magazine* and *The New York Times* have both devoted generous amounts of space to sympathetically considering the anti-Stratford arguments[1]. The Smithsonian Institution in 2002 held a seminar titled "Who Wrote Shakespeare?" The best-read article in the British magazine *History Today* was one examining the authorship question. Even *Scientific American* entered the fray with an article proposing that the person portrayed in the famous Martin Droeshout engraving[2] might actually be—I weep to say it—Elizabeth I. Perhaps the most extraordinary development of all is that Shakespeare's Globe Theater in London—built as a monument for his plays and with aspirations to be a world-class study center—became, under the

NOTES

Skill:
Central or Main
Idea

Based on the first sentence I know that Bryson's main idea will address the Shakespeare debate. Since he is not referring to himself, I can infer that Bryson does not agree that someone other than Shakespeare created these works.

---

1. **anti-Stratford arguments** referring to the idea that William Shakespeare of Stratford was not the real author of the plays attributed to him
2. **the famous Martin Droeshout engraving** a famous portrait of Shakespeare engraved by Martin Droeshout appearing on the title page of the collection of Shakespeare's plays published in 1623

NOTES

Skill:
Connotation and
Denotation

Bryson calls Wright's description of Shakespeare 'wildly imaginative." This is an insult since historians write about facts. In fact, "unimpeachable" means reliable, which tells me he takes issue with Rubinstein's imagination.

Skill:
Informational Text
Elements

Bryson uses records from that time period as evidence to support his argument. This record lends credibility and refutes assumptions made by the opposition.

stewardship of the artistic director Mark Rylance, a kind of clearinghouse for anti-Stratford sentiment.

4 So it needs to be said that nearly all of the anti-Shakespeare sentiment— actually all of it, every bit—involves manipulative scholarship or sweeping misstatements of fact. Shakespeare "never owned a book," a writer for *The New York Times* gravely informed readers in one doubting article in 2002. The statement cannot actually be refuted, for we know nothing about his incidental possessions. But the writer might just as well have suggested that Shakespeare never owned a pair of shoes or pants. For all the evidence tells us, he spent his life unclothed as well as bookless, but it is probable that what is lacking is the evidence, not the apparel or the books.

5 Daniel Wright, a professor at Concordia University in Portland, Oregon, and an active anti-Stratfordian, wrote in *Harper's Magazine* that Shakespeare was "a simple, untutored wool and grain merchant" and "a rather ordinary man who had no connection to the literary world." Such statements can only be characterized as wildly imaginative. Similarly, in the normally **unimpeachable** *History Today*, William D. Rubinstein, a professor at the University of Wales at Aberystwyth, stated in the opening paragraph of his anti-Shakespeare survey: "Of the seventy-five known contemporary documents in which Shakespeare is named, not one concerns his career as an author."

6 That is not even close to being so. In the Master of the Revels' accounts for 1604-1605—that is, the record of plays performed before the king, about as official a record as a record can be—Shakespeare is named seven times as the author of plays performed before James I. He is identified on the title pages as the author of the sonnets and in the dedications of two poems. He is named as author on several quarto[3] editions of his plays, by Francis Meres in *Palladis Tamia*, and by Robert Greene in the *Groat's-Worth of Wit*. John Webster identifies him as one of the great playwrights of the age in his preface to *The White Devil*.

7 The only absence among contemporary records is not of documents connecting Shakespeare to his works but of documents connecting any other human being to them. As the Shakespeare scholar Jonathan Bate has pointed out, virtually no one "in Shakespeare's lifetime or for the first two hundred years after his death expressed the slightest doubt about his authorship."

Excerpted from Shakespeare: The World As Stage by Bill Bryson, published by HarperCollins Publishers.

---

3. **quarto** a book printed on a full sheet that is folded twice to produce four leaves; Shakespeare's works were published in quarto or folio format (a larger, taller book)

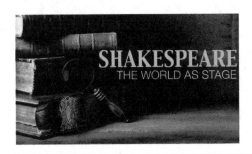

First Read

Read *Shakespeare: The World as Stage*. After you read, complete the Think Questions below.

☁ THINK QUESTIONS

1. Why does the author list sources of media coverage of the authorship controversy at the beginning of the selection? Cite evidence from the text to support your answer.

2. What is the author's response to the claim that Shakespeare "never owned a book"? What tone does he use in his response? Support your answer with evidence from the text.

3. How does the author conclude this excerpt? What does that tell you about Bryson's view of the authorship debate? Support your inference with evidence from the text.

4. Use context clues to determine the meaning of the word **provincial** as it is used in *Shakespeare: The World as Stage*. Write your definition of *provincial* here and describe how you determined the meaning.

5. Use your knowledge of word parts and the context clues provided in the text to determine the meaning of **unimpeachable**. Write your definition of *unimpeachable* and describe how you determined the meaning.

Please note that excerpts and passages in the StudySync® library and this workbook are intended as touchstones to generate interest in an author's work. The excerpts and passages do not substitute for the reading of entire texts, and StudySync® strongly recommends that students seek out and purchase the whole literary or informational work in order to experience it as the author intended. Links to online resellers are available in our digital library. In addition, complete works may be ordered through an authorized reseller by filling out and returning to StudySync® the order form enclosed in this workbook.

Reading & Writing Companion

277

Skill:
Central or Main Idea

Use the Checklist to analyze Central or Main Idea in *Shakespeare: The World as Stage*. Refer to the sample student annotations about Central or Main Idea in the text.

••• CHECKLIST FOR CENTRAL OR MAIN IDEA

In order to identify two or more central ideas of a text, note the following:

- ✓ key details in each paragraph or section of text, distinguishing what they have in common

- ✓ the main idea in each paragraph or group of paragraphs

- ✓ whether the details contain information that could indicate more than one main idea in a text

  - a science text, for example, may provide information about a specific environment and also a message on ecological awareness

  - a biography may contain equally important ideas about a person's achievements, influence, and the time period in which the person lives or lived

- ✓ when each central idea emerges

- ✓ ways that the central ideas interact and build on one another

To determine two or more central ideas of a text and analyze their development over the course of the text, including how they interact and build on one another to provide a complex analysis, consider the following questions:

- ✓ What main idea(s) do the details in each paragraphs explain or describe?

- ✓ What central or main ideas do all the paragraphs support?

- ✓ How do the central ideas interact and build on one another? How does this affect when they emerge?

- ✓ How might you provide an objective summary of the text? What details would you include?

Skill:
Central or Main Idea

Reread paragraphs 6 and 7 from *Shakespeare: The World as Stage*. Then, using the Checklist on the previous page, answer the multiple-choice questions below.

⟳ YOUR TURN

1. Which of the following sentences best summarizes these two paragraphs?

   ○ A. For two hundred years after Shakespeare's death, no one questioned whether he was the original author of his works.

   ○ B. People who choose to question Shakespeare's authorship are free to do so, but they willfully ignore the facts.

   ○ C. Not only is there historical evidence of Shakespeare's authorship, there also is no historical evidence of anyone else having authored these plays.

   ○ D. Scholars continue to question Shakespeare's authorship, based on growing evidence.

2. Which sentence or phrase from the passage does NOT offer clear evidence supporting Bryson's main idea?

   ○ A. As the Shakespeare scholar Jonathan Bate has pointed out, virtually no one "in Shakespeare's lifetime or for the first two hundred years after his death expressed the slightest doubt about his authorship."

   ○ B. The only absence among contemporary records is not of documents connecting Shakespeare to his works but of documents connecting any other human being to them.

   ○ C. In the Master of the Revels' accounts for 1604–1605 — that is, the record of plays performed before the king, about as official a record as a record can be — Shakespeare is named seven times as the author of plays performed before James I.

   ○ D. He is named as author on several quarto editions of his plays, by Francis Meres in *Palladis Tamia*, and by Robert Greene in the *Groat's-Worth of Wit*.

3. In what ways does Bryson mostly develop his main idea?

○ A. By providing a study of Shakespeare's works and share what he learned with a larger audience.

○ B. By persuading his audience to become familiar with 17th century literature.

○ C. By providing evidence of Shakespeare's authorship.

○ D. By ridiculing those who question Shakespeare's authorship.

Skill:
Connotation and Denotation

Use the Checklist to analyze Connotation and Denotation in *Shakespeare: The World as Stage.* Refer to the sample student annotations about Connotation and Denotation in the text.

••• CHECKLIST FOR CONNOTATION AND DENOTATION

1. In order to identify the denotative meanings of words, use the following steps:

   ✓ first, note unfamiliar words and phrases, key words used to describe important individuals, events, and ideas, or words that inspire an emotional reaction

   ✓ next, determine and note the denotative meaning of words by consulting a reference material such as a dictionary, glossary, or thesaurus

   ✓ finally, analyze nuances in the meaning of words with similar denotations

2. To better understand the meaning of words and phrases as they are used in a text, including connotative meanings, use the following questions as a guide:

   ✓ What is the genre or subject of the text? Based on context, what do you think the meaning of the word is intended to be?

   ✓ Is your inference the same or different from the dictionary definition?

   ✓ Does the word create a positive, negative, or neutral emotion?

   ✓ What synonyms or alternative phrasing help you describe the connotative meaning of the word?

3. To determine the meaning of words and phrases as they are used in a text, including connotative meanings, use the following questions as a guide:

   ✓ What is the denotative meaning of the word? Is that denotative meaning correct in context?

   ✓ What possible positive, neutral, or negative connotations might the word have, depending on context?

   ✓ What textual details signal a particular connotation for the word?

Please note that excerpts and passages in the StudySync® library and this workbook are intended as touchstones to generate interest in an author's work. The excerpts and passages do not substitute for the reading of entire texts, and StudySync® strongly recommends that students seek out and purchase the whole literary or informational work in order to experience it as the author intended. Links to online resellers are available in our digital library. In addition, complete works may be ordered through an authorized reseller by filling out and returning to StudySync® the order form enclosed in this workbook.

Reading & Writing Companion   **281**

Skill:
Connotation and Denotation

Reread paragraphs 1 and 2 from *Shakespeare: The World as Stage.* Then, using the Checklist on the previous page, answer the multiple-choice questions below.

⟳ YOUR TURN

1. What is the meaning of *insatiable* as it is used in paragraph 1 of the text?

   ○ A. limited

   ○ B. loose

   ○ C. unexplained

   ○ D. relentless

2. Read the following dictionary entry:

   in·sist \In·sist

   verb

   1. demand something forcefully, not accepting refusal.
   2. demand forcefully to have something.
   3. persist in doing something even though it is annoying or odd.

   Decide which definition and explanation best matches *insist* and its connotations in *Shakespeare: A World As Stage.*

   ○ A. As used in paragraph 1, insist means to demand something forcefully.

   ○ B. As used in paragraph 1, insist means to do something even if it is annoying.

   ○ C. As used in paragraph 1, insist means to not accept a refusal.

   ○ D. As used in paragraph 1, insist means to do something odd.

3. Which of the following words used in paragraph 2 most denotes that the author believes anti-Stratfordians are stubborn with their ideas, despite contrary evidence?

○ A. presumption

○ B. greater talent

○ C. publicly

○ D. insisting

Please note that excerpts and passages in the StudySync® library and this workbook are intended as touchstones to generate interest in an author's work. The excerpts and passages do not substitute for the reading of entire texts, and StudySync® strongly recommends that students seek out and purchase the whole literary or informational work in order to experience it as the author intended. Links to online resellers are available in our digital library. In addition, complete works may be ordered through an authorized reseller by filling out and returning to StudySync® the order form enclosed in this workbook.

Reading & Writing
Companion

283

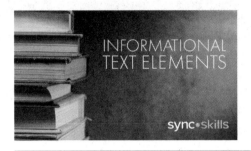

Skill:
Informational Text Elements

Use the Checklist to analyze Informational Text Elements in *Shakespeare: The World as Stage*. Refer to the sample student annotations about Informational Text Elements in the text.

••• CHECKLIST FOR INFORMATIONAL TEXT ELEMENTS

In order to identify a complex set of ideas or sequence of events, note the following:

✓ key details in the text that provide information about individuals, events, and ideas

✓ interactions between specific individuals, ideas, or events

✓ important developments over the course of the text

✓ transition words and phrases that signal interactions between individuals, events, and ideas, such as *because, as a consequence,* or *as a result.*

✓ similarities and differences between different types of information in the text by comparing and contrasting facts and opinions

To analyze a complex set of ideas or sequence of events and explain how specific individuals, ideas, or events interact and develop over the course of the text, consider the following questions:

✓ How does the order in which ideas or events are presented affect the connections between them?

✓ How do specific individuals, ideas, or events interact and develop over the course of the text?

✓ What other features, if any, help you to analyze the events, ideas, or individuals in the text?

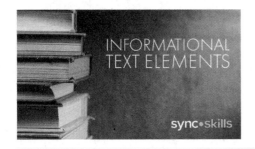

Skill:
Informational Text Elements

Reread paragraphs 4 and 5 from *Shakespeare: The World as Stage*. Then, using the Checklist on the previous page, answer the multiple-choice questions below.

↻ YOUR TURN

1. When the author states that "The statement cannot actually be refuted," he means—

   ○ A. To acknowledge the lack of information about Shakespeare.

   ○ B. There is no evidence, only assumption and opinion to support the notion that Shakespeare never owned a book.

   ○ C. To persuade the reader to make assumptions about Shakespeare.

   ○ D. To manipulate scholarly opinion on the subject.

2. What is most likely the reason Bryson provides various examples of anti-Shakespearean sentiment?

   ○ A. To evoke emotion.

   ○ B. To create confusion among complex ideas.

   ○ C. To educate the reader on the subject matter.

   ○ D. To explain opposing viewpoints and refute claims.

3. In paragraph 5, the author tells us that Daniel Wright is a "professor at Concordia University in Portland, Oregon and an active anti-Stratfordian." What function does this information play within the text?

   ○ A. To establish Wright as a credible source on Shakespeare.

   ○ B. To include a member of academia in his essay.

   ○ C. To present Wright's professional details in order to later refute his opinion-based claims.

   ○ D. To present a scholarly opinion in support of the author's claim.

Close Read

Reread *Shakespeare: The World as Stage*. As you reread, complete the Skills Focus questions below. Then use your answers and annotations from the questions to help you complete the Write activity.

◎ SKILLS FOCUS

1. What is Bryson's central idea in Paragraph 4? How does Bryson's tone in the paragraph help develop the central idea? Highlight evidence to support your ideas and use the annotation tool to write your response.

2. In the second paragraph, what does Bryson mean when he refers to Shakespeare as a "lightly educated provincial"? What connotation does that phrase have, and what does it tell you about Bryson's viewpoint? Highlight evidence in the text and use the annotation tool to explain the phrase.

3. Why does Bryson list the professions of Daniel Wright and William D. Rubinstein in Paragraph 5? What is his purpose for including the long list of media outlets in Paragraph 3? How do these details support his central idea? Highlight evidence from the text and make annotations to support your ideas.

4. Identify an opposing opinion Bryson considers, and the argument he forges in response. Explain how his rebuttal contributes to the effectiveness of the text. How does it support his main idea? Cite evidence from the text to support your answer.

5. What are the truths about Shakespeare and the scholarship surrounding Shakespeare that the author is defending in this excerpt? Why does this truth matter?

✏ WRITE

ANALYSIS: Bryson takes a strong, transparent view on the subject of Shakespearean authorship from the beginning of the excerpt, and maintains it throughout. What is Bryson's main idea regarding the authorship debate? What are the key pieces of evidence and structures he uses to make his point? Cite specific evidence from the text to support of your claim.

Hamlet and His Problems

ARGUMENTATIVE TEXT
T. S. Eliot
1919

Introduction

Written in 1919, this essay by writer T. S. Eliot (1888–1965) urges critics to analyze *Hamlet* through the lens of New Criticism, which views a text outside its history or performance. Eliot's essay addresses the concept of finding the "objective correlative," a technique used to evoke emotion in an audience.

"The grounds of *Hamlet's* failure are not immediately obvious."

1 Few critics have even admitted that *Hamlet* the play is the primary problem, and Hamlet the character only secondary. And Hamlet the character has had an especial temptation for that most dangerous type of critic: the critic with a mind which is naturally of the creative order, but which through some weakness in creative power exercises itself in criticism instead. These minds often find in Hamlet a **vicarious** existence for their own artistic realization. Such a mind had Goethe, who made of Hamlet a Werther; and such had Coleridge, who made of Hamlet a Coleridge; and probably neither of these men in writing about Hamlet remembered that his first business was to study a work of art. The kind of criticism that Goethe and Coleridge produced, in writing of Hamlet, is the most misleading kind possible. For they both possessed unquestionable critical insight, and both make their critical aberrations the more plausible by the substitution—of their own Hamlet for Shakespeare's—which their creative gift effects. We should be thankful that Walter Pater did not fix his attention on this play.

T. S. Eliot, 1951

2 Two recent writers, Mr. J. M. Robertson and Professor Stoll of the University of Minnesota, have issued small books which can be praised for moving in the other direction. Mr. Stoll performs a service in recalling to our attention the labours of the critics of the seventeenth and eighteenth centuries, observing that they knew less about psychology than more recent Hamlet critics, but they were nearer in spirit to Shakespeare's art; and as they insisted on the importance of the effect of the whole rather than on the importance of the leading character, they were nearer, in their old-fashioned way, to the secret of dramatic art in general.

3 *Qua*[1] work of art, the work of art cannot be interpreted; there is nothing to interpret; we can only criticize it according to standards, in comparison to

1. **Qua** (Latin) as being

other works of art; and for "interpretation" the chief task is the presentation of relevant historical facts which the reader is not assumed to know. Mr. Robertson points out, very pertinently, how critics have failed in their "interpretation" of Hamlet by ignoring what ought to be very obvious: that *Hamlet* is a **stratification**, that it represents the efforts of a series of men, each making what he could out of the work of his predecessors. The *Hamlet* of Shakespeare will appear to us very differently if, instead of treating the whole action of the play as due to Shakespeare's design, we perceive his *Hamlet* to be superposed upon much cruder material which persists even in the final form.

4 We know that there was an older play by Thomas Kyd, that extraordinary dramatic (if not poetic) genius who was in all probability the author of two plays so dissimilar as the *Spanish Tragedy* and *Arden of Feversham;* and what this play was like we can guess from three clues: from the *Spanish Tragedy* itself, from the tale of Belleforest upon which Kyd's *Hamlet* must have been based, and from a version acted in Germany in Shakespeare's lifetime which bears strong evidence of having been adapted from the earlier, not from the later, play. From these three sources it is clear that in the earlier play the motive was a revenge-motive simply; that the action or delay is caused, as in the *Spanish Tragedy*, solely by the difficulty of assassinating a monarch surrounded by guards; and that the "madness" of Hamlet was feigned in order to escape suspicion, and successfully. In the final play of Shakespeare, on the other hand, there is a motive which is more important than that of revenge, and which explicitly "blunts" the latter; the delay in revenge is unexplained on grounds of necessity or expediency; and the effect of the "madness" is not to lull but to arouse the king's suspicion. The alteration is not complete enough, however, to be convincing. Furthermore, there are verbal parallels so close to the *Spanish Tragedy* as to leave no doubt that in places Shakespeare was merely *revising* the text of Kyd. And finally there are unexplained scenes—the Polonius-Laertes and the Polonius-Reynaldo scenes—for which there is little excuse; these scenes are not in the verse style of Kyd, and not beyond doubt in the style of Shakespeare. These Mr. Robertson believes to be scenes in the original play of Kyd reworked by a third hand, perhaps Chapman, before Shakespeare touched the play. And he concludes, with very strong show of reason, that the original play of Kyd was, like certain other revenge plays, in two parts of five acts each. The upshot of Mr. Robertson's examination is, we believe, irrefragable: that Shakespeare's *Hamlet,* so far as it is Shakespeare's, is a play dealing with the effect of a mother's guilt upon her son, and that Shakespeare was unable to impose this motive successfully upon the **"intractable"** material of the old play.

5 Of the intractability there can be no doubt. So far from being Shakespeare's masterpiece, the play is most certainly an artistic failure. In several ways the

play is puzzling, and disquieting as is none of the others. Of all the plays it is the longest and is possibly the one on which Shakespeare spent most pains; and yet he has left in it **superfluous** and inconsistent scenes which even hasty revision should have noticed. The versification is variable. Lines like:

6   Look, the morn, in russet mantle clad,
     Walks o'er the dew of yon high eastern hill,

7   are of the Shakespeare of *Romeo and Juliet.* The lines in Act v. sc. ii.,

8   Sir, in my heart there was a kind of fighting
     That would not let me sleep. . .
     Up from my cabin,
     My sea-gown scarf'd about me, in the dark
     Grop'd I to find out them: had my desire;
     Finger'd their packet;

9   are of his quite mature. Both workmanship and thought are in an unstable condition. We are surely justified in attributing the play, with that other profoundly interesting play of "intractable" material and astonishing versification, *Measure for Measure,* to a period of crisis, after which follow the tragic successes which culminate in *Coriolanus. Coriolanus* may be not as "interesting" as *Hamlet,* but it is, with *Antony and Cleopatra,* Shakespeare's most assured artistic success. And probably more people have thought *Hamlet* a work of art because they found it interesting, than have found it interesting because it is a work of art. It is the "Mona Lisa" of literature.

10   The grounds of *Hamlet's* failure are not immediately obvious. Mr. Robertson is undoubtedly correct in concluding that the essential emotion of the play is the feeling of a son towards a guilty mother:

11   "[Hamlet's] tone is that of one who has suffered tortures on the score of his mother's degradation. . . . The guilt of a mother is an almost intolerable motive for drama, but it had to be maintained and emphasized to supply a psychological solution, or rather a hint of one."

12   This, however, is by no means the whole story. It is not merely the "guilt of a mother" that cannot be handled as Shakespeare handled the suspicion of Othello, the infatuation of Antony, or the pride of Coriolanus. The subject might conceivably have expanded into a tragedy like these, intelligible, self-complete, in the sunlight. *Hamlet,* like the sonnets, is full of some stuff that the writer could not drag to light, contemplate, or manipulate into art. And when we search for this feeling, we find it, as in the sonnets, very difficult to localize. You cannot point to it in the speeches; indeed, if you examine the two famous soliloquies you see the versification of Shakespeare, but a content which

might be claimed by another, perhaps by the author of the *Revenge of Bussy d'Ambois,* Act v. sc. i. We find Shakespeare's *Hamlet* not in the action, not in any quotations that we might select, so much as in an unmistakable tone which is unmistakably not in the earlier play.

13 The only way of expressing emotion in the form of art is by finding an "objective correlative"; in other words, a set of objects, a situation, a chain of events which shall be the formula of that *particular* emotion; such that when the external facts, which must terminate in sensory experience, are given, the emotion is immediately evoked. If you examine any of Shakespeare's more successful tragedies, you will find this exact equivalence; you will find that the state of mind of Lady Macbeth walking in her sleep has been communicated to you by a skilful accumulation of imagined sensory impressions; the words of Macbeth on hearing of his wife's death strike us as if, given the sequence of events, these words were automatically released by the last event in the series. The artistic "inevitability" lies in this complete adequacy of the external to the emotion; and this is precisely what is deficient in *Hamlet*. Hamlet (the man) is dominated by an emotion which is inexpressible, because it is in excess of the facts as they appear. And the supposed identity of Hamlet with his author is genuine to this point: that Hamlet's bafflement at the absence of objective equivalent to his feelings is a prolongation of the bafflement of his creator in the face of his artistic problem. Hamlet is up against the difficulty that his disgust is occasioned by his mother, but that his mother is not an adequate equivalent for it; his disgust envelops and exceeds her. It is thus a feeling which he cannot understand; he cannot objectify it, and it therefore remains to poison life and obstruct action. None of the possible actions can satisfy it; and nothing that Shakespeare can do with the plot can express Hamlet for him. And it must be noticed that the very nature of the *données*[2] of the problem precludes objective equivalence. To have heightened the criminality of Gertrude would have been to provide the formula for a totally different emotion in Hamlet; it is just *because* her character is so negative and insignificant that she arouses in Hamlet the feeling which she is incapable of representing.

14 The "madness" of Hamlet lay to Shakespeare's hand; in the earlier play a simple **ruse**, and to the end, we may presume, understood as a ruse by the audience. For Shakespeare it is less than madness and more than feigned. The levity of Hamlet, his repetition of phrase, his puns, are not part of a deliberate plan of dissimulation, but a form of emotional relief. In the character Hamlet it is the buffoonery of an emotion which can find no outlet in action; in the dramatist it is the buffoonery of an emotion which he cannot express in art. The intense feeling, ecstatic or terrible, without an object or exceeding its object, is something which every person of sensibility has known; it is

---

2. **données** (French) basic facts

NOTES

doubtless a study to pathologists. It often occurs in adolescence: the ordinary person puts these feelings to sleep, or trims down his feeling to fit the business world; the artist keeps it alive by his ability to intensify the world to his emotions. The Hamlet of Laforgue is an adolescent; the Hamlet of Shakespeare is not, he has not that explanation and excuse. We must simply admit that here Shakespeare tackled a problem which proved too much for him. Why he attempted it at all is an insoluble puzzle; under compulsion of what experience he attempted to express the inexpressibly horrible, we cannot ever know. We need a great many facts in his biography; and we should like to know whether, and when, and after or at the same time as what personal experience, he read Montaigne, II. xii., *Apologie de Raimond Sebond*. We should have, finally, to know something which is by hypothesis unknowable, for we assume it to be an experience which, in the manner indicated, exceeded the facts. We should have to understand things which Shakespeare did not understand himself.

✏ WRITE

EXPLANATORY ESSAY: In the essay "Hamlet and His Problems," T. S. Eliot makes the claim that Shakespeare's play *Hamlet* is "an artistic failure." Why does he make this claim? What ideas and examples does he use to support this claim? Write a response in which you answer these questions. Remember to use evidence from the text to support your response.

Hamlet
(Scenes from Acts I, II, III)

DRAMA
William Shakespeare
1601

Introduction

The Tragedy of Hamlet, Prince of Denmark by William Shakespeare (ca. 1564–1616) is a vivid portrayal of madness, rich with themes of treachery and revenge. His father the King's death, and his mother's immediate remarriage to his uncle throws Hamlet into existential turmoil—a struggle for personal meaning and grueling internal strife that threatens to consume him. A ghost, once played by Shakespeare himself around 1602, visits the Prince. Hamlet's soliloquies, exemplifying the best of Shakespeare's eloquent and clever language, raise unanswerable questions and explore the reality of being human in one of the

"To be, or not to be, that is the question . . ."

NOTES

1 *Hamlet has returned home from studying in Wittenberg to attend his father's funeral. Still in deep mourning, Hamlet is appalled by his mother's hasty remarriage to the dead King's brother, who has assumed the throne and persists in calling him "son." The circumstances drive Hamlet to voice his first passionate soliloquy.*

From Act I, Scene ii:

Hamlet: son to the late King Hamlet, and nephew to the present King
Claudius: King of Denmark
Gertrude: Queen of Denmark, and mother to Hamlet
Polonius: Lord Chamberlain
Laertes: son to Polonius

Location: Elsinore, the castle

Skill:
Dramatic Elements
and Structure

The aside reveals
Hamlet's negative
feelings toward his
uncle that motivate him
to want to avenge his
father's death later in
the play.

Also, the author's use
of an aside creates a
relationship between the
audience and Hamlet.

2 KING: Take thy fair hour, Laertes, time be thine,
3 And thy best graces spend it at thy will!
4 But now, my cousin Hamlet, and my son—

5 HAMLET: *[Aside]* A little more than kin, and less than kind.

6 KING: How is it that the clouds still hang on you?

7 HAMLET: Not so, my lord, I am too much in the sun.

8 QUEEN: Good Hamlet, cast thy nighted color off,
9 And let thine eye look like a friend on Denmark.
10 Do not for ever with thy vailed lids
11 Seek for thy noble father in the dust.
12 Thou know'st 'tis common, all that lives must die,
13 Passing through nature to eternity.

14 HAMLET: Ay, madam, it is common.

NOTES

15 QUEEN: If it be,
16 Why seems it so particular with thee?

17 HAMLET: Seems, madam? Nay, it is, I know not "seems."
18 'Tis not alone my inky cloak, good mother,
19 Nor customary suits of solemn black,
20 Nor windy suspiration of forc'd breath,
21 No, nor the fruitful river in the eye,
22 Nor the dejected havior of the visage,
23 Together with all forms, moods, shapes of grief,
24 That can denote me truly. These indeed seem,
25 For they are actions that a man might play,
26 But I have that within which passes show,
27 These but the **trappings** and the suits of woe.

28 KING: 'Tis sweet and commendable in your nature, Hamlet,
29 To give these mourning duties to your father.
30 But you must know your father lost a father,
31 That father lost, lost his, and the survivor bound
32 In **filial** obligation for some term
33 To do obsequious sorrow. But to persever
34 In obstinate condolement is a course
35 Of impious stubbornness, 'tis unmanly grief,
36 It shows a will most incorrect to heaven,
37 A heart unfortified, or mind impatient,
38 An understanding simple and unschool'd:
39 For what we know must be, and is as common
40 As any the most vulgar thing to sense,
41 Why should we in our peevish opposition
42 Take it to heart? Fie, 'tis a fault to heaven,
43 A fault against the dead, a fault to nature,
44 To reason most absurd, whose common theme
45 Is death of fathers, and who still hath cried,
46 From the first corse till he that died to-day,
47 "This must be so." We pray you, throw to earth
48 This unprevailing woe, and think of us
49 As of a father, for let the world take note
50 You are the most immediate to our throne,
51 And with no less nobility of love
52 Than that which dearest father bears his son
53 Do I impart toward you. For your intent
54 In going back to school in Wittenberg,
55 It is most **retrograde** to our desire,
56 And we beseech you, bend you to remain

NOTES

57 Here in the cheer and comfort of our eye,
58 Our chiefest courtier, cousin, and our son.

59 QUEEN: Let not thy mother lose her prayers, Hamlet,
60 I pray thee stay with us, go not to Wittenberg.

61 HAMLET: I shall in all my best obey you, madam.

62 KING: Why, 'tis a loving and a fair reply.
63 Be as ourself in Denmark. Madam, come.
64 This gentle and unforc'd accord of Hamlet
65 Sits smiling to my heart, in grace whereof,
66 No jocund health that Denmark drinks to-day,
67 But the great cannon to the clouds shall tell,
68 And the King's rouse the heaven shall bruit again,
69 Respeaking earthly thunder. Come away.

70 [Flourish. Exeunt all but HAMLET.]

71 HAMLET: O that this too too solid flesh would melt,
72 Thaw and resolve itself into a dew!
73 Or that the Everlasting had not fix'd
74 His canon 'gainst self-slaughter! O God, God,
75 How weary, stale, flat and unprofitable
76 Seem to me all the uses of this world!
77 Fie on't, ah fie! 'tis an unweeded garden
78 That grows to seed, things rank and gross in nature
79 Possess it merely. That it should come to this!
80 But two months dead, nay, not so much, not two.
81 So excellent a king, that was to this
82 Hyperion[1]—to a satyr[2], so loving to my mother
83 That he might not beteem the winds of heaven
84 Visit her face too roughly. Heaven and earth,
85 Must I remember? Why, she would hang on him
86 As if increase of appetite had grown
87 By what it fed on, and yet, within a month—
88 Let me not think on't! Frailty, thy name is woman!—
89 A little month, or ere those shoes were old
90 With which she followed my poor father's body,
91 Like Niobe, all tears—why, she, even she—
92 O, God, a beast that wants discourse of reason

Skill:
Dramatic Elements
and Structure

Alone on stage, Hamlet wishes he were dead because he thinks his life has lost all meaning. His soliloquy and the stage direction work together to reveal how disgusted he is with his mother's marriage to his uncle.

---

1. **Hyperion** the sun-god
2. **satyr** In Greek mythology, a lustful, drunken god of the woods, represented as a half man-half horse or goat.

93 Would have mourn'd longer—married with my uncle,
94 My father's brother, but no more like my father
95 Than I to Hercules. Within a month,
96 Ere yet the salt of most unrighteous tears
97 Had left the flushing in her galled eyes,
98 She married—O most wicked speed: to post
99 With such dexterity to incestuous sheets,
100 It is not, nor it cannot come to good,
101 But break my heart, for I must hold my tongue.

From Act II, Scene ii:

102 *Hamlet has been visited by an apparition claiming to be the ghost of his*
father, who urges Hamlet to avenge his father's murder. Hamlet swears he
will obey, but hesitates. Watching a group of traveling players perform the
murder of Priam, king of Troy, Hamlet compares one actor's passionate
portrayal of Hecuba, Priam's grieving widow, to his own inaction.

103 HAMLET: O, what a rogue and peasant slave am I!
104 Is it not monstrous that this player here,
105 But in a fiction, in a dream of passion,
106 Could force his soul so to his own conceit
107 That from her working all his visage wann'd,
108 Tears in his eyes, distraction in his aspect,

Hamlet and his father's ghost, by Henry Fuseli.

109 A broken voice, an' his whole function suiting
110 With forms to his conceit? And all for nothing,
111 For Hecuba!
112 What's Hecuba to him, or he to Hecuba,
113 That he should weep for her? What would he do
114 Had he the motive and the cue for passion
115 That I have? He would drown the stage with tears,
116 And cleave the general ear with horrid speech,
117 Make mad the guilty, and appall the free,
118 Confound the ignorant, and amaze indeed
119 The very faculties of eyes and ears. Yet I,
120 A dull and muddy-mettled rascal, peak[3]
121 Like John-a-dreams[4], unpregnant of[5] my cause,

---

3. **peak** to mope
4. **John-a-dreams** a nickname for a daydreamer
5. **unpregnant of** unquickened, or unmoved, by

122 And can say nothing; no, not for a king,
123 Upon whose property and most dear life
124 A damn'd defeat was made. Am I a coward?
125 Who calls me villain, breaks my pate across,
126 Plucks off my beard, and blows it in my face,
127 Tweaks me by the nose, gives me the lie i' the throat
128 As deep as to the lungs? Who does me this?
129 Hah, 'swounds, I should take it; for it cannot be
130 But I am pigeon-liver'd, and lack gall
131 To make oppression bitter, or ere this
132 I should 'a' fatted all the region kites
133 With this slave's offal. Bloody, bawdy villain!
134 Remorseless, treacherous, lecherous, kindless villain!
135 Why, what an ass am I! This is most brave,
136 That I, the son of a dear father murthered,
137 Prompted to my revenge by heaven and hell,
138 Must, like a whore unpack my heart with words,
139 And fall a-cursing like a very drab,
140 A stallion. Fie upon't, foh!
141 About, my brains! Hum—I have heard
142 That guilty creatures sitting at a play
143 Have by the very cunning of the scene
144 Been struck so to the soul, that presently
145 They have proclaim'd their malefactions:
146 For murther, though it have no tongue, will speak
147 With most miraculous organ. I'll have these players
148 Play something like the murther of my father
149 Before mine uncle. I'll observe his looks,
150 I'll tent⁶ him to the quick. If 'a do blench⁷,
151 I know my course. The spirit that I have seen
152 May be the dev'l, and the dev'l hath power
153 T' assume a pleasing shape, yea, and perhaps,
154 Out of my weakness and my melancholy,
155 As he is very potent with such spirits,
156 Abuses me to damn me. I'll have grounds
157 More relative than this—the play's the thing
158 Wherein I'll catch the conscience of the King.

From Act III, Scene i:

159 *Hamlet has been acting mad in front of his family and the court. The King and Polonius hope that Hamlet's strange behavior stems from his love for*

---

6. **tent** probe
7. **blench** flinch

Polonius's daughter, Ophelia, and they spy on the young couple in order to confirm their suspicions. While hidden, they catch Hamlet in a private moment of anguished contemplation.

160 HAMLET: To be, or not to be, that is the question:
161 Whether 'tis nobler in the mind to suffer
162 The slings and arrows of outrageous fortune,
163 Or to take arms against a sea of troubles,
164 And by opposing, end them. To die, to sleep—
165 No more, and by a sleep to say we end
166 The heart-ache and the thousand natural shocks
167 That flesh is heir to; 'tis a consummation
168 Devoutly to be wish'd. To die, to sleep—
169 To sleep, perchance to dream—ay, there's the rub,
170 For in that sleep of death what dreams may come,
171 When we have shuffled off this mortal coil,
172 Must give us pause; there's the respect
173 That makes calamity of so long life:
174 For who would bear the whips and scorns of time,
175 Th' oppressor's wrong, the proud man's contumely,
176 The pangs of despis'd love, the law's delay,
177 The **insolence** of office, and the spurns
178 That patient merit of th' unworthy takes,
179 When he himself might his quietus make
180 With a bare bodkin[8]; who would fardels[9] bear,
181 To grunt and sweat under a weary life,
182 But that the dread of something after death,
183 The undiscover'd country, from whose bourn
184 No traveller returns, puzzles the will,
185 And makes us rather bear those ills we have,
186 Than fly to others that we know not of?
187 Thus conscience does make cowards of us all,
188 And thus the native hue of resolution
189 Is sicklied o'er with the pale cast of thought,
190 And enterprises of great pith and moment
191 With this regard their currents turn awry,
192 And lose the name of action.—Soft you now,
193 The fair Ophelia!—Nymph, in thy orisons[10]
194 Be all my sins remembered.

195 OPHELIA: Good my lord,

Skill:
Media

The film shows Hamlet looking at the ocean. His words are heard before he is on screen. He holds a dagger when he says "end them." The film makes Hamlet's suicidal thoughts clearer than I originally read in Shakespeare's words.

8. **bare bodkin** mere dagger
9. **fardels** a burden in the form of a bundle
10. **orisons** prayers

196   How does your honor for this many a day?

197   HAMLET: I humbly thank you. Well, well, well.

198   OPHELIA: My lord, I have remembrances of yours
199   That I have longèd long to redeliver.
200   I pray you now receive them.

201   HAMLET: No, not I. I never gave you aught.

202   OPHELIA: My honored lord, you know right well you did,
203   And with them, words of so sweet breath composed
204   As made the things more rich. Their perfume lost,
205   Take these again, for to the noble mind
206   Rich gifts wax poor when givers prove unkind.
207   There, my lord.

208   HAMLET: Ha, ha, are you honest?

209   OPHELIA: My lord?

210   HAMLET: Are you fair?

211   OPHELIA: What means your lordship?

212   HAMLET: That if you be honest and fair, your honesty should admit no
        discourse to your beauty.

213   OPHELIA: Could beauty, my lord, have better commerce than with honesty?

214   HAMLET: Ay, truly, for the power of beauty will sooner transform honesty from
        what it is to a bawd than the force of honesty can translate beauty into his
        likeness. This was sometime a paradox, but now the time gives it proof. I did
        love you once.

215   OPHELIA: Indeed, my lord, you made me believe so.

216   HAMLET: You should not have believed me, for virtue cannot so inoculate our
        old stock but we shall relish of it. I loved you not.

217   OPHELIA: I was the more deceived.

218   HAMLET: Get thee to a nunnery. Why wouldst thou be a breeder of sinners?
        I am myself indifferent honest, but yet I could accuse me of such things that it
        were better my mother had not borne me.

219　I am very proud, revengeful, ambitious, with more offences at my beck than I have thoughts to put them in, imagination to give them shape, or time to act them in. What should such fellows as I do crawling between earth and heaven? We are arrant knaves, all. Believe none of us. Go thy ways to a nunnery. Where's your father?

220　OPHELIA: At home, my lord.

221　HAMLET: Let the doors be shut upon him, that he may play the fool no where but in 's own house. Farewell.

222　OPHELIA: O, help him, you sweet heavens!

223　HAMLET: If thou dost marry, I'll give thee this plague for thy dowry. Be thou as chaste as ice, as pure as snow, thou shalt not escape calumny. Get thee to a nunnery, go. Farewell. Or, if thou wilt needs marry, marry a fool, for wise men know well enough what monsters you make of them. To a nunnery, go, and quickly too. Farewell.

224　OPHELIA: Heavenly powers, restore him!

225　HAMLET: I have heard of your paintings too, well enough. God has given you one face and you make yourselves another. You jig and amble, and you lisp, you nickname God's creatures and make your wantonness your ignorance. Go to, I'll no more on 't. It hath made me mad. I say, we will have no more marriages. Those that are married already, all but one, shall live. The rest shall keep as they are. To a nunnery, go.

226　[*Exit HAMLET.*]

227　OPHELIA: Oh, what a noble mind is here o'erthrown!—
228　The courtier's, soldier's, scholar's, eye, tongue, sword,
229　Th' expectancy and rose of the fair state,
230　The glass of fashion and the mould of form,
231　Th' observed of all observers, quite, quite down!
232　And I, of ladies most deject and wretched,
233　That sucked the honey of his music vows,
234　Now see that noble and most sovereign reason
235　Like sweet bells jangled, out of tune and harsh;
236　That unmatched form and feature of blown youth
237　Blasted with ecstasy. Oh, woe is me,
238　T' have seen what I have seen, see what I see!

From Act III, Scene iii:

A room in the Castle.

239 *[Enter KING, ROSENCRANTZ, and GUILDENSTERN.]*

240 KING: I like him not; nor stands it safe with us
241 To let his madness range. Therefore prepare you;
242 I your commission will forthwith dispatch,
243 And he to England shall along with you:
244 The terms of our estate may not endure
245 Hazard so near us as doth hourly grow
246 Out of his lunacies.

247 GUILDENSTERN: We will ourselves provide:
248 Most holy and religious fear it is
249 To keep those many many bodies safe
250 That live and feed upon your majesty.

251 ROSENCRANTZ: The single and peculiar life is bound,
252 With all the strength and armour of the mind,
253 To keep itself from 'noyance; but much more
254 That spirit upon whose weal depend and rest
255 The lives of many. The cease of majesty
256 Dies not alone; but like a gulf doth draw
257 What's near it with it: it is a massy wheel,
258 Fix'd on the summit of the highest mount,
259 To whose huge spokes ten thousand lesser things
260 Are mortis'd and adjoin'd; which, when it falls,
261 Each small annexment, petty consequence,
262 Attends the **boisterous** ruin. Never alone
263 Did the king sigh, but with a general groan.

264 KING: Arm you, I pray you, to this speedy voyage;
265 For we will fetters put upon this fear,
266 Which now goes too free-footed.

267 ROSENCRANTZ and GUILDENSTERN: We will haste us.

268 *[Exeunt ROSENCRANTZ and GUILDENSTERN.]*

269 *[Enter POLONIUS.]*

270 POLONIUS: My lord, he's going to his mother's closet:
271 Behind the arras I'll convey myself
272 To hear the process; I'll warrant she'll tax him home:
273 And, as you said, and wisely was it said,
274 'Tis meet that some more audience than a mother,
275 Since nature makes them partial, should o'erhear

276 The speech, of vantage. Fare you well, my liege:
277 I'll call upon you ere you go to bed,
278 And tell you what I know.

279 KING: Thanks, dear my lord.

280 *[Exit POLONIUS.]*

281 O, my offence is rank, it smells to heaven;
282 It hath the primal eldest curse upon't,—
283 A brother's murder!—Pray can I not,
284 Though inclination be as sharp as will:
285 My stronger guilt defeats my strong intent;
286 And, like a man to double business bound,
287 I stand in pause where I shall first begin,
288 And both neglect. What if this cursed hand
289 Were thicker than itself with brother's blood,—
290 Is there not rain enough in the sweet heavens
291 To wash it white as snow? Whereto serves mercy
292 But to confront the visage of offence?
293 And what's in prayer but this twofold force,—
294 To be forestalled ere we come to fall,
295 Or pardon'd being down? Then I'll look up;
296 My fault is past. But, O, what form of prayer
297 Can serve my turn? Forgive me my foul murder!—
298 That cannot be; since I am still possess'd
299 Of those effects for which I did the murder,—
300 My crown, mine own ambition, and my queen.
301 May one be pardon'd and retain the offence?
302 In the corrupted currents of this world
303 Offence's gilded hand may shove by justice;
304 And oft 'tis seen the wicked prize itself
305 Buys out the law; but 'tis not so above;
306 There is no shuffling;—there the action lies
307 In his true nature; and we ourselves compell'd,
308 Even to the teeth and forehead of our faults,
309 To give in evidence. What then? what rests?
310 Try what repentance can: what can it not?
311 Yet what can it when one cannot repent?
312 O wretched state! O bosom black as death!
313 O limed soul, that, struggling to be free,
314 Art more engag'd! Help, angels! Make assay:
315 Bow, stubborn knees; and, heart, with strings of steel,

Skill:
Language, Style,
and Audience

The King describes the
murder of his brother
as so "rank" that the
smell rises to heaven.
But "my offence is
rank" can also mean
that the King's
"offence," or crime, is
to achieve rank.

316 Be soft as sinews of the new-born babe!

317 All may be well.

318 *[Retires and kneels.]*

319 *[Enter Hamlet.]*

320 HAMLET: Now might I do it pat, now he is praying;

321 And now I'll do't;—and so he goes to heaven;

322 And so am I reveng'd.—that would be scann'd:

323 A villain kills my father; and for that,

324 I, his sole son, do this same villain send

325 To heaven.

326 O, this is hire and salary, not revenge.

327 He took my father grossly, full of bread;

328 With all his crimes broad blown, as flush as May;

329 And how his audit stands, who knows save heaven?

330 But in our circumstance and course of thought,

331 'Tis heavy with him: and am I, then, reveng'd,

332 To take him in the purging of his soul,

333 When he is fit and season'd for his passage?

334 No.

335 Up, sword, and know thou a more horrid hent:

336 When he is drunk asleep; or in his rage;

337 Or in the incestuous pleasure of his bed;

338 At gaming, swearing; or about some act

339 That has no relish of salvation in't;—

340 Then trip him, that his heels may kick at heaven;

341 And that his soul may be as damn'd and black

342 As hell, whereto it goes. My mother stays:

343 This physic but prolongs thy sickly days.

344 *[Exit.]*

345 *[The King rises and advances.]*

346 KING: My words fly up, my thoughts remain below:

347 Words without thoughts never to heaven go.

348 *[Exit.]*

First Read

Read *Hamlet*. After you read, complete the Think Questions below.

☁ THINK QUESTIONS

1. In Act I, how do King Claudius and Queen Gertrude try to reason with Hamlet? What does Hamlet's soliloquy suggest about his response to their reasoning? Cite evidence from the text to support your response.

2. In Act II, what key comparison does Hamlet draw between himself and the players, confirming that he is a coward? Cite evidence from the text to support your answer.

3. In Act III, Scene i, what does Hamlet mean when he says, "To be, or not to be, that is the question"? Cite evidence from the text to support your answer.

4. Review the King's lines in Act I, Scene ii, that begin, "Tis sweet and commendable . . ." Use context to determine the meaning of the word **filial** as it is used in the fifth line. Explain how context helped you determine the meaning of the word.

5. Use context clues to determine a preliminary definition of **retrograde**. Write your definition here, and then verify your preliminary definition by checking a dictionary.

Please note that excerpts and passages in the StudySync® library and this workbook are intended as touchstones to generate interest in an author's work. The excerpts and passages do not substitute for the reading of entire texts, and StudySync® strongly recommends that students seek out and purchase the whole literary or informational work in order to experience it as the author intended. Links to online resellers are available in our digital library. In addition, complete works may be ordered through an authorized reseller by filling out and returning to StudySync® the order form enclosed in this workbook.

Reading & Writing Companion **305**

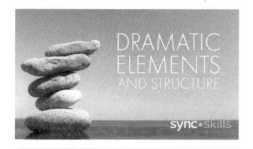

Skill:
Dramatic Elements and Structure

Use the Checklist to analyze Dramatic Elements and Structure in *Hamlet*. Refer to the sample student annotations about Dramatic Elements and Structure in the text.

••• CHECKLIST FOR DRAMATIC ELEMENTS AND STRUCTURE

In order to determine the author's choices regarding the development of a drama, note the following:

- ✓ the names of all the characters, how they are introduced, and their relationships with one another

- ✓ character development, including personality traits, motivations, decisions each character makes, and the actions they take

- ✓ the setting(s) of the story and how it influences the characters and the events of the plot

- ✓ how character choices and dialogue affect the plot

- ✓ the stage directions and how they are used to reveal character and plot development

To analyze the impact of the author's choices regarding how to develop and relate elements of a story or drama, consider the following questions:

- ✓ How does the order of events in the play affect the development of the drama?

- ✓ How are characters introduced, and what does it reveal about them?

- ✓ In what ways do the characters change over the course of the drama?

- ✓ How do the choices the characters make help advance the plot?

- ✓ How does the setting affect the characters and plot?

- ✓ How do the characters' actions help develop the theme or message of the play?

Copyright © BookheadEd Learning, LLC

Skill:
Dramatic Elements and Structure

Reread lines 102–126 from *Hamlet*. Then, using the Checklist on the previous page, answer the multiple-choice questions below.

⟳ YOUR TURN

1. This scene is from the second act of Hamlet. The author's choice to use a soliloquy at this point in the play helps advance the plot by —

   ○ A. making the audience approve of Hamlet's plan to get revenge on his family later in the play.

   ○ B. allowing Hamlet's family to find out what he is plotting, which enables them to foil his plan.

   ○ C. creating a mood of forgiveness that will affect Hamlet's actions toward his uncle and mother.

   ○ D. creating tension in the rising action of the play as the audience learns of Hamlet's plan for revenge.

2. The author's choice to use a soliloquy in this part of the play is effective because it —

   ○ A. leaves no question in the audience's mind that Hamlet, alone on stage, is revealing his own inner thoughts and feelings.

   ○ B. allows Hamlet to be alone on stage so that he can tell the audience directly that he enjoys putting on plays.

   ○ C. gives Hamlet a chance to get the audience to react to the claim that he is a rogue and a villain.

   ○ D. gives other actors a chance to be off stage so they can prepare for future scenes.

Skill:
Language, Style, and Audience

Use the Checklist to analyze Language, Style, and Audience in *Hamlet*. Refer to the sample student annotations about Language, Style, and Audience in the text.

••• CHECKLIST FOR LANGUAGE, STYLE, AND AUDIENCE

In order to determine an author's style and possible intended audience, do the following:

✓ identify and define any unfamiliar words or phrases that have multiple meanings

✓ identify language that is particularly fresh, engaging, or beautiful

✓ analyze the surrounding words and phrases as well as the context in which the specific words are being used

✓ note the audience—both intended and unintended—and possible reactions to the author's word choice and style

✓ examine your reaction to the author's word choice and how the author's choice affected your reaction

To analyze the impact of a specific word choice on meaning, including words with multiple meanings or language that is particularly fresh, engaging, or beautiful, consider the following questions:

✓ How does the author's use of fresh, engaging, or beautiful language enhance or change what is being described? How would a specific phrase or sentence sound different or shift in meaning if a synonym were used?

✓ How do the rhyme scheme, meter, and other poetic language affect the meaning?

✓ How does word choice, including different possible meanings from other countries, help determine meaning?

✓ How does Shakespeare use poetic techniques, multiple-meaning words, and language that appeals to emotions to craft a message or idea?

✓ How would the text be different if another type of technique or other words were used?

Skill:
Language, Style, and Audience

Reread lines 195–225 from *Hamlet*. Then, using the Checklist on the previous page, answer the multiple-choice questions below.

⟳ YOUR TURN

1. What impact does Hamlet's repeated command of Ophelia to go "to a nunnery" have on the meaning of this scene?

   ○ A. The repetition shows how much Hamlet now regrets having never given anything to Ophelia.

   ○ B. The repetition highlights the tense relationship that Hamlet and Ophelia have always had.

   ○ C. The repetition explains that Hamlet no longer finds Ophelia beautiful.

   ○ D. The repetition reinforces how much Hamlet now distrusts Ophelia.

2. Which statement best explains how the word "fair" is used in this scene?

   ○ A. The word "fair" refers to Ophelia's lack of beauty and judgement.

   ○ B. Hamlet uses the word "fair" to link Ophelia's beauty with what he sees as her lack of honesty.

   ○ C. Hamlet introduces the idea of being "fair" because Ophelia calls his gifts unkind.

   ○ D. The word "fair" refers to the open and honest relationship that Ophelia and Hamlet used to have.

Please note that excerpts and passages in the StudySync® library and this workbook are intended as touchstones to generate interest in an author's work. The excerpts and passages do not substitute for the reading of entire texts, and StudySync® strongly recommends that students seek out and purchase the whole literary or informational work in order to experience it as the author intended. Links to online resellers are available in our digital library. In addition, complete works may be ordered through an authorized reseller by filling out and returning to StudySync® the order form enclosed in this workbook.

Reading & Writing
Companion

309

Skill: Media

Use the Checklist to analyze Media in *Hamlet*. Refer to the sample student annotations about Media in the text.

••• CHECKLIST FOR MEDIA

Before analyzing multiple interpretations of a story, drama, or poem, note the following:

✓ similarities and differences in different media, such as the live production of a play or a recorded novel or poetry

✓ the different time periods and cultures in which the source material and interpretations were produced

To analyze multiple interpretations of a story, drama, or poem, evaluating how each version interprets the source text, consider the following questions:

✓ How does each version interpret the source text? What are the main similarities and differences between the two (or more) versions?

✓ In what ways does the medium affect the interpretations of the source text?

✓ If each version is from a different time period and/or culture, what does each version reveal about the time period and culture in which it was written?

✓ Does information about the time period and culture allow you to make any inferences about the authors' objectives or intentions?

Skill:
Media

Reread lines 169–186 from *Hamlet*. Then, using the Checklist on the previous page, answer the multiple-choice questions below.

⟳ YOUR TURN

1. How does Sonnet Man explain the idea of having "To grunt and sweat under a weary life" (line 181)?

   ○ A. Sonnet Man says the line out loud, which helps the listener and viewer know what he means by "a weary life."

   ○ B. Sonnet Man's version shows people fighting to help the listener and viewer see the experiences of someone with "a weary life."

   ○ C. Sonnet Man's version uses voice-over with photographs on the screen to help the listener and viewer understand the line.

   ○ D. Sonnet Man translates the line into his own words to help the listener and viewer understand what he means.

2. Which statement best explains how Sonnet Man interprets Shakespeare's text?

   ○ A. Sonnet Man breaks down the idea of Hamlet having an internal discussion by including the presence of others on the screen.

   ○ B. Sonnet Man's version translates the original words into words more commonly used and understood today.

   ○ C. Sonnet Man's version removes the explicit reference to suicide that was in the original.

   ○ D. Sonnet Man focuses less on Hamlet and more on the other characters in the play.

Please note that excerpts and passages in the StudySync® library and this workbook are intended as touchstones to generate interest in an author's work. The excerpts and passages do not substitute for the reading of entire texts, and StudySync® strongly recommends that students seek out and purchase the whole literary or informational work in order to experience it as the author intended. Links to online resellers are available in our digital library. In addition, complete works may be ordered through an authorized reseller by filling out and returning to StudySync® the order form enclosed in this workbook.

Reading & Writing Companion   **311**

Close Read

Reread *Hamlet*. As you reread, complete the Skills Focus questions below. Then use your answers and annotations from the questions to help you complete the Write activity.

◎ SKILLS FOCUS

1. Identify an important stage direction in Act III, Scene iii, of the play. Explain how this stage direction works together with the dialogue to develop the character of Hamlet.

2. Read lines 312 through 316 in Act III, Scene iii. Knowing that "limed" refers to a bird trapped with a lime-based paste, what do you think Shakespeare suggests, denotatively and connotatively, by using the phrase "limed soul" in line 313?

3. Read lines 75 through 79 of Act I, Scene ii, and explain how the overall meaning of Hamlet's soliloquy is affected by the word choice and tone of these lines.

4. Rewatch the "To be or not to be" speech as interpreted by Laurence Olivier and the Sonnet Man. Explain how Olivier's version is similar to and different from Sonnet Man's version. How do both versions relate back to Shakespeare's version? What does each version of the speech reveal about the time period and culture from which it came?

5. Throughout the play, Hamlet is deeply upset by his challenging situation: his father is dead, and he cannot trust anyone around him. Highlight two moments in which you believe Hamlet reveals his true self amidst these challenges. Explain why you chose these moments, and support your answer with textual evidence from other parts of the excerpt.

✏ WRITE

LITERARY ANALYSIS: A soliloquy is a speech in which a character thinks out loud while alone onstage. Hamlet's three soliloquies in the excerpt offer the reader a window into Hamlet's feelings concerning his father, mother, uncle, and especially himself. How does each soliloquy express Hamlet's conflicted feelings in a unique way? Be sure to use textual evidence to support your analysis.

Reading & Writing Companion

The Postmaster

FICTION
Rabindranath Tagore
1918

Introduction

studysync

Acclaimed Bengali poet, novelist, playwright, and composer, Rabindranath Tagore (1861–1941) was the first non-European Nobel Prize laureate. Today, the Indian, Bangladeshi, and Sri Lankan national anthems are all based on his writings. In "The Postmaster," one of Tagore's most memorable short stories, a postmaster moves from the city of Calcutta to the village of Ulapur and befriends a young orphan. What follows is a moving meditation on the nature of loneliness and love.

"At any rate, the postmaster had but little company; nor had he much to do."

NOTES

1   The postmaster first took up his duties in the village of Ulapur. Though the village was a small one, there was an indigo factory near by, and the proprietor, an Englishman, had managed to get a post office established.

2   Our postmaster belonged to Calcutta. He felt like a fish out of water in this remote village. His office and living-room were in a dark thatched shed, not far from a green, slimy pond, surrounded on all sides by a dense growth.

Drawing of 19th century Calcutta, India, from a 19th century print, from *The Age We Live In: A History of the Nineteenth Century*

3   The men employed in the indigo factory had no leisure; moreover, they were hardly desirable companions for decent folk. Nor is a Calcutta boy an adept in the art of associating with others. Among strangers he appears either proud or ill at ease. At any rate, the postmaster had but little company; nor had he much to do.

Skill:
Theme

The postmaster does not enjoy his new setting. He can't appreciate life in the village. It seems he feels isolated and that life here is something to be endured. This suggests isolation is a theme.

4   At times he tried his hand at writing a verse or two. That the movement of the leaves and the clouds of the sky were enough to fill life with joy—such were the sentiments to which he sought to give expression. But God knows that the poor fellow would have felt it as the gift of a new life, if some genie of the Arabian Nights had in one night swept away the trees, leaves and all, and replaced them with a macadamised road, hiding the clouds from view with rows of tall houses.

5   The postmaster's salary was small. He had to cook his own meals, which he used to share with Ratan, an orphan girl of the village, who did odd jobs for him.

6   When in the evening the smoke began to curl up from the village cowsheds, and the cicalas chirped in every bush; when the mendicants[1] of the Baül sect sang their shrill songs in their daily meeting-place, when any poet, who had attempted to watch the movement of the leaves in the dense bamboo

___

1. **mendicants** members of a religious order who have taken a vow of poverty

thickets, would have felt a ghostly shiver run down his back, the postmaster would light his little lamp, and call out "Ratan."

7 Ratan would sit outside waiting for this call, and, instead of coming in at once, would reply, "Did you call me, sir?"

8 "What are you doing?" the postmaster would ask.

9 "I must be going to light the kitchen fire," would be the answer.

10 And the postmaster would say: "Oh, let the kitchen fire be for awhile; light me my pipe first."

11 At last Ratan would enter, with puffed-out cheeks, vigorously blowing into a flame a live coal to light the tobacco. This would give the postmaster an opportunity of conversing. "Well, Ratan," perhaps he would begin, "do you remember anything of your mother?" That was a fertile subject. Ratan partly remembered, and partly didn't. Her father had been fonder of her than her mother; him she recollected more vividly. He used to come home in the evening after his work, and one or two evenings stood out more clearly than others, like pictures in her memory. Ratan would sit on the floor near the postmaster's feet, as memories crowded in upon her. She called to mind a little brother that she had—and how on some bygone cloudy day she had played at fishing with him on the edge of the pond, with a twig for a make-believe fishing-rod. Such little incidents would drive out greater events from her mind. Thus, as they talked, it would often get very late, and the postmaster would feel too lazy to do any cooking at all. Ratan would then hastily light the fire, and toast some unleavened bread, which, with the cold remnants of the morning meal, was enough for their supper.

12 On some evenings, seated at his desk in the corner of the big empty shed, the postmaster too would call up memories of his own home, of his mother and his sister, of those for whom in his **exile** his heart was sad,—memories which were always haunting him, but which he could not talk about with the men of the factory, though he found himself naturally recalling them aloud in the presence of the simple little girl. And so it came about that the girl would allude to his people as mother, brother, and sister, as if she had known them all her life. In fact, she had a complete picture of each one of them painted in her little heart.

13 One noon, during a break in the rains, there was a cool soft breeze blowing; the smell of the damp grass and leaves in the hot sun felt like the warm breathing of the tired earth on one's body. A persistent bird went on all the afternoon repeating the burden of its one complaint in Nature's audience chamber.

14 The postmaster had nothing to do. The shimmer of the freshly washed leaves, and the banked-up remnants of the retreating rain-clouds were sights to see;

Skill:
Story Elements

Ratan, an orphan, somewhat recalls her parents. She sits on the floor like a favorite pet. This shows how economic setting influences themes of love, loss, and family.

Skill:
Theme

The postmaster is homesick and overwhelmed by memories of his family. This deep connection to his past and his inability to share his feelings with the men in his village show that he is isolated from them but not from the little girl.

Copyright © BookheadEd Learning, LLC

and the postmaster was watching them and thinking to himself: "Oh, if only some kindred soul were near—just one loving human being whom I could hold near my heart!" This was exactly, he went on to think, what that bird was trying to say, and it was the same feeling which the murmuring leaves were striving to express. But no one knows, or would believe, that such an idea might also take possession of an ill-paid village postmaster in the deep, silent mid-day interval of his work.

15   The postmaster sighed, and called out "Ratan." Ratan was then sprawling beneath the guava-tree, busily engaged in eating unripe guavas. At the voice of her master, she ran up breathlessly, saying: "Were you calling me, Dada?" "I was thinking," said the postmaster, "of teaching you to read." And then for the rest of the afternoon he taught her the alphabet.

16   Thus, in a very short time, Ratan had got as far as the double consonants.

17   It seemed as though the showers of the season would never end. Canals, ditches, and hollows were all overflowing with water. Day and night the patter of rain was heard, and the croaking of frogs. The village roads became impassable, and marketing had to be done in punts.

18   One heavily clouded morning, the postmaster's little pupil had been long waiting outside the door for her call, but, not hearing it as usual, she took up her dog-eared book, and slowly entered the room. She found her master stretched out on his bed, and, thinking that he was resting, she was about to retire on tip-toe, when she suddenly heard her name—"Ratan!" She turned at once and asked: "Were you sleeping, Dada?" The postmaster in a plaintive voice said: "I am not well. Feel my head; is it very hot?"

19   In the loneliness of his exile, and in the gloom of the rains, his ailing body needed a little tender nursing. He longed to remember the touch on the forehead of soft hands with tinkling bracelets, to imagine the presence of loving womanhood, the nearness of mother and sister. And the exile was not disappointed. Ratan ceased to be a little girl. She at once stepped into the post of mother, called in the village doctor, gave the patient his pills at the proper intervals, sat up all night by his pillow, cooked his gruel for him, and every now and then asked: "Are you feeling a little better, Dada?"

20   It was some time before the postmaster, with weakened body, was able to leave his sick-bed. "No more of this," said he with decision. "I must get a transfer." He at once wrote off to Calcutta an application for a transfer, on the ground of the unhealthiness of the place.

21   Relieved from her duties as nurse, Ratan again took up her old place outside the door. But she no longer heard the same old call. She would sometimes peep inside furtively to find the postmaster sitting on his chair, or stretched on his bed, and staring absent-mindedly into the air. While Ratan was awaiting her call, the postmaster was awaiting a reply to his application. The girl read

Copyright © BookheadEd Learning, LLC

NOTES

her old lessons over and over again,—her great fear was lest, when the call came, she might be found wanting in the double consonants. At last, after a week, the call did come one evening. With an overflowing heart Ratan rushed into the room with her—"Were you calling me, Dada?"

22   The postmaster said: "I am going away to-morrow, Ratan."

23   "Where are you going, Dada?"

24   "I am going home."

25   "When will you come back?"

26   "I am not coming back."

27   Ratan asked no other question. The postmaster, of his own accord, went on to tell her that his application for a transfer had been rejected, so he had **resigned** his post and was going home. For a long time neither of them spoke another word. The lamp went on dimly burning, and from a leak in one corner of the thatch water dripped steadily into an earthen vessel on the floor beneath it.

28   After a while Ratan rose, and went off to the kitchen to prepare the meal; but she was not so quick about it as on other days. Many new things to think of had entered her little brain. When the postmaster had finished his supper, the girl suddenly asked him: "Dada, will you take me to your home?"

29   The postmaster laughed. "What an idea!" said he; but he did not think it necessary to explain to the girl wherein lay the absurdity.

30   That whole night, in her waking and in her dreams, the postmaster's laughing reply haunted her—"What an idea!"

31   On getting up in the morning, the postmaster found his bath ready. He had stuck to his Calcutta habit of bathing in water drawn and kept in pitchers, instead of taking a plunge in the river as was the custom of the village. For some reason or other, the girl could not ask him about the time of his departure, so she had fetched the water from the river long before sunrise, that it should be ready as early as he might want it. After the bath came a call for Ratan. She entered noiselessly, and looked silently into her master's face for orders. The master said: "You need not be anxious about my going away, Ratan; I shall tell my successor to look after you." These words were kindly meant, no doubt: but **inscrutable** are the ways of a woman's heart!

32   Ratan had borne many a scolding from her master without complaint, but these kind words she could not bear. She burst out weeping, and said: "No, no, you need not tell anybody anything at all about me; I don't want to stay on here."

Skill:
Summarizing

Ratan is shocked. Her relationship to him is not valuable enough for him to stay.

This section reminds me of earlier events in the story. The postmaster was never happy in Ulapur.

33 The postmaster was **dumbfounded**. He had never seen Ratan like this before.

34 The new incumbent duly arrived, and the postmaster, having given over charge, prepared to depart. Just before starting he called Ratan and said: "Here is something for you; I hope it will keep you for some little time." He brought out from his pocket the whole of his month's salary, retaining only a **trifle** for his travelling expenses. Then Ratan fell at his feet and cried: "Oh, Dada, I pray you, don't give me anything, don't in any way trouble about me," and then she ran away out of sight.

35 The postmaster heaved a sigh, took up his carpet bag, put his umbrella over his shoulder, and, accompanied by a man carrying his many-coloured tin trunk, he slowly made for the boat.

36 When he got in and the boat was under way, and the rain-swollen river, like a stream of tears welling up from the earth, swirled and sobbed at her bows, then he felt a pain at heart; the grief-stricken face of a village girl seemed to represent for him the great unspoken pervading grief of Mother Earth herself. At one time he had an impulse to go back, and bring away along with him that lonesome waif, forsaken of the world. But the wind had just filled the sails, the boat had got well into the middle of the turbulent current, and already the village was left behind, and its outlying burning-ground came in sight.

37 So the traveller, borne on the breast of the swift-flowing river, consoled himself with philosophical reflections on the numberless meetings and partings going on in the world—on death, the great parting, from which none returns.

38 But Ratan had no philosophy. She was wandering about the post office in a flood of tears. It may be that she had still a lurking hope in some corner of her heart that her Dada would return, and that is why she could not tear herself away. Alas for our foolish human nature! Its fond mistakes are persistent. The dictates of reason take a long time to assert their own sway. The surest proofs meanwhile are disbelieved. False hope is clung to with all one's might and main, till a day comes when it has sucked the heart dry and it forcibly breaks through its bonds and departs. After that comes the misery of awakening, and then once again the longing to get back into the maze of the same mistakes.

First Read

Read "The Postmaster." After you read, complete the Think Questions below.

☁ THINK QUESTIONS

1. Does the postmaster seem well-adapted to his new home? Use evidence from the text to describe the postmaster's feelings about the village.

2. Based on the text, what can you infer about the life of an orphan in Ulapur? How is Ratan's life in Ulapur different from that of the postmaster? Be sure to cite specific passages from the text.

3. What role does nature, particularly the seasons and the weather, play in the story? Explain how the author uses natural imagery, referring to specific examples from the text in your response.

4. Use context to determine the meaning of the verb **resigned** as it is used in "The Postmaster." Write your definition of *resigned* here and explain how you arrived at it. Use specific examples from the text.

5. The Latin prefix *in-* means "not," and the Latin root "scrutari," means "to search or examine" Using this information and your knowledge of word patterns and relationships, write your best definition of the word **inscrutable** here.

Please note that excerpts and passages in the StudySync® library and this workbook are intended as touchstones to generate interest in an author's work. The excerpts and passages do not substitute for the reading of entire texts, and StudySync® strongly recommends that students seek out and purchase the whole literary or informational work in order to experience it as the author intended. Links to online resellers are available in our digital library. In addition, complete works may be ordered through an authorized reseller by filling out and returning to StudySync® the order form enclosed in this workbook.

Reading & Writing Companion   **319**

Skill:
Theme

Use the Checklist to analyze Theme in "The Postmaster." Refer to the sample student annotations about Theme in the text.

••• CHECKLIST FOR THEME

In order to identify two or more themes or central ideas of a text, note the following:

✓ the subject and how it relates to the themes in the text

✓ if one or more themes is stated directly in the text

✓ details in the text that help to reveal each theme:

- the title and chapter headings

- details about the setting

- the narrator's or speaker's tone

- characters' thoughts, actions, and dialogue

- the central conflict, climax, and resolution of the conflict

- shifts in characters, setting, or plot events

✓ when and how the themes interact with each other

To determine two or more themes or central ideas of a text and analyze their development over the course of the text, including how they interact and build on one another to produce a complex account, consider the following questions:

✓ What are the themes in the text? When do they emerge?

✓ How does each theme develop over the course of the text?

✓ How do the themes interact and build on one another?

Skill:
Theme

Reread paragraphs 23–32 from "The Postmaster." Then, using the Checklist on the previous page, answer the multiple-choice questions below.

⟳ YOUR TURN

1. This question has two parts. First, answer Part A. Then, answer Part B.

   Part A: Details about the setting in paragraph 27 help develop the theme of disconnection by—

   - ○ A. introducing the idea that the postmaster wants to go home.
   - ○ B. explaining why Ratan thinks the postmaster will come back.
   - ○ C. suggesting that the postmaster will be unhappy no matter where he lives.
   - ○ D. emphasizing how quiet and lonely the postmaster's home is.

   Part B: Which of the following quotes from the text BEST supports the answer in Part A?

   - ○ A. ". . . his application for a transfer had been rejected . . ."
   - ○ B. ". . . he had resigned his post and was going home."
   - ○ C. ". . . neither of them spoke another word."
   - ○ D. ". . . the thatch water dripped steadily into an earthen vessel . . ."

2. The characterization of the postmaster in paragraph 29 contributes to the theme of isolation from others by—

   - ○ A. showing he has a sense of humor and can laugh at himself.
   - ○ B. suggesting he thinks Ratan is part of the village life he is eager to leave.
   - ○ C. explaining why he thinks Ratan's idea is absurd.
   - ○ D. introducing the idea that Ratan would not like living in Calcutta.

3. The depiction of the postmaster in paragraphs 31–32 further develops the theme of isolation from others because they—

- ○ A. demonstrate how frequently he scolds Ratan.
- ○ B. illustrate his disconnect from the rituals of the villages as well as Ratan's feelings.
- ○ C. indicate that he is demanding about routines in the morning.
- ○ D. show that he cares about Ratan's work with the new postmaster.

Skill:
Story Elements

Use the Checklist to analyze Story Elements in "The Postmaster." Refer to the sample student annotations about Story Elements in the text.

••• CHECKLIST FOR STORY ELEMENTS

In order to identify the impact of the author's choices regarding how to develop and relate elements of a story or drama, note the following:

- ✓ where and when the story takes place, who the main characters are, and the main conflict, or problem, in the plot

- ✓ the order of the action

- ✓ how the characters are introduced and developed

- ✓ the impact that the author's choice of setting has on the characters and their attempt to solve the problem

- ✓ the point of view the author uses, and how this shapes what readers know about the characters in the story

To analyze the impact of the author's choices regarding how to develop and relate elements of a story or drama, consider the following questions:

- ✓ How does the author's choices affect the story elements? The development of the plot?

- ✓ How does the setting influence the characters?

- ✓ Which elements of the setting impact the plot, and in particular the problem the characters face and must solve?

- ✓ Are there any flashbacks or other story elements that have an effect on the development of events in the plot? How does the author's choice of utilizing a flashback affect this development?

- ✓ How does the author introduce and develop characters in the story? Why do you think they made these choices?

Skill:
Story Elements

Reread paragraphs 18 and 19 from "The Postmaster." Then, using the Checklist on the previous page, answer the multiple-choice questions below.

⟳ YOUR TURN

1. How does the economic setting affect the characterization of Ratan in this scene?

   ○ A. It suggests that Ratan has nothing better to do than care for the postmaster.
   ○ B. It hints that the postmaster should pay Ratan for the many services she provides.
   ○ C. It highlights the postmaster's position as an authority figure to Ratan.
   ○ D. It shows that women, even young ones like Ratan, were expected to care for men.

2. The setting of this scene affects the impact of the development of the plot by—

   ○ A. including a flashback to a conflict between the postmaster and his family.
   ○ B. introducing the inner conflict Ratan is experiencing about her role in the postmaster's life.
   ○ C. heightening the growing tension in the story through the depiction of the weather.
   ○ D. showing the climax of the story as the postmaster struggles to rely on Ratan for help.

3. Which statement best evaluates the way the author uses details about the economic context of the story to develop the theme in this scene?

   ○ A. The use of the word *Dada* clearly shows that the orphan Ratan has come to rely on the postmaster as much as he has come to rely on her, which suggests a theme of family.
   ○ B. The postmaster's inability to go to work in a tough economic climate due to sickness strongly develops themes of life's unfairness.
   ○ C. The doctor's visit clearly highlights that other men in the town are of a higher status than the postmaster, which introduces themes of jealousy.
   ○ D. Ratan's eagerness to take on a parental role to the postmaster strongly develops a theme relating to money and power.

Skill:
Summarizing

Use the Checklist to analyze Summarizing in "The Postmaster." Refer to the sample student annotations about Summarizing in the text.

••• CHECKLIST FOR SUMMARIZING

In order to provide an objective summary of a text, note the following:

- ✓ answers to the basic questions *who*, *what*, *where*, *when*, *why*, and *how*

- ✓ in literature or nonfiction, note how two or more themes or central ideas are developed over the course of the text, and how they interact and build on one another to produce a complex account

- ✓ stay objective, and do not add your own personal thoughts, judgments, or opinions to the summary

To provide an objective summary of a text, consider the following questions:

- ✓ What are the answers to basic *who*, *what*, *where*, *when*, *why*, and *how* questions in literature and works of nonfiction?

- ✓ Does my summary include how two or more themes or central ideas are developed over the course of the text, and how they interact and build on one another in my summary?

- ✓ Is my summary objective, or have I added my own thoughts, judgments, and personal opinions?

Please note that excerpts and passages in the StudySync® library and this workbook are intended as touchstones to generate interest in an author's work. The excerpts and passages do not substitute for the reading of entire texts, and StudySync® strongly recommends that students seek out and purchase the whole literary or informational work in order to experience it as the author intended. Links to online resellers are available in our digital library. In addition, complete works may be ordered through an authorized reseller by filling out and returning to StudySync® the order form enclosed in this workbook.

Reading & Writing
Companion

325

Skill:
Summarizing

Reread paragraphs 19–25 from the text. Then, using the Checklist on the previous page, answer the multiple-choice questions below.

♺ YOUR TURN

1. What is the most important idea in paragraph 21?

   ○ A. Decisions are a result of both our inner feelings and reality.
   ○ B. Being lonely causes illness.
   ○ C. Resettling in a new place can cause depression and be grueling on the body.
   ○ D. People make poor decisions when they are sick.

2. Which of the following selections best identifies two themes present in the section of text?

   ○ A. "At the voice of her master, she ran up breathlessly, saying: "Were you calling me, Dada?"
   ○ B. "While Ratan was awaiting her call, the postmaster was awaiting a reply to his application."
   ○ C. "Relieved from her duties as nurse, Ratan again took up her old place outside the door. But she no longer heard the same old call."
   ○ D. "In the loneliness of his exile, and in the gloom of the rains, his ailing body needed a little tender nursing."

3. Which statement below is an objective summary of the text?

   ○ A. The postmaster feels bored and lonely in the new village.
   ○ B. Ratan provides the postmaster with some comfort, but this does not cause him to stay.
   ○ C. The postmaster longs for life in Calcutta and this desire to belong outweighs a perceived obligation to Ratan or his post.
   ○ D. The postmaster's sudden departure is selfish and provides little comfort to Ratan.

Close Read

Reread "The Postmaster." As you reread, complete the Skills Focus questions below. Then use your answers and annotations from the questions to help you complete the Write activity.

◎ SKILLS FOCUS

1. In the first four paragraphs, find descriptions of setting—namely, the village of Ulapur and the city of Calcutta. Explain how these descriptions help characterize the postmaster.

2. In paragraphs 1-12, highlight details that show what kind of people the postmaster and Ratan are. How does the narrator want you to feel about each character based on the descriptions he uses in the story? In your annotations, explain how the author's use of language develops the story's themes.

3. Highlight details that show the economic context of the story. Explain how much the characters' wealth, or lack of it, reveals their true character.

4. Highlight elements in "The Postmaster" which answer its basic who, what, where, when, why and how questions. In an annotation, write a brief, objective summary of the text, being sure to note at least two themes developed throughout the text.

5. The last paragraph directly states some themes of the story, particularly as it pertains to the ways circumstances can inform the choices people make. Highlight and restate these themes in your own words, noting how they build on one another. How do the postmaster and Ratan illustrate these themes? How do they reveal their true selves through the decisions they make?

✏ WRITE

COMPARE AND CONTRAST: Write a response comparing and contrasting the postmaster and Ratan's relationship with the village. How do their connections to place impact the story and reveal the text's themes? Be sure to use both evidence from the text and your own original **commentary** to support your analysis.

A Letter to NFL GMs

ARGUMENTATIVE TEXT

Shaquem Griffin

2018

Introduction

Time and time again, Shaquem Griffin (b. 1995) has been told that he doesn't have what it takes to play the punishing game of football. In this open letter to the general managers of the National Football League, Griffin opens up about how he's fought against adversity ever since a congenital illness prevented his left hand from fully developing. From the trash-talk of other players to the humiliation of being ignored by teams and coaches alike, Griffin traces how his life's setbacks have helped to define and strengthen his character. Several weeks after the publication of this letter, Shaquem Griffin was selected in the fifth round of the 2018 NFL Draft by the

"Nobody was ever going to tell me that I couldn't be great."

NOTES

Dear NFL GMs,

1   Everything you need to know about me you can learn by going back to when I was eight years old.

2   So let me take you there.

3   It was a Friday night in St. Petersburg, Florida, and I was sleeping — or at least I was trying to. My mind was going crazy because my twin brother, Shaquill, and I had a football game the next morning. He was in the room with me, and he couldn't sleep either, because if we won the next day, we'd be in the playoffs. I had my covers pulled up over my royal blue home jersey — that's right, I was *sleeping* in it. When I was a kid, I always slept in my football jersey the night before a game. That's how ready I was to play every Saturday.

4   So the next morning, when we got to the field — since it was youth football and there were weight **restrictions** — we had to weigh in. And I don't know if they still do it this way, but back then, each coach would weight the opposing team's players, and if you were too heavy or too light, you weren't eligible to play. I had to drop a couple of pounds to make weight for that game, and I had weighed myself the night before and again that morning, so I knew I was good to go.

5   But when the opposing coach weighed me, he said I was too heavy.

6   He told me I couldn't play.

7   So I was heartbroken, right? I mean, I was *devastated*. My coach put his arm around me, told me everything was gonna be O.K. and took me back into our locker room and weighed me himself.

8   This time, I was *not* overweight.

Please note that excerpts and passages in the StudySync® library and this workbook are intended as touchstones to generate interest in an author's work. The excerpts and passages do not substitute for the reading of entire texts, and StudySync® strongly recommends that students seek out and purchase the whole literary or informational work in order to experience it as the author intended. Links to online resellers are available in our digital library. In addition, complete works may be ordered through an authorized reseller by filling out and returning to StudySync® the order form enclosed in this workbook.

Reading & Writing Companion   **329**

9   I was thinking the other coach's scale must be broken or something. It didn't even occur to me that somebody might **deliberately** try to keep me off the football field. I was just a little kid, you know? Too young to understand that people got motives.

10   So my coach took me back over to the guy who weighed me in so we could do it again, and — now, this is a long time ago, so I don't remember exactly what was said, but basically, the opposing coach said that it wasn't about my weight.

11   It was about my *hand*.

12   He said I shouldn't have been allowed to play football *at all*.

13   Because football is for two-handed players.

14   Mind you, I didn't even know this guy. So I didn't know why he had a problem with me playing. I had been playing for a few years and I was pretty good, so maybe he just wanted to keep one of our team's better players off the field so his team had a better chance to win. I honestly don't know.

15   But this was the first time I ever had to deal with somebody telling me I shouldn't — or couldn't — do something because of my hand. Like I was defective or something. Like I didn't belong.

16   And that was the moment I realized I was always going to have to prove people wrong.

. . .

17   I'm not going to get into an explanation of the condition I was born with that prevented the fingers of my left hand from fully developing. Or talk about the

time when I was four years old and I tried to cut my own fingers off with a kitchen knife because I was in constant pain. Or about when I got my left hand amputated shortly after. That's stuff you probably already know about anyway — and if you don't, you can Google it. The story is out there.

And it's not some sob story or anything like that. It's not even a sad story — at least not to me.

18 It's just . . . *my* story.

19 I'm blessed to have thick skin. But I'm even more blessed to have a family that never let me make excuses and who raised me to never listen to anybody who told me I couldn't do something — especially because of my hand.

20 My dad used to build all kinds of **contraptions** to help me lift weights. We had this one thing — we called it "the book," and it was basically a piece of wood wrapped up in some cloth that I would hold up against the bar with my left arm when I bench pressed so my arms would be even. We had another block that I used for stuff like dips and push-ups, and I had chains and other straps to hold dumbbells for things like curls and shrugs.

21 And my dad used to work me, Shaquill and our older brother, Andre, hard.

22 In our backyard, we had a couple of stacks of cinder blocks with a stick across the top, like a hurdle. And when we would run routes, we would have to jump over the hurdle and do other obstacles mid-route. Then my dad would throw us the ball, and he'd throw it *hard*, right at our chest. And every time we dropped it, he would say, "Nothing comes easy."

23 That was kind of his motto — not just for me, but for all of us.

24 *Nothing comes easy.*

25 Man . . . I hated those workouts. There were definitely times when I wanted to quit. Sometimes, when my dad threw the ball so hard that it bounced off my chest or it hit me in the face, I would be like, "I don't wanna do this anymore."

26 But he never let me quit.

27 "You'll thank me one day," he'd say.

28 At the time, I didn't believe him. Now, I understand, and I thank him every chance I get, because all that work in the backyard helped me to develop the mentality that I can handle anything — that whatever you come at me with, I can come back at you even harder.

29 That's what I did that day when that youth coach told me I shouldn't be playing football.

30 I ended up being allowed to play that day, and I remember it like it was yesterday. It was near the end of the game, and we were ahead. I was on defense, playing linebacker. The outside receiver ran a slant route, and I read the play, jumped the route, dove in the air and caught the ball, flipping over onto my back to secure it before I hit the ground. It was the first time I had ever intercepted a pass in a game, and it basically sealed the win for us and sent us to the playoffs.

31 I got up and ran off the field, holding the ball up in the air with my one good hand and thinking that from that moment forward, nobody was ever going to tell me that I didn't belong on a football field.

32 And nobody was ever going to tell me that I couldn't be great.

33 I rode that mentality all the way through high school.

34 I got picked on because of my hand and I had guys trash-talk me and stuff like that, but most of the time, I just ignored it. On the football field, I got off to kind of a slow start adjusting to the high school game, but eventually I grew to be a leader and a team captain.

35 But right here, instead of talking about the success I've had, I think I would rather tell you about some of the more difficult times in my life — the lowest points. Because I think that's when true character shows. That's when you find out who people really are — what they're really made of.

36 And the lowest points for me came when I was in college.

37 I went to UCF thinking I was going to play as a freshman, and everybody was going to know my name. I was so confident.

38 But it wasn't like that at all.

39 My freshman year, I got redshirted[1]. The following year, I played well in the spring and worked my way up to second string on the depth chart.

_____

1. **redshirted** in college athletics, being "redshirted" means having one's participation delayed or suspended in order to increase the length of eligibility for the program

40   Then, right before the season-opener against Penn State, I got bumped down to third string.

41   The next week, I got moved to the scout team.

42   And nobody told me why.

43   Whenever I asked one of the coaches why I was being demoted, they just said things like, "Keep working," and, "Stay focused," and, "Your time will come."

44   So that's basically what I did for my first three years at UCF.

45   I think the hardest part about those first few years was watching Shaquill play on Saturdays. We've always told each other since we were kids that no matter what either of us is doing, we live through each other. His success is my success, and vice versa. And we meant that.

46   I didn't travel with the team much those first few years. When it came time for the team to go on the road, my brother and our two roommates, who were also on the team, all went. So on Saturdays, it was just me, alone in our dorm[2] room watching the game. Sometimes the game wasn't even on ESPN or FOX or anything, so I had to stream it on my laptop. I'd be sitting there on the couch, alone, the whole dorm silent except for the game commentary as I was watching my brother play . . . and living through him.

47   I used to tell my mom all the time that college was a negative place for me. Not UCF in general — I love my school and I'll represent it forever. It was just . . . that dorm room, man.

Unit 412, Room C.

48   I spent so much time those first three years in Orlando sitting in that room, wondering why I wasn't getting an opportunity to play on Saturdays. It got to

2. **dorm** short for dormitory, a facility where college students live

Please note that excerpts and passages in the StudySync® library and this workbook are intended as touchstones to generate interest in an author's work. The excerpts and passages do not substitute for the reading of entire texts, and StudySync® strongly recommends that students seek out and purchase the whole literary or informational work in order to experience it as the author intended. Links to online resellers are available in our digital library. In addition, complete works may be ordered through an authorized reseller by filling out and returning to StudySync® the order form enclosed in this workbook.

Reading & Writing
Companion

333

NOTES

the point where that dorm was just so full of negative **vibes**, because I pretty much kept everything to myself. I didn't really talk to anybody about what I was feeling — especially not to Shaquill.

49　It's a tough spot to be in, right? I mean, my twin brother was doing his thing. The dream was happening for him, and he was earning every single bit of it, working hard and showing out on the field.

50　I wanted that for myself so badly, and even though I felt like I was good enough, and I was doing everything my coaches asked me to, I wasn't even getting an opportunity. And the last thing I wanted to do was dump all my negativity on Shaquill and bring him down. So I made sure I was always positive around him. I never talked to him about how I was feeling those first three years.

51　The lowest of the lows was probably the summer before my third season, when the coaches had most of the guys stay in Orlando to work out while other guys went home for the summer.

52　They kept Shaquill at UCF for the summer.

53　They sent me home to St. Petersburg.

54　It was the first time Shaquill and I had ever really been apart.

55　I spent that summer working with my dad and Andre. My dad has a tow truck, so I would wake up at 7 a.m. and go to work with him, towing cars. I would get off around 6 p.m. and go to my old high school to work out with the track team, then I'd meet up with Andre around 8 p.m. and work with him until midnight, cleaning offices at the local Chevy dealership.

56　I did that every day, Monday through Saturday, for the entire summer.

57　I remember one time, when I was working with my dad, we towed this one guy's car, and when we dropped it off, the guy pulled a five-dollar bill out of his pocket and went to hand it to me. But before I took it, he pulled it back and ripped it in half. He gave me one half and put the other half back in his pocket. I didn't know if I was supposed to laugh or if I should have been mad. I just kind of looked at the guy.

58　He looked back at me and said, "Keep on working, son. Because nothing comes easy."

59　I still have that ripped-up five-dollar bill somewhere at my parents' house because I never want to forget what that guy said to me that day — it was the same thing my dad always used to say when I was a kid.

60   *Nothing comes easy.*

61   And looking back, at the time, I think I needed to be reminded of that. Because if sitting in my dorm room alone and watching games on my laptop was a low point, towing cars and cleaning out trash cans in those office cubicles at night was even worse.

62   Honestly, that summer was the first and only time since I was a little kid jumping hurdles and trying to catch rockets from my dad in the backyard that I thought about quitting football.

63   Those were pretty dark times for me.

64   Then, after I went back to UCF for my third season and we went 0–12, Coach Frost came in and brought me back into the light.

65   You probably know what happened next: Over the next two seasons, Coach Frost turned an 0–12 program into an undefeated, national championship team. (That's right, I said national championship team. And nobody can convince me otherwise.)

66   Along the way, he gave me the opportunity I had been waiting for ever since I first arrived at UCF.

67   And I took advantage of it.

68   I think that what I did on the field, especially this past season, speaks for itself. So I don't feel like I need to get into all that. I'll let the tape do the talking.

69   Besides, I don't define myself by my successes.

70   I define myself by **adversity,** and how I've persevered.

• • •

71   I don't sleep in my jersey the night before games anymore. But I did sleep at the football facility for basically the whole preseason camp this last season. I went out and bought a blow-up mattress and a comforter, and then I went to Publix and stocked up on drinks and snacks and stuff so I had everything I needed. And instead of going back and forth to my dorm during camp, I slept at the football facility and lifted weights and watched extra film at night.

72   I just knew it was going to be my last camp at UCF, so I wanted to get the full experience, you know?

73   I just think that as guys progress through their football careers, they start thinking about the game differently. They start thinking about getting their

Please note that excerpts and passages in the StudySync® library and this workbook are intended as touchstones to generate interest in an author's work. The excerpts and passages do not substitute for the reading of entire texts, and StudySync® strongly recommends that students seek out and purchase the whole literary or informational work in order to experience it as the author intended. Links to online resellers are available in our digital library. In addition, complete works may be ordered through an authorized reseller by filling out and returning to StudySync® the order form enclosed in this workbook.

Reading & Writing Companion   **335**

college paid for, or making it to the NFL so they can take care of their families. They start looking at it as a job — and they should, because to excel at the highest levels, you have to take the game seriously. It's a big responsibility.

74   But I think some guys forget about why they started playing back when they were kids — how they loved the game so much that they'd sleep in their jersey the night before a game.

75   I started playing football because I loved it. And yeah, just like anybody else, my view of the game has definitely changed as I've gotten older.

76   But it hasn't turned into a job or an obligation.

77   It's developed into a *purpose*.

78   I've had people doubt me my whole life, and I know that there are a lot of kids out there with various deformities or birth defects or whatever labels people want to put on them, and they're going to be doubted, too. And I'm convinced that God has put me on this earth for a reason, and that reason is to show people that it doesn't matter what anybody else says, because people are going to doubt you **regardless**. That's a fact of life for everybody, but especially for those with birth defects or other so-called disabilities.

79   The important thing is that you don't doubt *yourself*.

80   I feel like all the boys and girls out there with birth defects . . . we have our own little nation, and we've got to support each other, because everybody in this world deserves to show what they can do without anybody telling them they *can't*.

81   I know there are some scouts and coaches — and even some of you GMs out there — who are probably doubting me, and that's O.K. I get it. I only have one hand, and because of that, there have always been people who have questioned whether or not I could play this game.

82   If you're one of those GMs who believes that I can play in the NFL, I just want to say thank you. I appreciate you, and I'm excited for the opportunity to play for you and prove you right.

83   And if one you're of those who is doubting me . . . well, I want to thank you, too. Because you're what keeps me motivated every day to work hard and play even harder.

84   Back when I was eight years old, I played because I loved the game. I still do. But now, I also play because I believe it's my purpose. I know that it won't come easy. Nothing comes easy. But I will fulfill that purpose. I have no doubt.

85　Sincerely,

86　Shaquem Griffin
University of Central Florida
2017 National Champions (13–0)

By Shaquem Griffin, 2018. Used by permission of The Players' Tribune.

✏ WRITE

EXPLANATORY ESSAY: Why do you think Shaquem Griffin chose to write an open letter to general managers in the NFL? What is Griffin's point of view in the letter and how does he use his personal experiences to defend it? What do you think he hoped to accomplish by publishing this letter online? Write a response in which you answer these questions. Remember to use textual evidence to support your response.

Please note that excerpts and passages in the StudySync® library and this workbook are intended as touchstones to generate interest in an author's work. The excerpts and passages do not substitute for the reading of entire texts, and StudySync® strongly recommends that students seek out and purchase the whole literary or informational work in order to experience it as the author intended. Links to online resellers are available in our digital library. In addition, complete works may be ordered through an authorized reseller by filling out and returning to StudySync® the order form enclosed in this workbook.

Reading & Writing Companion　337

Men We Reaped: A Memoir

INFORMATIONAL TEXT
Jesmyn Ward
2013

Introduction

Jesmyn Ward (b. 1977) grew up in DeLisle, Mississippi, a small rural town along the Gulf Coast. She was the first woman to win the National Book Award twice: in 2011, for her second novel, *Salvage the Bones*, as well as for her third novel, 2017's *Sing, Unburied, Sing*. Ward's writing primarily focuses on the lives of the people in the communities where she grew up. She is known for creating honest, robust, complicated characters, and for her portrayals of life along the Gulf Coast with all of its lyricism and mystery. *Men We Reaped: A Memoir* traces Ward's search for meaning after her world was turned upside down by the violent deaths of her brother and four close personal friends over a four-year

"Somebody died here."

Prologue

1   Whenever my mother drove us from coastal Mississippi to New Orleans to visit my father on the weekend, she would say, "Lock the doors." After my mother and father split for the last time before they divorced, my father moved to New Orleans, while we remained in DeLisle, Mississippi.

2   My father's first house in the Crescent City was a modest one-bedroom, painted yellow, with bars on the window. It was in Shrewsbury, a small Black neighborhood that spread under and to the north of the causeway overpass. The house was **bounded** by a fenced industrial yard to the north and by the rushing, plunking sound of the cars on the elevated interstate to the south. I was the oldest of four, and since I was the oldest, I was the one who bossed my one brother, Joshua, and my two sisters, Nerissa and Charine, and my cousin Aldon, who lived with us for years, to arrange my father's extra sheets and sofa cushion into pallets on the living room floor so we all had enough room to sleep. My parents, who were attempting to reconcile and would fail, slept in the only bedroom. Joshua insisted that there was a ghost in the house, and at night we'd lie on our backs in the TV-less living room, watch the barred shadows slink across the walls, and wait for something to change, for something that wasn't supposed to be there, to move.

3   "Somebody died here," Josh said.

4   "How you know?" I said.

5   "Daddy told me," he said.

6   "You just trying to scare us," I said. What I didn't say: *It's working.*

7   I was in junior high then, in the late eighties and early nineties, and I attended a majority White, Episcopalian Mississippi private school. I was a small-town girl, and my classmates in Mississippi were as provincial as I was. My classmates called New Orleans the "murder capital." They told horror stories about White people being shot while unloading groceries from their cars. Gang **initiations**, they said. What was unspoken in this conversation—and,

given the racist proclivities of more than a few of my classmates, I'm surprised that it was unspoken—was that these gangsters, ruthlessly violent and untethered by common human decency, were Black. My school peers would often glance at me when they spoke about Black people. I was a scholarship kid, only attending the school because my mother was a maid for a few wealthy families on the Mississippi coast who sponsored my tuition. For most of my junior high and high school years, I was the only Black girl in the school. Whenever my classmates spoke about Black people or New Orleans and tried to not look at me but inevitably did, I stared back at them and thought about the young men I knew from New Orleans, my father's half brothers.

8   Uncle Bookie was our favorite of my father's half brothers. He and his brothers had spent their lives in the neighborhoods my classmates most feared. Uncle Bookie looked the most like the grandfather I'd barely known, who'd died of a **stroke** at age fifty. He had a chest like a barrel, and his eyes closed when he smiled. On hot days, Uncle Bookie would walk us through Shrewsbury toward the highway in the sky, to a ramshackle shotgun house, maroon in my memory, that stood on the corner. The lady who lived in the house sold ice pops out of the back. They were liquid sugar, and melted too quickly in the heat. On the walk to her yard, he'd crack jokes, gather more kids, lead us over the melting asphalt like a hood pied piper[1]. Once our ice pops melted to syrup in their cardboard cups, once Joshua and I had licked the sugar water from our hands and arms, Uncle Bookie would play games with us in the street: kickball, football, and basketball. He laughed when the football hit one of us in the mouth, leaving it sore and swollen, his eyes slit to the thin side of a penny. On some days he would take us with our father and his pit bull to the park under the highway. There, my father fought his dog against other dogs. The other men who watched or coaxed their dogs to savagery were dark and sweat-glazed as their animals in the heat. My brother and I always stood close to our uncle. We grabbed his forearms, holding tightly, flinching as the cars boomed overhead and the animals ripped at each other. Afterward, the dogs panted and smiled while they bled, and my brother and I relaxed our grip on our uncle, and were happy to leave the shadowed world and the threat of a dog lunging outside the fighting circle.

9   "Daddy ain't tell you no story about nobody dying in here," I said.

10   "Yeah, he did," Joshua said.

11   "You telling it," Aldon said.

12   When I was in high school, I could not reconcile the myth of New Orleans to the reality, but I knew that there was truth somewhere. My father and mother

---

1. **pied piper** a folkloric character who leads people into trouble or calamity by offering false promises

sat in the front seat of the car during those early nineties visits, when they were still married but separated, when they still had the easy rapport that years of marriage engenders, and they talked about shootings, about beatings, about murder. They gave the violence of New Orleans many names. We never saw any of that when we visited my father. But we listened to the chain-link fence rattle in the industrial yard next to my father's house and the night stretched on interminably, and we listened to my brother tell us ghost stories.

13   Yet we knew another New Orleans existed. We saw that when we piled into my mother's car and rode past the red brick projects scattered through New Orleans, two-story buildings with sagging iron balconies, massive old trees standing like sentinels at each side of the buildings, women gesticulating and scratching their heads, small dark children playing angrily, happily, sulking on the broken sidewalks. I eyed the young men through the car window. Men in sagging pants with their heads bent together, murmuring, ducking into corner stores that sold poboys shrimp oyster. I wondered what the men were talking about. I wondered who they were. I wondered what their lives were like. I wondered if they were murderers. At night on my father's living room floor, I asked Joshua again.

14   "What Daddy say happen?" I said.

15   "Said somebody got shot," Joshua said.

16   "What somebody?"

17   "A man," he said to the ceiling. Charine burrowed into my side.

18   "Shut up," Nerissa said. Aldon sighed.

19   When we left my father to go home to DeLisle, as we did every Sunday, I was sad. We all were sad, I think, even my mother, who was trying to make their marriage work, despite the distance and the years of infidelity. She'd even been contemplating moving to New Orleans, a city she hated. I missed my father. I didn't want to return to school in Mississippi on Monday morning, to walk through the glass doors to the large, fluorescent-lit classrooms, the old desks, my classmates perched on the backs of them, wearing collared shirts and khaki shorts, their legs spread, their eyeliner blue. I didn't want them to look at me after saying something about Black people, didn't want to have to avert my eyes so they didn't see me studying them, studying the entitlement they wore like another piece of clothing. Our drive home took us through New Orleans East, across the Isle Sauvage bayou[2], over the gray murmur of Lake Pontchartrain, through the billboards and strip malls of Slidell into

2. **bayou** In parts of the Southern U.S., an area of marshy, slow-moving water connected to a river or lake.

Mississippi. We took I-10 past the pine wall of Stennis Space Center, past Bay St. Louis, past Diamondhead to DeLisle. Once there, we would have exited the long, pitted highway, driven past Du Pont, shielded like Stennis behind its wall of pine trees, past the railroad tracks, past the small wooden houses set in small fields and small sandy yards, trees setting the porches in shade. Here horses stood still in fields, munching grass, seeking cool. Goats chewed fence posts.

20 DeLisle and Pass Christian, the two towns where all of my family hails from, are not New Orleans. Pass Christian squats beside the man-made beach of the Gulf of Mexico alongside Long Beach, the Bay of St. Louis at its back, while DeLisle hugs the back of the Bay of St. Louis before spreading away and thinning further upcountry. The streets of both towns are sleepy through much of the barely bearable summer, and through much of the winter, when temperatures hover near freezing. In DeLisle during the summers, there are sometimes crowds on Sundays at the county park because younger people come out to play basketball and play music from their cars. In the spring, the older people gather at the local baseball field, where Negro leagues from throughout the South come to play. On Halloween, children still walk or ride on the backs of pickup trucks through the neighborhood from house to house to trick-or-treat. On All Saints Day[3], families gather around loved ones' graves, bring nylon and canvas folding chairs to sit in after they've cleaned headstones and sandy plots, arranged potted mums, and shared food. They talk into the evening, burn fires, wave away the last of the fall gnats. This is not a murder capital.

21 Most of the Black families in DeLisle have lived there as far back as they can remember, including mine, in houses many of them built themselves. These houses, small shotguns and A-frames, were built in waves, the oldest in the thirties by our great-grandparents, the next in the fifties by our grandparents, the next in the seventies and eighties by our parents, who used contractors. These modest houses, ours included, had two to three bedrooms with gravel and dirt driveways and rabbit hutches and scupadine vineyards in the back. Poor and working-class, but proud. There is no public housing at all in DeLisle, and the project housing that existed before Hurricane Katrina in Pass Christian consisted of several small redbrick duplexes and a few subdivisions with single-family homes, which housed some Black people, some Vietnamese. Now, seven years after Katrina, developers build two- and three-bedroom houses up on fifteen- to twenty-foot stilts where this public housing stood, and these houses fill quickly with those still displaced from the storm, or young adults from Pass Christian and DeLisle who want to live in their hometown. Hurricane Katrina made that impossible for several years, since it

3. **All Saints Day** in Western Christianity, a celebration that immediately follows All Hallows' Eve (Halloween)

razed most of the housing in Pass Christian, and decimated what was closest to the bayou in DeLisle. Coming home to DeLisle as an adult has been harder for this reason, a concrete one. And then there are abstract reasons, too.

22 As Joshua said when we were kids hunting down ghosts: Somebody died here. From 2000 to 2004, five Black young men I grew up with died, all violently, in seemingly unrelated deaths. The first was my brother, Joshua, in October 2000. The second was Ronald in December 2002. The third was C. J. in January 2004. The fourth was Demond in February 2004. The last was Roger in June 2004. That's a brutal list, in its immediacy and its **relentlessness**, and it's a list that silences people. It silenced me for a long time. To say this is difficult is understatement; telling this story is the hardest thing I've ever done. But my ghosts were once people, and I cannot forget that. I cannot forget that when I am walking the streets of DeLisle, streets that seem even barer since Katrina. Streets that seem even more empty since all these deaths, where instead of hearing my friends or my brother playing music from their cars at the county park, the only sound I hear is a tortured parrot that one of my cousins owns, a parrot that screams so loudly it sounds through the neighborhood, a scream like a wounded child, from a cage so small the parrot's crest barely clears the top of the cage while its tail brushes the bottom. Sometimes when that parrot screams, sounding its rage and grief, I wonder at my neighborhood's silence. I wonder why silence is the sound of our subsumed rage, our accumulated grief. I decide this is not right, that I must give voice to this story. I'm telling you: there's a ghost in here, Joshua said. Because this is my story just as it is the story of those lost young men, and because this is my family's story just as it is my community's story, it is not straightforward. To tell it, I must tell the story of my town, and the history of my community. And then I must revisit each of the five young black men who died: follow them backward in time, from Rog's death to Demond's death to C. J.'s death to Ronald's death to my brother's death. At the same time, I must tell this story forward through time, so between those chapters where my friends and my brother live and speak and breathe again for a few paltry pages, I must write about my family and how I grew up. My hope is that learning something about our lives and the lives of the people in my community will mean that when I get to the heart, when my marches forward through the past and backward from the present meet in the middle with my brother's death, I'll understand a bit better why this epidemic happened, about how the history of racism and economic inequality and lapsed public and personal responsibility festered and turned sour and spread here. Hopefully, I'll understand why my brother died while I live, and why I've been saddled with this rotten story.

© Jesmyn Ward, 2013, *Men We Reaped*, Bloomsbury Publishing, Inc.

WRITE

LITERARY ANALYSIS: This excerpt contains descriptions of multiple settings that were significant in the author's life. Write a response in which you evaluate how the social and economic context of the settings influences the characterization and plot. Remember to use textual evidence to support your response.

Extended Writing Project and Grammar

EXTENDED WRITING PROJECT
NARRATIVE WRITING

Narrative Writing Process: Plan

PLAN	DRAFT	REVISE	EDIT AND PUBLISH

Great leaders the world over have emerged from troubled times to champion causes and to safeguard the lives of others. In fiction, the same is true: the worst of times may make a hero from a most unassuming character. This is evident in narratives that reach into the past, those that grapple with the circumstances of today, and those that look to the future here on Earth or among the stars.

WRITING PROMPT

How do leaders rise up and guide others?

Select an issue in today's society that is causing conflict in your own life or among groups of people. Write a personal or fictional narrative about this conflict. If you are writing a personal narrative, explain how this conflict has affected your life or the lives of your friends or family. Then, describe how you or someone in your life has demonstrated leadership skills in response to this conflict. If you are writing a fictional narrative, create a fictional character who belongs to one of the groups involved in this conflict and develop a plot outline set in the present or near future in which this character moves from being a passive member to a powerful leader of the group. Using that outline, write a narrative that shows this character's transformation and the effect this transformation has on the conflict. Be sure your narrative includes the following:

- a plot with a beginning, middle, and end
- a clear setting
- characters and dialogue
- a distinct conflict and resolution
- a clear theme

Introduction to Narrative Writing

Narrative writing tells a story of experiences or events that have been imagined by a writer or that have happened in real life. Good narrative writing effectively uses genre characteristics and craft such as relevant descriptive details and a purposeful structure with a series of events that includes a beginning, middle, and end. The characteristics of narrative writing include:

- setting
- characters

- plot
- theme

- point of view

In addition to these characteristics, narrative writers carefully craft their work through their use of dialogue, details, word choice, and figurative language. These choices help to shape the tone, mood, and overall style of the text. Effective narratives combine these genre characteristics and craft to engage the reader.

As you continue with this Extended Writing Project, you'll receive more instruction and practice in crafting each of the characteristics of narrative writing to create your own narrative.

Please note that excerpts and passages in the StudySync® library and this workbook are intended as touchstones to generate interest in an author's work. The excerpts and passages do not substitute for the reading of entire texts, and StudySync® strongly recommends that students seek out and purchase the whole literary or informational work in order to experience it as the author intended. Links to online resellers are available in our digital library. In addition, complete works may be ordered through an authorized reseller by filling out and returning to StudySync® the order form enclosed in this workbook.

Reading & Writing Companion   **347**

Before you get started on your own personal or fictional narrative, read this narrative that one student, Isaiah, wrote in response to the writing prompt. As you read the Model, highlight and annotate the features of narrative writing that Isaiah included in his narrative.

NOTES

☰ STUDENT MODEL

Daisy's Hero

1   David stood next to the hospital bed. The thick shade on the window kept out the sunshine, so the room was dim and cold. The sour smell of cleaning supplies and sickness burned his nostrils. The steady beep of the heart monitor was interrupted only by his parents' whispers. David watched as Daisy slept. The same question played on an endless loop in his head. How did this happen again? Daisy was 11 years old now. The cancer had been gone for seven years. David had studied the topic in his honors biology class, so he understood how cancer cells are formed and spread. Still, as he looked down at his little sister, he couldn't understand how the leukemia could come back after all this time.

2   Lost in his thoughts, David caught only bits of information from his parents' conversation with the doctor. The bad news hovered in the air like an angry wasp, and David hoped that by keeping still and quiet, he could trick it into flying away and leaving his family alone. He caught the words "aggressive" and "experimental treatment." The cancer was worse this time. It was stronger and more resistant to treatment. David wrapped his hand around Daisy's wrist. She had never seemed smaller. He closed his eyes and wished for a miracle. He had never wished more fervently for anything in his life, not even that time he almost won tickets to the World Series.

3   When Daisy came home from the hospital, the family had already made some changes. David helped turn their home office into a bedroom. The hospital bed they rented looked intimidating next to the old wooden desk and bookcases, so David lovingly filled the room with Daisy's stuffed animals. His mom left her bookkeeping job since Daisy couldn't go to school anymore. His dad started working a second job at a 24-hour supermarket to make up for the lost income. The medical bills overflowed their mailbox, and money grew

tight. David tried to keep a positive attitude, but every time he heard Daisy wheeze, "I'm just so tired," his outlook grew a little more bleak.

4   On one blustery February morning, it became clear to David that the family was in trouble.

5   David was alone in his room when his dad came through the door. "Son, I'm afraid I have some bad news," he began.

6   David's heart rate shot up immediately. "About Daisy?" he blurted. "Is she okay?"

7   His father offered a weak smile. "Your sister is okay. This has nothing to do with her. Your mother and I were up all night crunching the numbers, and we just don't have the money for your spring training trip and new uniform this year. I'm sorry."

8   That meant he couldn't play baseball this season, his last in high school. David knew that the family needed to make sacrifices for Daisy, but he couldn't help but feel angry that he had to give up the one thing he truly loved. David quickly turned away to hide his face. He wanted to shout that this wasn't fair. Hadn't their life changed enough? Didn't they understand that he needed this final season with his team? Was it too much to ask for something for himself for once?

9   "It's okay," he exhaled as his father left the room.

10   A month later, as David and his mother were driving home from school, they heard a loud bang and the car came to a stop in the middle of the road. After an expensive emergency tow and a mechanic's inspection, they learned that the engine would need to be replaced. The estimate was more than $2000. It was the family's only car. With Daisy's medical bills, they couldn't afford to spend that kind of money on repairs. But without the car, they couldn't take Daisy to get her cancer treatments. David's guilt over feeling upset about baseball was immediate and crushing. He was wrong to be selfish when his family was counting on him to be strong. He gently placed his arm around his mother's shoulders and gave her a tight squeeze.

11   "It'll be okay, Mom," he said brightly. "I swear."

12   Now he just had to find a way to keep that promise.

Please note that excerpts and passages in the StudySync® library and this workbook are intended as touchstones to generate interest in an author's work. The excerpts and passages do not substitute for the reading of entire texts, and StudySync® strongly recommends that students seek out and purchase the whole literary or informational work in order to experience it as the author intended. Links to online resellers are available in our digital library. In addition, complete works may be ordered through an authorized reseller by filling out and returning to StudySync® the order form enclosed in this workbook.

Reading & Writing Companion   349

13   David had been avoiding his baseball teammates since his unexpected retirement. Stories about preseason practices kept him away from their lunch tables, and it was painful to watch them head off to the field after school. But after three years of playing together, his former teammates were still his best friends and the only people he knew he could count on for help.

14   The locker room looked the same as it had the last time David entered it. The harsh overhead lights reflected off the red metal lockers, and the floor was just as mysteriously damp as it had always been. He took careful and deliberate steps, pausing only for a moment to glance at the locker that should have been his. His coach was the first to spot him.

15   "David!" Coach Warner boomed. "I hope this means you're coming back to the team."

16   "Not quite, Coach," David could feel everyone staring at him. Suddenly shy, he lowered his voice and asked, "Can we talk in your office for a minute?"

17   When David and Coach Warner emerged from the office a few minutes later, they had a plan. The team would host a fundraiser for David's family. Now all they needed were volunteers. Coach had barely finished his speech before every team member's hand was in the air. David beamed.

18   The fundraiser was a success. The team raised enough money to pay for the car repairs with a bit left over to cover some of Daisy's medical bills. That night at the dinner table, David's dad clapped him on the back and said, "You saved the day, son. How does it feel to be a hero?"

19   David flashed a smile as he thought about everything that had happened. "Don't be silly, Dad. I'm no hero. But I think I figured out what I want to do with my spare time now that I'm not playing baseball. I found a local organization that helps families who are dealing with childhood cancers, and I volunteered to help. I'm going to lead the team on a new fundraiser for another family. Coach says he'll help me do a new one next year when I'm home from college for spring break."

20   Daisy reached up from her wheelchair and grabbed David's hand. "Say whatever you want, big brother, but you'll always be my hero."

WRITE

Writers often take notes about story ideas before they sit down to write. Think about what you've learned so far about organizing narrative writing to help you begin prewriting.

- **Purpose:** What issue do you want to write about, and why is it a problem?

- **Audience:** Who is your audience, and what message do you want to express to your audience?

- **Setting:** Where and when will your story be set? What kinds of problems might the characters face? How might the setting of your story affect the characters and problem?

- **Characters:** What types of characters would you like to write about in your narrative?

- **Plot:** What events will lead to the resolution of the conflict while keeping a reader engaged?

- **Theme/Reflection:** If you are writing an imagined narrative, what general message about life do you want to express? If you are writing a real narrative, what careful thoughts about the significance of your experience will you include?

- **Point of View:** From which point of view should your story be told, and why?

Response Instructions

Use the questions in the bulleted list to write a one-paragraph summary. Your summary should describe what will happen in your narrative.

Don't worry about including all of the details now; focus only on the most essential and important elements. You will refer to this short summary as you continue through the steps of the writing process.

Please note that excerpts and passages in the StudySync® library and this workbook are intended as touchstones to generate interest in an author's work. The excerpts and passages do not substitute for the reading of entire texts, and StudySync® strongly recommends that students seek out and purchase the whole literary or informational work in order to experience it as the author intended. Links to online resellers are available in our digital library. In addition, complete works may be ordered through an authorized reseller by filling out and returning to StudySync® the order form enclosed in this workbook.

Reading & Writing Companion

351

ORGANIZING
NARRATIVE WRITING

sync skills

Skill:
Organizing Narrative Writing

••• CHECKLIST FOR ORGANIZING NARRATIVE WRITING

As you consider how to organize your writing for your narrative, use the following questions as a guide:

- Who is the narrator, and who are the characters in the story?
- Will the story be told from one or multiple points of view?
- Where will the story take place?
- Have I created a problem that characters will have to face and resolve, while noting its significance to the characters?
- Have I created a smooth progression of experiences or plot events, building toward a particular outcome?

Here are some strategies to help you create a smooth progression of experiences or events in your narrative:

- Establish a context

  > choose a setting and a problem that characters will have to face and resolve, noting its significance to the characters

  > decide how the conflict will be resolved

    o the problem often builds to a climax, when the characters are forced to take action

- Introduce a narrator and/or characters

  > characters can be introduced all at once or over the course of the narrative

  > choose the role each character will play in the story

  > choose one or multiple points of view, either first or third person

    o a first-person narrator can be a participant or character in the story

    o a third-person narrator tells the story as an outside observer

YOUR TURN

While identifying the problem that his characters will need to face in his narrative, Isaiah writes, "The main character's sister is very sick. He is sad." How would you change this statement of the problem to involve more characters? Choose the best revision of the statement.

○ A. The main character's sister has cancer, and the medical bills require the family to make sacrifices.

○ B. The main character's sister has cancer, and he is in denial and considers running away.

○ C. The main character's sister has cancer, and she spends most of her time in the hospital.

○ D. The main character's sister has cancer, and he doesn't know how to help her.

YOUR TURN

Complete the chart below by writing a short summary of what will happen in each section of your narrative.

Narrative Sequence	Event
Exposition	
Rising Action	
Climax	
Falling Action	
Resolution	

Narrative Writing Process: Draft

PLAN	DRAFT	REVISE	EDIT AND PUBLISH

You have already made progress toward writing your narrative. Now it is time to draft your narrative.

✏ WRITE

Use your plan and other responses in your Binder to draft your narrative. You may also have new ideas as you begin drafting. Feel free to explore those new ideas as you have them. You can also ask yourself these questions to ensure that your writing is focused, organized, and detailed:

Draft Checklist:

☐ **Purpose and Focus:** Have I made my conflict clear to readers? Have I included only relevant information and nothing extraneous that might confuse my readers?

☐ **Organization:** Does the sequence of events in my story make sense? Will readers be engaged by the organization and want to keep reading to find out what happens next?

☐ **Ideas and Details:** Does my writing include engaging ideas and details? Will my readers be able to easily understand descriptions of characters, settings, or events?

Before you submit your draft, read it over carefully. You want to be sure that you've responded to all aspects of the prompt.

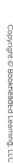

Here is Isaiah's fictional narrative. As you read, notice how Isaiah develops his draft to be focused, organized, and detailed. As he continues to revise and edit his narrative, he will find and improve weak spots in his writing, as well as correct any language or punctuation mistakes.

☰ STUDENT MODEL: FIRST DRAFT

~~David stood next to the hospital bed and watch as Daisy slept. The same question play on a loop in his head, how did this happen again? Daisy was 11 years old now. The cancer had been gone for seven years. David had been studied the topic in its honors biology class, so he understood how cancer cells work. Still, as he looked down at her little sister, he couldn't understand how the lukeamia could come back after all this time.~~

David stood next to the hospital bed. The thick shade on the window kept out the sunshine, so the room was dim and cold. The sour smell of cleaning supplies and sickness burned his nostrils. The steady beep of the heart monitor was interrupted only by his parents' whispers. David watched as Daisy slept. The same question played on an endless loop in his head. How did this happen again? Daisy was 11 years old now. The cancer had been gone for seven years. David had studied the topic in his honors biology class, so he understood how cancer cells are formed and spread. Still, as he looked down at his little sister, he couldn't understand how the leukemia could come back after all this time.

The bad news was a shock. The cancer was worse this time. It was strongest and more resistent to treatment. David held her sister's hand. She had never seemed small. He wished for a miracle.

David helped turn their home office into a bedroom. He helped his mom organize her room. His dad started working a second job at a 24-hour supermarket to make up for the lost income. Money grew tight. David did his best to stay optimistic, but each time he looked at his sister, he grew more afraid.

~~One morning, it became clearly to David that the family was in trouble.~~

~~"I'm afraid I have some bad news," he began.~~

Skill:
Story Beginnings

Isaiah decides to create a more engaging beginning. He wants readers to feel as if they are in the hospital with David. So he adds sight, smell, and sound details to help readers visualize the scene and connect with David.

~~David felt scared. Bad news was probably about Daisy. She had been going to get cancer treatments for a while now, it had been working. He wanted to hear only good news about it.~~

~~"About Daisy?" he asked. "Is she okay?"~~

~~His father offers a week smile. "Your sister is okay. This has nothing to do with it. Your mother and I were up all night crunching the numbers, and we just don't have the money for your spring training trip and new uniform this year. I'm sorry."~~

~~David quick turned away to hide his face. He wanted to shout that this wasn't fair. Hadn't our life changed enough? Didn't he understand that he needed this final season with his team? Was it too much to ask for something for himself for once.~~

~~"It's okay," he said as their father left the room.~~

On one blustery February morning, it became clear to David that the family was in trouble.

David was alone in his room when his dad came through the door. "Son, I'm afraid I have some bad news," he began.

David's heart rate shot up immediately. "About Daisy?" he blurted. "Is she okay?"

His father offered a weak smile. "Your sister is okay. This has nothing to do with her. Your mother and I were up all night crunching the numbers, and we just don't have the money for your spring training trip and new uniform this year. I'm sorry."

That meant he couldn't play baseball this season, his last in high school. David knew that the family needed to make sacrifices for Daisy, but he couldn't help but feel angry that he had to give up the one thing he truly loved. David quickly turned away to hide his face. He wanted to shout that this wasn't fair. Hadn't their life changed enough? Didn't they understand that he needed this final season with his team? Was it too much to ask for something for himself for once?

"It's okay," he exhaled as his father left the room.

Skill:
Descriptive Details

Isaiah realizes that he should add descriptive details to help readers picture the setting in this section of his narrative. So he adds details about where and when the conversation takes place.

Skill:
Narrative Techniques

In this section, Isaiah decides to improve the characterization and dialogue and adjust the pacing. He wants readers to feel David's initial panic and understand his reaction to what his dad says.

~~They heard a loud bang and the car came to a stop in the middle of the road. After an expensiver emergency tow and a mechanic's inspection, they learned that the engine would need to be replaced. The same thing happened to one of David's friends last year. The estimate was more than $2000. It was the family's only car. With Daisy's medical bills, they couldn't afford to spend that kind of money on repairs. But without the car, they couldn't take Daisy to get her cancer treatments. He gently placed his arm around his mother's shoulders and gave her a tight squeeze.~~

A month later, as David and his mother were driving home from school, they heard a loud bang and the car came to a stop in the middle of the road. After an expensive emergency tow and a mechanic's inspection, they learned that the engine would need to be replaced. The estimate was more than $2000. It was the family's only car. With Daisy's medical bills, they couldn't afford to spend that kind of money on repairs. But without the car, they couldn't take Daisy to get her cancer treatments. David's guilt over feeling upset about baseball was immediate and crushing. He was wrong to be selfish when his family was counting on him to be strong. He gently placed his arm around his mother's shoulders and gave her a tight squeeze.

"It'll be okay, Mom," she said brightly. "I swear."

Now he just had to find a way to keep that promise.

David has been avoiding his baseball teammates since his unexpected retirement. Stories about preseason practices kept him away from their lunch tables, and it was painful to watch them head off to the field after school. But after three years of playing together, his former teamates were still your best friends and the only people you knew he could count on for help.

The locker room is looking the same as it had the last time David entered it. The harsh overhead lights reflect off the red metal lockers, and the floor was just as mysterious damp as it has always been. He took careful and deliburet steps, pausing only for a moment to glance at the locker that should have been ours. His coach was the first to spot it.

 Skill:
Transitions

Isaiah notes that the change in setting and time is unclear in this section. He decides to use transitions to signal a shift in time and place.

NOTES

"David! I hope this means you're coming back to the team."

"Not quiet, Coach," David could feel everyone staring at him. Sudden shy, he lowers his voice and asks, "Can we talk in your office for a minute?"

David and Coach Warner agree that the team could host a fundraiser to help David's family. Coach and David discussed the details. Coach had barely finished his speech before every team member's hand was in the air. David beamed. The team would host a fundraiser for David's family. He remembered how much fun it was to be part of the team.

The fundraiser was a success. The team raised enough money to pay for the car repairs with a bit left over to cover some of Daisy's medical bills. David's dad was so proud of them. He said to David, You saved the day, son. How does it feel to be a hero?"

~~David is smiling as he thought about everything that has happened. I think I figured out what I want to do with my spare time now that I'm not playing baseball. I found a local organization that helps families who are dealing with childhood cancers, and I am going to help. I'm going to lead the team. We will do a new fundraiser for another family. Coach says he'll help me do a new one next year. I will be home from college for spring break."~~

~~Daisy couldn't hide her excitment. She was proud to have a brother that would help him in this way.~~

David flashed a smile as he thought about everything that had happened. "Don't be silly, Dad. I'm no hero. But I think I figured out what I want to do with my spare time now that I'm not playing baseball. I found a local organization that helps families who are dealing with childhood cancers, and I volunteered to help. I'm going to lead the team on a new fundraiser for another family. Coach says he'll help me do a new one next year when I'm home from college for spring break."

Daisy reached up from her wheelchair and grabbed David's hand. "Say whatever you want, big brother, but you'll always be my hero."

Skill:
Conclusions

Isaiah adds dialogue that allows David and Daisy to share their thoughts and feelings. By doing so, Isaiah helps readers better understand the characters and the significance of the events in the story.

Skill:
Story Beginnings

••• CHECKLIST FOR STORY BEGINNINGS

Before you write the beginning of your narrative, ask yourself the following questions:

- What information does my reader need to know at the beginning of the story about the narrator, main character, setting, and conflict?

- What will happen to my character in the story?

- Should I establish either a single narrator or multiple points of view?

There are many ways to help you engage and orient your reader. Here are some questions and methods to help you present a problem, situation, or observation and its significance, introduce a narrator and/or characters, and establish one or multiple point(s) of view:

- Action

    > What action could help reveal information about my character or conflict?

    > How might an exciting moment or observation and its significance grab my reader's attention?

    > How could a character's reaction help set the mood?

- Description

    > Does my story take place in a special location or specific time period?

    > How can describing a location or character grab my reader's attention? What powerful emotions can I use?

- Dialogue

    > What dialogue would help my reader understand the setting or the conflict?

    > How could a character's internal thoughts provide information for my reader?

- Information

    > Would a surprising statement grab a reader's attention?

> What details will help my reader understand the character, conflict, or setting?

- Point of view

  > one point of view: first person or third person—third-person omniscient or third-person limited

  > multiple points of view, introducing more than one narrator or character to tell the story

⟳ YOUR TURN

Below is the first paragraph of Isaiah's narrative draft. Choose the best answer to each question about his story beginning.

> David stood next to the hospital bed and watch as Daisy slept. The same question play on a loop in his head, how did this happen again? Daisy was 11 years old now. The cancer had been gone for seven years. David had been studied the topic in its honors biology class, so he understood how cancer cells work. Still, as he looked down at her little sister, he couldn't understand how the lukeamia could come back after all this time.

1. Which line could you add to Isaiah's first paragraph to better show the relationship David has with his sister and establish a stronger conflict?

   ○ A. David is frustrated by the number of hospital personnel in his sister's room.

   ○ B. David is concerned that the doctors have misdiagnosed his sister's cancer.

   ○ C. David notices his sister is shivering as she sleeps and finds a blanket in the closet to wrap around her.

   ○ D. David's coach contacts his parents about quitting the baseball team.

2. How does the last sentence in the paragraph help the reader better understand the main character?

   ○ A. Even though he understands how cancer works, he doesn't want it to be true that the cancer has returned.

   ○ B. The detail "he looked down at" his little sister helps the reader understand that David does not respect his sister.

   ○ C. It provides background information on David's knowledge of cancer.

   ○ D. It tells the reader that his sister has been in remission for years.

✎ WRITE

Use the questions in the checklist to revise the beginning of your narrative.

Skill:
Narrative Techniques

As you begin to develop the techniques you will use in your narrative, ask yourself the following questions:

- Is it clear which character is talking in a dialogue?

- Is the pacing of events suitable and effective?

- Which literary devices can strengthen descriptions of the characters or plot events? How can I use personal reflection to develop my narrative?

- What additional characters and/or events might help to develop the narrative?

Here are some methods that can help you use dialogue, description, pacing, reflection, and multiple plot lines to develop experiences, events, and/or characters in your narrative:

- use character dialogue to explain events or actions

  > use quotation marks correctly

  > include identifying names as needed before or after quotation marks

- use description so the reader can visualize the characters, setting, and other elements

  > descriptions should contribute to the reader's understanding of the element being described

- use pacing effectively

  > for a quick pace, use limited description, short paragraphs, brief dialogue, and simpler sentences

  > for a slower pace, use detailed description, longer paragraphs, and complex sentence structures

- use reflection to comment on the overall message

  > include a character's or personal inner thoughts or insights

- create multiple plot lines that further develop the narrative's message

  > include characters, events, or other elements that will further develop the plot

- use any combination of the techniques above

YOUR TURN

Choose the best answer to each question.

1. Below is a section from a previous draft of Isaiah's story in which the setting is unclear. How should he rewrite the underlined sentence to clarify the setting of the scene?

> <u>David followed Coach Warner into the room and sat down on a chair.</u> He noticed that his palms were starting to sweat. He was nervous.

   ○ A. David followed Coach Warner into his office and sat down on a cold metal folding chair.

   ○ B. David said, "Hi, Coach," before following the man into the room and sitting down on a chair.

   ○ C. David followed Coach Warner, a middle-aged man, into the room and sat down on a chair.

   ○ D. David felt his heart beat faster as he followed Coach Warner into the room and sat down on a chair.

2. Isaiah wants to improve the dialogue in a previous draft of his story. In the excerpt below, what change should he make to improve the dialogue so that it shows the characters' feelings?

> (1) David listened to his parents' conversation. The doctor explained, "The cancer is more aggressive this time."
> (2) David could hear his mother's gasp. Then she said, "Is there anything we can do?"
> (3) "There's an experimental treatment we can try," the doctor stated calmly.
> (4) "We'll do anything!" David's father cried.

   ○ A. Change *explained* to *shouted* in paragraph 1.

   ○ B. Change *said* to *squeaked* in paragraph 2.

   ○ C. Change *stated* to *whispered* in paragraph 3.

   ○ D. Change *cried* to *cheered* in paragraph 4.

 WRITE

Use the questions in the checklist for narrative techniques to revise a section of your narrative.

Skill:
Transitions

••• CHECKLIST FOR TRANSITIONS

Before you revise your current draft to include transitions, think about:

- the order of plot events
- how events build to create a unified story, build a specific mood, and work toward a particular outcome

Next, reread your current draft and note areas in your narrative where:

- the order of events is unclear or illogical
- changes in time or setting are confusing or unclear. Look for:

  > sudden jumps

  > missing or illogical plot events or outcome(s)

  > moments where the mood does not connect to the development of plot events

Revise your draft to use a variety of techniques to sequence events so that they build on one another to create a coherent whole and build toward a particular mood and outcome, using the following questions as a guide:

- What other techniques could I use so that events in my story build on one another, creating a coherent whole?
- Does the sequence of events in my story build toward a particular mood and outcome?

  > For example, you can build the mood of your story by creating a sense of mystery or suspense.

  > For example, you can build toward a particular outcome by showing character growth or by developing a resolution.

- Are there better transitional words, phrases, or clauses that I can use to show shifts in time or setting and relationships between experiences and events?

⟳ YOUR TURN

How could Isaiah revise this paragraph from a draft of his narrative to clarify David's feelings and the mood of his story? Choose the best answer to the question.

> Before she came home, David helped turn their home office into a bedroom. He helped his mom organize her room. His dad started working a second job at a 24-hour supermarket to make up for the lost income. Money grew tight. David did his best to stay optimistic, but each time he looked at his sister, he grew more afraid.

- ○ A. Isaiah could add dialogue between the hospital staff and David to clarify David's feelings and the mood of the story.
- ○ B. Isaiah could use phrases like *first* and *secondly* to clarify the feelings David has toward his sister.
- ○ C. Isaiah could compare his sister's current condition to her initial leukemia diagnosis seven years ago.
- ○ D. Isaiah could provide David's internal dialogue or thoughts to clarify his protagonist's feelings and the mood of the story.

⟳ YOUR TURN

Read the paragraph below. Then, using the checklist on the previous page, revise the paragraph in order to strengthen transitions and create a more coherent whole.

Paragraph	Revision
She was at a loss for words, but wanted to speak. It wasn't very often that words did not come to her. The snow fell in clumps. It made her tired just thinking about it all.	

Skill:
Descriptive Details

••• CHECKLIST FOR DESCRIPTIVE DETAILS

First, reread the draft of your narrative and identify the following:

- places where descriptive details are needed to convey experiences and events
- vague, general, or overused words and phrases
- places where you want to tell how something looks, sounds, feels, smells, or tastes, such as:

  > experiences

  > events

  > settings

  > characters

Use telling details, sensory language, and precise words and phrases to convey a vivid picture of the experiences, events, setting, and/or characters, using the following questions as a guide:

- What experiences and events do I want to convey in my writing?
- Have I included telling details that help reveal the experiences and events in the story?
- How do I want the characters and setting portrayed?
- How can I use sensory language—or words that appeal to the sense of sight, sound, touch, smell, or taste—so that readers can clearly visualize the experiences, events, setting, and/or characters in my story?
- What can I refine or revise in my word choice to make sure the reader can picture what is taking place?

↻ YOUR TURN

Choose the best answer to each question.

1. Isaiah would like to add a descriptive sound detail to this sentence from a previous draft. Which sentence best adds a sound detail to his sentence?

> David was alone in his room.

- ○ A. David was alone in his room, surrounded by the stench of old sweat socks.
- ○ B. David was alone in his room when the door started to creak open slowly.
- ○ C. David was alone in his room, playing a video game without distractions.
- ○ D. David was alone in his room, too depressed to notice the sunshine streaming through his window.

2. Isaiah wants to add a detail to better establish the setting of part of his story. Which sentence should he add to the excerpt below from a previous draft to help readers visualize the setting?

> The hazy gray sky matched David's mood. The last thing he wanted to do was ask the baseball team for help. He tried to ignore the sounds of laughter coming from their table, but he couldn't.

- ○ A. He needed to catch their attention before the bell rang and he lost his opportunity.
- ○ B. The mouth-watering scent of the tacos they were enjoying made him regret his choice of a peanut butter sandwich.
- ○ C. Their matching uniforms and wide smiles made David ache to be part of the baseball team again.
- ○ D. The cafeteria was teeming with students hanging out with their friends, but David was all alone.

✏ WRITE

Use the questions in the checklist for descriptive details to revise a section of your narrative.

Skill:
Conclusions

••• CHECKLIST FOR CONCLUSIONS

Before you write your conclusion, ask yourself the following questions:

- What important details should I include in my conclusion?
- What other thoughts and feelings could the characters share with readers in the conclusion?
- Should I express the importance of the events in my narrative through dialogue or a character's actions?

Below are two strategies to help you provide a conclusion that follows from and reflects on what is experienced, observed, or resolved over the course of the narrative:

- Peer Discussion

  > After you have written your introduction and body paragraphs, talk with a partner about possible endings for your narrative.

  > Summarize the events in the narrative through the narrator or one of the characters.

  > Describe the narrator's observations about the events they experienced.

  > Reveal to readers why the experiences in the narrative matter through a character's reflections.

  > Write your conclusion.

- Freewriting

  > Freewrite for 10 minutes about what you might include in your conclusion. Don't worry about grammar, punctuation, or having fully formed ideas. The point of freewriting is to discover ideas.

  > Review your notes, and think about how you want to end your story.

  > Summarize the events in the narrative through the narrator or one of the characters.

  > Describe the narrator's observations about the events they experienced.

  > Reveal to readers why the experiences in the narrative matter through a character's reflections.

  > Write your conclusion.

YOUR TURN

Below are Isaiah's revised concluding paragraphs. Choose the best answer to each question about his conclusion.

> The fundraiser was a success. The team raised enough money to pay for the car repairs with a bit left over to cover some of Daisy's medical bills. That night at the dinner table, David's dad clapped him on the back and said, "You saved the day, son. How does it feel to be a hero?"
>
> David flashed a smile as he thought about everything that had happened. "Don't be silly, Dad. I'm no hero. But I think I figured out what I want to do with my spare time now that I'm not playing baseball. I found a local organization that helps families who are dealing with childhood cancers, and I volunteered to help. I'm going to lead the team on a new fundraiser for another family. Coach says he'll help me do a new one next year when I'm home from college for spring break."
>
> Daisy reached up from her wheelchair and grabbed David's hand. "Say whatever you want, big brother, but you'll always be my hero."

1. What effect does the dialogue have in the conclusion of the story?

   ○ A. It shows that David and his father have finally come to some sort of agreement.
   ○ B. It reminds the reader that David and his coach have a strong relationship despite his quitting the baseball team.
   ○ C. It reveals a father's thoughts about his son and provides a resolution to a family problem.
   ○ D. It reinforces the theme of family.

2. Which sentence in the revised conclusion best shows what Isaiah learned about writing conclusions?

   ○ A. "The fundraiser was a success."
   ○ B. "David flashed a smile as he thought about everything that had happened."
   ○ C. "I'm going to lead the team on a new fundraiser for another family."
   ○ D. "Daisy reached up from her wheelchair and grabbed David's hand. 'Say whatever you want, big brother, but you'll always be my hero.'"

WRITE

Use the questions in the checklist for conclusions to revise the ending of your narrative.

Narrative Writing Process: Revise

PLAN	DRAFT	REVISE	EDIT AND PUBLISH

You have written a draft of your narrative. You have also received input from your peers about how to improve it. Now you are going to revise your draft.

◀◀ REVISION GUIDE

Examine your draft to find areas for revision. Keep in mind your purpose and audience as you revise for clarity, development, organization, and style. Use the guide below to help you review:

Review	Revise	Example
Clarity		
Label each piece of dialogue so you know who is speaking. Annotate any places where it is unclear who is speaking.	Use the character's name to show who is speaking, or add description about the speaker.	"David!" Coach Warner boomed. "I hope this means you're coming back to the team."
Development		
Identify moments that develop a distinct conflict. Annotate places where you feel the impact of the conflict is not clear.	Focus on a single event and add descriptive details, such as sounds, visual descriptions, and characters' thoughts and feelings, to show how the conflict impacts the characters.	But without the car, they couldn't take Daisy to get her cancer treatments. David's guilt over feeling upset about baseball was immediate and crushing. He was wrong to be selfish when his family was counting on him to be strong. He gently placed his arm around his mother's shoulders and gave her a tight squeeze.

Review	Revise	Example
Organization		
Explain your story in one or two sentences. Reread and annotate any places that don't match your explanation.	Rewrite the events in the correct sequence. Delete events that are not essential to the story.	Coach had barely finished his speech before every team member's hand was in the air. David beamed. ~~The team would host a fundraiser for David's family. He remembered how much fun it was to be part of the team.~~
Style: Word Choice		
Identify every form of the verb *to be* (*am, is, are, was, were, be, being, been*).	Select sentences to rewrite using action verbs.	"I found a local organization that helps families who are dealing with childhood cancers, and I ~~am going~~ volunteered to help."
Style: Sentence Fluency		
Think about a key event where you want your reader to feel a specific emotion. Long sentences can draw out a moment and make a reader think; short sentences can show urgent actions or danger.	Rewrite a key event making your sentences longer or shorter to achieve the emotion you want your reader to feel.	"I'm going to lead the team~~:~~ on ~~We will do~~ a new fundraiser for another family. Coach says he'll help me do a new one next year~~.~~ ~~I will be~~ when I'm home from college for spring break."

✎ WRITE

Use the revision guide, as well as your peer reviews, to help you evaluate your narrative to determine areas that should be revised.

Grammar: Modifiers

Most adjectives and adverbs have three degrees: the positive, or base, form; the comparative form; and the superlative form. The base form cannot be used to make a comparison. The comparative form compares two things. The superlative form compares three or more things.

In general, you can form the comparative by adding -er and the superlative by adding -est. (In some cases a spelling change is required.)

Comparative	Superlative
Last night when I spoke with you about the fall of Rome, I knew at that moment that troops of the United States and our Allies were crossing the Channel in another and **greater** operation. D-Day Prayer	So far from it, that, after surveying the history of woman, I cannot help agreeing with the **severest** satirist, considering the sex as the weakest as well as the most oppressed half of the species. . . . A Vindication of the Rights of Woman

Use *more* and *most* (or *less* and *least* for the opposite) to form the degrees of comparison in the following situations:

Rule	Example
adverbs that end in *-ly*	Did they murder each other **more gently** because in the woods sweet songbirds sang? Grendel
modifiers of three or more syllables	Perhaps the **most extraordinary** development of all is that Shakespeare's Globe Theater in London—built as a monument for his plays and with aspirations to be a world-class study center—became, under the stewardship of the artistic director Mark Rylance, a kind of clearinghouse for anti-Stratford sentiment. Shakespeare: The World As Stage

↻ YOUR TURN

1. How should this sentence be changed?

   > In the 1960s, when *Silent Spring* was published, many people believed that pesticides were safe than the insects they were meant to kill.

   - ○ A. In the 1960s, when *Silent Spring* was published, many people believed that pesticides were safest than the insects they were meant to kill.
   - ○ B. In the 1960s, when *Silent Spring* was published, many people believed that pesticides were safer than the insects they were meant to kill.
   - ○ C. In the 1960s, when *Silent Spring* was published, many people believed that pesticides were more safe than the insects they were meant to kill.
   - ○ D. No change needs to be made to this sentence.

2. How should this sentence be changed?

   > Birds appeared to be sensitive to the effects of pesticides than other animals.

   - ○ A. Birds appeared more to be sensitive to the effects of pesticides than other animals.
   - ○ B. Birds appeared to be sensitive to the effects of pesticides rather than other animals.
   - ○ C. Birds appeared to be more sensitive to the effects of pesticides than other animals.
   - ○ D. No change needs to be made to this sentence.

3. How should this sentence be changed?

   > The most powerfully of all these chemicals, DDT was banned in the United States.

   - ○ A. The powerfully of all these chemicals, DDT was banned in the United States.
   - ○ B. The most powerful of all these chemicals, DDT was banned in the United States.
   - ○ C. The most powerfullest of all these chemicals, DDT was banned in the United States.
   - ○ D. No change needs to be made to this sentence.

Grammar: Pronoun-Antecedent Agreement

A pronoun is a word that takes the place of a noun mentioned earlier. The noun is the pronoun's antecedent. A pronoun must agree in number, gender, and person with its antecedent.

Sometimes a pronoun has another pronoun as its antecedent. When that is the case, the two pronouns should also agree in person. These pairs of pronouns agree in person: *you/your, he/his, she/her, they/their*.

When the antecedent of a pronoun is a collective noun, such as *class* or *team*, the number of the pronoun depends on whether the collective noun is used as singular or plural. The sentence should make clear that *team*, for example, refers either to individual members of the team or to the team as a single unit.

Text	Pronoun	Antecedent
We hold these truths to be self-evident, that all **men** are created equal, that **they** are endowed by **their** Creator with certain unalienable Rights, that among these are Life, Liberty, and the pursuit of Happiness. The Declaration of Independence	they their	men
When a **woman** has five grown-up daughters **she** ought to give over thinking of **her** own beauty. Pride and Prejudice	she her	woman
Heathcliff had knelt on one knee to embrace her; **he** attempted to rise, but she seized **his** hair, and kept **him** down. Wuthering Heights	he his him	Heathcliff
I take the **world** as I find **it**, in trade and everything else. Middlemarch	it	world

Note that the antecedent should be clear.

Clear	Unclear	Explanation
Park in the garage and lock the **car**.	When you put the car in the garage, don't forget to lock **it**.	The pronoun *it* could refer to either the car or the garage.

↻ YOUR TURN

1. How should this sentence be changed?

> They swam to the far shore where you could find shells.

- ○ A. They swam to the far shore where she could find shells.
- ○ B. They swam to the far shore where it could find shells.
- ○ C. They swam to the far shore where they could find shells.
- ○ D. No change needs to be made to this sentence.

2. How should this sentence be changed?

> Robert Louis Stevenson started traveling to improve his health and soon began writing novels that would leave their impression on millions of readers.

- ○ A. Robert Louis Stevenson started traveling to improve their health and soon began writing novels that would leave their impression on millions of readers.
- ○ B. Robert Louis Stevenson started traveling to improve our health and soon began writing novels that would leave their impression on millions of readers.
- ○ C. Robert Louis Stevenson started traveling to improve his health and soon began writing novels that would leave its impression on millions of readers.
- ○ D. No change needs to be made to this sentence.

3. How should this sentence be changed?

> The class had their first meeting yesterday.

- ○ A. The class had its first meeting yesterday.
- ○ B. The class had your first meeting yesterday.
- ○ C. The class had my first meeting yesterday.
- ○ D. No change needs to be made to this sentence.

4. How should this sentence be changed?

> Since my father enjoyed his birthday party so much, I was glad I had not forgotten it.

- ○ A. Since my father enjoyed his birthday party so much, I was glad I had not forgotten you.
- ○ B. Since my father enjoyed his birthday party so much, I was glad I had not forgotten his birthday.
- ○ C. Since my father enjoyed his birthday party so much, I was glad I had not forgotten.
- ○ D. No change needs to be made to this sentence.

Grammar:
Basic Spelling Rules II

Follow these rules to avoid making some common spelling mistakes.

Rule	Text
If a one-syllable word ends in a single consonant preceded by a single vowel, double the final consonant before adding a suffix that begins with a vowel, such as -*ed* or -*ing*.	"Stand up," said Arthur, and he **clapped** his hands for a page to take away the seat. The Once and Future King
Double the final consonant if the last syllable of the word is accented and the accent does not move after the suffix is added.	And I feel that notwithstanding the past that my presence here is one additional bit of evidence that the American Dream need not forever be **deferred**. 1976 Democratic National Convention Keynote Address, by Barbara Jordan
Do not double the final consonant if the last syllable of the word is not accented or if the accent moves when the suffix is added.	Since then, when he had **happened** to see the sun come up in the country or on the water, he had often **remembered** the young Swedish girl and her milking pails. O Pioneers!
Do not double the final consonant if the suffix begins with a consonant. However, when adding -*ness* to a word that ends in *n*, keep the *n*.	I like him not; nor stands it safe with us / To let his **madness** range. Hamlet
Do not double the final consonant when adding suffixes if two vowels come before the final consonant or if the word ends in two consonants.	With **straining** eagerness Catherine gazed towards the entrance of her chamber. Wuthering Heights
When forming compound words, keep the original spelling of both words.	After the **sunsets** and the **dooryards** and the sprinkled streets, . . . The Love Song of J. Alfred Prufrock

↻ YOUR TURN

1. How should this sentence be changed?

> After being admited to college, Jerome deferred enrolling for one year so he could work to earn money for tuition.

- ○ A. After being admitted to college, Jerome deferred enrolling for one year so he could work to earn money for tuition.
- ○ B. After being admited to college, Jerome defered enrolling for one year so he could work to earn money for tuition.
- ○ C. After being admited to college, Jerome deferred enroling for one year so he could work to earn money for tuition.
- ○ D. No change needs to be made to this sentence.

2. How should this sentence be changed?

> Fariba was thrilled when she discoverred she had won the coveted scholarship to attend the prestigious university.

- ○ A. Fariba was thriled when she discoverred she had won the coveted scholarship to attend the prestigious university.
- ○ B. Fariba was thrilled when she discovered she had won the coveted scholarship to attend the prestigious university.
- ○ C. Fariba was thrilled when she discoverred she had won the covetted scholarship to attend the prestigious university.
- ○ D. No change needs to be made to this sentence.

3. How should this sentence be changed?

> The busy mom strapped her toddler into the shopping cart at the supermarket and headed down the first aisle.

- ○ A. The busy mom straped her toddler into the shopping cart at the supermarket and headed down the first aisle.
- ○ B. The busy mom strapped her toddler into the shoping cart at the supermarket and headed down the first aisle.
- ○ C. The busy mom strapped her toddler into the shopping cart at the super market and headed down the first aisle.
- ○ D. No change needs to be made to this sentence.

Narrative Writing Process: Edit and Publish

PLAN	DRAFT	REVISE	EDIT AND PUBLISH

You have revised your fictional or personal narrative based on your peer feedback and your own examination.

Now, it is time to edit your narrative. When you revised, you focused on the content of your narrative. You probably looked at your story's beginning, narrative techniques, transitions, descriptive details, and conclusion. When you edit, you focus on the mechanics of your story, paying close attention to things like grammar and punctuation.

Use the checklist below to guide you as you edit:

☐ Have I followed all the basic rules for correct spelling?

☐ Do my pronouns and antecedents agree?

☐ Have I used both comparative and superlative modifiers correctly?

☐ Have I used a consistent verb tense throughout the story?

☐ Do I have any sentence fragments or run-on sentences?

Notice some edits Isaiah has made:

- Changed his verb tense to maintain consistency

- Corrected commonly misspelled words

- Changed pronouns to agree with their antecedents

Please note that excerpts and passages in the StudySync® library and this workbook are intended as touchstones to generate interest in an author's work. The excerpts and passages do not substitute for the reading of entire texts, and StudySync® strongly recommends that students seek out and purchase the whole literary or informational work in order to experience it as the author intended. Links to online resellers are available in our digital library. In addition, complete works may be ordered through an authorized reseller by filling out and returning to StudySync® the order form enclosed in this workbook.

Reading & Writing Companion   **377**

David ~~has~~ had been avoiding his baseball teammates since his unexpected retirement. Stories about preseason practices kept him away from their lunch tables, and it was painful to watch them head off to the field after school. But after three years of playing together, his former ~~teamates~~ teammates were still ~~your~~ his best friends and the only people ~~you~~ he knew he could count on for help.

The locker room ~~is looking~~ looked the same as it had the last time David entered it. The harsh overhead lights ~~reflect~~ reflected off the red metal lockers, and the floor was just as mysteriously damp as it ~~has~~ had always been. He took careful and ~~deliburet~~ deliberate steps, pausing only for a moment to glance at the locker that should have been ~~ours~~ his. His coach was the first to spot ~~it~~ him.

✏ WRITE

Use the questions on the previous page, as well as your peer reviews, to help you evaluate your narrative to determine areas that need editing. Then, edit your narrative to correct those errors.

Once you have made all your corrections, you are ready to publish your work. You can distribute your writing to family and friends, hang it on a bulletin board, or post it on your blog. If you publish online, share the link with your family, friends, and classmates.

The Legend of Carman

FICTION

Introduction

This short story revisits an ancient Irish myth about an Athenian sorceress named Carman and her three sons—Dub, Dother, and Dian. Once Carman sees the fertile green fields of Ireland, she decides to conquer the current rulers, the Tuatha Dé Dannan, and make the land her home, but her sons' bad

VOCABULARY

progeny
offspring or children

callous
not sensitive; unsympathetic

usurp
to take power using illegal means

NO IMAGE PROVIDED

deplorable
worthy of criticism or regret

treason
the crime of betraying one's country

NOTES

≡ READ

1 Hearken! Attend the tale of noble Carman, the fair. Hold your tongues. Listen closely to her sorrowful story.

2 Carman, the raven-haired warrior woman from Athens, was a wonder. The gods blessed this battle-tested beauty with magic powers. Her three sons, a rank of rapacious offspring, were always with her. Dub, the Black-Hearted, had a soul as dark as the deepest cavern. Dother, the Evil, hated everything. Dian, the Violent, was a walking nightmare, leaving a bevy of victims wherever he traveled. Carman and her sons had been searching for land to conquer when she heard news of skirmishes on the shores of Ireland. Despite her great gifts, she never could have guessed that their next voyage would be her last. Not even her most skillful spell could save her from her sons' selfish mistake.

3 The Tuatha Dé Dannan had recently descended upon Ireland's emerald shores. Their name means "tribe of the gods," and gods they were. The Tuatha Dé Dannan came to the coast of Connemara in clouds of mist. Some

say they sailed into the harbor like men and burned their boats, creating smoke that spread out across the land. Others swear that they came down from the heavens on dark clouds like a fine rain. These supernatural beings brought with them three days and three nights of complete darkness, a harbinger of changes to come. No one knows the true story of how the Tuatha Dé Dannan arrived in Ireland. But everyone knows how they fought their way across the land until it was theirs.

4   Carman saw an opportunity when she heard about the recent unrest. Perhaps she and her power-hungry **progeny** could **usurp** the new leaders. Barely rested from their last battle, they boarded a boat and sailed toward their next conquest.

5   Carman and her sons came upon the southern shore of Ireland in their mighty vessel. She marveled at the green land that lay before them. Countless cattle and crops covered the countryside. She decided that her clan could be content living on that coast. "Soon," she said to the terrible trio, "all you see will be ours." The Black-Hearted, the Evil, and the Violent raised their swords, preparing to take the land by force. But wise and noble Carman knew a better way. She called upon her ancient powers and cast a spell across the land. Her magic turned green to gray. The crops withered away at her words. The soil under the shriveled roots would live to grow plants again, but the Irish would be too weak with hunger to fight. They would need Carman to reverse the spell, so they would welcome her as their queen.

6   But Carman would not succeed. The brothers did not obey their orders. As Carman slept, they laid siege to the nearest village. Their actions drew the attention of the Tuatha Dé Dannan. Before morning, the brothers were captured and given the choice between death or exile. They deserted Carman to save themselves. As punishment for her sons' crimes, fair Carman was sealed in a tomb and buried alive. Her sons' **treason** burned in her chest like a thousand flames. Her cry of grief echoed across the cliffs as breath left her body. Carman's anguish revealed her remorse and reversed her spell. The farms became more bountiful than ever before. The Irish were satisfied by the sorceress's sacrifice.

7   Too late, the Irish realized that Carman was not as **callous** as her sons. Deeply affected by her **deplorable** death and her final act of mercy, the townspeople held a festival in her honor. The land where her brave bones are buried was renamed Carman to pay tribute to this noble woman's memory.

First Read

Read the story. After you read, complete the Think Questions below.

☁ THINK QUESTIONS

1. Who are the main characters in the story? Include their relationship in your response.

    The main characters are _____.

    Their relationship is _____.

2. Write two or three sentences describing Carman's plan to take the land from the Tuatha Dé Dannan.

    Carman's plan is _____

    _____.

3. Why does Carman fail to take the land from the Tuatha Dé Dannan? Cite a line from the text as evidence.

    Carman fails to take the land because _____

    _____.

4. Use context to confirm the meaning of the word *deplorable* as it is used in "The Legend of Carman." Write your definition of *deplorable* here.

    Deplorable means _____.

    A context clue is _____.

5. What is another way to say that a person is *callous*?

    A person is callous when _____

    _____.

Skill:
Analyzing Expressions

★ DEFINE

When you read, you may find English expressions that you do not know. An **expression** is a group of words that communicates an idea. Three types of expressions are idioms, sayings, and figurative language. They can be difficult to understand because the meanings of the words are different from their **literal**, or usual, meanings.

An **idiom** is an expression that is commonly known among a group of people. For example, "It's raining cats and dogs" means it is raining heavily. **Sayings** are short expressions that contain advice or wisdom. For instance, "Don't count your chickens before they hatch" means do not plan on something good happening before it happens. **Figurative** language is when you describe something by comparing it with something else, either directly (using the words *like* or *as*) or indirectly. For example, "I'm as hungry as a horse" means I'm very hungry. None of the expressions are about actual animals.

••• CHECKLIST FOR ANALYZING EXPRESSIONS

To determine the meaning of an expression, remember the following:

✓ If you find a confusing group of words, it may be an expression. The meaning of words in expressions may not be their literal meaning.

- Ask yourself: Is this confusing because the words are new? Or because the words do not make sense together?

✓ Determining the overall meaning may require that you use one or more of the following:

- context clues

- a dictionary or other resource

- teacher or peer support

✓ Highlight important information before and after the expression to look for clues.

⟳ YOUR TURN

Read the following excerpt from "The Legend of Carman." Then, complete the multiple-choice questions below.

---

from **"The Legend of Carman"**

But Carman would not succeed. The brothers did not obey their orders. As Carman slept, they laid siege to the nearest village. Their actions drew the attention of the Tuatha Dé Dannan. Before morning, the brothers were captured and given the choice between death or exile. They deserted Carman to save themselves. As punishment for her sons' crimes, fair Carman was sealed in a tomb and buried alive. Her sons' treason burned in her chest like a thousand flames. Her cry of grief echoed across the cliffs as breath left her body. Carman's anguish revealed her remorse and reversed her spell. The farms became more bountiful than ever before. The Irish were satisfied by the sorceress's sacrifice.

---

1. What is the meaning of the expression "Her sons' treason burned in her chest like a thousand flames"?

   ○ A. Carmen is annoyed by her sons' betrayal.

   ○ B. Carman is not affected by her sons' betrayal.

   ○ C. Carman feels physical pain being buried alive.

   ○ D. Carmen feels extreme emotional distress because of her sons' betrayal.

2. A sentence that best supports the correct answer to question 1 is:

   ○ A. "Before morning, the brothers were captured and given the choice between death or exile."

   ○ B. "As punishment for her sons' crimes, fair Carman was sealed in a tomb and buried alive."

   ○ C. "Her cry of grief echoed across the cliffs as breath left her body."

   ○ D. "The farms became more bountiful than ever before."

3. Which phrase best describes the expression featured in question 1?

   ○ A. an idiom

   ○ B. figurative language

   ○ C. literal language

   ○ D. a saying

Skill:
Sharing Information

★ DEFINE

Sharing information involves asking for and giving information. The process of sharing information with other students can help all students learn more and better understand a text or a topic. You can share information when you participate in **brief** discussions or **extended** speaking assignments.

••• CHECKLIST FOR SHARING INFORMATION

When you have to speak for an extended period of time, as in a discussion, you ask for and share information. To ask for and share information, you may use the following sentence frames:

✓ To ask for information:

- What do you think about _____?

- Do you agree that _____?

- What is your understanding of _____?

✓ To give information:

- I think _____.

- I agree because _____.

- My understanding is _____.

YOUR TURN

Watch the *We Choose to Go to the Moon* StudySyncTV episode. After watching, sort the following statements from the episode into the chart below. Differentiate between statements that introduce text evidence and statements that express ideas about text evidence.

	Statement Options
A	"He points out that we've got all these great scientists, but there's still so much more to learn."
B	"Yeah. But Kennedy is sending mixed messages."
C	"Kennedy was a competitive guy!"
D	"He was talking about gaining scientific knowledge."
E	"So that's Kennedy's real motivation behind this moon-landing goal."
F	"I think he had other motivations besides gaining scientific knowledge."

Introduces Text Evidence	Expresses Ideas About Text Evidence

Close Read

✏️ **WRITE**

PERSONAL RESPONSE: In "The Legend of Carman," the actions of Carman and her sons lead to Carman's death. Who bears the greatest responsibility for her death? Write a paragraph in which you explain your opinion. Build your case on information from the story. Pay attention to and edit for the spelling rules of suffixes and English spelling patterns.

Use the checklist below to guide you as you write.

☐ Who is most responsible for Carman's death?

☐ Why is that your opinion?

☐ What information from the story supports your opinion?

Use the sentence frames to organize and write your personal response.

In my opinion, _____ (is/are)

responsible for Carman's death. I think so because _____

_____ .

Information from the story that supports my opinion includes _____

_____ .

Carman is put to death because _____

_____ .

Long Live King Chazz

FICTION

Introduction

In this humorous short story, a beloved monarch dies suddenly, and his young, uneducated six-year-old son is forced to take the throne. Once in power, King Chazz acts as any six-year-old might, outlawing bedtimes and broccoli. In the complications that arise during King Chazz's rule, the author offers satirical commentary on contemporary politics and the motivations of political leaders.

VOCABULARY

succession

the process of replacement for offices, ranks, or titles

competent

able to satisfactorily master and complete a task

welfare

the state of being well, such as being happy, healthy, or successful

delegation

a group of people chosen to represent others and make decisions

factions

small groups that share opinions that are in conflict with a larger group and with one another

 READ

NOTES

1   A great tragedy occurred one day in the small but majestic kingdom of Abrearia. Our beloved His Royal Highness King Chaderick IV died suddenly of a cold he caught while hunting wild boar in a thunderstorm. His advisers warned him against holding the hunt in such dangerous conditions. But the Annual Wild Boar Hunt has been held on the fourth Sunday after the third full moon in the second season for the past 300 years. He refused to reschedule. It was a terrible loss for our proud nation.

2   However, from even the darkest night arises the brightest sun. King Chaderick's son, His Royal Highness King Chaderick V, has inherited the throne. Stronger than a team of oxen and more brilliant than the brightest diamond, he is truly an awe-inspiring king.

3   Some critics have opposed the rules of **succession** that have allowed King Chazz, as the monarch prefers to be called, to assume the throne at the age of six. But these small-minded complainers fail to see the depths of the king's

wisdom. Some say he has been ignoring the nation's **welfare** to promote his own agenda. That is not true. For instance, his first official decree made it illegal for anyone to go to sleep before midnight. This was not merely a guise to avoid his own 8 o'clock bedtime. On the contrary, he was showing tremendous selflessness. He sacrificed his own rest so that the nation's engineers, inventors, and musicians could continue their work late into the night without disturbing their sleeping children. Likewise, his second decree outlawed the production and sale of green vegetables. This was not because he himself believes them to be icky. Rather, it is his forward-thinking attempt to inspire the country's farmers to create better-tasting crops. Such efforts will undoubtedly boost trade. What a visionary!

4   Yet, treasonous **factions** have suggested the king might not be the best man for the job. Just because the king has never set foot outside the palace doesn't mean he's out of touch with the people. And just because he doesn't read that well yet doesn't mean he's not capable of writing laws. Luckily for our **competent** leader, our country is governed by divine right. King Chazz was chosen to rule. We would remind any opponents to remember it is our duty to serve our king.

5   Still, those who doubt the king's abilities hounded the palace with protests until King Chazz magnanimously agreed to take on a special adviser. King Chazz set up a **delegation** to look for the sharpest legal minds and most brilliant economists. They visited universities and top corporations. They interviewed distinguished judges and local government officials. They scoured the countryside until they found the best of the best and brought the top candidates to the palace.

6   Every citizen came to witness the king's assessment of these talented individuals. King Chazz lined them up on a stage. Everyone waited to hear the criteria he would use to select the person who would help him run the country. The crowd was abuzz with guesses. Would they have to answer a series of questions or prove their physical strength?

7   King Chazz silenced the crowd and announced that the candidates would participate in a screaming contest. He explained, "For whoever screams the loudest is clearly demonstrating the most passion for our great nation and therefore deserves to hold this important position."

8   One by one, the candidates let out their most ear-piercing cries until tragedy struck a second time. The king's eardrums were indeed pierced. He pulled his too-big crown down to protect his ears, but it was too late. His sense of hearing was lost forever. But this is not a tale of woe. No longer haunted by the criticisms of this earthly realm, King Chazz was finally free to govern as he saw fit. He passed his next royal decree (exiling dentists from the kingdom) without hearing a word of opposition.

 First Read

Read the story. After you read, complete the Think Questions below.

☁ THINK QUESTIONS

1. What happened to King Chaderick IV? What happened as a result of this event?

   King Chadwick IV _____.

   As a result, _____.

2. What were the first two decrees, or laws, that King Chazz passed after he became king?

   The first decree was _____.

   The second decree was _____.

3. What was King Chazz's plan to choose an adviser? Explain in two or three sentences.

   King Chazz's plan was _____

   _____.

4. Use context to confirm the meaning of the word *delegation* as it is used in "Long Live King Chazz."
   Write your definition of *delegation* here.

   Delegation means _____.

   A context clue is _____.

5. What is another way to say that King Chazz has been ignoring the nation's *welfare*?

   King Chazz has been ignoring the nation's _____

   _____.

Please note that excerpts and passages in the StudySync® library and this workbook are intended as touchstones to generate interest in an author's work. The excerpts and passages do not substitute for the reading of entire texts, and StudySync® strongly recommends that students seek out and purchase the whole literary or informational work in order to experience it as the author intended. Links to online resellers are available in our digital library. In addition, complete works may be ordered through an authorized reseller by filling out and returning to StudySync® the order form enclosed in this workbook.

Reading & Writing Companion   **391**

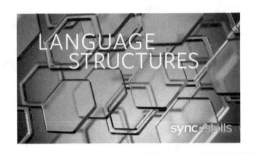

Skill:
Language Structures

★ DEFINE

In every language, there are rules that tell how to **structure** sentences. These rules define the correct order of words. In the English language, for example, a **basic** structure for sentences is subject, verb, and object. Some sentences have more **complicated** structures.

You will encounter both basic and complicated **language structures** in the classroom materials you read. Being familiar with language structures will help you better understand the text.

••• CHECKLIST FOR LANGUAGE STRUCTURES

To improve your comprehension of language structures, do the following:

✓ Monitor your understanding.

- Ask yourself: Why do I not understand this sentence? Is it because I do not understand some of the words? Or is it because I do not understand the way the words are ordered in the sentence?

✓ Break down the sentence into its parts.

- Pay attention to comparatives and superlatives. The **comparative** form compares two things. The **superlative** form compares more than two things.

- Ask yourself: Are there comparatives or superlatives in this sentence? What are they comparing?

✓ Confirm your understanding with a peer or teacher.

YOUR TURN

Read each adjective below. Then, complete the chart by matching each adjective with its comparative and superlative form.

Adjectives				
lighter	softest	most careful	happiest	softer
best	lightest	happier	better	more careful

Adjective	Comparative	Superlative
soft		
careful		
light		
good		
happy		

Please note that excerpts and passages in the StudySync® library and this workbook are intended as touchstones to generate interest in an author's work. The excerpts and passages do not substitute for the reading of entire texts, and StudySync® strongly recommends that students seek out and purchase the whole literary or informational work in order to experience it as the author intended. Links to online resellers are available in our digital library. In addition, complete works may be ordered through an authorized reseller by filling out and returning to StudySync® the order form enclosed in this workbook.

Reading & Writing Companion 393

Skill:
Main Ideas and Details

★ DEFINE

The **main ideas** are the most important ideas of a paragraph, a section, or an entire text. The **supporting details** are details that describe or explain the main ideas.

To **distinguish** between the main ideas and the supporting details, you will need to decide what information is the most important and supports or explains the main ideas.

••• CHECKLIST FOR MAIN IDEA AND DETAILS

In order to distinguish between main ideas and supporting details, do the following:

✓ Preview the text. Look at headings, topic sentences, and boldface vocabulary.

- Ask yourself: What seem to be the main ideas in this text?

✓ Read the text.

- Ask yourself: What are the most important ideas? What details support or explain the most important ideas?

✓ Take notes or use a graphic organizer to distinguish between main ideas and supporting details.

⟳ YOUR TURN

Read the following from "Long Live King Chazz." Then, complete the multiple-choice questions below.

---

from **"Long Live King Chazz"**

Some critics have opposed the rules of succession that have allowed King Chazz, as the monarch prefers to be called, to assume the throne at the age of six. But these small-minded complainers fail to see the depths of the king's wisdom. Some say he has been ignoring the nation's welfare to promote his own agenda. That is not true. For instance, his first official decree made it illegal for anyone to go to sleep before midnight. This was not merely a guise to avoid his own 8 o'clock bedtime. On the contrary, he was showing tremendous selflessness. He sacrificed his own rest so that the nation's engineers, inventors, and musicians could continue their work late into the night without disturbing their sleeping children. Likewise, his second decree outlawed the production and sale of green vegetables. This was not because he himself believes them to be icky. Rather, it is his forward-thinking attempt to inspire the country's farmers to create better-tasting crops. Such efforts will undoubtedly boost trade. What a visionary!

---

1. What is the main idea of the paragraph?

    ○ A. King Chazz is a child who knows how to make great laws.
    ○ B. Many people support King Chazz's first two laws.
    ○ C. King Chazz's first two laws are so bad that they are actually funny.

2. Which detail best supports the main idea?

    ○ A. "Some critics have opposed the rules of succession..."
    ○ B. "But these small-minded complainers fail to see the depths of the king's wisdom."
    ○ C. "Some say he has been ignoring the nation's welfare to promote his own agenda."

3. Which detail does <u>not</u> support the main idea?

    ○ A. "This was not merely a guise to avoid his own 8 o'clock bedtime. On the contrary, he was showing tremendous selflessness."
    ○ B. "For instance, his first official decree made it illegal for anyone to go to sleep before midnight."
    ○ C. "What a visionary!"

Close Read

Copyright © BookheadEd Learning, LLC

✏ WRITE

NARRATIVE: In "Long Live King Chazz," the new king is described as awe-inspiring. Imagine you live in King Chazz's kingdom and that you, in fact, do find him to be an amazing ruler. Write the king a letter and tell him why you find him so awe-inspiring. Provide details from the story that support your main idea. Pay attention to and edit for verb tenses.

Use the checklist below to guide you as you write.

☐ What qualities make King Chazz a good leader?

☐ How do King Chazz's laws help the people in his kingdom?

☐ Which verb tense will you use to write this letter?

Use the sentence frames to organize and write your narrative.

To His Royal Highness King Chazz, I just want to say that I think you are leading our kingdom in the right

direction. No other _____

_____

has the courage to make such _____ policies. For example, your decision to _____

_____

is awe-inspiring. Now, everyone has _____. Our country needs more leaders like you who are

willing to try _____. _____!

Sincerely,

studysync®

UNIT 3

Against the Wind

How do leaders fight for their ideas?

Genre Focus: ARGUMENTATIVE

Texts

 PAIRED READINGS

Extended Writing Project and Grammar

English Language Learner Resources

How do leaders fight for their ideas?

SUSAN B. ANTHONY

In the late 1800s, women in the United States did not yet have the right to vote. Famed women's suffrage activist Susan B. Anthony (1820–1906) set out to change that. After being arrested for casting an illegal vote in the presidential election of 1872, Anthony drafted a speech arguing that she had committed no crime and delivered it in each of the 29 postal districts in Monroe County, New York. The speech was so effective that the prosecution requested a change of venue.

FREDERICK DOUGLASS

A vital leader in the abolitionist movement, Frederick Douglass (1818–1895) was the first African American to serve as a United States official and was nominated for vice president of the United States. He was well-regarded in his time as a brilliant and eloquent speaker. Douglass's autobiographical writings, including *Narrative of the Life of Frederick Douglass, An American Slave* (1845), offer a portrait of slavery from the point of view of the enslaved, a much-needed contribution to literature that continues to be widely read.

FOUNDING FATHERS

The Founding Fathers of the United States used both words and weapons to create a nation. In documents such as the Declaration of Independence and the Constitution, they detailed the reasoning for the American colonists' revolt against British rule and the King of England, and described how they intended to form and structure their new government. Carefully, they defined and established how that government would function—what it could do, and, perhaps more importantly, what it could not.

LILI'UOKALANI

During her brief reign as Hawaii's monarch, Lili'uokalani (1838–1917) fiercely opposed the annexation of the islands by the United States. In 1893, a pro-American political party forced her to abdicate the throne. Following a series of insurrections and counter-insurrections, she finally signed a formal abdication in 1895 to protect her supporters from persecution. The annexation of Hawaii occurred in 1898. The same year, Lili'uokalani published *Hawaii's Story by Hawaii's Queen* and composed the song, "Aloha Oe," still popular in the islands today.

JAMES MADISON

A Founding Father of the United States and the fourth American president, James Madison (1751–1836) was the leading advocate for a strong federal government. He earned the nickname "Father of the Constitution" after penning the first drafts of both the U.S. Constitution and the Bill of Rights. In *The Federalist Papers*, Madison—along with John Jay and Alexander Hamilton—fought for the ratification of their Constitution, arguing that only a robust central government could protect the rights of its people.

NELSON MANDELA

Nelson Mandela (1918–2013) led the emancipation of South Africa from white minority rule and became the country's first democratically-elected president in 1994. His election came after he served twenty-seven years in prison on charges of conspiracy to overthrow the South African government. In his 1962 trial testimony, he indicted the state-sanctioned system of apartheid, voicing his opposition to this system of enforced segregation. His reputation grew steadily while he was in prison and he became an international emblem of freedom and democracy.

THOMAS PAINE

An intellectual and political theorist, Thomas Paine (1737–1809) was one of the leading figures urging the American colonies to fight for their independence from Britain. Through his pamphlet *Common Sense*, Paine deftly communicated the ideas of the American Revolution to common farmers and academics alike. His writing proved so influential that future president John Adams remarked, "without the pen of the author of *Common Sense*, the sword of Washington would have been raised in vain."

JONATHAN SWIFT

Considered the greatest prose satirist in English literature, Jonathan Swift (1667–1745) is best known for his deadpan, ironic style. In *Gulliver's Travels*—widely regarded as his masterpiece—Swift employed his caustic wit as he critiqued human nature and the society of his time. By Swift's own account, he wrote *Gulliver's Travels* in order "to vex the world rather than divert it." Vexed or not, the public embraced Swift's work and it has become the most widely held work of Irish literature in libraries around the world.

PHILLIS WHEATLEY

Taken from her home in West Africa and enslaved in America at age seven, Phillis Wheatley (1753–1784) became one of the best-known poets in pre-19th century America. After being purchased by a prominent Boston family, Wheatley learned to read and write and immersed herself in British literature and the Greek and Latin classics. At the age of eighteen, she became the first published African American poet in modern times. An abolitionist, Wheatley used her poetry to advance the cause of freedom for enslaved people.

ZITKÁLA-ŠÁ

Born in South Dakota, Zitkála-Šá or Red Bird (1876–1938) was the daughter of a Yankton Sioux mother and a German American father. Much of her writing addresses the conflict she felt as a child between her Native American heritage and the dominant culture. In 1926, she founded the National Council of American Indians, and became an influential spokesperson for Native American rights, advocating for cultural preservation and reforms in education and healthcare.

The Enlightenment

Introduction

This introduction provides readers with the historical and cultural context of the period of Enlightenment literature. The scientific progress that marked the 16th and 17th centuries paved the way for the Enlightenment, which is generally defined as the age of philosophy that figured most prominently in Europe during the 18th century. It was a time of scientific and social progress that fostered the foundations of the United States of America.

"Truth is not singular and does not come from a higher power."

A Reading of Voltaire's Tragedy *L'Orpheline de la Chine in the Salon of Madame Geoffrin*; painting of a French "salon" where intellectuals would gather to discuss literature and philosophy, by Anicet Charles Gabriel Lemonnier, ca. 1800

1   Just as the word *Renaissance* signifies the development of humanism in many different countries over several centuries, the term *Enlightenment* encompasses many thinkers and refers more to an idea than a specific time and place. Broadly defined, the Enlightenment is the age of **philosophy** that followed the scientific advancements of the Renaissance, spanning the late-17th to early-19th centuries. The period was influential in Europe, especially in France, and in the American colonies.

2   Known as the Age of Reason, the Enlightenment period was characterized by the belief that philosophy, which included the natural and social sciences, had the power to improve human life. In his essay "An Answer to the Question: What is Enlightenment?" (1784), German philosopher Immanuel Kant, defines "enlightenment" as the movement of humans toward maturity. The mark of this maturity, according to Kant, is thinking for oneself. He believed that people could rely on their own intellect to figure out what to believe and how to act. Like Kant, other thinkers of the period also promoted new ways of thinking about truth, freedom, and equality, which ultimately ignited political

Please note that excerpts and passages in the StudySync® library and this workbook are intended as touchstones to generate interest in an author's work. The excerpts and passages do not substitute for the reading of entire texts, and StudySync® strongly recommends that students seek out and purchase the whole literary or informational work in order to experience it as the author intended. Links to online resellers are available in our digital library. In addition, complete works may be ordered through an authorized reseller by filling out and returning to StudySync® the order form enclosed in this workbook.

Reading & Writing Companion 403

movements and gave rise to the two most important revolutions in the 18th century: The American (1775) and the French (1789).

Philosophy with Revolutionary Consequences

3   Many scholars consider the center of the Enlightenment to be an informal society known as the *philosophes*. These French thinkers **collaborated** during the middle decades of the eighteenth century, producing the *Encyclopedia,* which was published in 28 volumes over 21 years (1751–1772). Over 140 people submitted more than 70,000 articles. The aim of the *Encyclopedia* was to compile human knowledge in a range of subjects to pass onto future generations. Many of the social sciences we have today— history, anthropology, psychology, and sociology—have their roots in the eighteenth century, particularly in the ideas set forth in the *Encyclopedia.* The *Encyclopedia* was edited by Denis Diderot and Jean La Rond d'Alembert, and it was censored by the ruling class in France. The project exists largely because of Diderot's determination. It can be seen as a symbol of the Enlightenment because of its collaborative nature and its resistance to traditional power structures.

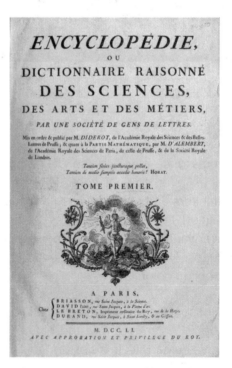

Encyclopédie, ou dictionnaire raisonné des sciences, des arts et des métiers, title page of the *Encyclopedia* including an illustration of an angel surrounded by books and scientific instruments, 1751

4   The social and political unrest of the time period influenced (and was influenced by) Enlightenment **ideals**. Many thinkers reexamined traditional ideas about how societies should be structured. The period originated theories of social contracts, which propose that individuals consent to be governed. This idea—that the right to rule is granted by individuals—contrasted sharply with the belief that monarchs possessed a divine right to rule. People wanted to think for themselves and have a say in how their governments functioned. This progress, some believed, meant that traditional structures, such as the monarchy, the privileged ruling class, and the political power of the Catholic Church, had to be removed.

5   The clash between the new and the traditional violently erupted with the famous Storming of the Bastille on July 14, 1789, which marked the beginning of the French Revolution. Although the Enlightenment-era revolutions were historic moments and successful in many ways, they did not always result in a more equal and free society. The French revolutionaries, for example, wanted to replace the monarchy with a government by the people. The high ideals of the period did not, however, translate into a lasting democracy. Violence continued throughout the 1790s, leading eventually to Napoleon Bonaparte reestablishing monarchical rule and crowning himself emperor in 1804. It would require multiple attempts before a stable democratic government would be established in France.

The Storming of the Bastille by Jean-Pierre Houël, 1789

Enlightenment Philosophy in America

6   Enlightenment ideals in general, and the work of John Locke in particular, inspired American colonists and the Founding Fathers. The second paragraph of the Declaration of Independence states that "We hold these truths to be self-evident, that all men are created equal, that they are endowed by their Creator with certain unalienable Rights, that among these are Life, Liberty and the pursuit of Happiness." The Founding Fathers wrote this sentence to

Copyright © BookheadEd Learning, LLC

NOTES

justify their revolt against British control of the colonies. Almost a century earlier, in his *Two Treatises on Government* (1689), Locke had similarly argued for the existence of "natural rights" and for the equality of all adults. No person, including the king, had the right to "harm another in his life, Health, Liberty or Possessions." Locke believed the power of any government came from the people, and the people had the right to overthrow any government that violated people's natural rights.

7 Thomas Paine's *Common Sense*, a pamphlet published in 1776, explains why the colonies should separate from Great Britain. It also explores what a new and independent American government would look like. Paine writes, "If there is any true cause of fear respecting independence, it is because no plan is yet laid down. Men do not see their way out." In many ways, American thinkers and statesmen applied Enlightenment ideals to the situation faced by the colonists. By doing so, the colonists could "see their way out."

8 Although this new government sought to treat all citizens as equals, not everyone was allowed to be a "citizen," such as Native Americans, women, immigrants, and slaves. For many people, rights were not guaranteed by law until the 20th century. Women, for example, were not allowed to vote until the 19th Amendment was passed in 1920. The rights of African Americans and other **minorities** were not protected by federal law until the Civil Rights Act of 1964 and the Voting Rights Act of 1965. Enlightenment theories valued freedom and equality, but in practice these rights were guaranteed only for specific people.

Enlightenment in the Arts

9 Much of the Enlightenment focused on the nature of experience, the influence of science, the role of reason, and the formation of new social and political systems, and visual and literary arts were not as much at the forefront. The focus on order did, however, still influence the visual arts, which emphasized symmetry and simplicity and viewed art as an intellectual pursuit more so than an emotional one. Many Enlightenment thinkers discussed theories of aesthetics, or the nature of beauty. The age of philosophy was also the age of criticism. Philosophers developed specific criteria that could be used to determine whether an object should be considered beautiful. Much of the art during this time period was Neoclassical. Writers, musicians, painters, sculptors, and architects found inspiration in the classical beauty of Ancient Greece and the Roman Empire.

Frontispiece to Phillis Wheatley's *Poems on Various Subjects,* this portrait of Phillis Wheatley includes an inscription referring to her as "Servant to Mr. John Wheatley of Boston," by Scorpio Moorhead, 1773.

10 In America, poets discussed the themes of freedom, equality, and liberty in poems that followed the strict rules of traditional rhyme and meter. Phillis Wheatley, for example, often composed poems using heroic couplets, or two rhyming lines of iambic pentameter. Wheatley also read **profusely**, including the Bible, John Milton's *Paradise Lost*, and the Greek and Latin classics of Virgil, Ovid, and Homer. These texts served as her inspiration and echoes of them can be seen in her work. The most well-known poet of the American Revolution was Philip Morin Freneau. Freneau was also a journalist and established a newspaper called the *National Gazette* to promote the ideas of Thomas Jefferson. Freneau's nature poems pay close attention to the American landscape and, in many ways, mark the transition from Enlightenment literature to the literary period that directly followed—Romanticism. Freneau's political poems were often satires, but Freneau routinely incorporated the ideals of the American Revolution into his work.

George Washington by Jean-Antoine Houdon, 1785

Copyright © Bookheaded Learning, LLC

NOTES

11 **Major Concepts**

- **The Pursuit of Truth**—Most Enlightenment philosophy centers on the idea of "Truth" and the work of humans to understand it. Enlightenment thinkers developed the ideas of empiricism, which hold that we gain knowledge through direct observation and sensory experience, and which are considered the cornerstone of modern scientific experimentation. They held that truth is not singular and does not come from a higher power. It is an abstract concept, but it is worthy of study. Through careful observation, experimentation, and logic, humans can better understand "Truth," and this understanding can improve the human condition. The study of truth involves many different fields of knowledge—the natural world, the human body, human behavior, the role of governments, and the formation of just societies.

- **The Pursuit of Liberty**—The revolutions that took place during the 18th century sought to create free and equal societies that respected the will of the people. Although these ideals did not always work out in reality, the pursuit of liberty was a powerful force for progress and change. Themes of liberty and freedom are explored throughout the literary and informational texts of the time period. Artists and philosophers looked back to Ancient Greece and Rome to find inspiration in these great civilizations. They respected the wisdom and reason of ancient philosophers as they looked toward the future, imagining new knowledge, technology, and structures that could continue to improve human life.

12 **Style and Form**

- **Rhetoric and Rhetorical Devices** — Rhetoric is the art of speaking and writing persuasively. Classical rhetoric uses three types of appeals: *logos*, an appeal to logic; *pathos*, an appeal to the emotions of the audience; and *ethos*, an appeal based on the author's expertise. Authors and speakers often use rhetorical devices, such as similes, metaphors, alliteration, allusions, and repetition, to help them persuade their audience. These techniques help readers and listeners better understand and relate to what an author is trying to say.

- **Neoclassicism**— Much of the art during the 18th century included allusions, or references, to earlier ideas, images, and figures. Many of these referred to figures and stories from Ancient Greece and Rome. Particularly in America, poets and writers discussed hope for the New World by alluding to the past. In addition, rather than experimenting with new poetic forms, poets most often composed their works using traditional forms. Artists rose to the challenge of exploring themes with far-reaching implications, such as liberty, justice, and independence, within the confines of strict rules about rhyme and meter.

- **Satire** — Satire is a way of criticizing something—a person, an idea, a tradition, a political structure, a social custom—by making it ridiculous. Creating a satire often requires verbal irony, or stating one thing and meaning the opposite. The Enlightenment's focus on improving human life often involved noticing what needed to be changed. Satirists highlighted these necessary changes by presenting the ridiculousness of things as they were. Writer Jonathan Swift defined a specific deadpan, or deliberately unexpressive, style of satire. His fictional *Gulliver's Travels* is an account of the strange customs Gulliver encounters; however, they reflect British society as Swift observed it. For instance, Swift mocks the cronyism of Britain's political parties when he shows the Lilliputians making court appointments based solely on style of a person's shoes.

13 Both the achievements and failures of the Enlightenment changed the course of history and continue to influence societies and governments around the world today. The Enlightenment's focus on the scientific method and the pursuit of knowledge ushered in an age of rapid industrialization, the effects of which, from the incredible developments in technology and medicine to the challenges posed by pollution, are important aspects of the 21st century. The French and American Revolutions inspired hope, but they also caused a backlash, reinforcing in many ways the very structures that they sought to change. Although the American Revolution was successful, the Enlightenment ideals of equality were not equally applied. Many groups were, and would continue to be, excluded from the equality and justice promised by one of the preeminent texts of the Enlightenment, the Constitution of the United States of America.

14 Although many writers and artists of the 19th century would go on to reject Enlightenment aesthetics and embrace a new movement, Romanticism, instead, the Enlightenment had an undeniable cultural impact. Governmental sponsorship of scientific pursuits and the emphasis on learning led to significant changes that are still felt today. From questioning the divine right of kings, to embracing modes of inquiry that still underlie the scientific method, the Enlightenment changed the way people related to the world around them. Likewise, Swiftian satire can still be seen in a wide variety of media. Movies, television, websites, online newspapers, blogs, and tweets all satirize politicians, celebrities, mainstream news outlets, and countless other aspects of modern life. Just as in the age of philosophy, we continue to pursue truth and liberty, hoping to make human experience just a little better each day.

Please note that excerpts and passages in the StudySync® library and this workbook are intended as touchstones to generate interest in an author's work. The excerpts and passages do not substitute for the reading of entire texts, and StudySync® strongly recommends that students seek out and purchase the whole literary or informational work in order to experience it as the author intended. Links to online resellers are available in our digital library. In addition, complete works may be ordered through an authorized reseller by filling out and returning to StudySync® the order form enclosed in this workbook.

Reading & Writing Companion 409

LITERARY FOCUS:
THE ENLIGHTENMENT

Literary Focus

Read "Literary Focus: The Enlightenment." After you read, complete the Think Questions below.

☁ THINK QUESTIONS

1. What were the main goals of the Enlightenment? Cite evidence from the text to support your answer.

2. How did Enlightenment ideals affect the United States of America? Cite evidence from the text to support your answer.

3. According to the author, in what ways did the Enlightenment fail to achieve its goals? Cite evidence from the text to support your answer.

4. Use context clues to determine the meaning of *collaborated*. Write your best definition here, and describe which clues helped you come to it.

5. Use context clues to determine the meaning of *profusely*. Write its definition here. Then, check your definition with a print or digital dictionary.

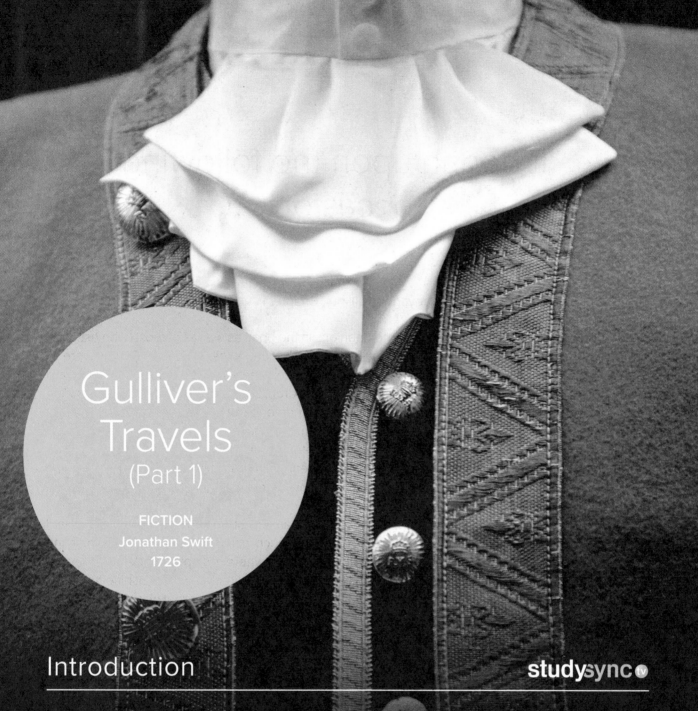

Gulliver's Travels
(Part 1)

FICTION
Jonathan Swift
1726

Introduction

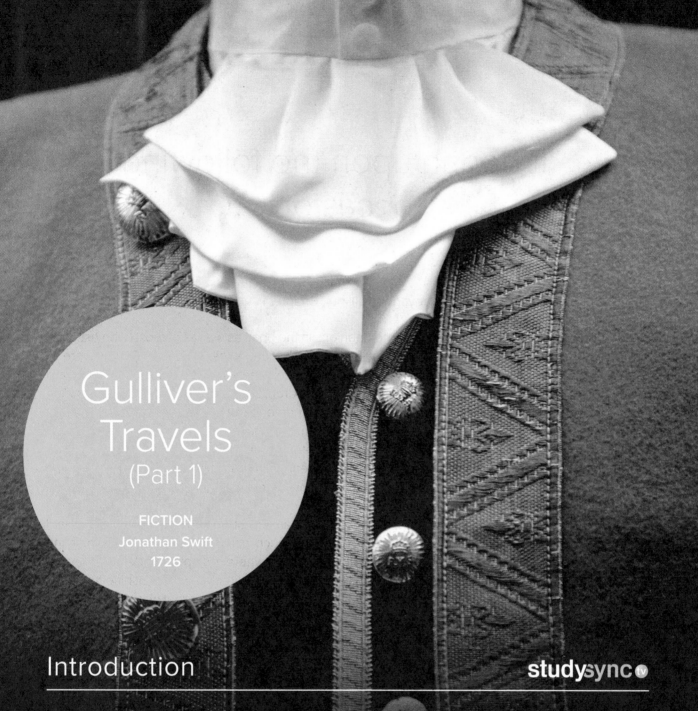

studysync tv

Gulliver's Travels is a masterpiece of satire, critiquing the popular 18th-century Enlightenment notion that advances in human society are the result of reason and logic alone. Through Lemuel Gulliver's voyages to fantastical lands, author Jonathan Swift (1667–1745) suggests the importance of religion and compassion in the guidance of human affairs. In this excerpt from Part I, Swift offers a thinly veiled mockery of 18th-century English politics: Lilliput, an island of miniature people engaged in ridiculous conflicts, is likely to symbolize the Kingdom of England, with the two major political parties of England—the Tories and Whigs—represented by Lilliput's High Heels and Low Heels. Rival island Blefuscu symbolizes the Kingdom

"It began upon the following occasion."

Copyright © BookheadEd Learning, LLC

NOTES

Skill:
Word Meaning

What is a vessel? It is the object of a prepositional phrase, so I know it's a noun. I see words like boat, swam, and tide. These are context clues that a vessel relates to the sea, but I'm still not sure of its exact meaning.

from Part I: A Voyage to Lilliput, Chapter I

1   What became of my companions in the boat, as well as of those who escaped on the rock, or were left in the vessel, I cannot tell; but conclude they were all lost. For my own part, I swam as fortune directed me, and was pushed forward by wind and tide. I often let my legs drop, and could feel no bottom; but when I was almost gone, and able to struggle no longer, I found myself within my depth; and by this time the storm was much abated. The declivity was so small, that I walked near a mile before I got to the shore, which I conjectured was about eight o'clock in the evening. I then advanced forward near half a mile, but could not discover any sign of houses or inhabitants; at least I was in so weak a condition, that I did not observe them. I was extremely tired, and with that, and the heat of the weather, and about half a pint of brandy that I drank as I left the ship, I found myself much inclined to sleep. I lay down on the grass, which was very short and soft, where I slept sounder than ever I remembered to have done in my life, and, as I reckoned, about nine hours; for when I awaked, it was just day-light. I attempted to rise, but was not able to stir: for, as I happened to lie on my back, I found my arms and legs were strongly fastened on each side to the ground; and my hair, which was long and thick, tied down in the same manner. I likewise felt several slender **ligatures** across my body, from my arm-pits to my thighs. I could only look upwards; the sun began to grow hot, and the light offended my eyes. I heard a confused noise about me; but in the posture I lay, could see nothing except the sky.

2   In a little time I felt something alive moving on my left leg, which advancing gently forward over my breast, came almost up to my chin; when, bending my eyes downwards as much as I could, I perceived it to be a human creature not six inches high, with a bow and arrow in his hands, and a quiver at his back. In the mean time, I felt at least forty more of the same kind (as I

Gulliver held prisoner and tied down by the people of Lilliput, published c.1880

conjectured) following the first. I was in the utmost astonishment, and roared so loud, that they all ran back in a fright; and some of them, as I was afterwards told, were hurt with the falls they got by leaping from my sides upon the ground. However, they soon returned, and one of them, who ventured so far as to get a full sight of my face, lifting up his hands and eyes by way of admiration, cried out in a shrill but distinct voice, *Hekinah degul*: the others repeated the same words several times, but then I knew not what they meant. I lay all this while, as the reader may believe, in great uneasiness.

3   At length, struggling to get loose, I had the fortune to break the strings, and wrench out the pegs that fastened my left arm to the ground; for, by lifting it up to my face, I discovered the methods they had taken to bind me, and at the same time with a violent pull, which gave me excessive pain, I a little loosened the strings that tied down my hair on the left side, so that I was just able to turn my head about two inches. But the creatures ran off a second time, before I could seize them; whereupon there was a great shout in a very shrill accent, and after it ceased I heard one of them cry aloud *Tolgo phonac*; when in an instant I felt above a hundred arrows **discharged** on my left hand, which, pricked me like so many needles; and besides, they shot another flight into the air, as we do bombs in Europe, whereof many, I suppose, fell on my body, (though I felt them not), and some on my face, which I immediately covered with my left hand. When this shower of arrows was over, I fell a groaning with grief and pain; and then striving again to get loose, they discharged another volley larger than the first, and some of them attempted with spears to stick me in the sides; but by good luck I had on a buff jerkin, which they could not pierce.

4   I thought it the most prudent method to lie still, and my design was to continue so till night, when, my left hand being already loose, I could easily free myself: and as for the inhabitants, I had reason to believe I might be a match for the greatest army they could bring against me, if they were all of the same size with him that I saw. But fortune disposed otherwise of me. When the people observed I was quiet, they discharged no more arrows; but, by the noise I heard, I knew their numbers increased; and about four yards from me, over against my right ear, I heard a knocking for above an hour, like that of people at work; when turning my head that way, as well as the pegs and strings would permit me, I saw a stage erected about a foot and a half from the ground, capable of holding four of the inhabitants, with two or three ladders to mount it: from whence one of them, who seemed to be a person of quality, made me a long speech, whereof I understood not one syllable. But I should have mentioned, that before the principal person began his oration, he cried out three times, *Langro dehul san* (these words and the former were afterwards repeated and explained to me); whereupon, immediately, about fifty of the inhabitants came and cut the strings that fastened the left side of my head, which gave me the liberty of turning it to the right, and of observing

Skill:
Media

I see a similarity in how both versions poke fun at leaders. The "principal person" in the book and the king in the cartoon both appear to be more concerned with pomp and circumstance than with effective communication.

NOTES

the person and gesture of him that was to speak. He appeared to be of a middle age, and taller than any of the other three who attended him, whereof one was a page[1] that held up his train, and seemed to be somewhat longer than my middle finger; the other two stood one on each side to support him. He acted every part of an orator, and I could observe many periods of threatenings, and others of promises, pity, and kindness.

5   I answered in a few words, but in the most submissive manner, lifting up my left hand, and both my eyes to the sun, as calling him for a witness; and being almost famished with hunger, having not eaten a morsel for some hours before I left the ship, I found the demands of nature so strong upon me, that I could not forbear showing my impatience (perhaps against the strict rules of decency) by putting my finger frequently to my mouth, to signify that I wanted food. The *hurgo* (for so they call a great lord, as I afterwards learnt) understood me very well. He descended from the stage, and commanded that several ladders should be applied to my sides, on which above a hundred of the inhabitants mounted and walked towards my mouth, laden with baskets full of meat, which had been provided and sent thither by the king's orders, upon the first intelligence he received of me. I observed there was the flesh of several animals, but could not distinguish them by the taste. There were shoulders, legs, and loins, shaped like those of mutton, and very well dressed, but smaller than the wings of a lark. I ate them by two or three at a mouthful, and took three loaves at a time, about the bigness of musket bullets.

. . .

6   It seems, that upon the first moment I was discovered sleeping on the ground, after my landing, the emperor had early notice of it by an express; and determined in council, that I should be tied in the manner I have related, (which was done in the night while I slept;) that plenty of meat and drink should be sent to me, and a machine prepared to carry me to the capital city.

7   This resolution perhaps may appear very bold and dangerous, and I am confident would not be imitated by any prince in Europe on the like occasion. However, in my opinion, it was extremely **prudent**, as well as generous: for, supposing these people had endeavoured to kill me with their spears and arrows, while I was asleep, I should certainly have awaked with the first sense of smart, which might so far have roused my rage and strength, as to have enabled me to break the strings wherewith I was tied; after which, as they were not able to make resistance, so they could expect no mercy.

. . .

1. **a page** a court servant

Copyright © BookheadEd Learning, LLC

from Part I: A Voyage to Lilliput, Chapter IV

• • •

8   One morning, about a fortnight[2] after I had obtained my liberty, Reldresal, principal secretary (as they style him) for private affairs, came to my house attended only by one servant. He ordered his coach to wait at a distance, and desired I would give him an hours audience; which I readily consented to, on account of his quality and personal merits, as well as of the many good offices he had done me during my solicitations at court. I offered to lie down that he might the more conveniently reach my ear, but he chose rather to let me hold him in my hand during our conversation.

9   He began with compliments on my liberty; said "he might pretend to some merit in it;" but, however, added, "that if it had not been for the present situation of things at court, perhaps I might not have obtained it so soon. For," said he, "as flourishing a condition as we may appear to be in to foreigners, we labour under two mighty evils: a violent faction at home, and the danger of an invasion, by a most potent enemy, from abroad.

10 As to the first, you are to understand, that for about seventy moons past there have been two struggling parties in this empire, under the names of *Tramecksan* and *Slamecksan*, from the high and low heels of their shoes, by which they distinguish themselves. It is alleged, indeed, that the high heels are most agreeable to our ancient constitution; but, however this be, his majesty has determined to make use only of low heels in the administration of the government, and all offices in the gift of the crown, as you cannot but observe; and particularly that his majesty's imperial heels are lower at least by a *drurr* than any of his court (*drurr* is a measure about the fourteenth part of an inch). The **animosities** between these two parties run so high, that they will neither eat, nor drink, nor talk with each other. We compute the *Tramecksan*, or high heels, to exceed us in number; but the power is wholly on our side. We apprehend his imperial highness, the heir to the crown, to have some tendency towards the high heels; at least we can plainly discover that one of his heels is higher than the other, which gives him a hobble in his gait.

Skill:
Point of View

The political parties have silly, similar names. Heel height is a significant difference between the parties. This makes me think of political debates I've heard, and it makes me wonder if Swift is being critical of politics.

11 Now, in the midst of these intestine disquiets, we are threatened with an invasion from the island of Blefuscu, which is the other great empire of the universe, almost as large and powerful as this of his majesty. For as to what we have heard you affirm, that there are other kingdoms and states in the world inhabited by human creatures as large as yourself, our philosophers are in much doubt, and would rather conjecture that you dropped from the

2. **fortnight** (British) two weeks

NOTES

moon, or one of the stars; because it is certain, that a hundred mortals of your bulk would in a short time destroy all the fruits and cattle of his majesty's dominions: besides, our histories of six thousand moons make no mention of any other regions than the two great empires of Lilliput and Blefuscu. Which two mighty powers have, as I was going to tell you, been engaged in a most obstinate war for six-and-thirty moons past.

12   It began upon the following occasion. It is allowed on all hands, that the primitive way of breaking eggs, before we eat them, was upon the larger end; but his present majesty's grandfather, while he was a boy, going to eat an egg, and breaking it according to the ancient practice, happened to cut one of his fingers. Whereupon the emperor his father published an edict, commanding all his subjects, upon great penalties, to break the smaller end of their eggs. The people so highly resented this law, that our histories tell us, there have been six rebellions raised on that account; wherein one emperor lost his life, and another his crown.

13   These civil commotions were constantly fomented by the monarchs of Blefuscu; and when they were quelled, the exiles always fled for refuge to that empire. It is computed that eleven thousand persons have at several times suffered death, rather than submit to break their eggs at the smaller end. Many hundred large volumes have been published upon this controversy: but the books of the Big-endians have been long forbidden, and the whole party rendered incapable by law of holding employments. During the course of these troubles, the emperors of Blefuscu did frequently expostulate by their ambassadors, accusing us of making a schism in religion, by offending against a fundamental doctrine of our great prophet Lustrog, in the fifty-fourth chapter of the Blundecral (which is their Alcoran[3]).

14   This, however, is thought to be a mere strain upon the text; for the words are these: 'that all true believers break their eggs at the convenient end.' And which is the convenient end, seems, in my humble opinion to be left to every man's conscience, or at least in the power of the chief magistrate to determine. Now, the Big-endian exiles have found so much credit in the emperor of Blefuscu's court, and so much private assistance and encouragement from their party here at home, that a bloody war has been carried on between the two empires for six-and-thirty moons, with various success; during which time we have lost forty capital ships, and a much greater number of smaller vessels, together with thirty thousand of our best seamen and soldiers; and the damage received by the enemy is reckoned to be somewhat greater than ours. However, they have now equipped a numerous fleet, and are just preparing to make a descent upon us; and his imperial majesty, placing great

---

3. **Alcoran** an archaic name for the Koran, Islam's sacred text

confidence in your valour and strength, has commanded me to lay this account of his affairs before you."

15   I desired the secretary to present my humble duty to the emperor; and to let him know, "that I thought it would not become me, who was a foreigner, to interfere with parties; but I was ready, with the hazard of my life, to defend his person and state against all invaders."

First Read

Read *Gulliver's Travels*. After you read, complete the Think Questions below.

☁ THINK QUESTIONS

1. Why did the small people of Lilliput first try to attack Gulliver but then provide him with food? Use evidence from the text to support your answer.

2. Write two or three sentences describing the two political parties in Lilliput. Be sure to include specific details from the text in your answer.

3. Why does Reldresal believe that his people face "the danger of an invasion" from outside? Cite specific evidence from the text to support your answer.

4. Read the following dictionary entry:

   discharge
   dis•charge /dis'CHärj/ *verb*

   1. to remove or tell someone to leave
   2. to fire or shoot
   3. to relieve oneself of an obligation or duty
   4. to fulfill, perform, or execute a duty

   Which definition most closely matches the meaning of **discharged** as it is used in paragraphs 3 and 4 of the excerpt? Explain why you made this choice.

5. Use the context clues provided in paragraph 10 of the passage to determine the meaning of **animosities**. Write your definition of *animosities* here and explain how you came to it.

Skill:
Point of View

Use the Checklist to analyze Point of View in *Gulliver's Travels*. Refer to the sample student annotations about Point of View in the text.

••• CHECKLIST FOR POINT OF VIEW

In order to determine a narrator's point of view through what is directly stated versus what is really meant, note the following:

✓ literary techniques intended to provide humor or criticism. Examples include:

- sarcasm, or the use of language that says one thing but means the opposite

- irony, or a contrast between what one expects to happen and what happens

- understatement, or an instance where a character deliberately makes a situation seem less important or serious than it is

- satire, or the use of humor, irony, exaggeration, or ridicule to expose and criticize people's foolishness or vices

✓ possible critiques an author might be making about contemporary society

✓ an unreliable narrator or character whose point of view cannot be trusted

To analyze a case in which grasping a point of view requires distinguishing what is directly stated in a text from what is really meant, consider the following questions.

✓ How does the cultural lens and experiences of the narrator shape his point of view? How does it shape what he says and how he says it?

✓ Is the narrator reliable? Why?

✓ How does the narrator's point of view contribute to a non-literal understanding of the text?

✓ How does the use of satire add meaning to the story?

Skill:
Point of View

Reread paragraphs 13 and 14 of *Gulliver's Travels*. Then, using the Checklist on the previous page, answer the multiple-choice questions below.

↻ YOUR TURN

1. Which of these quotations most effectively shows how the author uses humor to make the reader think the Lilliputians are foolish?

   ○ A. "These civil commotions were constantly fomented by the monarchs of Blefuscu."
   ○ B. "It is computed that eleven thousand persons have at several times suffered death, rather than submit to break their eggs at the smaller end."
   ○ C. "A bloody war has been carried on between the two empires for six-and-thirty moons."
   ○ D. "However, they have now equipped a numerous fleet, and are just preparing to make a descent upon us."

2. Swift mocks warfare by —

   ○ A. telling how long the war between the empires has lasted.
   ○ B. describing the ships and soldiers employed by each side.
   ○ C. using silly-sounding words to name the countries.
   ○ D. showing that the war began over an ambiguous sentence.

Skill:
Media

Use the Checklist to analyze Media in *Gulliver's Travels*. Refer to the sample student annotations about Media in the text.

••• CHECKLIST FOR MEDIA

Before analyzing multiple interpretations of a story, drama, or poem, note the following:

✓ similarities and differences in different media, such as the live production of a play or a recorded novel or poetry

✓ the different time periods and cultures in which the source material and interpretations were produced

To analyze multiple interpretations of a story, drama, or poem, evaluating how each version interprets the source text, consider the following questions:

✓ How does each version interpret the source text? What are the main similarities and differences between the two (or more) versions?

✓ In what ways does the medium affect the interpretations of the source text?

✓ If each version is from a different time period and/or culture, what does each version reveal about the time period and culture in which it was written?

✓ Does information about the time period and culture allow you to make any inferences about the authors' objectives or intentions?

Skill:
Media

Reread paragraph 4 of *Gulliver's Travels* and compare it with a segment of the Gulliver's Travels cartoon. Then, using the Checklist on the previous page, answer the multiple-choice questions below.

↻ YOUR TURN

1. The book version of *Gulliver's Travels* is more for adults, while the cartoon is more for children. What aspect of the video demonstrates this?

   ○ A. The manner in which Gulliver is restrained.

   ○ B. The townspeople's fear of Gulliver.

   ○ C. The difference in size between Gulliver and the Lilliputians.

   ○ D. The music and sound effects during the battle scene.

2. The king in the cartoon displays that he is out of touch with reality when he warns Gulliver, "You'll pay for this!" (2:30), even though he has no way of making Gulliver pay for anything. Which quote from the book suggests a similar avoidance of reality?

   ○ A. "I saw a stage erected about a foot and a half from the ground. . ."

   ○ B. ". . .before the principal person began his oration, he cried out three times, Langro dehul san. . ."

   ○ C. "He appeared to be of a middle age, and taller than any of the other three who attended him. . ."

   ○ D. "I could observe many periods of threatenings, and others of promises, pity, and kindness."

Skill:
Word Meaning

Use the Checklist to analyze Word Meaning in *Gulliver's Travels*. Refer to the sample student annotations about Word Meaning in the text.

••• CHECKLIST FOR WORD MEANING

In order to find the pronunciation of a word or determine or clarify its precise meaning, do the following:

- ✓ determine the word's part of speech

- ✓ use context clues to make an inferred meaning of the word or phrase

- ✓ consult a dictionary to verify your preliminary determination of the meaning of a word or phrase

- ✓ decide which definition makes sense within the context of the text

In order to determine or clarify a word's part of speech, do the following:

- ✓ determine what the word is describing

- ✓ identify how the word is being used in the phrase or sentence

To determine or clarify the etymology or standard usage of a word, consider the following questions:

- ✓ How formal or informal is this word?

- ✓ What is the word describing? What inferred meanings can I make?

- ✓ In what context is the word being used?

- ✓ Is this slang? Is it an example of vernacular? In what other contexts might this word be used?

Skill:
Word Meaning

Reread the end of the opening paragraph of Part I of *Gulliver's Travels* and the dictionary entry below to determine the answers to the follow-up questions.

⟳ YOUR TURN

offend / ə-'fend- / *transitive verb*
1. a. To break or disregard something, as the law   b. to cause pain or discomfort to
2. *obsolete*: to cause to sin or fall
3. to cause a person or group to feel angry or upset by something said or done

Origin: Middle English *offenden* "to assail, violate, displease, hurt the feelings of," borrowed from Anglo-French & Latin; Anglo-French *offendre*, borrowed from Latin *offendere*, "to strike against, stumble (upon), trouble, break a rule, displease, annoy"

1. This question has two parts. First, answer Part A. Then, answer Part B.

   Part A: Which definition best fits the way *offended* is used in paragraph 2?

   ○ A. Definition 1.a   ○ B. Definition 1.b   ○ C. Definition 2   ○ D. Definition 3

   Part B: Which phrase is a clue to the meaning of the word *offended*?

   ○ A. "several slender ligatures"   ○ B. "heard a confused noise"

   ○ C. "arm-pits to my thighs"   ○ D. "sun began to grow hot"

2. What is the word origin of the word *offend*?

   ○ A. Middle English, Anglo-French, and Latin   ○ B. Latin, French, and Greek

   ○ C. German and Anglo-French   ○ D. cannot be determined

3. Which of the following parts of the entry provides the pronunciation of the word?

   ○ A. *obsolete*: to cause to sin or fall

   ○ B. Origin: Middle English offenden "to assail, violate, displease, hurt the feelings of,"

   ○ C. transitive verb   ○ D. ə-'fend-

Close Read

Reread *Gulliver's Travels*. As you reread, complete the Skills Focus questions below. Then use your answers and annotations from the questions to help you complete the Write activity.

◎ SKILLS FOCUS

1. Identify a passage that you found funny in *Part 1: A Voyage to Lilliput*. Explain what the author's point of view might be in this moment, and what makes this moment satirical.

2. Identify a passage in which Swift is satirizing society's very narrow understanding of the surrounding world. Explain why his choice to use the Lilliputians to make this point of view clear is effective.

3. In the cartoon you watched, the Lilliputians speak English, whereas in Jonathan Swift's original writing they speak an unknown language that we read in italics. How does having the Lilliputians speak in a way that you can understand change your experience of the story? In what ways does it deepen your understanding of the text?

4. The word *submit* can have multiple meanings. Read paragraph 13 to see how it is used in this context: "It is computed that eleven thousand persons have at several times suffered death, rather than submit to break their eggs at the smaller end." Given your own knowledge of the word, context clues, and the following definition, what do you think is the best interpretation of this word as it is used here? How does the word add humor and a satirical tone to the story?

5. With *Gulliver's Travels*, Jonathan Swift aimed to satirize European leaders by re-creating their ridiculous behaviors in a fantastical setting. In what ways do we see leaders fighting for their ideas in *Gulliver's Travels*? Are these ideas always worth fighting for? Use textual evidence to support your answer.

✐ WRITE

PERSONAL RESPONSE: Jonathan Swift's original version of *Gulliver's Travels* is a transparent satire of the European society he lived in. If you were to create a movie version of *Gulliver's Travels* with the purpose of satirizing leaders or famous people in contemporary American society, what changes would you make to the story? Select one scene you would change. Describe how you would make the movie interpretation of the scene different from the scene in the book to better satirize current leaders or celebrities.

Liberty Tree

POETRY
Thomas Paine
1775

Introduction

Thomas Paine (1737–1809), a political activist and a Founding Father, played a pivotal role in the American independence movement. Born in England, Paine's political theories were greatly influenced by Enlightenment ideas concerning the precedence of human rights. Although he is known more for his informational pamphlets, such as *Common Sense* and *The Crisis,* Paine also wrote the political poem "Liberty Tree," inspired by a famous elm tree that stood near Boston Common.

"Unmindful of names or distinction they came . . ."

1   In a chariot of light from the regions of day,
2   The Goddess of Liberty[1] came;
3   Ten thousand **celestials**[2] directed the way
4   And hither conducted the dame.
5   A fair budding branch from the gardens above,
6   Where millions with millions agree,
7   She brought in her hand as a pledge of her love,
8   And the plant she named *Liberty Tree*.

Samuel Adams and the Sons of Liberty gather under the Liberty Tree in Boston, hanging small dolls and effigies of British rulers from the branches.

9   The celestial **exotic** struck deep in the ground,
10 Like a native it flourished and bore;
11 The fame of its fruit drew the nations around,
12 To seek out this peaceable shore.
13 Unmindful of names or distinction they came,
14 For freemen like brothers agree;
15 With one spirit endued, they one friendship pursued,
16 And their temple was *Liberty Tree*.

17 Beneath this fair tree, like the **patriarchs** of old,
18 Their bread in contentment they ate,
19 **Unvexed** with the troubles of silver and gold,
20 The cares of the grand and the great.
21 With timber and tar they Old England supplied,
22 And supported her power on the sea;
23 Her battles they fought, without getting a groat,[3]
24 For the honor of *Liberty Tree*.

25 But hear, O ye swains, 'tis a tale most **profane**,
26 How all the tyrannical powers,
27 Kings, Commons, and Lords, are uniting amain

---

1. **Goddess of Liberty** the Roman goddess Libertas is the ancestor of modern personifications of liberty as a woman, as seen in the U.S., France, and other nations
2. **celestials** stars or heavens
3. **groat** in medieval times, an English coin

28 To cut down this guardian of ours;
29 From the east to the west blow the trumpet to arms
30 Through the land let the sound of it flee,
31 Let the far and the near, all unite with a cheer,
32 In defence of our *Liberty Tree*.

✏ WRITE

In "Liberty Tree," Thomas Paine uses the central image of the Liberty Tree. What is the overall effect of this image? How does this central image support the poem's meaning?

To His Excellency, General Washington

POETRY
Phillis Wheatley
1775

Introduction

When she was only seven or eight years old, Phillis Wheatley (1753–1784) was captured in Africa by slave traders and brought to America. By the time she was twelve, Wheatley was reading Greek and Latin classics and studying difficult passages from the Bible. She soon began writing poetry, publishing her first poem when she was just thirteen years of age. In 1775, when General George Washington traveled to Boston to assume leadership of the Continental Army, Wheatley wrote this poem about Washington and sent it to him. Washington was so honored by Wheatley's poem that he later invited her to visit him. This text is accompanied by Howard Chandler Christy's 1940 oil-on-canvas painting, *Scene at the Signing of the Constitution of the United States*, which currently hangs in the House of Representatives wing of the U.S. Capitol Building.

"Columbia's scenes of glorious toils I write."

1   Celestial choir! enthron'd in realms of light,
2   Columbia's[1] scenes of glorious toils I write.
3   While freedom's cause her anxious breast alarms,
4   She flashes dreadful in **refulgent** arms.
5   See mother earth her offspring's fate bemoan,
6   And nations gaze at scenes before unknown!
7   See the bright beams of heaven's revolving light
8   Involved in sorrows and the veil of night!

9   The Goddess comes, she moves divinely fair,
10 Olive and laurel binds Her golden hair:
11 Wherever **shines** this native[2] of the skies,
12 Unnumber'd charms and recent **graces** rise.

13 Muse[3]! Bow propitious while my pen relates
14 How pour her armies through a thousand gates,
15 As when Eolus[4] heaven's fair face deforms,
16 Enwrapp'd in tempest and a night of storms;
17 Astonish'd ocean feels the wild uproar,
18 The refluent surges beat the sounding shore;
19 Or think as leaves in Autumn's golden reign,
20 Such, and so many, moves the warrior's train.
21 In bright array they seek the work of war,
22 Where high unfurl'd the **ensign** waves in air.
23 Shall I to Washington their praise recite?
24 Enough thou know'st them in the fields of fight.
25 Thee, first in peace and honors—we demand
26 The grace and glory of thy **martial** band.
27 Fam'd for thy valour, for thy virtues more,
28 Hear every tongue thy guardian aid implore!

---

1. **Columbia** an early name for what is now called America.
2. **native** a person whose birthplace or origin is a specific place
3. **Muse** any of the nine goddesses from Greek mythology who guide the arts and sciences, often prayed to when someone is in need of inspiration
4. **Eolus** the Greek mythological god of wind

29 One century scarce perform'd its destined round,
30 When Gallic[5] powers Columbia's fury found;
31 And so may you, whoever dares disgrace
32 The land of freedom's heaven-defended race!
33 Fix'd are the eyes of nations on the scales,
34 For in their hopes Columbia's arm prevails.
35 Anon Britannia droops the pensive head,
36 While round increase the rising hills of dead.
37 Ah! Cruel blindness to Columbia's state!
38 Lament thy thirst of boundless power too late.

39 Proceed, great chief, with virtue on thy side,
40 Thy ev'ry action let the Goddess guide.
41 A crown, a mansion, and a throne that shine,
42 With gold unfading, WASHINGTON! Be thine.

 Skill:
Theme

Columbia's "fury," or anger, is focused on the British "powers." America's people are defended by heaven. Anyone who disrespects America will face her "fury" as well.

---

5. **Gallic** related to the Gauls, an ancient people from France

First Read

Read "To His Excellency, General Washington." After you read, complete the Think Questions below.

☁ THINK QUESTIONS

1. Columbia is a name used historically for a personification of the United States. How does the speaker describe Columbia in the first and second stanzas? Cite evidence from the text to support your answer.

2. What two things does the speaker compare in the first half of the third stanza? What is the effect of this comparison? Support your response with evidence from the text.

3. To whom is the last stanza addressed? What is the speaker's message to this person? Cite evidence from the poem to support your response.

4. Use context to determine the meaning of the word **ensign** as it is used in "To His Excellency, General Washington." Write your definition of *ensign* here and explain how you determined it.

5. Use context to determine the meaning of the word **martial** as it is used in "To His Excellency, General Washington." Write your definition of *martial* here and explain how you determined it.

Skill:
Compare and Contrast

Use the Checklist to analyze Compare and Contrast in "To His Excellency, General Washington." Refer to the sample student annotations about Compare and Contrast in the text.

••• CHECKLIST FOR COMPARE AND CONTRAST

In order to determine how to compare and contrast texts from the same period, and how these texts treat similar themes or topics, use the following steps:

- ✓ first, identify two or more foundational works of American literature written during the eighteenth-, nineteenth- or early-twentieth-century

- ✓ next, identify the topic and theme in each work, and any central or recurring topics the author presents

- ✓ after, explain how each text reflects and represents the time period in which it was written, including its historical events, customs, beliefs, or social norms

- ✓ finally, explain the similarities or differences between two or more texts that are written during the same time period and address related themes and topics

To demonstrate knowledge of eighteenth-, nineteenth- and early-twentieth-century foundational works of American literature, consider the following questions:

- ✓ Are the texts from the same time period in American literature?

- ✓ In what ways does each text reflect and represent the time period in which it was written?

- ✓ How does each work treat themes or topics representative of the time period in which it was written?

- ✓ How is the treatment of the themes or topics in these literary works similar and different?

Skill:
Compare and Contrast

Reread stanza 5 (lines 39–42) of "To His Excellency, George Washington" and stanza 3 from "The Liberty Tree" (lines 17–24). Then, using the Checklist on the previous page, answer the multiple-choice questions below.

↻ YOUR TURN

1. What theme, common to the literary period of The Enlightenment, do you see in these lines from both poems?

   ○ A. England will survive with or without colonial America.
   ○ B. Free and equal societies respect the will of the people.
   ○ C. The fight for a free and independent America is virtuous.
   ○ D. Humans gain knowledge through direct observation.

2. Which statement best describes the use of allusion in both poems?

   ○ A. Allusion is used to express the danger of rebelling against Great Britain.
   ○ B. Allusion is used to indirectly praise George Washington and the Founding Fathers.
   ○ C. Allusion is used to remind readers of the power and influence of Greek mythology.
   ○ D. Allusion is used to express the honor of independence, and the evil of British rule.

Skill:
Theme

Use the Checklist to analyze Theme in "To His Excellency, General Washington." Refer to the sample student annotations about Theme in the text.

••• CHECKLIST FOR THEME

In order to identify two or more themes or central ideas of a text, note the following:

✓ the subject and how it relates to the themes in the text

✓ if one or more themes is stated directly in the text

✓ details in the text that help to reveal each theme:

- the title and chapter headings
- details about the setting
- the narrator's or speaker's tone
- characters' thoughts, actions, and dialogue
- the central conflict, climax, and resolution of the conflict
- shifts in characters, setting, or plot events

✓ when the themes interact with each other

To determine two or more themes or central ideas of a text and analyze their development over the course of the text, including how they interact and build on one another to produce a complex account, consider the following questions:

✓ What are the themes in the text? When do they emerge?

✓ How does each theme develop over the course of the text?

✓ How do the themes interact and build on one another?

Skill:
Theme

Reread lines 33–42 of "To His Excellency, General Washington." Then, using the Checklist on the previous page, answer the multiple-choice questions below.

⟳ YOUR TURN

1. Which statement best explains the meaning of "Anon Britannia droops the pensive head, / While round increase the rising hills of dead"?

    ○ A. Britannia will fear failure as the number of her fallen soldiers grows ever higher.

    ○ B. Britannia's leaders are not smart enough to defeat America's great army.

    ○ C. Both sides will see a great number of fallen soldiers as a result of the war.

    ○ D. America's victory is certain because she has more troops who are willing to fight.

2. Which statement best explains how the figure of Washington relates to the theme that good triumphs over evil?

    ○ A. Washington knows the world is watching the war between America and Britain.

    ○ B. The promise of future glory inspires Washington to be a great leader.

    ○ C. Washington's warriors are better prepared for battle than Britain's soldiers.

    ○ D. Washington is a virtuous leader capable of leading America to victory.

Close Read

Reread "To His Excellency, General Washington." As you reread, complete the Skills Focus questions below. Then use your answers and annotations from the questions to help you complete the Write activity.

◎ SKILLS FOCUS

1. What themes common to American poetry in the late eighteenth century are present in the first two stanzas of Wheatley's poem? Highlight evidence from the text and explain your reasoning using the annotation tool.

2. How does the Goddess Columbia change and evolve over the course of Wheatley's poem? What does this tell us about the theme of divine protection?

3. How do Wheatley and Paine use mythological and religious figures to further their themes? Highlight and annotate examples in the text to support your claim.

4. How do Wheatley and Paine represent leaders who fight for their ideas and values? Highlight evidence in "To His Excellency, General Washington" to support your claim.

✎ WRITE

COMPARE AND CONTRAST: Which themes about freedom or the American Revolution are explored in "To His Excellency, General Washington"? How are these themes similar to or different than those in "Liberty Tree"? Which figures and images seem to overlap? Support your writing with textual evidence from "To His Excellency, General Washington."

Please note that excerpts and passages in the StudySync® library and this workbook are intended as touchstones to generate interest in an author's work. The excerpts and passages do not substitute for the reading of entire texts, and StudySync® strongly recommends that students seek out and purchase the whole literary or informational work in order to experience it as the author intended. Links to online resellers are available in our digital library. In addition, complete works may be ordered through an authorized reseller by filling out and returning to StudySync® the order form enclosed in this workbook.

Reading & Writing Companion 437

Preamble to the Constitution and the Bill of Rights

INFORMATIONAL TEXT
Gouverneur Morris,
James Madison, et al.
1787

Introduction

The Founding Fathers of the United States used both words and weapons to create a nation. Pamphlets such as *The Crisis* and *Common Sense*, along with documents such as *The Federalist Papers*, helped to drive public opinion around the time of the Revolutionary War. The most important of these documents are the Declaration of Independence, the Constitution of the United States of America, and the Bill of Rights (the first ten amendments to the United States Constitution). These documents detailed the reasoning for the American colonists' revolt against British rule and the King of England and described how they intended to form and structure their new government. Carefully, they defined and established how that government would function—what it could do, and perhaps more

"We, the People of the United States, in Order to form a more perfect Union, establish . . ."

Preamble to the United States Constitution[1] and First Ten Amendments[2] (The Bill of Rights) 1787–1791.

The Preamble to the Constitution

1 Preamble:

We, the People of the United States, in Order to form a more perfect Union, establish Justice, insure domestic **Tranquility**, provide for the common defence, promote the general Welfare, and secure the Blessings of Liberty to ourselves and our Posterity, do ordain and establish this Constitution of the United States of America.

2 Amendment I:

Congress[3] shall make no law respecting the establishment of religion, or prohibiting the free exercise thereof; or **abridging** the freedom of speech, or of the press; or the right of people peaceably to assemble, and to petition the Government for a **redress** of grievances.

3 Amendment II:

A well regulated Militia, being necessary to the security of a free State, the right of the people to keep and bear Arms, shall not be infringed.

4 Amendment III:

No Soldier shall, in time of peace be quartered in any house, without the consent of the Owner, nor in time of war, but in a manner to be prescribed by law.

---

1. **constitution** the laws and practices of a country that allocate the responsibilities of a government
2. **amendments** a formal change made to a legal document
3. **Congress** the legislative branch of the government, consisting of the Senate and House of Representatives

NOTES

5   Amendment IV:

The right of the people to be secure in their persons, houses, papers, and effects, against unreasonable searches and seizures, shall not be violated, and no Warrants shall issue, but upon probable cause, supported by Oath or affirmation, and particularly describing the place to be searched, and the persons or things to be seized.

6   Amendment V:

No person shall be held to answer for a capital, or otherwise infamous crime, unless on a presentment or indictment of a Grand Jury, except in cases arising in the land or naval forces, or in the Militia, when in actual service in time of War or public danger; nor shall any person be subject for the same offence to be twice put in jeopardy of life or limb; nor shall be **compelled** in any criminal case to be a witness against himself, nor be deprived of life, liberty, or property, without due process of law; nor shall private property be taken for public use, without just compensation.

7   Amendment VI:

In all criminal prosecutions, the accused shall enjoy the right to a speedy and public trial, by an impartial jury of the State and district wherein the crime shall have been committed, which district shall have been previously ascertained by law, and to be informed of the nature and cause of the accusation; to be confronted with the witnesses against him; to have compulsory process for **obtaining** witnesses in his favor, and to have the Assistance of Counsel for his defence.

8   Amendment VII:

In Suits at common law, where the value in controversy shall exceed twenty dollars, the right of trial by jury shall be preserved, and no fact tried by a jury, shall be otherwise re-examined in any Court of the United States, than according to the rules of the common law.

9   Amendment VIII:

Excessive bail shall not be required, nor excessive fines imposed, nor cruel and unusual punishments inflicted.

10   Amendment IX:

The enumeration in the Constitution, of certain rights, shall not be construed to deny or disparage others retained by the people.

11   Amendment X:

The powers not delegated to the United States by the Constitution, nor prohibited by it to the States, are reserved to the States respectively, or to the people.

WRITE

EXPLANATORY ESSAY: The Constitution is a statement of "how we choose to rule ourselves." What are the goals established in the Preamble and how do the amendments in the Bill of Rights advance those goals? Connect the goals of the Preamble to three amendments of your choosing. Remember to use textual evidence to support your response.

Please note that excerpts and passages in the StudySync® library and this workbook are intended as touchstones to generate interest in an author's work. The excerpts and passages do not substitute for the reading of entire texts, and StudySync® strongly recommends that students seek out and purchase the whole literary or informational work in order to experience it as the author intended. Links to online resellers are available in our digital library. In addition, complete works may be ordered through an authorized reseller by filling out and returning to StudySync® the order form enclosed in this workbook.

Reading & Writing Companion   441

United States v. The Amistad

ARGUMENTATIVE TEXT
U.S. Supreme Court
1841

Introduction

United States v. The Amistad is a famous U.S. Supreme Court case from 1841 in which the Court had to decide whether to grant freedom to Africans who were kidnapped by Spanish slave traders. The Africans led a violent rebellion aboard the Spanish ship *La Amistad*, and were eventually apprehended near Long Island, New York. *Amistad* was a complicated case that involved international parties, including British and Spanish interests. The Spanish owners of the ship demanded their "property" be returned and cited Pinckney's Treaty of 1795, which established friendship between the United States and Spain, as the legal basis for their claim. John Quincy Adams, who served as the sixth President of the United States, argued before the Supreme Court for the freedom of the Africans.

"Is that the principle on which these United States stand before the world?"

from John Quincy Adams' oral argument in favor of the defendants:

NOTES

1 There is the principle, on which a particular decision is demanded from this Court, by the Official Journal of the Executive, on behalf of the southern states? Is that a principle recognized by this Court? Is it the principle of that Declaration [of Independence]? It is alleged in the Official Journal, that war gives the right to take the life of our enemy, and that this confers a right to make him a slave, on account of having spared his life. Is that the principle on which these United States stand before the world? That Declaration says that every man is "endowed by his Creator with certain inalienable rights," and that among these are "life, liberty, and the pursuit of happiness." If these rights are inalienable, they are incompatible with the rights of the victor to take the life of his enemy in war, or to spare his life and make him a slave. If this principle is sound, it reduces to brute force all the rights of man. It places all the sacred relations of life at the power of the strongest. No man has a right to life or liberty, if he has an enemy able to take them from him. There is the principle. There is the whole argument of this paper. Now I do not deny that the only principle upon which a color of right can be attributed to the condition of slavery is by assuming that the natural state of man is war. The bright intellect of the South, clearly saw, that without this principle for a corner stone, he had no foundation for his argument. He assumes it therefore without a blush, as Hobbes[1] assumed it to prove that government and **despotism** are synonymous words. I will not here discuss the right or the rights of slavery, but I say that the doctrine of Hobbes, that War is the natural state of man, has for ages been exploded, as equally disclaimed and rejected by the philosopher and the Christian. That it is

Portrait of Joseph Cinque (1813–1879) who led the mutiny and revolt in 1839 of fellow slaves on the ship Amistad, late nineteenth century.

Skill: Primary and Secondary Sources

John Quincy Adams poses these questions to the Supreme Court during the time period in which the document was written, so this must be a primary source document. Adams intends to argue using the Declaration of Independence as a foundational text.

Skill: Reasons and Evidence

Adams argues in favor of maintaining the rights of the defendants. He refers to the Declaration of Independence to support his argument. His argument is logical given the language of "inalienable rights" in the Declaration.

---

1. **Hobbes** English philosopher Thomas Hobbes (1588–1679) argued, in *Leviathan*, that the natural state of humankind is chaos and the best solution is a monarch or sovereign leader

utterly incompatible with any theory of human rights, and especially with the rights which the Declaration of Independence proclaims as self-evident truths. The moment you come, to the Declaration of Independence, that every man has a right to life and liberty, an inalienable right, this case is decided. I ask nothing more in behalf of these unfortunate men, than this Declaration.

From the majority opinion of the Court, delivered by Justice Joseph Story:

2   It has been argued on behalf of the United States, that the Court are bound to deliver them up, according to the treaty of 1795, with Spain, which has in this particular been continued in full force, by the treaty of 1819, ratified in 1821. The sixth article of that treaty, seems to have had, principally, in view cases where the property of the subjects of either state had been taken possession of within the territorial jurisdiction of the other, during war. The eighth article provides for cases where the shipping of the inhabitants of either state are forced, through stress of weather, pursuit of pirates, or enemies, or any other urgent necessity, to seek shelter in the ports of the other. There may well be some doubt entertained, whether the present case, in its actual circumstances, falls within the purview of this article. But it does not seem necessary, for reasons hereafter stated, absolutely to decide it. The ninth article provides, "that all ships and merchandise, of what nature soever, which shall be rescued out of the hands of any pirates or robbers, on the high seas, shall be brought into some port of either state, and shall be delivered to the custody of the officers of that port, in order to be taken care of and restored entire to the true **proprietor,** as soon as due and sufficient proof shall be made concerning the property thereof." This is the article on which the main reliance is placed on behalf of the United States, for the restitution of these negroes. To bring the case within the article, it is essential to establish, First, that these negroes, under all the circumstances, fall within the description of merchandise, in the sense of the treaty. Secondly, That there has been a rescue of them on the high seas, out of the hands of the pirates and robbers; which, in the present case, can only be, by showing that they themselves are pirates and robbers; and, Thirdly, that Ruiz and Montez, the asserted proprietors, are the true proprietors, and have established their title by competent proof.

3   If these negroes were, at the time, lawfully held as slaves under the laws of Spain, and recognised by those laws as property capable of being lawfully bought and sold; we see no reason why they may not justly be deemed within the intent of the treaty, to be included under the denomination of merchandise, and, as such, ought to be restored to the claimants: for, upon that point, the laws of Spain would seem to furnish the proper rule of interpretation. But, admitting this, it is clear, in our opinion, that neither of the other essential facts and requisites has been established in proof; and the

onus probandi[2] of both lies upon the claimants to give rise to the *casus foederis*[3]. It is plain beyond controversy, if we examine the evidence, that these negroes never were the lawful slaves of Ruiz or Montez, or of any other Spanish subjects. They are natives of Africa, and were kidnapped there, and were unlawfully transported to Cuba, in violation of the laws and treaties of Spain, and the most solemn edicts and declarations of that government. By those laws, and treaties, and edicts, the African slave trade is utterly abolished; the dealing in that trade is deemed a **heinous** crime; and the negroes thereby introduced into the dominions of Spain, are declared to be free. Ruiz and Montez are proved to have made the pretended purchase of these negroes, with a full knowledge of all the circumstances. And so **cogent** and irresistible is the evidence in this respect, that the District Attorney[4] has admitted in open Court, upon the record, that these negroes were native Africans, and recently imported into Cuba, as alleged in their answers to the libels in the case. The supposed proprietary interest of Ruiz and Montez, is completely displaced, if we are at liberty to look at the evidence of the admissions of the District Attorney.

. . .

4 It is also a most important consideration in the present case, which ought not to be lost sight of, that, supposing these African negroes not to be slaves, but kidnapped, and free negroes, the treaty with Spain cannot be obligatory upon them; and the United States are bound to respect their rights as much as those of Spanish subjects. The conflict of rights between the parties under such circumstances, becomes positive and inevitable, and must be decided upon the eternal principles of justice and international law. If the contest were about any goods on board of this ship, to which American citizens asserted a title, which was denied by the Spanish claimants, there could be no doubt of the right of such American citizens to **litigate** their claims before any competent American tribunal[5], notwithstanding the treaty with Spain. A fortiori[6], the doctrine must apply where human life and human liberty are in issue; and constitute the very essence of the controversy. The treaty with Spain never could have intended to take away the equal rights of all foreigners, who should contest their claims before any of our Courts, to equal justice; or to deprive such foreigners of the protection given them by other treaties, or by the general law of nations. Upon the merits of the case, then, there does not seem to us to be any ground for doubt, that these negroes ought to be deemed free; and that the Spanish treaty interposes no obstacle to the just assertion of their rights.

2. **onus probandi** (Latin) burden of proof
3. **casus foederis** (Latin) case for the alliance
4. **district attorney** the chief prosecutor in a local area or county
5. **tribunal** a forum that considers matters of justice; a jury
6. **a fortiori** (Latin) from the stronger argument

First Read

Read *United States v. The Amistad*. After you read, complete the Think Questions below.

THINK QUESTIONS

1. How does John Quincy Adams argue that principles in the Declaration of Independence overpower claims made by victors in wartime? Support your answer with textual evidence.

2. (a) What three key questions does Justice Joseph Story identify as the test to whether or not the enslaved passengers on *The Amistad* are subject to Pinckney's Treaty of 1795? (b) How do these questions relate to Adams's argument? Support your answer with evidence from the text.

3. In his first paragraph, Justice Story explains the implications of Pinckney's Treaty of 1795. However, in his second and third paragraphs, he highlights the problems with upholding the treaty. Briefly explain his reasons below. How does this relate to Adams's argument, and what can you infer from this opinion about how courts in the United States apply the principle of natural rights?

4. Use context to determine the meaning of the word **proprietor** as it is used in *United States v. The Amistad*. Write your definition of "proprietor" here and tell how you found it.

5. The verb **litigate** means "to make a situation the subject of a lawsuit." Adding the noun suffix "-ion" creates the word "litigation." What does "litigation" mean?

Skill:
Primary and Secondary Sources

Use the Checklist to analyze Primary and Secondary Sources in *United States v. The Amistad*. Refer to the sample student annotations about Primary and Secondary Sources in the text.

••• CHECKLIST FOR PRIMARY AND SECONDARY SOURCES

In order to differentiate between primary and secondary sources, do the following:

✓ examine the source, noting the title, author, and date of publication

✓ identify the genre of the source

- examples of primary sources include letters, diaries, journals, speeches, eyewitness interviews, oral histories, memoirs, and autobiographies

- examples of secondary sources include encyclopedia articles, newspaper and magazine articles, biographies, documentary films, history books, and textbooks

If the source meets one or more of the following criteria, it is considered a primary source:

✓ original, first-hand account of an event or time period

✓ writing that takes place during the event or time period

If the source meets one or more of the following criteria, it is considered a secondary source:

✓ a book or an article that analyzes and interprets primary sources

✓ a second-hand account of a historical event

✓ a book or an article that interprets or analyzes creative work

To analyze seventeenth-, eighteenth-, and nineteenth-century foundational U.S. documents of historical and literary significance, consider the following questions:

- ✓ How is the source reliable and credible?

- ✓ What is the purpose of this source?

- ✓ What historical themes, such as patriotism or heroism, are brought out in the source?

- ✓ How does the author use anecdotes, interviews, allusions, or other rhetorical features?

- ✓ What gives this source literary or historical significance?

Skill:
Primary and Secondary Sources

Reread the last paragraph of *United States v. The Amistad*. Then, using the Checklist on the previous page, answer the multiple-choice questions below.

YOUR TURN

1. What early American values are emphasized in the conclusion of Justice Joseph Story's argument?

   ○ A. Trade with foreign nations
   ○ B. Freedom and equal rights
   ○ C. Servitude and slavery
   ○ D. Conformity and individuality

2. What gives this text historical significance?

   ○ A. It was written during the time period the country was formed.
   ○ B. The case was tried by the U.S. Court, the highest court in the land.
   ○ C. It marks a moment where Africans revolted against their captors.
   ○ D. It marks a moment where the Constitution is understood as having application to all people in American soil.

Skill:
Reasons and Evidence

Review the Checklist for Reasons and Evidence below. Then read the Skill Model to examine how one student used the checklist to analyze reasons and evidence in *United States v. The Amistad*. As you read, identify the question from the checklist the student used for each annotation.

••• CHECKLIST FOR REASONS AND EVIDENCE

In order to delineate and evaluate the reasoning in seminal (influential) U.S. texts, note the following:

✓ the writer's position and how he or she uses legal reasoning to interpret the law

  • legal reasoning includes the thinking processes and strategies used by lawyers and judges when arguing and deciding legal cases, and is based on constitutional principles, or laws written down in the U.S. Constitution

✓ a Supreme Court judge that disagrees with the legal reasoning behind the majority opinion in a legal case writes a dissent, expressing opposition

  • a dissent must follow constitutional principles, or the laws set down in the Constitution

✓ determine whether the premise is based on legal reasoning and constitutional principles

To evaluate the reasoning in seminal (influential) U.S. texts, including the application of constitutional principles and use of legal reasoning, consider the following questions:

✓ What position does the writer take?

✓ How does the writer use constitutional principles and legal reasoning to support his or her position?

Skill:
Reasons and Evidence

Reread paragraph 4 of the text to determine the answers to the follow-up questions

↻ YOUR TURN

1. This question has two parts. First, answer Part A. Then, answer Part B.

   Part A: What reasoning leads Justice Story to the conclusion that the Africans should be freed?

   ○ A. Slavery is outlawed in New York, so the enslaved passengers are free.

   ○ B. Liberty is more important than a law or treaty.

   ○ C. The treaty cannot allow Spanish subjects to be held by other parties.

   ○ D. Africans were kidnapped and unlawfully held, therefore they should be freed.

   Part B: Which sentence or phrase from the passage provides the best evidence that supports your answer?

   ○ A. "The conflict of rights between the parties under such circumstances, becomes positive and inevitable, and must be decided upon the eternal principles of justice and international law."

   ○ B. "Supposing these African negroes not to be slaves, but kidnapped, and free negroes, the treaty with Spain cannot be obligatory upon them; and the United States are bound to respect their rights as much as those of Spanish subjects."

   ○ C. "If the contest were about any goods on board of this ship, to which American citizens asserted a title, which was denied by the Spanish claimants, there could be no doubt of the right of such American citizens to litigate their claims before any competent American tribunal, notwithstanding the treaty with Spain."

   ○ D. "A fortiori, the doctrine must apply where human life and human liberty are in issue; and constitute the very essence of the controversy."

Close Read

Reread *United States v. The Amistad*. As you reread, complete the Skills Focus questions below. Then use your answers and annotations from the questions to help you complete the Write activity.

◎ SKILLS FOCUS

1. How does this document highlight important American values? Identify examples throughout the text.

2. Recall that rhetoric is the art of speaking and writing persuasively. Reread Adams's argument and highlight at least three examples of rhetorical devices. Make annotations to explain the use of rhetoric and how it impacts his argument.

3. Toward the end of the excerpt from John Quincy Adams's oral argument, he concedes a point to his opposition, the plaintiffs: "Now I do not deny

that the only principle upon which a color of right can be attributed to the condition of slavery is by assuming that the natural state of man is war." Explain why Adams may have conceded this point and how this point relates to the larger pattern of reasoning in his argument. Evaluate the contribution of this point to his overall argument.

4. What connections can you make between how John Quincy Adams fights for his ideas and how leaders today do the same? How is the fight for equality similar or different in the 20th century?

✏ WRITE

ARGUMENTATIVE: Imagine you are John Quincy Adams. Write a speech that you would give to the media, outside on the courthouse steps, just following the verdict in the case (as indicated in the majority opinion of the Court delivered by Justice Story). Explain the meaning of the verdict, citing textual evidence from both Adams's argument and the majority opinion of the Court. Using sound and logical arguments, describe what further legal and social changes need to be made in the United States of the 1840s.

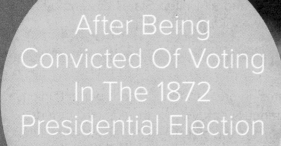

After Being
Convicted Of Voting
In The 1872
Presidential Election

ARGUMENTATIVE TEXT
Susan B. Anthony
1873

Introduction

In the late 1800s, women in the United States did not yet have the right to vote, and famed women's suffrage activist Susan B. Anthony (1820–1906) set out to change that. After being arrested for casting an illegal vote in the presidential election of 1872, Anthony drafted a speech arguing that she had committed no crime, and delivered it in each of the 29 postal districts in Monroe County, New York. The speech was so effective that the prosecution requested a change of venue.

"Being persons, then, women are citizens . . ."

NOTES

Stump Speech in all 29 postal districts of Monroe County, New York, in 1873

1 Friends and fellow citizens: I stand before you tonight under **indictment** for the alleged[1] crime of having voted at the last presidential election, without having a lawful right to vote. It shall be my work this evening to prove to you that in thus voting, I not only committed no crime, but, instead, simply exercised my citizen's rights, guaranteed to me and all United States citizens by the National Constitution, beyond the power of any state to deny. . . .

2 The preamble of the Federal Constitution says:

3 "We, the people of the United States, in order to form a more perfect union, establish justice, insure domestic tranquility, provide for the common defense, promote the general welfare, and secure the blessings of liberty to ourselves and our **posterity**, do ordain and establish this Constitution for the United States of America."

4 It was we, the people; not we, the white male citizens; nor yet we, the male citizens; but we, the whole people, who formed the Union. And we formed it, not to give the blessings of liberty, but to secure them; not to the half of ourselves and the half of our posterity, but to the whole people—women as well as men. And it is a downright mockery to talk to women of their enjoyment of the blessings of liberty while they are denied the use of the only means of securing them provided by this democratic-republican government—the ballot. . . .

5 For any state to make sex a qualification that must ever result in the **disfranchisement**[2] of one entire half of the people, is to pass a bill of attainder, or, an **ex post facto**[3] law, and is therefore a violation of the supreme law of the land. By it the blessings of liberty are forever withheld from women and their female posterity. . . .

---

1. **alleged** said to be true but not proven; supposed
2. **disfranchisement** denial of power, commonly power in the form of the right to vote
3. **ex post facto (Latin)** made or done after the fact; retroactive

6   To them this government has no just powers derived from the consent of the governed. To them this government is not a democracy. It is not a republic. It is an odious aristocracy[4]; a hateful **oligarchy**[5] of sex; the most hateful aristocracy ever established on the face of the globe; an oligarchy of wealth, where the rich govern the poor. An oligarchy of learning, where the educated govern the ignorant, or even an oligarchy of race, where the Saxon rules the African, might be endured; but this oligarchy of sex, which makes father, brothers, husband, sons, the oligarchs over the mother and sisters, the wife and daughters, of every household—which ordains all men sovereigns, all women subjects, carries dissension, discord, and rebellion into every home of the nation.

7   Webster, Worcester, and Bouvier all define a citizen to be a person in the United States, entitled to vote and hold office.

8   The only question left to be settled now is: Are women persons? And I hardly believe any of our opponents will have the hardihood to say they are not. Being persons, then, women are citizens; and no state has a right to make any law, or to enforce any old law, that shall abridge their privileges or immunities. Hence, every discrimination against women in the constitutions and laws of the several states is today null and void, precisely as is every one against Negroes.

✏ WRITE

ARGUMENTATIVE: You have just finished reading a famous persuasive speech by Susan B. Anthony. In your opinion, what made her argument so convincing? Write an argumentative (or persuasive) speech in which you convince your audience that Susan B. Anthony's argument gets stronger with each paragraph of her speech. Quote passages from the text to support your claims. Provide a concluding statement that follows from and supports the argument you present.

---

4. **aristocracy** a form of government in which power belongs to the nobility, or the upper class
5. **oligarchy** a government in which power is held by only a few people

Hawaii's Story by Hawaii's Queen

ARGUMENTATIVE TEXT
Lili'uokalani
1898

Introduction

Queen Lili'uokalani (1838–1917) was a composer and author, as well as the final reigning monarch of the Kingdom of Hawaii. Among other things, *Hawaii's Story by Hawaii's Queen* features a personal account of her final days on the throne before a group of sugar planters, backed by pro-American forces, led a coup to remove her from power. The excerpt here is from Lili'uokalani's official protest to a treaty signed on January 17, 1893, ceding powers to the United States. Hoping that President Grover Cleveland or his successor would be sympathetic to her cause, Lili'uokalani explains why the treaty is unconstitutional and appeals for help from the United States government. In 1898, shortly after President Cleveland left office, Hawaii was formally annexed as a territory of the United States.

"To him who judgeth righteously, I commit my cause."

NOTES

CHAPTER LV

MY OFFICIAL PROTEST TO THE TREATY

1 I, LILIUOKALANI of Hawaii, by the will of God named heir apparent on the tenth day of April, A. D. 1877, and by the grace of God Queen of the Hawaiian Islands on the seventeenth day of January, A. D. 1893, do hereby protest against the ratification of a certain treaty, which, so I am informed, has been signed at Washington by Messrs. Hatch, Thurston, and Kinney, purporting to cede those Islands to the territory and **dominion** of the United States. I declare such a treaty to be an act of wrong toward the native and part-native people of Hawaii, an invasion of the rights of the ruling chiefs, in violation of international rights both toward my people and toward friendly nations with whom they have made treaties, the perpetuation of the fraud whereby the constitutional government was overthrown and, finally, an act of gross injustice to me.

Queen Lili'uokalani of Hawaii, 1887

2 Because the official protests made by me on the seventeenth day of January, 1893, to the so-called Provisional Government was signed by me, and received by said government with the assurance that the case was referred to the United States of America for **arbitration.**

YIELDED TO AVOID BLOODSHED.

3 Because that protest and my communications to the United States Government immediately thereafter expressly declare that I yielded my authority to the forces of the United States in order to avoid bloodshed, and because I recognized the futility of a conflict with so formidable a power.

4   Because the President of the United States, the Secretary of State, and an envoy commissioned by them reported in official documents that my government was unlawfully coerced by the forces, diplomatic and naval, of the United States; that I was at the date of their investigations the constitutional ruler of my people.

5   Because such decision of the recognized magistrates of the United States was officially communicated to me and to Sanford B. Dole, and said Dole's resignation requested by Albert S. Willis, the recognized agent and minister of the Government of the United States.

6   Because neither the above-named commission nor the government which sends it has ever received any such authority from the registered voters of Hawaii, but **derives** its assumed powers from the so-called committee of public safety, organized on or about the seventeenth day of January, 1893, said committee being composed largely of persons claiming American citizenship, and not one single Hawaiian was a member thereof, or in any way participated in the demonstration leading to its existence.

7   Because my people, about forty thousand in number, have in no way been consulted by those, three thousand in number, who claim the right to destroy the independence of Hawaii. My people constitute four-fifths of the legally qualified voters of Hawaii, and excluding those imported for the demands of labor, about the same proportion of the inhabitants.

CIVIC AND HEREDITARY RIGHTS.

8   Because said treaty ignores, not only the civic rights of my people, but, further, the hereditary property of their chiefs. Of the 4,000,000 acres composing the territory said treaty offers to annex, 1,000,000 or 915,000 acres has in no way been heretofore recognized as other than the private property of the constitutional monarch, subject to a control in no way differing from other items of a private estate.

9   Because it is proposed by said treaty to **confiscate** said property, technically called the crown lands, those legally entitled thereto, either now or in succession, receiving no consideration whatever for estates, their title to which has been always undisputed, and which is legitimately in my name at this date.

10 Because said treaty ignores, not only all professions of perpetual amity and good faith made by the United States in former treaties with the sovereigns representing the Hawaiian people, but all treaties made by those sovereigns with other and friendly powers, and it is thereby in violation of international law.

11 Because, by treating with the parties claiming at this time the right to cede said territory of Hawaii, the Government of the United States receives such territory from the hands of those whom its own magistrates (legally elected by the people of the United States, and in office in 1893) pronounced fraudulently in power and unconstitutionally ruling Hawaii.

APPEALS TO PRESIDENT AND SENATE.

12 Therefore I, Liliuokalani of Hawaii, do hereby call upon the President of that nation, to whom alone I yielded my property and my authority, to withdraw said treaty (ceding said Islands) from further consideration. I ask the honorable Senate of the United States to decline to ratify said treaty, and I implore the people of this great and good nation, from whom my ancestors learned the Christian religion, to sustain their representatives in such acts of justice and equity as may be in accord with the principles of their fathers, and to the Almighty Ruler of the universe, to him who judgeth righteously, I commit my cause.

13 Done at Washington, District of Columbia, United States of America, this seventeenth day of June, in the year eighteen hundred and ninety-seven.

LILIUOKALANI.

JOSEPH HELELUHE.

WOKEKI HELELUHE   }   Witnesses to Signature."

JULIUS A. PALMER.[1]

14 In the matter of providing me with seats in the diplomatic gallery at the ceremonies of the inauguration, I have already expressed my gratitude to Secretary John Sherman. It is but just that I should repeat here my appreciation of the kind, **gallant,** and courteous treatment again received at his official hands. For although it was my directions that this document should be delivered to any person authorized to receive it, yet as soon as Secretary Sherman saw the cards of my commissioners, he at once accorded them a private audience.

15 My protest, and a like **remonstrance** made on behalf of the patriotic leagues of the Hawaiian people by Hon. Joseph Heleluhe as their authorized commissioner, were both placed in the secretary's hands by that gentleman; and Mr. Sherman read them both through. He then turned to Captain Palmer,

---

1. **Julius A. Palmer** an American ship captain and mycologist who was friends with Hawaiian Queen Lili'uokalani, and assisted her in opposing the annexation

and had an agreeable conversation on the points at issue, after which my commissioners retired. The accustomed tissue of falsehoods was woven about this interview; some stating that Secretary Sherman had refused to see my messengers, others again giving the names of some one or other of his **subordinates** with whom my commissioners had had an interview, and finally asserting that the protests went into the archives of the department without examination, and were pigeon-holed; all of which statements, it is needless to say, were untrue. Secretary Sherman by his action showed that, a skilled diplomatist, he had not forgotten to remain a gallant gentleman.

✏ WRITE

RESEARCH: Imagine that you are a reporter. Write an article about Queen Lili'uokalani's protest. Make sure that your article inspires the reader to be curious, and answers the questions of who, what, where, when, why, and how. Use evidence from the text and information acquired from your own research.

The Federalist Papers: No. 10

ARGUMENTATIVE TEXT
James Madison
1787

Introduction

Although the United States is a democracy in the sense that its government derives power from the people, the U.S. Constitution established a republic in which elected officials make policy decisions—rather than a system in which citizens decide on policy matters directly. James Madison addresses this and more in *The Federalist Papers*, a collection of 85 articles and essays published by Madison, Alexander Hamilton, and John Jay in 1787 and 1788 to promote ratification of the Constitution. Their wish was for a strong central government that could raise revenue through taxation and maintain law and order at a time when people feared political instability. Here, in Federalist No. 10, Madison argues that only a strong republican government will protect its citizens against dangerous factions of individuals motivated by their own political self-interests.

"Liberty is to faction what air is to fire, an aliment without which it instantly expires."

NOTES

Skill:
Primary and
Secondary
Sources

Madison was a founding father of the government and the Constitution was approved in 1787, the same year as he wrote this essay.

This is a primary source because it is written by someone who participated in forming our government.

Federalist No 10. The Same Subject Continued

The Union as a Safeguard Against Domestic Faction[1] and Insurrection

From the New York Packet. Friday, November 23, 1787.

MADISON

To the People of the State of New York:

1   Among the numerous advantages promised by a well-constructed Union, none deserves to be more accurately developed than its tendency to break and control the violence of faction. . . .Complaints are everywhere heard from our most considerate and virtuous citizens, equally the friends of public and private faith, and of public and personal liberty, that our governments are too unstable, that the public good[2] is disregarded in the conflicts of rival parties[3], and that measures are too often decided, not according to the rules of justice and the rights of the minor party, but by the superior force of an interested and overbearing majority. . . .

2   By a faction, I understand a number of citizens, whether amounting to a majority or a minority of the whole, who are united and actuated by some common impulse of passion, or of interest, adversed to the rights of other citizens, or to the permanent and aggregate interests of the community.

3   There are two methods of curing the mischiefs of faction: the one, by removing its causes; the other, by controlling its effects.

4   There are again two methods of removing the causes of faction: the one, by destroying the liberty which is essential to its existence; the other, by giving to every citizen the same opinions, the same passions, and the same interests.

---

1. **faction** a small group that shares opinions that are in conflict with a larger group
2. **public good** general benefit to the members of a society which cannot be reduced by use or kept exclusive from anyone in that society
3. **parties** formally organized political groups who participate in government

5   It could never be more truly said than of the first remedy, that it was worse than the disease. Liberty is to faction what air is to fire, an aliment without which it instantly expires. But it could not be less folly to abolish liberty, which is essential to political life, because it nourishes faction, than it would be to wish the annihilation of air, which is essential to animal life, because it imparts to fire its destructive agency.

6   The second **expedient** is as impracticable as the first would be unwise. As long as the reason of man continues fallible, and he is at liberty to exercise it, different opinions will be formed. As long as the connection subsists between his reason and his self-love, his opinions and his passions will have a **reciprocal** influence on each other; and the former will be objects to which the latter will attach themselves. The diversity in the faculties of men, from which the rights of property originate, is not less an insuperable obstacle to a uniformity of interests. The protection of these faculties is the first object of government. From the protection of different and unequal faculties of acquiring property, the possession of different degrees and kinds of property immediately results; and from the influence of these on the sentiments and views of the respective proprietors, ensues a division of the society into different interests and parties.

7   The latent causes of faction are thus sown in the nature of man; and we see them everywhere brought into different degrees of activity, according to the different circumstances of civil society. A zeal for different opinions concerning religion, concerning government, and many other points, as well of speculation as of practice; an attachment to different leaders ambitiously contending for pre-eminence and power; or to persons of other descriptions whose fortunes have been interesting to the human passions, have, in turn, divided mankind into parties, inflamed them with mutual animosity, and rendered them much more disposed to vex and oppress each other than to co-operate for their common good. So strong is this propensity of mankind to fall into mutual animosities, that where no substantial occasion presents itself, the most frivolous and fanciful distinctions have been sufficient to kindle their unfriendly passions and excite their most violent conflicts. But the most common and durable source of factions has been the various and unequal distribution of property. Those who hold and those who are without property have ever formed distinct interests in society. Those who are creditors, and those who are debtors, fall under a like discrimination. A landed interest, a manufacturing interest, a mercantile interest, a moneyed interest, with many lesser interests, grow up of necessity in civilized nations, and divide them into different classes, actuated by different sentiments and views. The regulation of these various and interfering interests forms the principal task of modern legislation, and involves the spirit of party and faction in the necessary and ordinary operations of the government.

• • •

Skill:
Language, Style,
and Audience

The metaphor clarifies that while dangerous, factions are "essential to political life". His argument is intended to address the audience's fears of factions, but also state that factions are necessary.

NOTES

8   The inference to which we are brought is, that the CAUSES of faction cannot be removed, and that relief is only to be sought in the means of controlling its EFFECTS.

9   If a faction consists of less than a majority, relief is supplied by the republican principle, which enables the majority to defeat its sinister views by regular vote. It may clog the administration, it may convulse the society; but it will be unable to execute and mask its violence under the forms of the Constitution. When a majority is included in a faction, the form of popular government, on the other hand, enables it to sacrifice to its ruling passion or interest both the public good and the rights of other citizens. To secure the public good and private rights against the danger of such a faction, and at the same time to preserve the spirit and the form of popular government, is then the great object to which our inquiries are directed.

. . .

10   A republic[4], by which I mean a government in which the scheme of representation takes place, opens a different prospect, and promises the cure for which we are seeking. Let us examine the points in which it varies from pure democracy, and we shall comprehend both the nature of the cure and the efficacy which it must derive from the Union.

11   The two great points of difference between a democracy and a republic are: first, the **delegation** of the government, in the latter, to a small number of citizens elected by the rest; secondly, the greater number of citizens, and greater sphere of country, over which the latter may be extended.

12   The effect of the first difference is, on the one hand, to refine and enlarge the public views, by passing them through the medium of a chosen body of citizens, whose wisdom may best discern the true interest of their country, and whose patriotism and love of justice will be least likely to sacrifice it to temporary or partial considerations. Under such a regulation, it may well happen that the public voice, pronounced by the representatives of the people, will be more **consonant** to the public good than if pronounced by the people themselves, convened for the purpose. . . .

13   The other point of difference is, the greater number of citizens and extent of territory which may be brought within the compass of republican than of democratic government; and it is this circumstance principally which renders factious combinations less to be dreaded in the former than in the latter. The smaller the society, the fewer probably will be the distinct parties and interests

4. **republic** a system of government in which the people elect representatives to make and enforce the law

NOTES

composing it; the fewer the distinct parties and interests, the more frequently will a majority be found of the same party; and the smaller the number of individuals composing a majority, and the smaller the compass within which they are placed, the more easily will they concert and execute their plans of oppression. Extend the sphere, and you take in a greater variety of parties and interests; you make it less probable that a majority of the whole will have a common motive to invade the rights of other citizens; or if such a common motive exists, it will be more difficult for all who feel it to discover their own strength, and to act in unison with each other. Besides other impediments, it may be remarked that, where there is a consciousness of unjust or dishonorable purposes, communication is always checked by distrust in proportion to the number whose concurrence is necessary.

· · ·

14 The influence of factious leaders may kindle a flame within their particular States, but will be unable to spread a general conflagration through the other States. A religious sect may degenerate into a political faction in a part of the Confederacy; but the variety of sects dispersed over the entire face of it must secure the national councils against any danger from that source. A rage for paper money, for an abolition of debts, for an equal division of property, or for any other improper or wicked project, will be less apt to pervade the whole body of the Union than a particular member of it; in the same proportion as such a malady is more likely to taint a particular county or district, than an entire State.

15 In the extent and proper structure of the Union, therefore, we behold a republican remedy for the diseases most incident to republican government. And according to the degree of pleasure and pride we feel in being republicans, ought to be our zeal in cherishing the spirit and supporting the character of Federalists.

Skill:
Arguments and
Claims

Madison appeals to fear, but provides a reasoned solution that does not dismiss the fear, but states how it will be contained, legally and in accordance with the constitution, by the republican form of government.

First Read

Read "The Federalist Papers: No. 10." After you read, complete the Think Questions below.

☁ THINK QUESTIONS

1. Reread the first paragraph. What are the three undesirable effects of factions?

2. Reread paragraphs 3 through 6. What are the two ways of controlling factions? Which method does Madison favor and why?

3. Reread the paragraph that begins "The effect of the first difference is." Why does Madison believe that chosen government representatives can control the effects of factions?

4. Locate the word **expedient** in the text. How does the adjective *second* in front of the word help you locate clues elsewhere in the text that can help you define the word? Follow that line of thinking and write a definition for *expedient*.

5. Locate the word **concert** in the next-to-last paragraph. You may recognize the word, but the most familiar definition from today doesn't match its use in this historical document. How might you determine its meaning in this passage if its usage is unfamiliar to you?

Skill: Primary and Secondary Sources

Use the Checklist to analyze Primary and Secondary Sources in "The Federalist Papers: No. 10." Refer to the sample student annotations about Primary and Secondary Sources in the text.

••• CHECKLIST FOR PRIMARY AND SECONDARY SOURCES

In order to differentiate between primary and secondary sources, do the following:

✓ examine the source, noting the title, author, and date of publication

✓ identify the genre of the source

- examples of primary sources include letters, diaries, journals, speeches, eyewitness interviews, oral histories, memoirs, and autobiographies

- examples of secondary sources include encyclopedia articles, newspaper and magazine articles, biographies, documentary films, history books, and textbooks

If the source meets one or more of the following criteria, it is considered a primary source:

✓ original, first-hand account of an event or time period

✓ writing that takes place during the event or time period

If the source meets one or more of the following criteria, it is considered a secondary source:

✓ a book or an article that analyzes and interprets primary sources

✓ a second-hand account of a historical event

✓ a book or an article that interprets or analyzes creative work

To analyze seventeenth-, eighteenth-, and nineteenth-century foundational U.S. documents of historical and literary significance, consider the following questions:

✓ How is the source reliable and credible?

✓ What is the purpose of this source?

✓ What historical themes, such as patriotism or heroism, are brought out in the source?

✓ How does the author use anecdotes, interviews, allusions, or other rhetorical features?

✓ What gives this source literary or historical significance?

Skill: Primary and Secondary Sources

sync•skills

Reread paragraph 13 of "The Federalist Papers: No. 10." Then, using the Checklist on the previous page, answer the multiple-choice questions below.

⟳ YOUR TURN

1. Which of the following statements best represents how Madison is supporting the purpose of the address in the passage?

   ○ A. By reducing the sphere of the central government, factions will dissolve.

   ○ B. With a greater variety of parties and interests, it is less likely that one faction becomes too powerful.

   ○ C. Citizens are less motivated to act if governed centrally.

   ○ D. Oppression exists in all forms of government.

2. How does Madison appeal to the importance of his argument?

   ○ A. He appeals to the fears citizens have in society.

   ○ B. He appeals to each citizen's sense of justice and fairness.

   ○ C. He appeals to the American values of liberty and equality.

   ○ D. He appeals to the ideals that value strong state governments.

Skill:
Arguments and Claims

Use the Checklist to analyze Arguments and Claims in "The Federalist Papers: No. 10." Refer to the sample student annotations about Arguments and Claims in the text.

••• CHECKLIST FOR ARGUMENTS AND CLAIMS

In order to delineate the premises, purposes, and arguments in works of public advocacy, note the following:

✓ legal reasoning includes the thinking processes and strategies used by lawyers and judges when arguing and deciding legal cases, and is based on constitutional principles, or laws written down in the U.S. Constitution

✓ in works of public advocacy, an individual or group tries to influence or support a cause or policy

✓ the premise, or the basis of the proposal the individual or group makes, must be based on logical reasoning and constitutional principles

✓ isolate the premise in a work of public advocacy

✓ identify the purpose of the text and the position the writer takes

✓ recognize how the author uses legal reasoning to interpret the law

✓ determine whether the premise is based on logical reasoning and constitutional principles

To evaluate the premises, purposes, and arguments in works of public advocacy, consider the following questions:

✓ What position does the writer take?

✓ How does the writer use legal reasoning to support his or her position?

✓ In a work of public advocacy, how does the individual or group try to influence or support a cause or policy?

Skill:
Arguments and Claims

Reread paragraph 11–12 of the text to determine the answers to the follow-up questions.

⟳ YOUR TURN

1. This question has two parts. First, answer Part A. Then, answer Part B.

   Part A: In the passage, what conclusion is drawn about a republic as a form of government?

   - ○ A. It reduces the number of distinct parties and special interests.
   - ○ B. It allows for different voices to coexist, making it unlikely that one party or faction will become too powerful.
   - ○ C. In a republic, one leader is appointed to rule over all factions.
   - ○ D. A republic is not an effective system of governance for larger societies, while a democracy can extend over a greater sphere.

   Part B: Which sentence or phrase from the passage best supports this conclusion?

   - ○ A. "The greater number of citizens, and greater sphere of country."
   - ○ B. "Whose patriotism and love of justice will be least likely to sacrifice it."
   - ○ C. "The other point of difference is, the greater number of citizens and extent of territory which may be brought within the compass of republican than of democratic government."
   - ○ D. "Extend the sphere, and you take in a greater variety of parties and interests; you make it less probable that a majority of the whole will have a common motive to invade the rights of other citizens."

Skill: Language, Style, and Audience

Use the Checklist to analyze Language, Style, and Audience in "The Federalist Papers: No. 10." Refer to the sample student annotations about Language, Style, and Audience in the text.

••• CHECKLIST FOR LANGUAGE, STYLE, AND AUDIENCE

In order to determine an author's style and possible intended audience, do the following:

✓ identify instances where the author uses key terms throughout the course of a text

✓ examine surrounding words and phrases to determine the context, connotation, style and tone of the term's usage

✓ analyze how the author's treatment of the key term affects the reader's understanding of the text

✓ note the audience and possible reactions to the author's word choice, style, and treatment of key terms

To analyze how an author's treatment of language and key terms affect the reader's understanding of the text, consider the following questions:

✓ How do the author's word choices enhance or change what is being described?

✓ How do the author's word choices affect the reader's understanding of key terms and ideas in the text?

✓ How do choices about language affect the author's style and audience?

✓ How often does the author use this term or terms?

Skill: Language, Style, and Audience

Reread paragraph 7 of "The Federalist Papers: No. 10." Then, using the Checklist on the previous page, answer the multiple-choice questions below.

↻ YOUR TURN

1. Which of the following statements best represents how Madison elaborates on the idea of factions in this passage?

   ○ A. Madison asserts that different interests will require legislation due to factions.
   ○ B. Madison identifies that those who are without property are one single faction.
   ○ C. Madison concludes that factions are inevitable.
   ○ D. Madison explains that factions are inevitable because of the unequal distribution of property.

2. How does Madison support his argument with this elaboration on the idea of factions?

   ○ A. Madison supports his argument by stating that factions are a normal challenge for any modern government, and a republic is the best solution.
   ○ B. Madison supports his argument by stating that factions create additional issues for states to debate prior to the ratification of the Constitution.
   ○ C. Madison supports his argument by limiting the examples of factions to property distribution.
   ○ D. Madison supports his argument by providing a path to legislation for addressing varied interests and sectors.

Close Read

Reread "The Federalist Papers: No. 10." As you reread, complete the Skills Focus questions below. Then use your answers and annotations from the questions to help you complete the Write activity.

◎ SKILLS FOCUS

1. "After Being Convicted of Voting in the 1872 Presidential Election", "Testimony Before the Credentials Committee, Democratic National Convention", and *The Federalist Papers* are all Primary Sources, written by speakers who were fighting for their ideals. How does "The Federalist Papers: No. 10" highlight places where you see themes and purposes that were specific to Early American History and Literature? Make sure to use textual evidence to support your response.

2. Reread the paragraph that begins "The other point of difference is. . ." What is Madison saying about small democracies versus larger republics? How does this support his overall argument? Highlight evidence in the text that will help you respond to this question, and comment on that evidence.

3. Highlight any passages that present an analogy about disease and cure. How does this analogy relate to Madison's central argument about factions?

4. Reread the paragraph that begins "The influence of factious leaders. . ." Highlight the analogy related to fire in that paragraph. Explain this analogy. Do you think the point that Madison is making about the threat to the nation's early identity is still true today?

5. In "The Federalist Papers: No. 10," Madison argues for his belief in establishing a republic for the United States of America. What is his approach to fighting for this ideal? How does the structure of his argument drive towards his goal and try to convince his audience?

✏ WRITE

ARGUMENTATIVE: Do you think Madison's arguments, concerns, and values are still relevant today? For example, do you think that factions, or groups that represent people who share the same interests and have a common political cause, are still likely to **agitate** against the public good today? Do you agree that elected politicians are enlightened individuals who can be trusted to make decisions for the public good, or is that an old-fashioned belief? Was Madison right, or was he just stuck in the beliefs of his historical moment? Select two points from Madison's essay and write a response in which you explain whether you think the points are still valid in today's society.

Self-Made Men

ARGUMENTATIVE TEXT
Frederick Douglass
1872

Introduction

I n his speech, "Self-Made Men," famed abolitionist and orator Frederick Douglass (1818-1895) articulated his view of what it means to be self-made. Douglass stresses that self-made individuals do not inherit their positions by birth or other fortunate circumstances, but instead achieve success through their own efforts. Furthermore, Douglass argues, while each individual is responsible for their own path, those paths are ultimately interconnected. Self-made individuals can't help but form part of a larger whole. Their success or failure affects that larger whole, just as the success or failure of a generation affects the generations to come.

"Properly speaking, there are in the world no such men as self-made men."

1   From man comes all that we know or can imagine of heaven and earth, of time and eternity. He is the **prolific** constituter of manners, morals, religions and governments. He spins them out as the spider spins his web, and they are coarse or fine, kind or cruel, according to the degree of intelligence reached by him at the period of their establishment. He compels us to contemplate his past with wonder and to survey his future with much the same feelings as those with which Columbus is supposed to have gazed westward over the sea. It is the faith of the race that in man there exists far outlying continents of power, thought and feeling, which remain to be discovered, explored, cultivated, made practical and glorified.

2   Mr. Emerson[1] has declared that it is natural to believe in great men. Whether this is a fact, or not, we do believe in them and worship them. The Visible God of the New Testament is revealed to us as a man of like passions with ourselves. We seek out our wisest and best man, the man who, by eloquence or the sword compels us to believe him such, and make him our leader, prophet, preacher and law giver. We do this, not because he is essentially different from us, but because of his identity with us. He is our best representative and reflects, on a colossal scale, the scale to which we would aspire, our highest aims, objects, powers and possibilities.

3   This natural reverence for all that is great in man, and this tendency to **deify** and worship him, though natural and the source of man's elevation, has not always shown itself wise but has often shown itself far otherwise than wise. It has often given us a wicked ruler for a righteous one, a false prophet for a true one, a corrupt preacher for a pure one, a man of war for a man of peace, and a distorted and vengeful image of God for an image of justice and mercy.

4   But it is not my purpose to attempt here any comprehensive and exhaustive theory or philosophy or the nature of manhood in all the range I have indicated. I am here to speak to you of a peculiar type of manhood under the title of "Self-Made Men."

1. **Mr. Emerson** in his famous essay "Self-Reliance," American writer and philosopher Ralph Waldo Emerson argued that following one's own individual will, rather than conforming to polite society, is the key to greatness

5   That there is, in more respects than one, something like a **solecism** in this title, I freely admit. Properly speaking, there are in the world no such men as self-made men. That term implies an individual independence of the past and present which can never exist.

6   Our best and most valued acquisitions have been obtained either from our contemporaries or from those who have preceded us in the field of thought and discovery. We have all either begged, borrowed or stolen. We have reaped where others have sown, and that which others have strown, we have gathered. It must in truth be said, though it may not accord well with self-conscious individuality and self-conceit, that no possible native force of character, and no depth of wealth and originality, can lift a man into absolute independence of his fellowmen, and no generation of men can be independent of the preceding generation. The brotherhood and inter-dependence of mankind are guarded and defended at all points. I believe in individuality, but individuals are, to the mass, like waves to the ocean. The highest order of genius is as dependent as is the lowest. It, like the loftiest waves of the sea, derives its power and greatness from the grandeur and vastness of the ocean of which it forms a part. We differ as the waves, but are one as the sea. To do something well does not necessarily imply the ability to do everything else equally well. If you can do in one direction that which I cannot do, I may in another direction, be able to do that which you cannot do. Thus the balance of power is kept comparatively even, and a self-acting brotherhood and inter-dependence is maintained.

7   Nevertheless, the title of my lecture is eminently descriptive of a class and is, moreover, a fit and convenient one for my purpose, in illustrating the idea which I have in view. In the order of discussion I shall adopt the style of an old-fashioned preacher and have a "firstly," a "secondly," a "thirdly," a "fourthly" and, possibly, a "conclusion."

8   My first is, "Who are self-made men?" My second is, "What is the true theory of their success?" My third is, "The advantages which self-made men derive from the manners and institutions of their surroundings," and my fourth is, "The grounds of the criticism to which they are, as a class, especially exposed."

9   On the first point I may say that, by the term "self-made men," I mean especially what, to the popular mind, the term least imports. Self-made men are the men who, under peculiar difficulties and without the ordinary helps of favoring circumstances, have attained knowledge, usefulness, power and position and have learned from themselves the best uses to which life can be put in this world, and in the exercises of these uses to build up worthy character. They are the men who owe little or nothing to birth, relationship, friendly surroundings; to wealth inherited or to early approved means of education; who are what they are, without the aid of any favoring conditions by which other men usually rise in the world and achieve great results. In fact they are the men who are not brought up but who are obliged to come up, not only without the voluntary assistance or friendly co-operation of society, but often in open and **derisive** defiance of all the efforts of society and the tendency of circumstances to

NOTES

repress, retard and keep them down. They are the men who, in a world of schools, academies, colleges and other institutions of learning, are often compelled by unfriendly circumstances to acquire their education elsewhere and, amidst unfavorable conditions, to hew out for themselves a way to success, and thus to become the architects of their own good fortunes. They are in a peculiar sense, indebted to themselves for themselves. If they have traveled far, they have made the road on which they have travelled. If they have ascended high, they have built their own ladder. From the depths of poverty such as these have often come. From the heartless pavements of large and crowded cities; barefooted, homeless, and friendless, they have come. From hunger, rags and destitution, they have come; motherless and fatherless, they have come, and may come. Flung overboard in the midnight storm on the broad and tempest-tossed ocean of life; left without ropes, planks, oars or life-preservers, they have bravely buffetted[2] the frowning billows and have risen in safety and life where others, supplied with the best appliances for safety and success, have fainted, despaired and gone down forever.

10 Such men as these, whether found in one position or another, whether in the college or in the factory; whether professors or plowmen; whether Caucasian or Indian; whether Anglo-Saxon or Anglo-African, are self-made men and are entitled to a certain measure of respect for their success and for proving to the world the grandest possibilities of human nature, of whatever variety of race or color.

11 Though a man of this class need not claim to be a hero or to be worshiped as such, there is genuine heroism in his struggle and something of sublimity and glory in his triumph. Every instance of such success is an example and a help to humanity. It, better than any mere assertion, gives us assurance of the latent powers and resources of simple and unaided manhood. It dignifies labor, honors application, lessens pain and depression, dispels gloom from the brow of the **destitute** and weariness from the heart of him about to faint, and enables man to take hold of the roughest and flintiest hardships incident to the battle of life, with a lighter heart, with higher hopes and a larger courage.

✏ WRITE

PERSONAL RESPONSE: Frederick Douglass is an important figure in the abolitionist movement. "Self-Made Men" is one of the author's most famous speeches. What is the message of the speech? Connect this message to your own experiences: how does this speech change your understanding of what it means to be a self-made person pursuing the American Dream? Support your response with evidence from the text as well as from your personal experiences.

2. **buffet** to strike repeatedly and harshly

I Am Prepared to Die

ARGUMENTATIVE TEXT
Nelson Mandela
1964

Introduction

In 1962, political leader Nelson Mandela (1918–2013) was arrested for participating in a conspiracy to overthrow the South African government. Nearly two years later, Mandela was sentenced to life in prison. In this excerpt from his trial testimony in Rivonia, Mandela indicts the state-sanctioned system of apartheid, explaining why he and several others plotted acts of guerilla warfare against his segregated nation. After serving 27 years in prison, Mandela became the first democratically elected president of South Africa. Many South Africans refer to him as *Madiba*, or "father of the nation."

"During my lifetime I have dedicated myself to this struggle of the African people."

from Nelson Mandela's Statement at the Rivonia Trial[1], 1964

1   South Africa is the richest country in Africa, and could be one of the richest countries in the world. But it is a land of extremes and remarkable **contrasts**. The whites enjoy what may well be the highest standard of living in the world, whilst Africans live in poverty and misery. Forty percent of the Africans live in hopelessly overcrowded and, in some cases, drought-stricken reserves, where soil erosion and the overworking of the soil makes it impossible for them to live properly off the land. Thirty percent are labourers, labour tenants[2], and squatters on white farms and work and live under conditions similar to those of the serfs[3] of the Middle Ages. The other thirty percent live in towns where they have developed economic and social habits which bring them closer in many respects to white standards. Yet most Africans, even in this group, are impoverished by low incomes and the high cost of living.

2   The highest-paid and the most **prosperous** section of urban African life is in Johannesburg. Yet their actual position is desperate. The latest figures were given on the 25th of March 1964 by Mr. Carr, Manager of the Johannesburg Non-European Affairs Department. The poverty datum line for the average African family in Johannesburg, according to Mr. Carr's department, is R42.84 per month. He showed that the average monthly wage is R32.24 and that forty-six percent of all African families in Johannesburg do not earn enough to keep them going.

3   Poverty goes hand in hand with **malnutrition** and disease. The incidence of malnutrition and deficiency diseases is very high amongst Africans. Tuberculosis, pellagra, kwashiorkor, gastroenteritis, and scurvy bring death and destruction of health. The incidence of infant mortality is one of the highest in the world. According to the Medical Officer of Health for Pretoria, it is estimated that tuberculosis kills forty people a day, almost all Africans, and

---

1. **Rivonia Trial** the criminal trial where Nelson Mandela and others were convicted of sabotage and sentenced to life in prison
2. **labour tenants** farm workers who are unpaid except for free residence on that farm and a portion of the land to work for himself
3. **serfs** members of the most servile class, usually bound to physical labor

in 1961 there were 58,491 new cases reported. These diseases, My Lord, not only destroy the vital organs of the body, but they result in retarded mental conditions and lack of initiative, and reduce powers of concentration. The secondary results of such conditions affect the whole community and the standard of work performed by Africans.

4   The complaint of Africans, however, is not only that they are poor and whites are rich, but that the laws which are made by the whites are designed to preserve this situation.

5   There are two ways to break out of poverty. The first is by formal education, and the second is by the worker acquiring a greater skill at his work and thus higher wages. As far as Africans are concerned, both these avenues of advancement are deliberately **curtailed** by legislation.

6   I ask the Court to remember that the present Government has always sought to **hamper** Africans in their search for education. One of their early acts, after coming into power, was to stop subsidies for African school feeding. Many African children who attended schools depended on this supplement to their diet. This was a cruel act.

7   There is compulsory education for all white children at virtually no cost to their parents, be they rich or poor. Similar facilities are not provided for the African children, though there are some who receive such assistance. African children, however, generally have to pay more for their schooling than whites. According to figures quoted by the South African Institute of Race Relations in its 1963 journal, approximately forty percent of African children in the age group between seven and fourteen do not attend school. For those who do attend school, the standards are vastly different from those afforded to white children. In 1960-61 the per capita[4] Government spending on African students at State-aided schools was estimated at R12.46. In the same years, the per capita spending on white children in the Cape Province (which are the only figures available to me) was R144.57. Although there are no figures available to me, it can be stated, without doubt, that the white children on whom R144.57 per head was being spent all came from wealthier homes than African children on whom R12.46 per head was being spent.

8   The quality of education is also different. According to the Bantu Educational Journal, only 5,660 African children in the whole of South Africa passed their Junior Certificate in 1962, and in that year only 362 passed matric[5]. This is presumably consistent with the policy of Bantu Education about which the present Prime Minister said, during the debate on the Bantu Education Bill in 1953 when he was Minister of Native Affairs:

---

4. **per capita** (Latin) for each person
5. **matric** the requirements for university admission

"When I have control of Native Education I will reform it so that Natives will be taught from childhood to realise that equality with Europeans is not for them. People who believe in equality are not desirable teachers for Natives. When my Department controls Native education it will know for what class of higher education a Native is fitted, and whether he will have a chance in life to use his knowledge."

9   The other main obstacle to the economic advancement of the African is the Industrial Colour Bar under which all the better paid, better jobs of industry are reserved for whites only. Moreover, Africans in the unskilled and semi-skilled occupations which are open to them are not allowed to form trade unions which have recognition under the Industrial Conciliation Act. This means that strikes of African workers are illegal, and that they are denied the right of collective bargaining which is permitted to the better-paid white workers. The discrimination in the policy of successive South African Governments towards African workers is demonstrated by the so-called 'civilized labour policy' under which sheltered, unskilled Government jobs are found for those white workers who cannot make the grade in industry, at wages far, which far exceed the earnings of the average African employee in industry.

10 The Government often answers its critics by saying that Africans in South Africa are economically better off than the inhabitants of the other countries in Africa. I do not know whether this statement is true and doubt whether any comparison can be made without having regard to the cost-of-living index in such countries. But even if it is true, as far as African people are concerned, it is irrelevant. Our complaint is not that we are poor by comparison with people in other countries, but that we are poor by comparison with white people in our own country, and that we are prevented by legislation from altering this imbalance.

11 The lack of human dignity experienced by Africans is the direct result of the policy of white supremacy. White supremacy **implies** black inferiority. Legislation designed to preserve white supremacy entrenches this notion. Menial tasks in South Africa are invariably performed by Africans. When anything has to be carried or cleaned the white man will look around for an African to do it for him, whether the African is employed by him or not. Because of this sort of attitude, whites tend to regard Africans as a separate breed. They do not look upon them as people with families of their own; they do not realise that we have emotions—that we fall in love like white people do; that we want to be with our wives and children like white people want to be with theirs; that we want to earn money, enough money to support our families properly, to feed and clothe them and send them to school. And what 'house-boy' or 'garden-boy' or labourer can ever hope to do this?

• • •

12 During my lifetime I have dedicated myself to this struggle of the African people. I have fought against white domination, and I have fought against black domination. I have cherished the ideal of a democratic and free society in which all persons live together in harmony and with equal opportunities. It is an ideal which I hope to live for and to achieve. But if needs be, it is an ideal for which I am prepared to die.

Prisoners raising their fists in protest from inside a prison car, carrying eight men, including Nelson Mandela, after being sentenced to life imprisonment for conspiracy, sabotage and treason, 1964

✏ WRITE

RHETORICAL ANALYSIS: The ancient Greek philosopher Aristotle wrote the *Rhetoric*, one of the most famous works on the art of persuasion. In the treatise, he outlines the main rhetorical appeals to an audience: ethos (author credibility), pathos (emotions), and logos (logic and reasoning). How does Mandela use these appeals to advance his argument? Use specific textual evidence to support your response.

Leadership During a Crisis

ARGUMENTATIVE TEXT
2018

Introduction

Conflict and crisis are inherent to human beings' competitive nature. But as the world becomes more crowded and its resources more limited, this also means that conflicts between various groups and interests are increasingly likely to occur. When examining the difficult choices made by leaders past and present, what patterns or lessons emerge? When and how have leaders resolved conflicts in a way that made their communities stronger, safer, and more at peace? Both essays present strong opinions about effective leadership. Which do you find more persuasive?

"In other words, does might indeed make right?"

NOTES

Leadership During a Crisis: Is Aggressiveness or Peacefulness More Effective?

Point: Whatever the Crisis May Be, It Must Always Be Addressed Peacefully

1   Imagine a playground full of children playing together—suddenly, a problem arises. A bigger kid wants to play with a certain toy, so he grabs it out of a smaller child's hands and runs away. Sure, the bigger child has the physical strength to do what he wants, but should that power **enable** him to achieve his goals by taking advantage of others? In other words, does might indeed make right?

2   A world history filled with conflict, colonization, slavery, and apartheid[1] might suggest that it does. With such a history, it can be tempting to meet force with force—an action that may even seem justified at times—but when faced with a crisis, the response of aggression is not the more effective tactic. In times of crisis, a leader must rise to oppose violent forces by engaging in deliberate actions that will bring about a *sustainable* resolution, and that can only be achieved through peaceful protests and negotiations.

Skill:
Informational
Text Structure

The author recognizes that some might think using only "peaceful tactics" does not work. The author poses a question that those who disagree might ask the author.

3   Some might view relying entirely on peaceful tactics as too idealistic. How can one depend only on a tactic that seeks to persuade those with power and privilege to reconcile their actions with the very ideals—such as freedom and justice—that they are **violating** or ignoring? But while the goal of peaceful tactics may be lofty, it is this very focus on ideals that gives it its strength. True peace or justice can only be achieved when the groups involved find common ground, which depends on shared ideals. Aggression militates against that, and worse still, can perpetuate cyclical violence. In fact, research has demonstrated that from 1900 to 2006, peaceful campaigns were twice as likely to bring about change as violent protests (Chenoweth, "My Talk"). In times of crisis, the use of peaceful tactics is the most successful way to build a moral movement that can lead to positive, sustainable change.

---

1. **apartheid** a policy of segregation and discrimination, particularly the state-sanctioned racial one of 20th-century South Africa

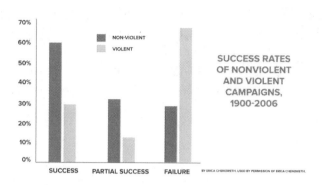

SUCCESS RATES OF NONVIOLENT AND VIOLENT CAMPAIGNS, 1900-2006

BY ERICA CHENOWETH. USED BY PERMISSION OF ERICA CHENOWETH.

 NOTES

 Skill: Media

The bar graph summarizes data from 1900–2006, showing that nonviolent campaigns were more successful. It summarizes a lot of data, but I wonder how the author defines "success" and "failure" in this context.

4   One way that peaceful actions can help achieve the goals of a movement is by highlighting the injustice they seek to **address**, namely through nonviolent direct action. This tactic creates a dynamic that compels members of the privileged and powerful groups in a society to question the status quo. This was employed by Mahatma Gandhi[2] during his Salt March, which compelled British colonialists to change their laws that forced Indians to purchase taxed salt, which was produced in India but controlled by the British (Nojeim 140). Nonviolent direct action was also especially useful to leaders of the Civil Rights Movement[3], who could use the media attention they received, especially on television, to force white Americans to face their most despicable values. These efforts to turn public opinion would help desegregate the South and enfranchise African Americans (Nojeim 214).

5   At the same time, peaceful, nonviolent actions can be restorative for those who participate in protest. In his book *Why We Can't Wait*, Dr. Martin Luther King, Jr. described the effect that joining the movement had on African Americans: "Nonviolence had tremendous psychological importance for the Negro. . . . The Negro was able to face his adversary, to concede him his physical advantage and to defeat him because the superior force of the oppressor had become powerless" (26). With a great deal of discipline and dedication, African Americans who participated in nonviolent direct action were able to exert agency in bringing about their own liberation, and being able to accomplish such a feat was empowering.

6   Another benefit of using peaceful means to address a crisis, particularly one that necessitates replacing members of a governing body, is that peaceful tactics are more likely to bring about the establishment of a democratic government. In her research on recent mass movements, political scientist Erica Chenoweth examined the success of both violent and nonviolent movements. In her blog post, "How Can We Know When Popular Movements Are Winning? Look to These Four Trends," which reported some of her

2. **Mahatma Gandhi** the Indian leader and activist who led the nonviolent movement against British rule of India
3. **Civil Rights Movement** the American movement in the 1950s and 1960s to give African-Americans the same rights as white people

NOTES

findings, she noted that "nonviolent resistance campaigns are ten times more likely to usher in democratic institutions than violent ones. And from 1900–2006, only 50% of democratic countries facing armed campaigns remained democratic in the aftermath. [Ninety percent] of democratic countries facing

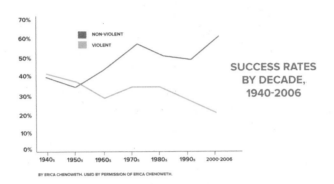

SUCCESS RATES BY DECADE, 1940-2006

BY ERICA CHENOWETH. USED BY PERMISSION OF ERICA CHENOWETH.

nonviolent resistance campaigns remained democratic after the campaign ended" ("How Can We Know").

7   Crisis forces leaders of social movements to make important decisions about how to address conflict and inequality. An important part of that decision-making process is to consider what sort of society, or world, one hopes to find on the other end of a struggle for peace or justice. History has shown us that violence has too often brought about more violence, and that cruelty is returned in kind, several times over. If leaders hope to change that dynamic, they must focus on using peaceful tactics to bring about a new, better world.

"Although it is an imperfect tactic, the threat or use of violence has utility in times of crisis."

Copyright © BookheadEd Learning, LLC

Counterpoint: In an Imperfect World, Turning the Other Cheek Cannot Always Be the Answer

8   In times of political and social crisis—when war has been waged or the oppressed can no longer bear injustice—leaders are faced with an age-old dilemma: what means will they use to resolve the problem? If history has taught us anything, it is that these decisions are both complicated and of great consequence. Thus, in times of crisis when urgency necessitates decisive action, it is imperative that leaders have the freedom to use whatever means effects the resolution they seek—even if that includes using violence.

9   Some will argue that the use or threat of violence only brings about more violence, and that this cyclical problem makes true peace or justice impossible. The perpetuation of violence is, indeed, an outcome that has been borne out many times in the past; however, it seems naïve to limit leaders only to peaceful tactics for the sake of avoiding this possible outcome. Anti-apartheid activist Nelson Mandela recognized that different tactics, even those requiring violence, are sometimes required to make sure leaders are effective in different situations: "Our approach was to empower the organization to be *effective* in its leadership. And if the adoption of nonviolence gave it that effectiveness, that efficiency, we would pursue nonviolence. But if the condition shows that nonviolence was not effective, we would use other means" (53). Achieving one's goals is most important—especially when lives and basic human and civil rights are at stake—and leaders must be able to adapt their tactics, with purpose, to protect their people. Although it is an imperfect tactic, the threat or use of violence has utility in times of crisis.

10 First, the threat of violence can be a useful deterrent. Even during the Civil Rights Movement, a movement characterized by nonviolence, some African Americans chose self-defense instead. In 1964, in Jonesboro, Louisiana, a group of African American men formed the Deacons for Defense and Justice, an armed group that operated in several towns protecting Congress of Racial

Equality (CORE) workers from the Ku Klux Klan[4], serving as bodyguards for activists and security at events. Occasionally, the deacons engaged in skirmishes with the Ku Klux Klan, but often their mere presence prevented the Ku Klux Klan from acting (Hill 3). In the end, their actions did more good than they **anticipated:** not only did they protect civil rights activists from violence, but they also empowered more local African Americans to defend themselves against white violence and eventually compelled the federal government to quell the violence perpetrated by the Ku Klux Klan.

**Skill:
Media**

The photo shows members of the Deacons for Defense and Justice taking a stand against the KKK. The photo does not show violence taking place; just people who are not afraid to confront the KKK.

11 Second, the use of violence is at times a simple necessity. In some cases, it may be the only way to thwart a violent attack or maintain one's sovereignty when negotiation or diplomacy has proven ineffective. World War II is a good example of a situation in which aggression became a necessity. When Germany began to annex land in other countries, Great Britain and France first tried to negotiate peace

Charles Sims, head of the Deacons for Defense and Justice, displays replicas of Ku Klux Klan robes, July 10, 1964

with Germany. In September of 1938, Great Britain, France, Germany, and Italy signed the Munich Agreement, which allowed Germany to take control of Sudetenland in Czechoslovakia in exchange for peace. Winston Churchill, who would later lead Great Britain in its conflict with Germany, quickly recognized the miscalculation in their actions; to him, the countries' imperilment was a **fait accompli**. In an address to the House of Commons on October 5, 1938, Churchill lamented, "Many people, no doubt, honestly believe that they are only giving away the interests of Czechoslovakia, whereas I fear we shall find that we have deeply compromised, and perhaps fatally endangered, the safety and even the independence of Great Britain and France." And he was right. The peace did not last long. In March of 1939, Germany violated the Munich Agreement by invading Czechoslovakia again. In September of that year, Germany invaded Poland, forcing France and Great Britain finally to declare war on Germany.

**Skill:
Technical
Language**

Examples of "tactics" here are "diplomacy, alliances, and neutrality." But all of these prove "ineffective," making war "necessary."

12 Germany would later violate a nonaggression agreement with the Soviet Union and declare war on the country, and the United States, which tried at first to remain neutral, would join the conflict after Japan, an ally of Germany, attacked Pearl Harbor. For Great Britain, France, the Soviet Union and the United States, diplomacy, alliances, and neutrality were ineffective tactics to address the threat Germany and its allies posed, and war became necessary.

---

4. **Ku Klux Klan** secretive groups of extremist white supremacists, known for wearing pointed, white hoods

13   Nations, groups, and individuals the world over have established relationships based on varying degrees of power, freedom, and privilege. They are constantly in **flux,** always becoming more and more complex. In an ideal world, leaders would be able to address the crises that result from negotiating these relationships through purely peaceful means. But we do not live in such a world, so sometimes addressing those crises requires more aggressive tactics.

First Read

Read "Leadership During a Crisis." After you read, complete the Think Questions below.

☁ THINK QUESTIONS

1. What is the author's view on the use of nonviolent conflict resolution in the Point essay? Cite specific evidence from the essay to support your answer.

2. In the Counterpoint essay, what is the author's view on the use of violence? Cite specific evidence from the essay to support your answer.

3. Provide one reason nonviolence can be effective and one reason violence can be effective in conflict resolution, according to the essays. Be sure to use specific evidence from the texts to support your answer.

4. Use context clues to determine the meaning of **violating** as it is used in paragraph 3 of the Point essay. Write your own definition of *violating* and explain how you figured it out.

5. The Latin word *fluere* means to flow. With this information in mind, what do you think the word **flux** means? Use context clues to support your thinking and write your best definition here.

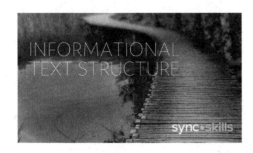

Skill:
Informational Text Structure

Use the Checklist to analyze Informational Text Structure in "Leadership During a Crisis." Refer to the sample student annotations about Informational Text Structure in the text.

••• CHECKLIST FOR INFORMATIONAL TEXT STRUCTURE

In order to determine the structure an author uses in his or her exposition or argument, note the following:

✓ where the author introduces and clarifies the argument

✓ sentences and paragraphs that reveal the text structure the author uses to frame the argument

✓ whether the text structure is effective in presenting all sides of the argument and makes the author's points clear, convincing, and engaging

To analyze and evaluate the effectiveness of the structure an author uses in his or her exposition or argument, including whether the structure makes points clear, convincing, and engaging, consider the following questions:

✓ Did I have to read a particular sentence or phrase over again? Where?

✓ Did I find myself distracted or uninterested while reading the text? When?

✓ Did the structure the author used make his or her points clear, convincing, and engaging? Why or why not?

✓ Was the author's exposition or argument effective? Why or why not?

Please note that excerpts and passages in the StudySync® library and this workbook are intended as touchstones to generate interest in an author's work. The excerpts and passages do not substitute for the reading of entire texts, and StudySync® strongly recommends that students seek out and purchase the whole literary or informational work in order to experience it as the author intended. Links to online resellers are available in our digital library. In addition, complete works may be ordered through an authorized reseller by filling out and returning to StudySync® the order form enclosed in this workbook.

Reading & Writing
Companion

491

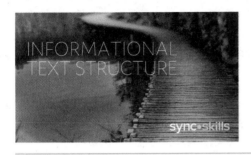

Skill:
Informational Text Structure

Reread paragraphs 1-2 of "Leadership During a Crisis." Then, using the Checklist on the previous page, answer the multiple-choice questions below.

♻ YOUR TURN

1. What is the purpose of the first sentence in paragraph 1?

   ○ A. to explain the author's point of view about solving problems

   ○ B. to describe the author's focus on important political and social movements

   ○ C. to encourage readers to question their assumptions about war

   ○ D. to get the reader thinking about how political and social crises can be solved

2. Why does the author use a quotation from Nelson Mandela in paragraph 2?

   ○ A. to explain the necessary characteristics of an effective leader

   ○ B. to support the idea that peaceful tactics do not work in all situations

   ○ C. to include an expert opinion about how to start an activist movement

   ○ D. to give an example of when violent tactics proved to be the most effective

Skill:
Media

Use the Checklist to analyze Media in "Leadership During a Crisis." Refer to the sample student annotations about Media in the text.

••• CHECKLIST FOR MEDIA

In order to determine how to integrate and evaluate multiple sources of information presented in different media or formats, note the following:

- ✓ the key elements in each source of information

- ✓ how each media or format, such as visual or quantitative, presents the sources of information

- ✓ what information is included or excluded in each media presentation

- ✓ the audience of each media presentation and the author's purpose

- ✓ the reliability and credibility of each presentation

To integrate and evaluate multiple sources of information presented in different media or formats as well as in words in order to address a question or solve a problem, consider the following questions:

- ✓ How is each media presentation reliable or credible?

- ✓ How can you use each media presentation?

- ✓ How can you integrate multiple sources of information presented in different media or formats to address a question or solve a problem?

Skill:
Media

Look at this line graph based on the research of Erica Chenoweth. Then, answer the multiple-choice questions that follow.

🔁 YOUR TURN

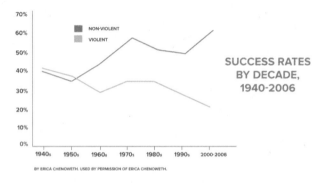

SUCCESS RATES
BY DECADE,
1940-2006

BY ERICA CHENOWETH. USED BY PERMISSION OF ERICA CHENOWETH.

1. If someone wanted to argue that violent tactics are more effective, which would be the best response to the graph above?

    ○ A. a different type of graph that better shows the same data

    ○ B. an analysis of why the data in the graph are misleading

    ○ C. a photograph showing the use of violent tactics

    ○ D. a quotation that makes violent tactics feel right

2. Which statement best explains when a photograph would be the most effective support for an author's topic?

    ○ A. An author is explaining how hurricanes develop and includes a photograph that shows the aftermath of a powerful hurricane.

    ○ B. An author is arguing for the importance of recycling and includes a photograph that shows a typical recycling center.

    ○ C. An author is arguing for the importance of protecting endangered species and includes a photograph of a baby tiger.

    ○ D. An author is explaining how to prepare for the college admissions process and includes a photograph of a famous university.

↻ YOUR TURN

3. Which statement best analyzes the graph to support an argument in favor of nonviolent protest?

- ○ A. The graph shows that, since the 1950s, violent protests have become increasingly unsuccessful.
- ○ B. The graph shows, through its use of colors, that violent protest is an aggressive practice that should end.
- ○ C. The graph shows that during the period from 1940 to 1950, violent protests were more successful.
- ○ D. The graph shows that, especially in recent years, violent protests are effective at least 10% of the time.

Please note that excerpts and passages in the StudySync® library and this workbook are intended as touchstones to generate interest in an author's work. The excerpts and passages do not substitute for the reading of entire texts, and StudySync® strongly recommends that students seek out and purchase the whole literary or informational work in order to experience it as the author intended. Links to online resellers are available in our digital library. In addition, complete works may be ordered through an authorized reseller by filling out and returning to StudySync® the order form enclosed in this workbook.

Reading & Writing Companion 495

Skill:
Technical Language

Use the Checklist to analyze Technical Language in "Leadership During a Crisis." Refer to the sample student annotations about Technical Language in the text.

••• CHECKLIST FOR TECHNICAL LANGUAGE

In order to determine the meaning of words and phrases as they are used in a text, including key terms and technical meanings, note the following:

✓   the subject of the book or article

✓   any unfamiliar words that you think might be technical terms

✓   words that have multiple meanings that change when used with a specific subject

✓   the possible contextual meaning of a word, or the definition from a dictionary

✓   key terms that are used repeatedly throughout the text

To determine the meaning of words and phrases as they are used in a text, including key terms and technical meanings, consider the following questions:

✓   What is the subject of the informational text?

✓   How does the use of technical language help establish the author as an authority on the subject?

✓   Are there any key terms or technical words that have an impact on the meaning and tone of the book or article?

✓   Does the author use the same term several times, refining its meaning and adding layers to it over the course of the text?

Skill:
Technical Language

Reread paragraphs 11 and 12 from "Counterpoint: In an Imperfect World, Turning the Other Cheek Cannot Always Be the Answer" and the following dictionary entry to determine the answers to the follow-up questions.

YOUR TURN

Violate

verb

1. To break or disregard
2. To do harm to a person or especially the chastity of
3. To fail to show proper respect for
4. To interrupt or remove

---

1. This question has two parts. First, answer Part A. Then, answer Part B.

   Part A: Which definition best fits how the word *violated* is used in the text?

   ○ A. definition 1
   ○ B. definition 2
   ○ C. definition 3
   ○ D. definition 4

   Part B: Which statement best explains how the use of the technical term *violate* supports the author's argument?

   ○ A. The author uses the word *violate* when discussing Germany and Czechoslovakia to explain why agreements are pointless.
   ○ B. The author uses the word *violate* in the context of World War II to defend the idea that peaceful solutions never last.
   ○ C. The author uses the word *violate* when discussing Germany and Czechoslovakia to highlight how many people were harmed during the invasion.
   ○ D. The author uses the word *violate* in the context of World War II to show how aggression might be the only response when agreements are broken.

Close Read

Reread "Leadership During a Crisis." As you reread, complete the Skills Focus questions below. Then use your answers and annotations from the questions to help you complete the Write activity.

◎ SKILLS FOCUS

1. Re-read the last two paragraphs of both the Point and Counterpoint essays. Which do you find more effective and convincing? Why? Use textual evidence to support your answer.

2. Note how, in the Point essay, the author uses historical examples and quotations as well as graphs and statistics to support their argument. What kinds of information would help support the Counterpoint argument? At which points in the essay would you think it most effective to include images, graphs, or statistics?

3. Identify an example of statistical evidence in the Point essay. Evaluate the effectiveness of the evidence and explain why you think it is or is not convincing.

4. Find three examples of the way *effective* is used in the Counterpoint essay. What does the author mean by the technical term *effective*? How is the word used differently in the different parts of the paragraph?

These two arguments propose two different ways that leaders should fight for their ideas, and the arguments offer different examples of how leaders have fought for their ideas in the past. Imagine you are a leader fighting for one of your ideas. What would you need to think about before deciding whether to use peaceful tactics or violent ones? What questions would you ask yourself? Use examples of leaders and facts from the text to support your answer.

✏ WRITE

DISCUSSION: Which side of the argument do you agree with? Why do you agree with that side? Do you fully agree with the writer, or do you notice any weaknesses in the writer's use of media, evidence, and counterarguments? Which argument is more substantial? To prepare for your debate, use the graphic organizer to write down your ideas about the prompt. Support your ideas with evidence from the text, referring to specific graphs, images, and examples. After your discussion you will write a reflection in the space below.

A Warrior's Daughter

FICTION
Zitkála-Šá
1921

Introduction

Zitkála-Šá, or Red Bird (1876–1938), was a Sioux writer and activist whose work appeared in *Harper's* and *Atlantic Monthly*. In much of her writing, Zitkála-Šá tells of her childhood struggles between her Native American heritage and the dominant culture. "A Warrior's Daughter" first appeared in *American Indian Stories*, a collection of allegorical fiction and childhood narratives to which Zitkála-Šá was a leading contributor. In "A Warrior's Daughter," she tells the story of a young Native American woman who shows admirable strength as she sets out to rescue her lover from captivity.

"This is the night of the dance."

1   IN THE afternoon shadow of a large tepee, with red-painted smoke lapels, sat a warrior father with crossed shins. His head was so **poised** that his eye swept easily the vast level land to the eastern horizon line.

2   He was the chieftain's bravest warrior. He had won by heroic deeds the privilege of staking his wigwam[1] within the great circle of tepees.

3   He was also one of the most generous gift givers to the toothless old people. For this he was entitled to the red-painted smoke lapels on his cone-shaped dwelling. He was proud of his honors. He never wearied of rehearsing nightly his own brave deeds. Though by wigwam fires he prated much of his high rank and widespread fame, his great joy was a wee black-eyed daughter of eight sturdy winters. Thus as he sat upon the soft grass, with his wife at his side, bent over her bead work, he was singing a dance song, and beat lightly the rhythm with his slender hands.

4   His shrewd eyes softened with pleasure as he watched the easy movements of the small body dancing on the green before him.

5   Tusee is taking her first dancing lesson. Her tightly-braided hair curves over both brown ears like a pair of crooked little horns which glisten in the summer sun.

6   With her snugly moccasined feet close together, and a wee hand at her belt to stay the long string of beads which hang from her bare neck, she bends her knees gently to the rhythm of her father's voice.

7   Now she ventures upon the earnest movement, slightly upward and sidewise, in a circle. At length the song drops into a closing **cadence**, and the little woman, clad in beaded deerskin, sits down beside the elder one. Like her mother, she sits upon her feet. In a brief moment the warrior repeats the last refrain. Again Tusee springs to her feet and dances to the swing of the few final measures.

---

1. **wigwam** a dome-shaped tent made by fastening material over a framework of poles, used by some North American Indigenous peoples

8   Just as the dance was finished, an elderly man, with short, thick hair loose about his square shoulders, rode into their presence from the rear, and leaped lightly from his pony's back.

9   Dropping the rawhide rein to the ground, he tossed himself lazily on the grass. "Hunhe, you have returned soon," said the warrior, while extending a hand to his little daughter.
Quickly the child ran to her father's side and cuddled close to him, while he tenderly placed a strong arm about her. Both father and child, eyeing the figure on the grass, waited to hear the man's report.

10 "It is true," began the man, with a stranger's accent. "This is the night of the dance."

11 "Hunha!" muttered the warrior with some surprise.

12 Propping himself upon his elbows, the man raised his face. His features were of the Southern type. From an enemy's camp he was taken captive long years ago by Tusee's father. But the unusual qualities of the slave had won the Sioux warrior's heart, and for the last three winters the man had had his freedom. He was made real man again. His hair was allowed to grow. However, he himself had chosen to stay in the warrior's family.

13 "Hunha!" again ejaculated the warrior father. Then turning to his little daughter, he asked,

14 "Tusee, do you hear that?"

15 "Yes, father, and I am going to dance tonight!"

16 With these words she bounded out of his arm and frolicked about in glee. Hereupon the proud mother's voice rang out in a chiding laugh.

17 "My child, in honor of your first dance your father must give a generous gift. His ponies are wild, and roam beyond the great hill. Pray, what has he fit to offer?" she questioned, the pair of puzzled eyes fixed upon her.

18 "A pony from the herd, mother, a fleet-footed pony from the herd!" Tusee shouted with sudden inspiration.

19 Pointing a small forefinger toward the man lying on the grass, she cried, "Uncle, you will go after the pony tomorrow!" And pleased with her solution of the problem, she skipped wildly about. Her childish faith in her elders was not conditioned by a knowledge of human limitations, but thought all things possible to grown-ups.

20 "Hähob!" exclaimed the mother, with a rising **inflection**, implying by the expletive that her child's **buoyant** spirit be not weighted with a denial.

21   Quickly to the hard request the man replied, "How! I go if Tusee tells me so!"

22   This delighted the little one, whose black eyes brimmed over with light. Standing in front of the strong man, she clapped her small, brown hands with joy.

23   "That makes me glad! My heart is good! Go, uncle, and bring a handsome pony!" she cried. In an instant she would have frisked away, but an impulse held her tilting where she stood. In the man's own tongue, for he had taught her many words and phrases, she exploded, "Thank you, good uncle, thank you!" then tore away from sheer excess of glee.

24   The proud warrior father, smiling and narrowing his eyes, muttered approval, "Howo! Hechetu!"

25   Like her mother, Tusee has finely pencilled eyebrows and slightly extended nostrils; but in her sturdiness of form she resembles her father.

26   A loyal daughter, she sits within her tepee making beaded deerskins for her father, while he longs to stave off her every suitor as all unworthy of his old heart's pride. But Tusee is not alone in her dwelling. Near the entrance-way a young brave is half reclining on a mat. In silence he watches the petals of a wild rose growing on the soft buckskin. Quickly the young woman slips the beads on the silvery sinew thread, and works them into the pretty flower design. Finally, in a low, deep voice, the young man begins:

27   "The sun is far past the zenith. It is now only a man's height above the western edge of land. I hurried hither to tell you tomorrow I join the war party."

28   He pauses for reply, but the maid's head drops lower over her deerskin, and her lips are more firmly drawn together. He continues:

29   "Last night in the moonlight I met your warrior father. He seemed to know I had just stepped forth from your tepee. I fear he did not like it, for though I greeted him, he was silent. I halted in his pathway. With what boldness I dared, while my heart was beating hard and fast, I asked him for his only daughter.

30   "Drawing himself erect to his tallest height, and gathering his loose robe more closely about his proud figure, he flashed a pair of piercing eyes upon me.

31   "'Young man,'" said he, with a cold, slow voice that chilled me to the marrow of my bones, 'hear me. Naught but an enemy's scalp-lock, plucked fresh with your own hand, will buy Tusee for your wife.' Then he turned on his heel and stalked away."

32   Tusee thrusts her work aside. With earnest eyes she scans her lover's face.

33 "My father's heart is really kind. He would know if you are brave and true," murmured the daughter, who wished no ill-will between her two loved ones.

34 Then rising to go, the youth holds out a right hand. "Grasp my hand once firmly before I go,
Hoye. Pray tell me, will you wait and watch for my return?"

35 Tusee only nods assent, for mere words are vain.

36 At early dawn the round camp-ground awakes into song. Men and women sing of bravery and of triumph. They inspire the swelling breasts of the painted warriors mounted on prancing ponies bedecked with the green branches of trees.

37 Riding slowly around the great ring of cone-shaped tepees, here and there, a loud-singing warrior swears to avenge a former wrong, and thrusts a bare brown arm against the purple east, calling the Great Spirit to hear his vow. All having made the circuit, the singing war party gallops away southward.

38 Astride their ponies laden with food and deerskins, brave elderly women follow after their warriors. Among the foremost rides a young woman in elaborately beaded buckskin dress.

39 Proudly mounted, she curbs with the single rawhide loop a wild-eyed pony.

40 It is Tusee on her father's warhorse. Thus the war party of Indian men and their faithful women vanish beyond the southern skyline.

41 A day's journey brings them very near the enemy's borderland. Nightfall finds a pair of twin tepees nestled in a deep ravine. Within one lounge the painted warriors, smoking their pipes and telling weird stories by the firelight, while in the other watchful women crouch uneasily about their center fire.

42 By the first gray light in the east the tepees are banished. They are gone. The warriors are in the enemy's camp, breaking dreams with their tomahawks. The women are hid away in secret places in the long thicketed ravine.

43 The day is far spent, the red sun is low over the west.

44 At length straggling warriors return, one by one, to the deep hollow. In the twilight they number their men. Three are missing. Of these absent ones two are dead; but the third one, a young man, is a captive to the foe.

45 "He-he!" lament the warriors, taking food in haste.

46 In silence each woman, with long strides, hurries to and fro, tying large bundles on her pony's back. Under cover of night the war party must hasten homeward. Motionless, with bowed head, sits a woman in her hiding-place. She grieves for her lover.

47   In bitterness of spirit she hears the warriors' murmuring words. With set teeth she plans to cheat the hated enemy of their captive. In the meanwhile low signals are given, and the war party, unaware of Tusee's absence, steal quietly away. The soft thud of pony-hoofs grows fainter and fainter. The gradual hush of the empty ravine whirrs noisily in the ear of the young woman. Alert for any sound of footfalls nigh, she holds her breath to listen. Her right hand rests on a long knife in her belt. Ah, yes, she knows where her pony is hid, but not yet has she need of him. Satisfied that no danger is nigh, she prowls forth from her place of hiding. With a panther's tread and pace she climbs the high ridge beyond the low ravine. From thence she spies the enemy's camp-fires.

48   Rooted to the barren bluff the slender woman's figure stands on the pinnacle of night, outlined against a starry sky. The cool night breeze wafts to her burning ear snatches of song and drum.

49   With desperate hate she bites her teeth.

50   Tusee beckons the stars to witness. With impassioned voice and uplifted face she pleads:

51   "Great Spirit, speed me to my lover's rescue! Give me swift cunning for a weapon this night! All-powerful Spirit, grant me my warrior-father's heart, strong to slay a foe and mighty to save a friend!"

52   In the midst of the enemy's camp-ground, underneath a temporary dance-house, are men and women in gala-day dress. It is late in the night, but the merry warriors bend and bow their nude, painted bodies before a bright center fire. To the lusty men's voices and the rhythmic throbbing drum, they leap and rebound with feathered headgears waving.

53   Women with red-painted cheeks and long, braided hair sit in a large half-circle against the willow railing. They, too, join in the singing, and rise to dance with their victorious warriors.

54   Amid this circular dance arena stands a prisoner bound to a post, haggard with shame and sorrow. He hangs his **disheveled** head.

55   He stares with unseeing eyes upon the bare earth at his feet. With jeers and smirking faces the dancers mock the Dakota captive. Rowdy braves and small boys hoot and yell in derision.
Silent among the noisy mob, a tall woman, leaning both elbows on the round willow railing, peers into the lighted arena. The dancing center fire shines bright into her handsome face, intensifying the night in her dark eyes. It breaks into myriad points upon her beaded dress. Unmindful of the surging throng jostling her at either side, she glares in upon the hateful, scoffing men. Suddenly she turns her head. Tittering maids whisper near her ear:

56 "There! There! See him now, sneering in the captive's face. 'Tis he who sprang upon the young man and dragged him by his long hair to yonder post. See! He is handsome! How gracefully he dances!"

57 The silent young woman looks toward the bound captive. She sees a warrior, scarce older than the captive, flourishing a tomahawk in the Dakota's face. A burning rage darts forth from her eyes and brands him for a victim of revenge. Her heart mutters within her breast, "Come, I wish to meet you, vile foe, who captured my lover and tortures him now with a living death."

58 Here the singers hush their voices, and the dancers scatter to their various resting-places along the willow ring. The victor gives a reluctant last twirl of his tomahawk, then, like the others, he leaves the center ground. With head and shoulders swaying from side to side, he carries a high-pointing chin toward the willow railing. Sitting down upon the ground with crossed legs, he fans himself with an outspread turkey wing.

59 Now and then he stops his haughty blinking to peep out of the corners of his eyes. He hears some one clearing her throat gently. It is unmistakably for his ear. The wing-fan swings irregularly to and fro. At length he turns a proud face over a bare shoulder and beholds a handsome woman smiling.

60 "Ah, she would speak to a hero!" thumps his heart wildly.

61 The singers raise their voices in **unison**. The music is irresistible. Again lunges the victor into the open arena. Again he leers into the captive's face. At every interval between the songs he returns to his resting-place. Here the young woman awaits him. As he approaches she smiles boldly into his eyes. He is pleased with her face and her smile.

62 Waving his wing-fan spasmodically in front of his face, he sits with his ears pricked up. He catches a low whisper. A hand taps him lightly on the shoulder. The handsome woman speaks to him in his own tongue. "Come out into the night. I wish to tell you who I am."

63 He must know what sweet words of praise the handsome woman has for him. With both hands he spreads the meshes of the loosely-woven willows, and crawls out unnoticed into the dark.

64 Before him stands the young woman. Beckoning him with a slender hand, she steps backward, away from the light and the restless throng of onlookers. He follows with impatient strides. She quickens her pace. He lengthens his strides. Then suddenly the woman turns from him and darts away with amazing speed. Clenching his fists and biting his lower lip, the young man runs after the fleeing woman. In his maddened pursuit he forgets the dance arena.

65 Beside a cluster of low bushes the woman halts. The young man, panting for breath and plunging headlong forward, whispers loud, "Pray tell me, are you a woman or an evil spirit to lure me away?"

66 Turning on heels firmly planted in the earth, the woman gives a wild spring forward, like a panther for its prey. In a husky voice she hissed between her teeth, "I am a Dakota woman!"
From her unerring long knife the enemy falls heavily at her feet. The Great Spirit heard Tusee's prayer on the hilltop. He gave her a warrior's strong heart to lessen the foe by one.

67 A bent old woman's figure, with a bundle like a grandchild slung on her back, walks round and round the dance-house. The wearied onlookers are leaving in twos and threes. The tired dancers creep out of the willow railing, and some go out at the entrance way, till the singers, too, rise from the drum and are trudging drowsily homeward. Within the arena the center fire lies broken in red embers. The night no longer lingers about the willow railing, but, hovering into the dance-house, covers here and there a snoring man whom sleep has overpowered where he sat.

68 The captive in his tight-binding rawhide ropes hangs in hopeless despair. Close about him the gloom of night is slowly crouching. Yet the last red, crackling embers cast a faint light upon his long black hair, and, shining through the thick mats, caress his wan face with undying hope.

69 Still about the dance-house the old woman prowls. Now the embers are gray with ashes.

70 The old bent woman appears at the entrance way. With a cautious, groping foot she enters.

71 Whispering between her teeth a lullaby for her sleeping child in her blanket, she searches for something forgotten.

72 Noisily snored the dreaming men in the darkest parts. As the lisping old woman draws nigh, the captive again opens his eyes.

73 A forefinger she presses to her lip. The young man arouses himself from his stupor. His senses belie him. Before his wide-open eyes the old bent figure straightens into its youthful stature. Tusee herself is beside him. With a stroke upward and downward she severs the cruel cords with her sharp blade. Dropping her blanket from her shoulders, so that it hangs from her girdled waist like a skirt, she shakes the large bundle into a light shawl for her lover. Quickly she spreads it over his bare back.

74 "Come!" she whispers, and turns to go; but the young man, numb and helpless, staggers nigh to falling.

75   The sight of his weakness makes her strong. A mighty power thrills her body. Stooping beneath his outstretched arms grasping at the air for support, Tusee lifts him upon her broad shoulders. With half-running, triumphant steps she carries him away into the open night.

✏ WRITE

PERSONAL RESPONSE: What do you think "A Warrior's Daughter" suggests about courage and determination? What cultivates those qualities in a leader? Consider the values and norms of the culture depicted in the story. Then write a response using textual evidence and original commentary to support your ideas.

Extended Writing Project and Grammar

EXTENDED WRITING PROJECT
ARGUMENTATIVE WRITING

Argumentative Writing Process: Plan

PLAN	DRAFT	REVISE	EDIT AND PUBLISH

Many leaders would say that they understand a truth that motivates them—something of which others may not be aware. The texts in this unit feature leaders who fight for ideals based on a truth, a set of facts that is motivating them.

WRITING PROMPT

What is one truth you are aware of that many members of your community don't know?

This could be a sad truth; for example, the water at your local beach is too polluted to swim in. Or it could be a happy truth; for example, the timid owner of a cleaning service left enough money in her will to fund two college scholarships. Write a persuasive essay with the intent of showing others how much this truth matters. If you are describing a problem that needs to be solved, include details about how the problem began and what could happen if it isn't solved. If you are calling attention to a valuable person or business, describe what the individual or business has contributed to the community. Arrange an interview with the figures involved and ask about their motivations. Be sure your persuasive essay includes the following:

- a thesis statement that makes a claim about the truth of something

- an explanation of how a problem arose or how a person or business succeeded

- vivid, energetic language that keeps readers involved

- a style that can heighten readers' emotions and make them accept your arguments

- a counterargument that you use to anticipate and defend against what readers opposed to your claim might say

- a strong conclusion that restates your position and gets readers on your side

Please note that excerpts and passages in the StudySync® library and this workbook are intended as touchstones to generate interest in an author's work. The excerpts and passages do not substitute for the reading of entire texts, and StudySync® strongly recommends that students seek out and purchase the whole literary or informational work in order to experience it as the author intended. Links to online resellers are available in our digital library. In addition, complete works may be ordered through an authorized reseller by filling out and returning to StudySync® the order form enclosed in this workbook.

Reading & Writing
Companion

509

Introduction to Argumentative Writing

Argumentative writing aims to persuade an audience to agree with a writer's point of view on a topic or issue. In an argumentative essay, a writer develops his or her argument and states a precise and informative claim. Then the writer provides relevant evidence and reasons to support it. Strong argumentative writing effectively uses genre characteristics and craft such as relevant evidence, rhetorical devices, and a clear organizational structure to persuade readers to accept and agree with the writer's claim. The characteristics of argumentative writing include:

- introduction

- thesis statement

- relevant evidence and reasons

- style and rhetorical devices

- transitions

- conclusion

In addition, argumentative writers carefully craft their work through the use of precise claims, counterarguments, and a strong, confident tone. The use of argumentative elements in an essay helps to make the text more persuasive. Effective arguments combine these genre characteristics and elements of the writer's craft to engage and convince the reader.

As you continue with this Extended Writing Project, you'll receive more instruction and practice in crafting each of the characteristics of argumentative writing to create your own argumentative essay.

Before you get started on your own argumentative essay, read this argumentative essay that one student, Kristen, wrote in response to the writing prompt. As you read the Model, highlight and annotate the features of argumentative writing that Kristen included in her argumentative essay.

☰ STUDENT MODEL

The Man in the House on Third Street

1 Everyone knows the old adage "You can't judge a book by its cover." Although this may be true, these words seldom stop people from making snap judgements based on appearances. We often base our first impressions on the way a person looks, but appearances can be deceiving. In my neighborhood, there is one house that everyone avoids. The lawn is overrun with tall grass and weeds. The owner's somber face discourages anyone who happens to walk by. Mr. Jenkins looks like a cranky, antisocial loner, but the truth is he's one of the bravest, most selfless men you'll ever meet—and he needs our help.

2 I first met Mr. Jenkins when I was selling tickets for my high school's drama club. I'd heard nasty rumors about the old man, so my breath caught in my throat as I knocked on his door. When he asked who I was, his gravelly voice sent a chill down my spine. After I told him about the drama club, though, a bright smile appeared on his face. He explained that his late wife loved musicals and invited me to talk more about how he could help. It turns out that Mr. Jenkins is a sweet, generous man who lost his wife in a car accident and has simply kept to himself ever since. His house and clothes are shabby because his military pension is small and he doesn't like spending money on himself. The more Mr. Jenkins shared about his life— stories about his marriage, his experiences overseas during the Korean War, and his loneliness—the more certain I became that everyone in the community needs to band together to help this wonderful man.

3 One problem with Mr. Jenkins's current situation is the most obvious to outsiders: his home needs immediate attention. Anyone who doesn't already know Mr. Jenkins could be easily scared away by the foot-tall grass in his yard. While it is true that maintenance is the homeowner's responsibility, the community must keep in mind that

the curb appeal of one home can affect the whole neighborhood. Most buyers are reluctant to purchase a home that looks unattractive. Some will even decide not to buy a home that is located near such an eyesore. On the other hand, people will pay more for a home that looks nice from the outside. As a matter of fact, doing a simple repair or planting some flowers can actually increase a home's suggested value. Consequently, property values in the whole neighborhood could improve if some local teenagers volunteered to mow the lawn regularly and plant some easy-to-maintain flowers. Community service is a graduation requirement at the local high school, so this act of kindness would help the teenagers and Mr. Jenkins alike. Plus, it would begin to build a relationship between Mr. Jenkins and the community.

4   Another problem Mr. Jenkins faces is a struggle to afford healthy food and quality clothing. Most of his pension is used to pay for healthcare costs, property taxes, and other monthly bills. Living on a fixed income makes it harder for older Americans like Mr. Jenkins to face unexpected costs or splurge on more expensive items. When I spoke with Mr. Jenkins, he mentioned that he usually uses the same canned or frozen ingredients to prepare all of his daily meals because it's cheap and easy. He may say that he doesn't mind the gastronomic redundancy, but it is heartbreaking to imagine him alone in his kitchen eating the same bland meal for breakfast, lunch, and dinner. Don't our senior citizens deserve better? Local families could help by sharing their meals with Mr. Jenkins. In addition, we could organize a neighborhood food and clothing drive to support Mr. Jenkins and other members of the community who struggle to make ends meet. Some may argue that since Mr. Jenkins is a veteran, the government is responsible for finding ways to assist him. Whereas there are several government programs designed to help veterans, funding and other support can be limited. Despite their best efforts to serve the community, these programs often have long wait lists, leaving veterans without the immediate assistance they need. Mr. Jenkins and others like him need our help now.

5   Even if a neighbor does not have extra food or clothing to offer, there is one key way that he or she can help Mr. Jenkins: spend time with him. Ever since Mrs. Jenkins passed away, Mr. Jenkins has had few visitors. Most of his days are passed in lonely silence. I learned so

much from Mr. Jenkins in the few hours I spent with him as he spoke eloquently about patriotic duty and sacrifice. I knew the facts about the Korean War, but I had no idea what it was like to risk your life in service of others. His words were moving and inspiring; they made me realize how much veterans like Mr. Jenkins give up in service to our country. It is our duty as Americans to honor veterans for their service. Mr. Jenkins devoted his life to serving others and never asked for anything in return. Mr. Jenkins says that he does not want to be a burden on the neighborhood, but spending time with such a man is far from burdensome; it's a privilege. We all should be proud to step up and help him.

6   Some truths are easy to see. You can look at the sky and tell if it's sunny or raining. Others are harder to divine. You can't intuit a person's whole story with one passing glance. The only way you can learn the truth of a person's experience is to sit down with him or her and listen. To many people in my community, Mr. Jenkins is the weird old man in the creepy house at the end of Third Street. But after spending an afternoon with him, I know the truth. Once other neighbors move beyond their flawed first impressions and spend some time with him, they will, too.

✏ WRITE

Writers often take notes about their ideas before they sit down to write. Think about what you've learned so far about argumentative writing to help you begin prewriting.

- **Purpose and Focus:** What topic do you want to write about, and why don't most people know about it?

- **Audience:** Who is your audience, and what idea do you want to express to them?

- **Introduction:** How will you introduce your topic? How will you engage an audience and preview what you plan to argue in your essay?

- **Thesis Statement:** What is your claim about the topic? How can you word your claim so it is clear to readers?

- **Reasons and Relevant Evidence:** What evidence will you use to support your claim? What facts, details, examples, and quotations will persuade your audience to agree with your claim?

- **Style:** What kinds of techniques and language will you use to persuade your audience? How can you appeal to your audience's sense of logic and emotions and gain their trust?

- **Transitions:** How will you smoothly transition from one idea to another within and across paragraphs?

- **Conclusion:** How will you wrap up your argument? How can you restate the main ideas in your argument without being redundant?

Response Instructions

Use the questions in the bulleted list to write a one-paragraph summary. Your summary should describe what you will argue in your argumentative essay.

Don't worry about including all of the details now; focus only on the most essential and important elements. You will refer to this short summary as you continue through the steps of the writing process.

Skill: Organizing Argumentative Writing

••• CHECKLIST FOR ORGANIZING ARGUMENTATIVE WRITING

As you consider how to organize your writing for your argumentative essay, use the following questions as a guide:

- What thesis statement will I provide in my introduction to introduce my claim?

- What other kinds of evidence could I find that would support my claim?

- What other types of information could I look for to establish the significance of my claim?

- Is there another approach I could use to distinguish my claim from any alternate or opposing claims?

- Did I choose an organizational structure that establishes clear relationships between claims and counterclaims?

Follow these steps to organize your argumentative essay in a way that logically sequences claim(s), counterclaims, reasons, and evidence:

- identify your precise, or specific, claim or claims and the evidence that supports them

- establish the significance of your claim

  > find what others may have written about the topic, and learn why they feel it is important

  > look for possible consequences or complications if something is done or is not accomplished

- distinguish the claim or claims from alternate or opposing claims

- find evidence that distinguishes counterclaims from your own claim

- choose an organizational structure that logically sequences and establishes clear relationships among claims, counterclaims, and the evidence presented to support your claims

YOUR TURN

Read the claims below. Then, complete the chart by writing the organizational structure that would best convey the ideas of each claim.

Organizational Structure Options			
compare and contrast	problem and solution	cause and effect	list advantages and disadvantages

Claim	Organizational Structure
Deep cuts to the federal budget will result in problems at the state and local levels.	
Athletes suffering from season-ending injuries may benefit from alternative medicine.	
The candidates running for school board president have more in common than parents may think.	
Dual language programs in elementary schools have proven to be both successful and challenging.	

↻ YOUR TURN

Complete the chart below by writing a short summary of what you will focus on in each section of your essay.

Outline	Summary
Introductory Statement	
Thesis	
How You Learned the Truth	
Body Paragraph 1	
Body Paragraph 2	
Body Paragraph 3	
Conclusion	

Skill:
Thesis Statement

••• CHECKLIST FOR THESIS STATEMENT

Before you begin writing your thesis statement, ask yourself the following questions:

- What is the prompt asking me to write about?
- What claim do I want to make about the topic of this essay?
- Is my claim precise and informative? How is it specific to my topic?
- How does my claim inform the reader about my topic?
- Does my thesis statement introduce the body of my essay?
- Where should I place my thesis statement?

Here are some methods to introduce and develop a topic as well as a precise and informative claim:

- think about your central claim of your essay
  - > identify a clear claim you want to introduce, thinking about:
    - o how closely your claim is related to your topic and how specific it is to your supporting details
    - o how your claim includes necessary information to guide the reader through your argument
- identify as many claims as you intend to prove
- write a thesis statement that lets the reader anticipate the content of your essay

Copyright © BookheadEd Learning, LLC

⟳ YOUR TURN

Read the sentences below. Then, complete the chart by sorting the sentences into two categories: effective thesis statements and ineffective thesis statements. Write the corresponding letter for each sentence in the appropriate column.

	Sentence Options
A	"Self-Made Men" recognizes that a man's success is intertwined with the success of those that came before him.
B	Swift uses irony and exaggeration to convey his message about European governments.
C	Douglass references the American dream in his speech.
D	"The Federalist Papers: No. 10" demonstrates that being true to your ideals is important.
E	Madison helped form our government.
F	*Gulliver's Travels* is about a man that gets shipwrecked in a strange land.

Effective Thesis Statement	Ineffective Thesis Statement

YOUR TURN

Write a thesis statement for each topic below. Remember to keep your thesis statements related to the topics.

Topic	Thesis Statement
Is school lunch healthy?	
Is college today affordable?	
Are objects or experiences more valuable?	

 WRITE

Use the questions in the checklist to plan and write your thesis statement.

Skill:
Reasons and Relevant Evidence

••• CHECKLIST FOR REASONS AND RELEVANT EVIDENCE

As you determine what reasons and relevant evidence you will need, use the following questions as a guide:

- What is my claim (or claims)? What are the strengths and limitations of my claim(s)?

- Have I presented more than one counterclaim (another claim that attempts to disprove the opposing opinion) from a credible source?

  - > What is the effect on the argument?

  - > What are the strengths and limitations of the counterclaim(s)?

  - > How might the counterclaim strengthen my claim?

- What relevant evidence do I have? Where could I add more support for my claim(s)?

- What do I know about the audience's:

  - > knowledge about my topic?

  - > concerns and values?

  - > possible biases about the subject matter?

Use the following steps to help you develop claims and counterclaims fairly and thoroughly:

- establish a claim and counterclaim and then evaluate:

  - > strengths and limitations of both

  - > any biases you have toward both

  - > any gaps in support for your claim(s), so that your support can be more thorough

- find the most relevant evidence that supports the claim and counterclaim

- consider your audience and their perspective on your topic. Determine:

  - > their probable prior knowledge about the topic

  - > their concerns and values

  - > any biases they may have toward the subject matter

  - > how you will approach your claim(s) to ensure your audience is engaged and has the background knowledge they need

↻ YOUR TURN

Read each claim in the chart below. Then, for each claim, complete the chart by writing the corresponding letter for a strength, limitation, and piece of relevant evidence in the appropriate column.

Strengths, Limitations, and Relevant Evidence Options	
A	Most children participate in video games on their own, with little to no interaction.
B	There are heartbreaking, accurate accounts of news events and honest personal stories.
C	School lunches vary depending on what is grown at school and what can be sourced locally.
D	With food allergies on the rise and children's food preferences varying from vegan to vegetarian, etc., school lunches should mirror science and the preferences of American school children today.
E	Everyone has had a school lunch they didn't eat or like.
F	31% of children or teenagers have shared a fake news story online.
G	Some children communicate with their peers and strategize during and after video game play.
H	Many people share only good times, making everyone think they live a perfect life.
I	Many effects of video games are still unknown, but American parents should be concerned that video games are known to make kids more aggressive and feel less inclined to socialize.

Claim	Strength	Limitation	Relevant Evidence
School lunches need to be improved.			
Video games isolate children.			
Most of what is posted on social media is not true.			

↻ YOUR TURN

Complete the chart by identifying the strengths, limitations, and relevant evidence for the counterclaims you will use to strengthen the argument in your essay.

Counterclaim	Strength	Limitation	Relevant Evidence

Argumentative Writing Process: Draft

| PLAN | DRAFT | REVISE | EDIT AND PUBLISH |

You have already made progress toward writing your argumentative essay. Now it is time to draft your argumentative essay.

✎ WRITE

Use your plan and other responses in your Binder to draft your argumentative essay. You may also have new ideas as you begin drafting. Feel free to explore those new ideas as you have them. You can also ask yourself these questions to ensure that your writing is focused and organized and has relevant evidence and elaboration to support your claim:

Draft Checklist:

☐ **Purpose and Focus:** Have I clearly stated my argument for readers? Have I included only relevant supporting evidence and nothing extraneous that might confuse my readers?

☐ **Organization:** Does the organizational structure in my essay make sense? Will readers be engaged by the organization and convinced by the way I present evidence? Does my writing flow together naturally, or is it choppy? Will my readers be able to easily follow and understand my ideas?

☐ **Evidence and Elaboration:** Where have I provided reasons and relevant evidence to support my claim?

Before you submit your draft, read it over carefully. You want to be sure that you've responded to all aspects of the prompt.

Here is Kristen's argumentative essay draft. As you read, notice how Kristen develops her draft to be focused and organized, with relevant evidence and elaboration to support her claim. As she continues to revise and edit her argumentative essay, she will find and improve weak spots in her writing, as well as correct any language or punctuation mistakes.

☰ STUDENT MODEL: FIRST DRAFT

NOTES

~~We often base our first impressions on the way a person looks but appearances can be deceiving. In my neighborhood, there is one house that every one avoids. The lawn is overrun with tall grass and weeds. The owner's sullen face discourages anyone who happens to walk by. He looks like a cranky, antisocial loner but the truth is he's one of the bravest, most selfless men you'll ever meet and he needs our help.~~

Everyone knows the old adage "You can't judge a book by its cover." Although this may be true, these words seldom stop people from making snap judgements based on appearances. We often base our first impressions on the way a person looks, but appearances can be deceiving. In my neighborhood, there is one house that everyone avoids. The lawn is overrun with tall grass and weeds. The owner's somber face discourages anyone who happens to walk by. Mr. Jenkins looks like a cranky, antisocial loner, but the truth is he's one of the bravest, most selfless men you'll ever meet—and he needs our help.

I first met Mr. Jenkins when I was selling tickets for my high school's drama club. I'd heard nasty rumors about him so my breath caught in my throat. When he asked who I was, his gravelly voice sent a chill down my spine. After I told him about the drama club, he explained that his late wife loved musicals and invited me to talk more about how he could help. It turns out that Mr. Jenkins is a sweet, generous man who lost his wife in a car accident. His house and clothes is shabby because his military pension is small and he doesn't like spending money on himself. The more Mr. Jenkins shared about his life, stories about his marriage, his experiances overseas during the Korean War, and his loneliness, the more I knew about him.

~~One problem with Mr. Jenkins's current situation is the most obvious to outsiders. His home needs immediate attention. Anyone who~~

Skill:
Introductions

Kristen wants to make her introduction more engaging. So she adds a strong hook to introduce her ideas about how appearances can be deceiving.

Reading & Writing
Companion

NOTES

Skill:
Transitions

Kristen realizes her paragraph should be more coherent. She adds transition words and phrases like on the other hand, as a matter of fact, *and* consequently *to create clear links between her ideas.*

~~don't already know Mr. Jenkins could be easily scared away by the foot-tall grass in his yard. While it is true that maintenance is the homeowner's responsibility the community must keep in mind that the curb appeal of one home can affect the whole neighborhood. Most buyers are reluctant to purchase a home that looks unattractive. Some will even decide not to buy a home that is located near such an eyesore. People will pay more for a home that looks nice from the outside. Doing a simple repair or planting some flowers can actually increase a home's suggested value. Property values in the whole neighborhood could improve if some local teenagers volunteered to mow the lawn regularly and plant some easy-to-maintain flowers. Community service is a graduation requirement at the local high school, so this act of kindness would help the teenagers and Mr. Jenkins alike. It would begin to build a relationship between Mr. Jenkins and the community.~~

One problem with Mr. Jenkins's current situation is the most obvious to outsiders: his home needs immediate attention. Anyone who doesn't already know Mr. Jenkins could be easily scared away by the foot-tall grass in his yard. While it is true that maintenance is the homeowner's responsibility, the community must keep in mind that the curb appeal of one home can affect the whole neighborhood. Most buyers are reluctant to purchase a home that looks unattractive. Some will even decide not to buy a home that is located near such an eyesore. On the other hand, people will pay more for a home that looks nice from the outside. As a matter of fact, doing a simple repair or planting some flowers can actually increase a home's suggested value. Consequently, property values in the whole neighborhood could improve if some local teenagers volunteered to mow the lawn regularly and plant some easy-to-maintain flowers. Community service is a graduation requirement at the local high school, so this act of kindness would help the teenagers and Mr. Jenkins alike. Plus, it would begin to build a relationship between Mr. Jenkins and the community.

A problem Mr. Jenkins faces is a struggle to afford healthy food and quality clothing. The problem is that most of his pension is used to pay for healthcare costs property taxes and other monthly bills. Another problem is that fixed income makes it harder for older Americans to face unexpected costs or splurge on more expensive items. When I spoke with Mr. Jenkins he mentioned that he usually uses the same ingredients to prepare all of his daily meals because it's cheep and easy. Local families could help by sharing their meals with Mr. Jenkins. In addition, we could organize a neighborhood food and clothing drive to help Mr. Jenkins and other members of the community who struggle to make ends meet. Mr. Jenkins and others like him need our help now.

Even if a neighbor does not have extra food or clothing to offer there is one key way that he or she can help Mr. Jenkins. Spend time with him. Ever since Mrs. Jenkins passed away, Mr. Jenkins has had few visitors. I learned so much from Mr. Jenkins in the few hours I spent with him. I knew the facts about the Korean War. I had no idea what it was like to risk your life in service of others. It is our duty as Americans to honor veterans for their service. His words were moving and inspiring, they made me realize how much veterans like Mr. Jenkins give up in service to our country. Mr. Jenkins devoted his life to serving others and never asked for anything in return. Mr. Jenkins say that he does not want to be a burden on the neighborhood, but spending time with such a man is far from burdensome, it's a privilege. We all should be glad to step up and help him.

~~To many people in my community, Mr. Jenkins is the weird old man in the creepy house at the end of Third Street. I took time out to get to know him. I know better.~~

Some truths are easy to see. You can look at the sky and tell if it's sunny or raining. Others are harder to divine. You can't intuit a person's whole story with one passing glance. The only way you can learn the truth of a person's experience is to sit down with him or her and listen. To many people in my community, Mr. Jenkins is the weird old man in the creepy house at the end of Third Street. But after spending an afternoon with him, I know the truth. Once other neighbors move beyond their flawed first impressions and spend some time with him, they will, too.

 Skill:
Conclusions

Kristen wants to strengthen her conclusion. She rephrases her ideas to reinforce the importance of the community's coming together to get to know and help Mr. Jenkins.

Please note that excerpts and passages in the StudySync® library and this workbook are intended as touchstones to generate interest in an author's work. The excerpts and passages do not substitute for the reading of entire texts, and StudySync® strongly recommends that students seek out and purchase the whole literary or informational work in order to experience it as the author intended. Links to online resellers are available in our digital library. In addition, complete works may be ordered through an authorized reseller by filling out and returning to StudySync® the order form enclosed in this workbook.

Reading & Writing Companion   527

Skill:
Introductions

••• CHECKLIST FOR INTRODUCTIONS

Before you write your introduction, ask yourself the following questions:

- What is my claim? In addition:

  > How can I make it more precise and informative?

  > Have I included why my claim is significant to discuss? How does it help the reader understand the topic better? What does it contribute to the conversation on my topic?

  > How can I distinguish my claim from alternate or opposing claims?

- How can I introduce my topic? Have I organized complex ideas, concepts, and information so that each new element builds on the previous element and creates a unified whole?

- How will you "hook" your reader's interest? You might:

  > start with an attention-grabbing statement

  > begin with an intriguing question

  > use descriptive words to set a scene

Below are two strategies to help you introduce your precise claim and topic clearly in your introduction:

- Peer Discussion

  > talk about your topic with a partner, explaining what you already know and your ideas about your topic

  > write notes about the ideas you have discussed and any new questions you may have

  > review your notes, and think about what your claim or controlling idea will be

  > briefly state your precise and informative claim, establishing why it is important—or what ideas you are contributing to your topic—and how it is different from other claims about your topic

  > write a possible "hook"

- Freewriting

  > freewrite for 10 minutes about your topic. Don't worry about grammar, punctuation, or having fully formed ideas. The point of freewriting is to discover ideas

  > review your notes, and think about what your claim or controlling idea will be

  > briefly state your precise and informative claim, establishing why it is important—or what ideas you are contributing to your topic—and how it is different from other claims about your topic

  > write a possible "hook"

YOUR TURN

In order to improve the draft of her introductory paragraph below, Kristen considers alternative "hooks" to engage her readers. Which of the following sentences would be the best alternative to start her introduction?

> We often base our first impressions on the way a person looks but appearances can be deceiving. In my neighborhood, there is one house that every one avoids. The lawn is overrun with tall grass and weeds. The owner's sullen face discourages anyone who happens to walk by. He looks like a cranky, antisocial loner but the truth is he's one of the bravest, most selfless men you'll ever meet and he needs our help.

- ○ A. Why are lawns such an important part of our community spirit and neighborhood beauty?
- ○ B. Due to the wet weather, the grass in our neighborhood is overgrown.
- ○ C. Vets are neglected.
- ○ D. Have you ever felt like people are judging you without really knowing you?

Please note that excerpts and passages in the StudySync® library and this workbook are intended as touchstones to generate interest in an author's work. The excerpts and passages do not substitute for the reading of entire texts, and StudySync® strongly recommends that students seek out and purchase the whole literary or informational work in order to experience it as the author intended. Links to online resellers are available in our digital library. In addition, complete works may be ordered through an authorized reseller by filling out and returning to StudySync® the order form enclosed in this workbook.

Reading & Writing
Companion

529

↻ YOUR TURN

Read the statements below. Then, match each statement with the correct essay component listed in the chart. Write the corresponding letter for each statement in the chart.

Statement Options	
A	Last year, a study estimated that around eight million metric tons of our plastic waste enter the oceans each year.
B	Indeed, the water bottle you just tossed in the street might end up in your local waterway.
C	Our oceans are dirty.
D	Plastics, pollution, and our carelessness are killing our waterways and the different species that inhabit them.
E	Did you know that some of your garbage is killing our oceans, lakes, and seas?

Essay Component	Statement
Claim	
Hook	
Thesis Statement	
Relevant Evidence	
Transition Sentence	

✏ WRITE

Use the questions in the checklist to revise the introduction of your argumentative essay.

Skill:
Transitions

••• CHECKLIST FOR TRANSITIONS

Before you revise your current draft to include transitions, think about:

- the key ideas you discuss in your body paragraphs
- the relationships among your claim(s), reasons, and evidence
- the relationship between your claim(s) and counterclaims
- the logical progression of your argument

Next, reread your current draft and note areas in your essay where:

- the relationships among your claim(s), counterclaims, and the reasons and evidence are unclear

- you could add linking words, vary sentence structure (or syntax), or include other transitional devices to make your argument more cohesive. Look for:

  > sudden jumps between your ideas

  > breaks between paragraphs where the ideas in the next paragraph are not logically following from the previous one

  > repetitive sentence structures

Revise your draft to use words, phrases, and clauses as well as varied syntax to link the major sections of the text, create cohesion, and clarify the relationships between claim(s) and reasons, between reasons and evidence, and between claim(s) and counterclaims, using the following questions as a guide:

- Are there unifying relationships between the claims, reasons, and the evidence I present in my argument?
- How do my claim(s) and counterclaim relate?
- Have I clarified, or made clear, these relationships?
- How can I link major sections of my essay using words, phrases, clauses, and varied syntax?

YOUR TURN

Choose the best answer to each question.

1. Below is a section from a previous draft of Kristen's essay. The connection between her claim, reasons, and evidence in the second and third sentences is unclear. What transition should Kristen add to the beginning of the third sentence to make her writing more coherent and appropriate for the purpose, topic, and context of her essay, as well as her audience?

> (1) No one expects to solve all of Mr. Jenkins's problems overnight. (2) Renovating a yard and planning a food and clothing drive can take weeks. (3) We can help Mr. Jenkins in simpler ways. (4) We can be his friends.

   ○ A. Particularly
   ○ B. As a result
   ○ C. In the meantime
   ○ D. Eventually

2. Below is a section from a previous draft of Kristen's essay. In the underlined sentence, Kristen did not use an appropriate transition to show the relationship between paragraphs. Which transition is the best replacement for the word *Likewise*? Choose the transition that makes her writing more coherent and is the most appropriate for the purpose, topic, and context of her essay, as well as her audience.

> Everyone needs help at one time or another. A strength of this community is the way we band together and help each other.
>
> Likewise, half of the residents of Maple Avenue pitched in to dig Mrs. Smith's car out of the snowbank last January. Each summer, community members volunteer as lifeguards at the local pool. If we can come together to support each other in these ways, why can't we help Mr. Jenkins?

   ○ A. For instance
   ○ B. Given these points
   ○ C. To say nothing of
   ○ D. Although this may be true

✎ **WRITE**

Use the questions in the checklist to revise your use of transitions in a section of your argumentative essay.

Skill:
Conclusions

••• CHECKLIST FOR CONCLUSIONS

Before you write your conclusion, ask yourself the following questions:

- How can I rephrase the thesis or main idea in my concluding section or statement? What impression can I make on my reader?

- How can I write my conclusion so that it supports and follows logically from my argument?

- Should I include a call to action?

- How can I conclude with a memorable comment?

Below are two strategies to help you provide a concluding statement or section that follows from and supports the argument presented:

- Peer Discussion

  > After you have written your introduction and body paragraphs, talk with a partner and tell them what you want readers to remember, writing notes about your discussion.

  > Review your notes, and think about what you wish to express in your conclusion.

  > Do not simply restate your claim or thesis statement. Rephrase your main idea to show the depth of your knowledge and the importance of your idea, and encourage readers to adopt your view.

  > Write your conclusion.

- Freewriting

  > Freewrite for 10 minutes about what you might include in your conclusion. Don't worry about grammar, punctuation, or having fully formed ideas. The point of freewriting is to discover ideas.

  > Review your notes, and think about what you wish to express in your conclusion.

  > Do not simply restate your claim or thesis statement. Rephrase your main idea to show the depth of your knowledge and the importance of your idea, and encourage readers to adopt your view.

  > Write your conclusion.

YOUR TURN

Choose the best answer to each question about Kristen's draft of her essay (see the Draft lesson).

1. Which of the following would be the most appropriate memorable comment to conclude Kristen's argumentative essay?

   ○ A. I've been wrong about many people and things in my life before. Mr. Jenkins serves as a reminder to be a better neighbor.

   ○ B. Be part of the solution, not the problem.

   ○ C. Neighbors need to stop making excuses and do what is right.

   ○ D. Who knows why things happen as they do. I know I met Mr. Jenkins for a reason.

2. Kristen considers starting her conclusion with the sentence "Veterans are the most important group for us to help in our community." Why would this not be the best opening sentence for her conclusion?

   ○ A. There is no evidence that there is a need to support veterans in her community.

   ○ B. It does not logically follow from and support her argument.

   ○ C. This statement excludes other groups in the community.

   ○ D. There are not enough veterans in the community to warrant her claim.

 WRITE

Use the questions in the checklist to revise the conclusion of your argumentative essay.

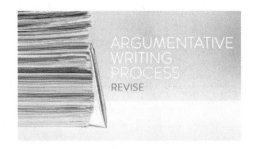

Argumentative Writing Process: Revise

PLAN	DRAFT	REVISE	EDIT AND PUBLISH

You have written a draft of your argumentative essay. You have also received input from your peers about how to improve it. Now you are going to revise your draft.

← REVISION GUIDE

Examine your draft to find areas for revision. Use the guide below to help you review:

Review	Revise	Example
Clarity		
Highlight a sentence in each paragraph that reminds the reader of your purpose in this essay.	Make sure the purpose is clear for your audience throughout the essay.	The more Mr. Jenkins shared about his life, stories about his marriage, his experiances overseas during the Korean War, and his loneliness, the more I knew about him. certain I became that everyone in the community needs to band together to help this wonderful man.
Development		
Identify the reasons that support your claim. Annotate places where you don't feel your reasoning is clearly explained.	Make sure you provide any information the audience may need to understand your argument.	Even if a neighbor does not have extra food or clothing to offer there is one key way that he or she can help Mr. Jenkins. Spend time with him. Ever since Mrs. Jenkins passed away, Mr. Jenkins has had few visitors. Most of his days are passed in lonely silence.

Review	Revise	Example
Organization		
Review your body paragraphs. Are they coherent? Identify and annotate any sentences within and across paragraphs that don't flow in a clear and logical way.	Rewrite the sentences so they appear in a clear and logical order.	~~It is our duty as Americans to honor veterans for their service.~~ His words were moving and inspiring, they made me realize how much veterans like Mr. Jenkins give up in service to our country. It is our duty as Americans to honor veterans for their service. Mr. Jenkins devoted his life to serving others and never asked for anything in return.
Style: Word Choice		
Identify any weak adjectives or verbs.	Replace weak adjectives and verbs with strong, descriptive adjectives and verbs.	In addition, we could organize a neighborhood food and clothing drive to ~~help~~ support Mr. Jenkins and other members of the community who struggle to make ends meet.
Style: Sentence Fluency		
Read aloud your writing and listen to the way the text sounds. Does it sound choppy? Or does it flow smoothly with rhythm, movement, and emphasis on important details and events?	Rewrite a key passage, making your sentences longer or shorter to achieve a better flow of writing and the effect you want your reader to feel.	To many people in my community, Mr. Jenkins is the weird old man in the creepy house at the end of Third Street. ~~I took time out to get to know him. I know better.~~ But after spending an afternoon with him, I know the truth. Once other neighbors move beyond their flawed first impressions and spend some time with him, they will, too.

✏ WRITE

Use the revision guide, as well as your peer reviews, to help you evaluate your argumentative essay to determine areas that should be revised.

 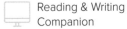

Skill:
Style

••• CHECKLIST FOR STYLE

First, reread the draft of your argumentative essay and identify the following:

- slang, colloquialisms, contractions, abbreviations, or a conversational tone
- places where you could use subject-specific or academic language in order to help persuade or inform your readers
- places where you could vary sentence structure and length, emphasizing compound, complex, and compound-complex sentences

   > for guidance on effective ways of varying syntax, reference a style guide

- statements that express judgment or emotion, rather than a balanced tone that relies on facts and evidence
- incorrect uses of the conventions of standard English for grammar, spelling, capitalization, and punctuation

Establish and maintain a formal style in your essay, using the following questions as a guide:

- Have I used a colloquial tone when appropriate and academic language when demonstrating my expertise and appealing to my reader's logic and reasoning?
- Have I used a consistent and strategic perspective (i.e., first person when describing personal experiences)?
- Have I maintained a balanced tone even when expressing my own judgments and emotions?
- Have I used varied sentence lengths and different sentence structures? Did I consider using reference sources to learn about effective ways of varying syntax?

   > Where should I make some sentences longer by using conjunctions to connect independent clauses, dependent clauses, and phrases?

   > Where should I make some sentences shorter by separating independent clauses?

- Did I follow the conventions of standard English?

Please note that excerpts and passages in the StudySync® library and this workbook are intended as touchstones to generate interest in an author's work. The excerpts and passages do not substitute for the reading of entire texts, and StudySync® strongly recommends that students seek out and purchase the whole literary or informational work in order to experience it as the author intended. Links to online resellers are available in our digital library. In addition, complete works may be ordered through an authorized reseller by filling out and returning to StudySync® the order form enclosed in this workbook.

Reading & Writing   537
Companion

⟳ YOUR TURN

Choose the best answer to each question.

1. Below is a section from another draft of Kristen's essay. How can she rewrite the underlined sentence to eliminate slang and non-academic language?

> Living on a dime makes it harder for older Americans. <u>When I chatted with Mr. Jenkins he mentioned that he usually uses the same ingredients to prepare all of his daily meals, which is mind-boggling to me.</u>

   ○ A. When I spoke with Mr. Jenkins he mentioned that he usually uses the same ingredients to prepare all of his daily meals, which is unsanitary.

   ○ B. When I spoke with Mr. Jenkins he mentioned that he usually uses the same ingredients to prepare all of his daily meals, which is mind-numbing to me.

   ○ C. When I spoke with Mr. Jenkins he mentioned that he usually uses the same ingredients to prepare all of his daily meals, which is perplexing to me.

   ○ D. When I chatted with Mr. Jenkins he mentioned that he usually uses the same ingredients to prepare all of his daily meals, which disturbed me.

2. Referring to a style guide, Kristen finds that the passive voice is not often used in academic writing because it makes the actor of the sentence unclear. How can she change the sentence below from the passive to the active voice?

> Mr. Jenkins's yard was populated by weeds.

   ○ A. The yard was not maintained by Mr. Jenkins.

   ○ B. Mr. Jenkins was blamed by his neighbors for neglecting his yard.

   ○ C. Weeds populated Mr. Jenkins's yard.

   ○ D. The yard was choked with weeds.

✎ WRITE

Use the checklist to revise a paragraph of your argumentative essay to improve the style.

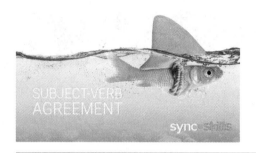

Grammar:
Subject-Verb Agreement

Every verb must agree with its subject in person and in number. The verb names an action or state of being; the subject tells what the sentence or clause is about.

A subject's **person** and **number** tell whether the sentence is about the speaker or writer (*I*), about the listener or reader (*you*), or about someone or something else (*he, she,* or *it*) and whether the subject is singular or plural. The form of a verb is determined by the person and number of its subject.

Most verbs have different forms only in the present tense and only for the third-person singular, when *-s* or *-es* is added to the base verb. Otherwise, the forms of the verbs are the same within each tense, regardless of the subject's person and number.

The linking verb *be* is an exception. It changes form in both the present and past tenses. The auxiliary verbs *be*, *have*, and *do* change form in verb phrases to show agreement with third-person subjects.

Text	Explanation
I grieve and **dare not show** my discontent . . . On Monsieur's Departure	When the subject is first-person singular, the verb is the regular form for that tense.
For all of that, **Captain Marvel is** a great character. DC Comics: Sixty Years of the World's Favorite Comic Book Heroes	When the subject is third-person singular, the correct form of *be* in the present tense is *is*.
Goody Cloyse, that excellent old Christian, **stood** in the early sunshine at her own lattice, catechizing a little girl who had brought her a pint of morning's milk. Young Goodman Brown	In the third-person singular, past tense, the verb does not change from its usual form. *Stood* is the past tense for *stand,* whatever the number and person of the subject.
Yet this **inconstancy is** such As **you** too **shall adore**; **I could not love** thee, Dear, so much, **Loved I** not Honor more. To Lucasta, Going to the Wars	Subject-verb agreement must be maintained within clauses, but the tense can change more than once within a sentence.

↻ YOUR TURN

1. How should this sentence be changed?

> These days a highly skilled multimedia creator have the tools to imagine and animate personal, highly idiosyncratic superheroes.

- ○ A. These days a highly skilled multimedia creator has the tools to imagine and animate personal, highly idiosyncratic superheroes.
- ○ B. These days a highly skilled multimedia creator have the tool to imagine and animate personal, highly idiosyncratic superheroes.
- ○ C. These days a highly skilled multimedia creators have the tools to imagine and animate personal, highly idiosyncratic superheroes.
- ○ D. No change needs to be made to this sentence.

2. How should this sentence be changed?

> Some modern stories, such as Aldous Huxley's *Brave New World,* is set in the not-too-distant future at a time when technology has become a tool of evil.

- ○ A. Some modern stories, such as Aldous Huxley's *Brave New World*, is set in the not-too-distant future at a time when technology becomes a tool of evil.
- ○ B. Some modern stories, such as Aldous Huxley's *Brave New World*, am set in the not-too-distant future at a time when technology has become a tool of evil.
- ○ C. Some modern stories, such as Aldous Huxley's *Brave New World*, are set in the not-too-distant future at a time when technology has become a tool of evil.
- ○ D. No change needs to be made to this sentence.

3. How should this sentence be changed?

> Although "A Voyage to Lilliput" is the only one of his adventures most people remember, Gulliver actually make many journeys to places equally improbable.

- ○ A. Although "A Voyage to Lilliput" am the only one of his adventures most people remember, Gulliver actually make many journeys to places equally improbable.
- ○ B. Although "A Voyage to Lilliput" is the only one of his adventures most people remember, Gulliver actually makes many journeys to places equally improbable.
- ○ C. Although "A Voyage to Lilliput" is the only one of his adventures most people remember, Gulliver actually make many journey to places equally improbable.
- ○ D. No change needs to be made to this sentence.

Grammar:
Commas

Commas can be used in the following situations:

Rule	Correctly Edited	Incorrectly Edited
Use commas to separate three or more words, phrases, or clauses in a list.	We should honor the student **who demonstrates great effort, who always completes his or her assignments on time,** and **who offers assistance to his or her peers.**	We should honor the student who demonstrates great effort who always completes his or her assignments on time and who offers assistance to his or her peers.
Two or more simple sentences can be connected to form a compound sentence by using a comma followed by a conjunction (such as *and, but, or, yet*).	The whale swam near our boat**, and** it raised a flipper out of the water.	The whale swam near our boat, it raised a flipper out of the water.
Commas are used to set off interjections and transition words.	Darcie's brother has blond hair, while her sister**, on the other hand,** has flaming red hair.	Darcie's brother has blond hair, while her sister on the other hand has flaming red hair.
Commas are used to set off introductory phrases from the main clause. Introductory phrases include prepositional and participial phrases.	**Scampering quickly across the busy road,** the groundhog avoided being hit by a car.	Scampering quickly across the busy road the groundhog avoided being hit by a car.
Commas are used to set off nonessential elements in a sentence. **Nonessential elements** can include relative clauses that are not required to understand the main meaning of a sentence.	Maria caught a steelhead, **which is a kind of trout,** on a fishing trip with her father.	Maria caught a steelhead which is a kind of trout on a fishing trip with her father.

YOUR TURN

1. How should this sentence be changed?

   > Well, the chocolate cake was loaded with calories but it sure did taste delicious!

   ○ A. Well the chocolate cake was loaded with calories but it sure did taste delicious!
   ○ B. Well, the chocolate cake was loaded with calories, but it sure did taste delicious!
   ○ C. Well, the chocolate cake was loaded with calories but, it sure did taste delicious!
   ○ D. No change needs to be made to this sentence.

2. How should this sentence be changed?

   > The Cajun menu features crayfish casserole, red beans and rice, and firecracker shrimp sandwiches.

   ○ A. The Cajun menu features crayfish casserole, red, beans and rice, and firecracker shrimp sandwiches.
   ○ B. The Cajun menu features crayfish casserole, red beans, and rice, and firecracker shrimp sandwiches.
   ○ C. The Cajun menu features crayfish casserole, red beans and rice, and firecracker, shrimp sandwiches.
   ○ D. No change needs to be made to this sentence.

3. How should this sentence be changed?

   > After a few hours, when the sun finally set and the temperature dropped Mikayla opened up the windows of her house and let the fresh air in.

   ○ A. After a few hours when the sun finally set and the temperature dropped Mikayla opened up the windows of her house and let the fresh air in.
   ○ B. After a few hours, when the sun finally set and the temperature dropped, Mikayla opened up the windows of her house and let the fresh air in.
   ○ C. After a few hours, when the sun finally set and the temperature dropped Mikayla opened up the windows of her house, and let the fresh air in.
   ○ D. No change needs to be made to this sentence.

Grammar: Semicolons, Colons, and Dashes

There are several ways to use a colon, but a colon must always follow a complete sentence.

Rule	Text
Use a colon to introduce a list after an independent clause.	The Britons immediately found themselves under attack from groups they thought of as barbarians: **the Irish from the west, the Picts from the north, and the Anglo-Saxons from across the North Sea.** Unsolved Mysteries of History: An Eye-Opening Investigation into the Most Baffling Events of All Time

A semicolon joins two independent clauses. Never use a semicolon with a coordinating conjunction.

Rule	Text
Use a semicolon to join two independent clauses that are closely connected.	There was never a castle here in the medieval sense; the fortified hill itself was the "castle," as elsewhere in southern and southwest England. Conversation with Geoffrey Ashe re: King Arthur
Use a semicolon to join two independent clauses with a conjunctive adverb (such as *however*) or another transition word or phrase (such as *in short*). A comma may follow the transition word or phrase.	Many technical careers are high-paying; **for instance,** the median salary for an air traffic controller is $124,540. Community Colleges vs. Technical Schools

A dash [—] looks like a long hyphen. Use a dash or dashes to show a sudden break or a change of thought, to emphasize a thought, or to give new information.

Rule	Text
Use one dash if the new thought or emphasized information is at the end of a sentence. If the new thought or emphasized information comes in the middle of a sentence, use two dashes to set it off.	There was just such a man when I was young—**an Austrian who invented a new way of life and convinced himself that he was the chap to make it work.** Once and Future King

⟳ YOUR TURN

1. How should this sentence be changed?

> The world's population is growing at an alarming rate—fast enough to double in only forty-three years!

- ○ A. The world's population is—growing at an alarming rate—fast enough to double in only forty-three years!
- ○ B. The world's population is growing—at an alarming rate—fast enough to double in only forty-three years!
- ○ C. The world's population is growing at an alarming rate; fast enough to double in only forty-three years!
- ○ D. No change needs to be made to this sentence.

2. How should this sentence be changed?

> Elvis Presley's hit singles include: "Heartbreak Hotel," "Hound Dog," and "Love Me Tender."

- ○ A. Elvis Presley's hit singles: "Heartbreak Hotel," "Hound Dog," and "Love Me Tender."
- ○ B. Elvis Presley's hit singles include; "Heartbreak Hotel," "Hound Dog," and "Love Me Tender."
- ○ C. Elvis Presley's hit singles include "Heartbreak Hotel," "Hound Dog," and "Love Me Tender."
- ○ D. No change needs to be made to this sentence.

3. How should this sentence be changed?

> Coffee is very popular in most countries: however, in a few, tea is the warm beverage of choice.

- ○ A. Coffee is very popular in most countries: however in a few, tea is the warm beverage of choice.
- ○ B. Coffee is very popular in most countries; however, in a few, tea is the warm beverage of choice.
- ○ C. Coffee is very popular in most countries: however, in a few, tea; is the warm beverage of choice.
- ○ D. No change needs to be made to this sentence.

Argumentative Writing Process: Edit and Publish

PLAN	DRAFT	REVISE	EDIT AND PUBLISH

You have revised your argumentative essay based on your peer feedback and your own examination.

Now, it is time to edit your argumentative essay. When you revised, you focused on the content of your argumentative essay. You probably looked at your use of reasons and relevant evidence to support your thesis statement, your introduction, conclusion, and transitions. When you edit, you focus on the mechanics of your essay, paying close attention to things like grammar and punctuation.

Use the checklist below to guide you as you edit:

☐ Have I followed all the rules for punctuating writing?

☐ Have I used commas, colons, semicolons, and dashes correctly?

☐ Do my subjects and verbs agree?

☐ Do I have any sentence fragments or run-on sentences?

☐ Have I spelled everything correctly?

Notice some edits Kristen has made:

- Corrected an error in subject-verb agreement
- Replaced commas with a set of dashes to set off information
- Corrected a spelling mistake

Please note that excerpts and passages in the StudySync® library and this workbook are intended as touchstones to generate interest in an author's work. The excerpts and passages do not substitute for the reading of entire texts, and StudySync® strongly recommends that students seek out and purchase the whole literary or informational work in order to experience it as the author intended. Links to online resellers are available in our digital library. In addition, complete works may be ordered through an authorized reseller by filling out and returning to StudySync® the order form enclosed in this workbook.

Reading & Writing Companion   545

I first met Mr. Jenkins when I was selling tickets for my high school's drama club. I'd heard nasty rumors about the old man, so my breath caught in my throat as I knocked on his door. When he asked who I was, his gravelly voice sent a chill down my spine. After I told him about the drama club, though, a bright smile appeared on his face. He explained that his late wife loved musicals and invited me to talk more about how he could help. It turns out that Mr. Jenkins is a sweet, generous man who lost his wife in a car accident and has simply kept to himself ever since. His house and clothes is are shabby because his military pension is small and he doesn't like spending money on himself. The more Mr. Jenkins shared about his life,—stories about his marriage, his experiances experiences overseas during the Korean War, and his loneliness,—the more certain I became that everyone in the community needs to band together to help this wonderful man.

✏ WRITE

Use the questions on the previous page, as well as your peer reviews, to help you evaluate your argumentative essay to determine areas that need editing. Then, edit your argumentative essay to correct those errors.

Once you have made all your corrections, you are ready to publish your work. You can distribute your writing to family and friends, hang it on a bulletin board, or post it on your blog. If you publish online, share the link with your family, friends, and classmates.

Emilia's Lament

FICTION

Introduction

This work of historical fiction is set in medieval Spain. It tells the story of a young woman named Emilia who looks out at the Mediterranean Sea and confesses her anxieties about her upcoming arranged marriage. Emilia reveals that her older sister's arranged marriage turned out differently than planned, and hopes she can avoid the same outcome.

V VOCABULARY

exhilarated

lively or excited; refreshed or invigorated

giddy

very happy or silly

turbulence

a state of agitation or confusion

mused

thought deeply; wondered

betrothed

a person to whom someone is promised to be married

NOTES

≡ READ

1 Emilia gazed out at the sapphire waters of the Mediterranean Sea. On most days, thinking about the world beyond the waves made her feel **exhilarated**. But today she wanted the still waters to mirror the **turbulence** she felt within her heart. Tomorrow she would be wed. She knew she was supposed to feel grateful. She remembered the joy her older sister felt the day before she was married in 1427. That was just a few years ago. On the other hand, she also knew the despair Maria had felt since her wedding day. She ranted at the sea.

2 "I do not understand why I have to do this. Didn't Mama and Papa learn anything from the mistake they made with Maria? Don't they see how unhappy she is? Maria and I stood together at this same window, dreaming about her future. We had not yet met Alfonzo, Maria's **betrothed**, but Papa and Mama told us he was a wealthy merchant from a respected family. They heard he was very handsome, generous, and kind to his mother. They swore he would be a perfect match for Maria.

3   "I feel so foolish to think about how **giddy** we felt imagining what Maria's life would be like once she was married. She would be the lady of her own household. That is to say, she would be free to do what we both desired more than anything else. She would finally be able to see the world beyond the vast Mediterranean Sea. But, in reality, Maria's world became smaller after her wedding. Yes, Alfonzo travels all the time, but he never takes Maria with him. Instead, he leaves her to care for his mother. Maria has to do everything by the old woman's rules. It was not the life our parents had been promised for their daughter. But it was too late."

4   After the family had learned the truth about Alfonzo, Emilia begged her father to let her choose a husband for herself. He rejected her plea. "That is not how the world works," he explained. "Although your happiness means everything to me, I have no sons to carry on our family name. It is the responsibility of my daughters to make connections with the right people so that our family tree can continue to thrive."

5   Emilia did not think her sister was thriving. On the contrary, Maria was wilting in front of their eyes. Every time Emilia saw her sister, she seemed smaller and quieter. When her father announced that Emilia, too, would marry a man she had never met, her heart shrank with fear. She worried that her life would turn out like Maria's had.

6   Meanwhile, Emilia's wedding day was almost here, and there was nothing she could do to change her future. Emilia **mused** to the sea air. "Mama and Papa have promised that Diego is different than Alfonzo. For instance, Diego makes his swords nearby. He must stay in town to run his shop, so he will not sail away and leave me alone. But how am I to know that he will not invent another reason to abandon me with our children? They say that he is kind. As an illustration, they recall tales told by his apprentices about his patience and generosity. But that does not prove that he will be kind and patient with a woman. There is so much about this arrangement that I do not understand, yet there is nothing I can do to stop it. I must send my fears out into the sea and accept my fate as Diego's wife. I do not know if Diego will be a good husband, but he may be. I must remember that I am not Maria, and he is not Alfonzo."

7   At the end of this declaration, Emilia stepped away from the window. She needed to get some rest. Her new life would begin tomorrow.

First Read

Read "Emilia's Lament." After you read, complete the Think Questions below.

☁ THINK QUESTIONS

1. Who is the main character in the story? What is the character's concern?

   The main character is _____.

   Her concern is _____.

2. Write two or three sentences describing the setting of the story.

   The setting is _____

   _____.

3. At the end of the story, how does the character feel about her situation? Include a line of textual evidence to support your claim.

   Emilia feels _____

   _____

   because "_____."

4. Use context to confirm the meaning of the word *mused* as it is used in "Emilia's Lament." Write your definition of *mused* here.

   Mused means _____.

   A context clue is _____.

5. What is another way to say that a person feels *giddy*?

   A person feels _____.

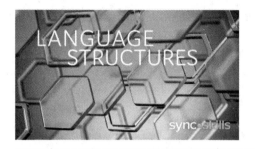

Skill:
Language Structures

★ DEFINE

In every language, there are rules that tell how to **structure** sentences. These rules define the correct order of words. In the English language, for example, a **basic** structure for sentences is subject, verb, and object. Some sentences have more **complicated** structures.

You will encounter both basic and complicated **language structures** in the classroom materials you read. Being familiar with language structures will help you better understand the text.

••• CHECKLIST FOR LANGUAGE STRUCTURES

To improve your comprehension of language structures, do the following:

 Monitor your understanding.

- Ask yourself: Why do I not understand this sentence? Is it because I do not understand some of the words? Or is it because I do not understand the way the words are ordered in the sentence?

✓ Pay attention to verbs followed by prepositions.

- A **verb** names an action.

  > Example: I **sit** on my chair.

  > This tells the reader what the subject of the sentence is doing (sitting).

- A **preposition** defines the relationship between two or more nouns or verbs in a sentence.

  > Example: I **sit** on my chair.

  > This tells the reader where the subject is doing the action (on a chair).

- Sometimes the preposition comes directly after the verb, but it can also be separated by another word.

  > Example: I **took** it **to** school with me.

- Sometimes the preposition changes the meaning of the verb. This is called a **phrasal verb.**

  > Example: The teacher liked to **call on** the students in the front of the class.

  > The phrasal verb *call on* means "to select someone to share information."

✓ Break down the sentence into its parts.

- Ask yourself: What words make up the verbs in this sentence? Is the verb followed by a preposition? How does this affect the meaning of the sentence?

✓ Confirm your understanding with a peer or teacher.

⟳ YOUR TURN

Read each sentence and notice the verb and preposition pairs. Then, sort each sentence into the correct category by writing the letter in the phrasal or non-phrasal verb column.

	Sentence Options
A	"Emilia mused to the sea air."
B	"She worried that her life would turn out like Maria's had."
C	Emilia's parents would not call off her wedding.
D	Emilia pleaded with her father to let her choose a husband.

Phrasal Verb	Non-Phrasal Verb

Please note that excerpts and passages in the StudySync® library and this workbook are intended as touchstones to generate interest in an author's work. The excerpts and passages do not substitute for the reading of entire texts, and StudySync® strongly recommends that students seek out and purchase the whole literary or informational work in order to experience it as the author intended. Links to online resellers are available in our digital library. In addition, complete works may be ordered through an authorized reseller by filling out and returning to StudySync® the order form enclosed in this workbook.

Reading & Writing
Companion
553

Skill: Drawing Inferences and Conclusions

★ DEFINE

Making **inferences** means connecting your experiences with what you read. Authors do not always tell readers directly everything that takes place in a story or text. You need to use clues to infer, or make a guess, about what is happening. To make an inference, first find facts, details, and examples in the text. Then think about what you already know. Combine the **textual evidence** with your **prior knowledge** to draw a **conclusion** about what the author is trying to communicate.

Making inferences and drawing conclusions can help you better understand what you are reading. It may also help you search for and find the author's message in the text.

••• CHECKLIST FOR DRAWING INFERENCES AND CONCLUSIONS

In order to make inferences and draw conclusions, do the following:

✓ Look for information that is missing from the text or that is not directly stated.

- Ask yourself: What is confusing? What is missing?

✓ Think about what you already know about the topic.

- Ask yourself: Have I had a similar experience in my life? Have I learned about this subject in another class?

✓ Combine clues from the text with prior knowledge to make an inference and draw a conclusion.

- Think: I can conclude _____, because the text says _____

  and I know that _____.

✓ Use textual evidence to support your inference and make sure that it is valid.

YOUR TURN

Read paragraphs 6 and 7 from "Emilia's Lament." Then, match the sentence endings to the correct sentence beginnings to complete the chart and draw a conclusion.

---

from **"Emilia's Lament"**

Meanwhile, Emilia's wedding day was almost here, and there was nothing she could do to change her future. Emilia mused to the sea air. "Mama and Papa have promised that Diego is different from Alfonzo. For instance, Diego makes his swords nearby. He must stay in town to run his shop, so he will not sail away and leave me alone. But how am I to know that he will not invent another reason to abandon me and our children? They say that he is kind. As an illustration, they recall tales told by his apprentices about his patience and generosity. But that does not prove he will be kind and patient with a woman. There is so much about this arrangement that I do not understand, yet there is nothing I can do to stop it. I must send my fears out into the sea and accept my fate as Diego's wife. I do not know if Diego will be a good husband, but he may be. I must remember that I am not Maria, and he is not Alfonzo."

At the end of this declaration, Emilia stepped away from the window. She needed to get some rest. Her new life would begin tomorrow.

Ending Options	
A	Emilia is feeling more optimistic about her parents' decision.
B	based on my prior knowledge, parents don't take back their decisions very easily.
C	"I am not Maria, and he is not Alfonzo."

Sentence Beginning	Sentence Ending
I can conclude that. . .	
Because the text says,. . .	
And, I know that. . .	

Close Read

✏️ **WRITE**

LITERARY ANALYSIS: At the beginning of the story, "Emilia's Lament," the main character is angry and worried. She will soon be married and concludes that her life will be as horrible as Maria's. By the end of the story, Emilia may have arrived at a different conclusion. Write a response in which you explain how Emilia came to this conclusion. Include examples of Emilia's inferences from the story to support your explanation. Pay attention to and edit for the possessive case.

Use the checklist below to guide you as you write.

☐ Does Emilia change the way she feels about her future, married to Diego?

☐ Do you have any prior knowledge about one of the topics in the text?

☐ What does Emilia conclude about her future, married to Diego?

Use the sentence frames to organize and write your literary analysis.

Emilia needed to shout her concerns to the sea because she was _____

about getting married. By the end of the story, Emilia feels _____

and concludes that she needs to _____.

Emilia makes several inferences about her future husband, Diego. For example, she assumes he is

_____

because " _____."

In another class, I learned that _____.

When I combine the textual evidence with my prior knowledge, I can conclude that Emilia

_____.

To Be a Queen

ARGUMENTATIVE TEXT

Introduction

Queen Elizabeth I was a famous woman, and not just because she was royalty in 16th-century England. She was only the second female to have complete control of the throne during that era. Elizabeth was a natural leader. However, despite her accomplishments as a woman who succeeded in a male-dominated role, some people scoff when she's compared to modern-day feminists who fight for women's rights. She was a queen, but now you have to

VOCABULARY

nation

a country

single

not married or in a serious romantic relationship

threat

a statement given with the intention to hurt or kill

barrier

an obstacle that prevents something

NOTES

≡ READ

To Be a Queen

Point: Queen Elizabeth I symbolizes a modern-day feminist.

1   She wore an elaborate gown instead of a skirt. She led a **nation** instead of a company. She lived during the 16th century instead of the 21st century. Those are the only differences between Queen Elizabeth I and a modern-day working woman. Queen Elizabeth I is remembered not only for her talents of ruling England, but for being a strong woman. Queen Elizabeth I symbolizes a modern-day feminist because of the way she led, lived, and paved the way for women.

2   To be a feminist, one must believe that men and women can do the same job, and Elizabeth definitely proved this to be true. She received death **threats** and numerous insults, but Queen Elizabeth led her country with confidence and pride. Although she had a counsel of male advisors, it was believed that she made all of the major decisions for the country by herself. Elizabeth spoke many languages, had a talent for international diplomacy, and managed people very well. Her time ruling England was even named "The Golden Era" because she helped solve many political, religious, and economic problems. Elizabeth's reign shows modern-day women that they can do anything, even rule a country.

3   Queen Elizabeth I also symbolizes a feminist because of how she chose to live her life. Her political advisors told Elizabeth that she must get married, but she did not listen. Elizabeth refused to take a husband because during the 16th century, a husband had control over his wife. Elizabeth strongly disagreed with this belief, so she decided to remain **single**. Queen Elizabeth I was proud of this decision and told the citizens of England that she was "married to her country" instead. Elizabeth was also responsible for making portraits popular. She would have her portraits painted to make her look strong and fierce. Elizabeth I, like a feminist, lived her life the way she wanted.

4   To this day, people regard Queen Elizabeth I as one of the strongest symbols of female power and feminism. Despite dealing with the pressures of society and even threats, she remained a powerful leader. Elizabeth paved the way for women to be the independent, intelligent, and fearless leaders they are today.

Counterpoint: Queen Elizabeth I does not represent feminism in the 21st century.

5   There's no doubt that Queen Elizabeth I was a strong, independent woman. She had to be confident in her role because she was only the second woman to rule England. In fact, Queen Elizabeth was a very successful queen during the late 16th century, but being a great leader and a powerful woman does not make a feminist. Today, a true feminist stands up for women's rights, breaks down **barriers**, and uses her power to change inequality. Queen Elizabeth I of England did not do any of these things, and therefore she cannot represent feminism in the 21st century.

6   Although she was a woman in power, Elizabeth did not do much for women's rights in England. The queen had a strong opinion about marriage in her life, but failed to support other women's choices about marriage. In order to get married, women still had to ask for permission. In addition, Queen Elizabeth I was not trying to support the women of England when she chose to stay single; rather, she decided to stay "married to her country" to support her political agenda. Elizabeth even posed for a portrait wearing a black and white dress to symbolize her purity in ruling the country. She used her decision to remain unmarried to prove that she was an honest politician, not to support other women's rights.

7   Queen Elizabeth I did not break down any barriers for women, either. In fact, the queen believed she was above all other women. Elizabeth thought that God had appointed her to be queen, and therefore she was more important than other women. A true feminist sees other women as part of a sisterhood, or a family that supports and uplifts each other. However, Elizabeth I did not use her power to help the female population, and she was infamous for being

jealous of other women. For example, she even executed her own female relative, Mary Queen of Scots.

8   Lastly, Queen Elizabeth I cannot be a feminist because she did not strive to change inequality. During her reign as queen, women were still considered second-class citizens compared to men. Even though it seemed progressive to have a female queen, Elizabeth represented a hierarchy. Instead of treating people as equals, Elizabeth and her government judged people on their status and ranking in society. Therefore, equality was never a mission for Queen Elizabeth I.

9   Is Queen Elizabeth I a strong, female leader in history? Absolutely. Is she a feminist? No. Feminists bend over backwards to fight for change and equal rights, leading the way for women to live up to their full potential in a society that limits them. Queen Elizabeth I was too focused on her own power to make any real changes for women. Therefore, she does not represent feminism in the 21st century.

First Read

Read "To Be a Queen." After you read, complete the Think Questions below.

☁ THINK QUESTIONS

1. What is the author's main argument in the Point section?

   The author's main argument is _____

   _____.

2. What is the author's main argument in the Counterpoint section?

   The author's main argument is _____

   _____.

3. What is one piece of evidence that both authors use in their argument? How do they use this evidence differently to support their claims?

   Both authors use _____.

   They use this differently by _____.

4. Use context to confirm the meaning of the word *barrier* as it is used in "To Be a Queen." Write your definition of *barrier* here.

   Barrier means _____.

   A context clue is _____.

5. What is another way to say that a person is *single*?

   A person is single when _____

   _____.

Reading & Writing
Companion

Skill:
Analyzing Expressions

 DEFINE

When you read, you may find English expressions that you do not know. An **expression** is a group of words that communicates an idea. Three types of expressions are idioms, sayings, and figurative language. They can be difficult to understand because the meanings of the words are different from their **literal,** or usual, meanings.

An **idiom** is an expression that is commonly known among a group of people. For example, "It's raining cats and dogs" means it is raining heavily. **Sayings** are short expressions that contain advice or wisdom. For instance, "Don't count your chickens before they hatch" means do not plan on something good happening before it happens. **Figurative** language is when you describe something by comparing it with something else, either directly (using the words *like* or *as*) or indirectly. For example, "I'm as hungry as a horse" means I'm very hungry. None of the expressions are about actual animals.

••• CHECKLIST FOR ANALYZING EXPRESSIONS

To determine the meaning of an expression, remember the following:

✓ If you find a confusing group of words, it may be an expression. The meaning of words in expressions may not be their literal meaning.

   • Ask yourself: Is this confusing because the words are new? Or because the words do not make sense together?

✓ Determining the overall meaning may require that you use one or more of the following:

   • context clues

   • a dictionary or other resource

   • teacher or peer support

✓ Highlight important information before and after the expression to look for clues.

⟳ YOUR TURN

Read paragraphs 7 and 9 from "To Be a Queen." Then, complete the multiple-choice questions below.

from **"To Be a Queen"**

7   Queen Elizabeth I did not break down any barriers for women, either. In fact, the queen believed she was above all other women. Elizabeth thought that God had appointed her to be queen, and therefore she was more important than other women. A true feminist sees other women as part of a sisterhood, or a family that supports and uplifts each other. However, Elizabeth I did not use her power to help the female population, and she was infamous for being jealous of other women. For example, she even executed her own female relative, Mary Queen of Scots.

. . .

9   Is Queen Elizabeth I a strong, female leader in history? Absolutely. Is she a feminist? No. Feminists bend over backwards to fight for change and equal rights, leading the way for women to live up to their full potential in a society that limits them. Queen Elizabeth I was too focused on her own power to make any real changes for women. Therefore, she does not represent feminism in the 21st century.

1. Which of the following quotations from paragraph 7 includes an idiom?

   ○ A. "Queen Elizabeth I did not break down any barriers for women, either."
   ○ B. "Elizabeth thought that God had appointed her to be queen, and therefore she was more important than other women."
   ○ C. "However, Elizabeth I did not use her power to help the female population, and she was infamous for being jealous of other women."
   ○ D. "For example, she even executed her own female relative, Mary Queen of Scots."

2. The idiom in Question 1 is referring to . . .

   ○ A. the walls around a castle keeping women out.
   ○ B. the social practices depriving women of equality.
   ○ C. the social practices depriving royalty of equality.
   ○ D. the locks placed on homes keeping women captive.

3. Which of the following quotations from paragraph 9 includes an idiom?

   ○ A. "Is Queen Elizabeth I a strong, female leader in history? Absolutely."
   ○ B. "Feminists bend over backwards to fight for change and equal rights, leading the way for women to live up to their full potential in a society that limits them."
   ○ C. "Queen Elizabeth I was too focused on her own power to make any real changes for women."
   ○ D. "Therefore, she does not represent feminism in the 21st century."

Please note that excerpts and passages in the StudySync® library and this workbook are intended as touchstones to generate interest in an author's work. The excerpts and passages do not substitute for the reading of entire texts, and StudySync® strongly recommends that students seek out and purchase the whole literary or informational work in order to experience it as the author intended. Links to online resellers are available in our digital library. In addition, complete works may be ordered through an authorized reseller by filling out and returning to StudySync® the order form enclosed in this workbook.

Reading & Writing Companion   563

4. This idiom means —

   ○ A. to complete a task easily.
   ○ B. to avoid change.
   ○ C. to discuss the options.
   ○ D. to make extreme efforts.

Skill: Comparing and Contrasting

★ DEFINE

To **compare** is to show how two or more pieces of information or literary elements in a text are similar. To **contrast** is to show how two or more pieces of information or literary elements in a text are different. By comparing and contrasting, you can better understand the **meaning** and the **purpose** of the text you are reading.

••• CHECKLIST FOR COMPARING AND CONTRASTING

In order to compare and contrast, do the following:

- ✓ Look for information or elements that you can compare and contrast.

  - • Ask yourself: How are these two things similar? How are they different?

- ✓ Look for signal words that indicate a compare-and-contrast relationship.

  - • Ask yourself: Are there any words that indicate the writer is trying to compare and contrast two or more things?

- ✓ Use a graphic organizer, such as a Venn diagram or chart, to compare and contrast information.

Please note that excerpts and passages in the StudySync® library and this workbook are intended as touchstones to generate interest in an author's work. The excerpts and passages do not substitute for the reading of entire texts, and StudySync® strongly recommends that students seek out and purchase the whole literary or informational work in order to experience it as the author intended. Links to online resellers are available in our digital library. In addition, complete works may be ordered through an authorized reseller by filling out and returning to StudySync® the order form enclosed in this workbook.

Reading & Writing Companion   **565**

↻ YOUR TURN

Read the following excerpts from "To Be a Queen." Then, complete the chart below to compare and contrast the passages.

---

from **"To Be a Queen"**

Point

Elizabeth was also responsible for making portraits popular. She would have her portraits painted to make her look strong and fierce. Elizabeth I, like a feminist, lived her life the way she wanted.

To this day, people regard Queen Elizabeth I as one of the strongest symbols of female power and feminism. Despite dealing with the pressures of society and even threats, she remained a powerful leader. Elizabeth paved the way for women to be the independent, intelligent, and fearless leaders they are today.

Counterpoint

Instead of treating people as equals, Elizabeth and her government judged people on their status and ranking in society. Therefore, equality was never a mission for Queen Elizabeth I.

Is Queen Elizabeth I a strong, female leader in history? Absolutely. Is she a feminist? No. Feminists bend over backwards to fight for change and equal rights, leading the way for women to live up to their full potential in a society that limits them. Queen Elizabeth I was too focused on her own power to make any real changes for women. Therefore, she does not represent feminism in the 21st century.

	Examples
A	Queen Elizabeth I was a powerful, female leader.
B	Queen Elizabeth I was too selfish with her power.
C	Queen Elizabeth I inspires modern-day women to be leaders.

Point	Both	Counterpoint

Close Read

✏ WRITE

ARGUMENTATIVE: One author argues that Elizabeth I was a feminist. Another author argues that she was not. Which argument do you agree with? Explain and justify your opinion using specific details from the text. Pay attention to and edit for *ie* and *ei* spelling rules.

Use the checklist below to guide you as you write.

☐ Which argument do you agree with?

☐ Why do you agree with this argument?

☐ What details from the text support your opinion?

Use the sentence frames to organize and write your argument.

I agree with the _____.

Queen Elizabeth I _____ a symbol of feminism because she _____

_____.

For example, "_____"

_____.

This _____ modern-day women to _____.

In her personal life, Queen Elizabeth I _____.

According to the text, "_____."

This choice _____

shows Queen Elizabeth I _____.

PHOTO/IMAGE CREDITS:

p. 397, ©iStock.com/kieferpix
p. 397, ©iStock.com/eyewave, ©iStock.com/subjug,
©iStock.com/Ivantsov, iStock.com/borchee, ©iStock.com/
seb_ra
p. 399, iStock/francescoch
p. 400, Susan B. Anthony - PhotoQuest/Contributor/
Archive Photos/Getty Images
p. 400, Frederick Douglass - Archive Photos/Library of
Congress/Stringer/Getty Images
p. 400, Founding Fathers - GraphicaArtis/Contributor/
Archive Photos/Getty Images
p. 400, Liliukalani - Bettmann/Contributor/Bettmann/Getty
Images
p. 400, James Madison - istock.com/GeorgiosArt
p. 401, Nelson Mandela - Ulrich Baumgarten/Contributor/
Ulrich Baumgarten/Getty
p. 401, Thomas Paine - Bettmann/Contributor/Bettmann/
Getty Images
p. 401, Johnathan Swift - istock.com/GeorgiosArt
p. 401, Phillis Wheatley - Culture Club/Contributor/Hulton
Archive/Getty Images
p. 401, Zitkala-Sa - Bettmann/Contributor/Bettmann/Getty
Images
p. 402, ©iStock.com/Creativeye99
p. 403, Public Domain
p. 404, Getty: Universal History Archive/Contributor/
Universal Images Group
p. 405, Getty: Photo Josse/Leemage/Contributor/Corbis
Historical
p. 407, Getty: Culture Club/Contributor/Hulton Archive
p. 407, Getty: ullstein bild Dtl./Contributor/ullstein bild
p. 410, ©iStock.com/Creativeye99
p. 411, ©iStock.com/Roberto A Sanchez
p. 412, Public domain
p. 418, ©iStock.com/Roberto A Sanchez
p. 419, ©iStock.com/yipengge
p. 420, ©iStock.com/yipengge
p. 421, ©iStock.com/Hohenhaus
p. 422, ©iStock.com/Hohenhaus
p. 423, ©iStock.com/janrysavy
p. 424, ©iStock.com/janrysavy
p. 425, ©iStock.com/Roberto A Sanchez
p. 426, ©iStock.com/enter89
p. 427, ©iStock.com/duncan1890
p. 429, ©iStock.com/MarkSkalny
p. 432, ©iStock.com/MarkSkalny
p. 433, ©iStock.com/
p. 434, ©iStock.com/
p. 435, ©iStock.com/Dominique_Lavoie
p. 436, ©iStock.com/Dominique_Lavoie
p. 437, ©iStock.com/MarkSkalny
p. 438, ©iStock.com/diegograndi
p. 439, ©iStock.com/giftlegacy
p. 442, wahahaz/iStock.com
p. 443, Interim Archives/Archive Photos/Getty Images
p. 446, wahahaz/iStock.com
p. 447, ©iStock.com/ThomasVogel
p. 449, ©iStock.com/ThomasVogel
p. 450, ©iStock.com/peepo
p. 451, ©iStock.com/peepo
p. 452, wahahaz/iStock.com
p. 453, Public Domain
p. 456, ©iStock.com/Karimpard
p. 457, Public Domain

p. 461, ©iStock.com/Bill Oxford
p. 466, ©iStock.com/Bill Oxford
p. 467, ©iStock.com/ThomasVogel
p. 468, ©iStock.com/ThomasVogel
p. 469, ©iStock.com/DNY59
p. 470, ©iStock.com/DNY59
p. 471, ©iStock.com/antoni_halim
p. 472, ©iStock.com/antoni_halim
p. 473, ©iStock.com/Bill Oxford
p. 474, ©iStock.com/DNY59
p. 478, ©istock.com/Devasahayam Chandra Dhas
p. 482, Public Domain
p. 483, ©istock.com/Tero Vesalainen
p. 485, StudySync Image
p. 486, StudySync Image
p. 488, Getty: Bettmann/Contributor/Bettmann
p. 490, ©istock.com/Tero Vesalainen
p. 491, ©iStock.com/Caval
p. 492, ©iStock.com/Caval
p. 493, ©iStock.com/Hohenhaus
p. 494, ©iStock.com/Hohenhaus
p. 494, StudySync Image
p. 496, ©iStock.com/Orla
p. 497, ©iStock.com/Orla
p. 498, ©istock.com/Tero Vesalainen
p. 499, ©istock.com/ThomasShanahan
p. 508, ©iStock.com/Martin Barraud
p. 509, ©iStock.com/Martin Barraud
p. 515, ©iStock.com/fstop123
p. 518, ©iStock.com/gopixa
p. 521, ©iStock.com/Dominik Pabis
p. 524, ©iStock.com/Martin Barraud
p. 528, ©iStock.com/bo1982
p. 531, ©iStock/Jeff_Hu
p. 533, ©iStock.com/stevedangers
p. 535, ©iStock.com/Martin Barraud
p. 537, ©iStock/Fodor90
p. 539, iStock.com/RomoloTavani
p. 541, iStock.com/wwing
p. 543, iStock.com/Piotr_roae
p. 545, ©iStock.com/Martin Barraud
p. 547, ©iStock.com/Imgorthand
p. 548, ©iStock.com/Susan Chiang
p. 548, ©iStock.com/Willowpix
p. 548, ©iStock.com/AnthonyRosenberg
p. 548, ©iStock.com/baona
p. 548, ©iStock.com/Alejandro Rivera
p. 550, ©iStock.com/Imgorthand
p. 551, ©iStock.com/BlackJack3D
p. 554, ©iStock.com/serggn
p. 556, ©iStock.com/Imgorthand
p. 557, ©iStock.com/nurulanga
p. 558, ©istock.com/scyther5
p. 558, ©istock.com/Tharakorn
p. 558, ©istock.com/m-imagephotography
p. 558, ©istock.com/Armastas
p. 561, ©iStock.com/nurulanga
p. 562, ©iStock.com/Ales_Utovko
p. 565, ©iStock.com/RazvanDP
p. 567, ©iStock.com/nurulanga

studysync®

Text Fulfillment Through StudySync

If you are interested in specific titles, please fill out the form below and we will check availability through our partners.

ORDER DETAILS

Date:

TITLE	AUTHOR	Paperback/ Hardcover	Specific Edition *If Applicable*	Quantity

SHIPPING INFORMATION

Contact:

Title:

School/District:

Address Line 1:

Address Line 2:

Zip or Postal Code:

Phone:

Mobile:

Email:

BILLING INFORMATION ☐ SAME AS SHIPPING

Contact:

Title:

School/District:

Address Line 1:

Address Line 2:

Zip or Postal Code:

Phone:

Mobile:

Email:

PAYMENT INFORMATION

☐ CREDIT CARD

Name on Card:

Card Number:

Expiration Date:

Security Code:

☐ PO

Purchase Order Number:

StudySync Text Fulfillment, BookheadEd Learning, LLC
610 Daniel Young Drive | Sonoma, CA 95476